The New Century Handbook of

# CLASSICAL GEOGRAPHY

The New Century Handbook of

# CLASSICAL GEOGRAPHY

edited by

Catherine B. Avery

APPLETON-CENTURY-CROFTS
Educational Division
MEREDITH CORPORATION
NEW YORK

*913*
*N*
*c. 1*

Selected from *The New Century Classical Handbook,*
edited by Catherine B. Avery
Copyright © 1962 by
APPLETON-CENTURY-CROFTS, INC.


72   73   74   75   76/10   9   8   7   6   5   4   3   2   1

Library of Congress Catalog Card Number:
78-189006

PRINTED IN THE UNITED STATES OF AMERICA
(X) 390-66930-X

# Preface

No less than the myths and literary works of the Classical World, the cities, mountains, rivers, and islands of the Mediterranean region have taken their place in the history of Western Civilization. Such sites in Greece, Italy, and Asia Minor as Mycenae, Delphi, Epidaurus, Marathon, Olympia, Paestum, Tarentum, and Halicarnassus were the focal points of historical events, rituals, and in myths, the activities of the gods.

THE NEW CENTURY HANDBOOK OF CLASSICAL GEOGRAPHY presents concise discussions of the major geographical locations, incorporating the facts *and* legends drawn from such diverse sources as modern archaeology and ancient poetry. The specialized format will prove helpful to the traveler, as he visits the areas that once formed the locus of civilization. Because the towns and waterways of classical times were so rich in stories, the student can learn from a volume devoted solely to geography the connection between environment and the formation of a culture, between the physical world and the world of the mind.

Most of the entries in THE NEW CENTURY HANDBOOK OF CLASSICAL GEOGRAPHY are derived from THE NEW CENTURY CLASSICAL HANDBOOK, published by Appleton-Century-Crofts in 1962. In a number of cases, information on finds that have been made since 1962 has beeen added, as well as completely new entries, such as the one on Akrotiri. Articles signed with the initials JJ were prepared by the late Jotham Johnson, Head of the Department of Classics, New York University, who served as Editorial Consultant for THE NEW CENTURY CLASSICAL HANDBOOK. Those signed with the initials AH and PM were prepared by Professors Abraham Holtz and Philip Mayerson of New York University.

Catherine B. Avery

# —A—

*Abae* (ā′bē). [Also: *Abai*.] In ancient geography, a city in Phocis, Greece, noted for its temple and oracle of Apollo. Looted and largely destroyed during one of the Persian invasions of Greece, it was later partly rebuilt under the Roman emperor Hadrian. Ruins of parts of the town still exist.

*Abdera* (ab-dir′a). A maritime city in Thrace on Cape Balastra, opposite the island of Thasus in NE Greece. According to legend, it was founded by Heracles, who had gone there to fetch the man-eating mares of Diomedes of Thrace, in memory of Heracles' servant Abderus who was slain by the mares while Heracles sought Diomedes. The city is now known to have been colonized (c650 B.C.) by people from Clazomenae. Destroyed some time before 550 B.C. by Thrace, it was resettled (c540 B.C.) by refugees from the Persian occupation of Teos, and became during the next 200 years one of the most prosperous of Greek cities. Thereafter it declined in importance, and the ancient city is now entirely in ruins. A small agricultural community still occupies part of the original site. The air of the region was thought in ancient times to cause people to become dull, and from this came a folk belief among the ancient Greeks that all Abderites were stupid. This conviction persisted despite the fact that a number of famous men, including Protagoras and Democritus, either were born in or were residents of Abdera.

*Abydos* (a-bī′dos) or *Abydus* (-dus). In ancient geography, a town in Mysia, Asia Minor, on the Hellespont. It was colonized by Ionians from Miletus. It was from Abydos that Leander swam across the Hellespont each night to visit his beloved Hero at Sestos. From Abydos Xerxes caused a double bridge to be constructed across the Hellespont by which

fat, fāte, fär, fåll, ȧsk, fãre; net, mē, hėr; pin, pīne; not, nōte, möve, nôr; up, lūte, pull; oi, oil; ou out; (lightened) ēlect, agōny, ūnite; (obscured) errant, ardent, actor; ch, chip; g, go; th, thin; ᵺ, then; y, you; (variable) d̠ as d or j, ș as s or sh, t̤ as t or ch, z̧ as z or zh.

1

his army could march into Europe to attack Greece. However, when it was completed a great storm arose and dashed the whole work to pieces. Xerxes was so angry when he learned of the destruction of the bridge that he gave orders for the Hellespont to receive 300 lashes, and that fetters should be hurled into it. Some say he ordered the waters of the Hellespont branded with a hot iron, and commanded those who carried out the task of lashing the water to say the following as they did so: "Thou bitter water, thy lord lays on thee this punishment because thou hast wronged him without a cause, having suffered no evil at his hands." When the waters had thus been punished, those who had been in charge of constructing the bridge had their heads cut off, new engineers were appointed and the work was recommenced. This time the bridge was made of boats—triremes and penteconters (50-oared ships). The keels of the boats ran parallel to the current of the Hellespont to ease the strain on the cables which fastened them together. The ships were also made fast with heavy anchors. In the middle of the strait a gap was left between the ships so that light vessels could pass through them into or out of the Euxine Sea. Sawn planks from tree trunks were laid on the cables and fastened to them, brushwood and earth were packed down on top of the planks to form a roadway, and on each side of the bridge a fence was raised high enough so that the animals passing across could not see the water and become frightened. When Xerxes learned in Sardis that the bridge was ready he set out with his vast army and arrived for the crossing. Now he took a golden goblet and poured a libation into the Hellespont as he prayed for success in his conquest of Greece. Then he cast the golden goblet, a golden bowl, and a sword into the waters. Perhaps this was to make amends for having scourged the waters, or perhaps this was an offering to the sun. Having carried out these rites his vast host successfully crossed over from Abydos into Europe. The people of Abydos did not accompany him into Greece; they were left behind to guard the bridge. However, when Xerxes returned, after the disaster of Salamis (480 B.C.), he found his bridge of boats had been scattered by storms, and this time he crossed back to Asia in his ships which had sailed back from Greece.

*Abyla* (ab'i-la̧). [Also: *Abyla Columna, Abyla Mons.*] A promontory in Africa, the modern Jebel Musa at Ceuta, opposite the ancient Calpe (the modern Gibraltar). One of the pillars supposed to have been set up by Heracles, either to narrow the opening between the ocean and the inner sea and keep ocean monsters out, or as a headland which he made by cutting a passage from the ocean into the inner sea, hitherto separated by a continuous range of mountains between the European and African continents.

*Acanthus* (a-kan'thus). In ancient geography, a town situated on the base of the peninsula of Acte in Chalcidice. It was colonized by Andros and allied to Athens. The Spartan general Brasidas moved to attack it in 424 B.C. The Acanthians allowed him to enter their city alone, to present reasons why they should surrender to him. It was time to harvest the grapes and they did not want to lose the vintage. Thus, "not being a bad speaker for a Lacedaemonian," the arguments of Brasidas persuaded them to revolt against Athens and to submit to Sparta.

*Acarnania* (ak-ar-nā'ni-a). In ancient geography, a division of Greece, bounded by the Ambracian Gulf on the N, by Amphilochia on the NE, by Aetolia on the E (partly separated by the Achelous River), and by the Ionian Sea on the W. Its ancient inhabitants were the Leleges and Curetes. They were considered rude mountaineers by the people of the Greek city-states, but were nevertheless regarded as Hellenes and as such were allowed to participate in the Panhellenic games.

*Achaea* (a-kē'a). [Also: *Achaia;* called *Achaea Phthiotis.*] In ancient geography, a small region in S Thessaly, containing Phthia. It was probably the original home of the Achaean people, and it retained its name as late as the time of Herodotus. According to tradition, this was the home of Deucalion, who with his wife survived the great flood sent by the gods to destroy wicked mankind. The land was ruled by Xuthus, son of Hellen and grandson of Deucalion. Xuthus left it to help the Athenians in a war. Later, Achaeus, son of Xuthus, returned and won back his father's realm for himself and named it Achaea.

*Achaea.* [Also: *Achaia;* original name, *Aegialus* or *Aegialea,* meaning "the Coast."] In ancient geography, a mountainous district in the Peloponnesus bordering on the Gulf of Corinth, N of Elis and Arcadia. According to tradition,

(obscured) errant, ardent, actor; ch, chip; g, go; th, thin; ŦH, then; y, you;
(variable) ḏ as d or j, ṣ as s or sh, ṭ as t or ch, ẓ as z or zh.

Achaeans from Argos and Lacedaemon under the leadership of Tisamenus, son of Orestes, invaded this land when they were driven from Argos and Lacedaemon by the Dorians. Driving out the Ionians who inhabited it, they took the land for themselves and named it Achaea.

*Acharnae* (ạ-kär'nē). Deme in Attica where the ivy plant was said to have first appeared. Here Dionysus Kissos *(Ivy)* and Dionysus Melpomenus *(Singer)* were invoked. Apollo Agyieus and Heracles were also worshiped here. It is the scene of Aristophanes' comedy, *The Acharnians.*

*Achelous* (ak-ẹ-lō'us). [Modern names, **Akheloos, Aspropotamos.**] River in NW Greece which rises in Epirus, in the Pindus Mountains, forms part of the boundary between what was ancient Aetolia and Acarnania, and flows into the Ionian Sea.

*Acheron* (ak'ẹ-ron). In ancient geography, the name of several small rivers in Greece, of which the chief (the modern Gurla) was in Thesprotia in Epirus. It flowed through Lake Acherusia, received the waters of the Cocytus (the modern Vuvos), and emptied into the Ionian Sea.

*Acherusia Palus* (ak-ẹ-rö'si-ạ pā'lus). [Eng. trans., "Acherusian Bog."] In ancient geography, the name of several small lakes supposed to be connected with the lower world. The most important were the lake through which the Acheron flowed, and one about 11 miles W of Naples, the modern Fusaro Lake. Like Acheron, the name came to be applied, in ancient literary usage, to the lower world itself.

*Acrae* (ak'rē). In ancient geography, a city of SE Sicily, situated about 20 miles inland and W of Syracuse. It was founded (664 B.C.) by colonists from Syracuse. Quarries near the ancient city are filled with tombs dating from various periods. The ancient city was built on a hill above the modern town of Palazzolo Acreide.

*Acragas* (ak'rạ-gạs). [Latin, **Agrigentum;** modern names, **Agrigento, Girgenti.**] In ancient geography, a city of Sicily, situated on a high hill near the shore on the SW coast of the island. It was founded c582 B.C. by colonists from the Dorian city of Gela. Shortly after its founding it was compelled to defend itself, perhaps under the tyrant Phalaris, from attacks by the Carthaginians (c560–550 B.C.). By the beginning of the 5th century B.C. it was a flourishing and prosperous city, called by Pindar "the fairest of mortal cities." It outstripped Gela and became second only to Syracuse among the Greek cities of Sicily. Under the tyrant Theron (died c472 B.C.) the city was greatly enlarged: its walls were extended to include both eastern and western summits, a water supply was provided, and the foundations were laid for a magnificent row of temples along the south wall between the rivers Acragas and Hypsas. Following the defeat of the Carthaginians at Himera (480 B.C.) the city flourished. In 472 B.C. the tyrants were overthrown and a democracy was established. A high degree of prosperity and even luxury was attained and the temples begun by Theron were completed. In 406 B.C. the Carthaginians besieged the city, which had refused immunity in return for neutrality in the struggle that Carthage now undertook to reduce and conquer Greek Sicily. After a siege of eight months, in which they were deserted by their allies and mercenaries, most of the inhabitants abandoned their city. Under cover of darkness they marched out, leaving those either unable or unwilling to go to be butchered by the Carthaginians under the command of Himilco, who sacked the city. It remained a Punic city until c340 B.C., when it was rewon and recolonized by Timoleon, the general sent by Corinth to rescue her colony of Syracuse. During the Punic Wars the city was sacked by the Romans (261 B.C.) and by the Carthaginians (255), and finally fell to Rome (210 B.C.). Many remains of the magnificent temples constructed in the 5th century B.C. are to be found on the site, including temples of Zeus, Heracles, Concordia, and Hera, as well as remains of the 4th century B.C. temples of Demeter, Castor and Pollux, and Hephaestus. The poet and philosopher Empedocles was a native of Acragas.

*Acroceraunia* (ak″rō-sē-rô′ni-ạ). [Also: *Akrokeraunia;* modern Greek, *Glossa;* Italian, *Linguetta.*] In ancient geography, a promontory projecting from what was then the NW part of Epirus (and is now SW Albania) into the Ionian Sea. The name has sometimes been incorrectly extended to the whole range of the Ceraunian Mountains.

*Acrocorinthus* (ak″rō-kō-rin′thus). [Also *Akrokorinthos, Acro-Corinth.*] Hill, about 1885 feet high in Greece, under the N slope of which lies the city of Corinth. According to legend, Poseidon and Helius struggled for control of the land about Corinth. Briareus awarded the hill to Helius. He in his turn gave it to Aphrodite. On the slopes of the hill were many temples and altars, and on the summit a temple of Aphrodite. The spring behind the temple was given to the city by the river-god Asopus to reward Sisyphus for informing him that it was Zeus who had carried off his daughter Aegina. Some say this spring and the Pirene spring are the same, that the water flows underground from one to the other. The hill, celebrated for its extensive view, is now covered with ruins. There are scanty remains of the ancient fortifications and of the celebrated temple of Aphrodite and other religious structures. In 1961 the discovery on the hill of remains of a 6th century B.C. sanctuary, probably one of Demeter, was reported. Excavation at the site uncovered three marble heads: two, probably from the 2nd century A.D., of young priestesses; the third, larger than life-size, originally had inset eyes and gilded hair and was possibly part of an acrolithic cult statue.

*Acropolis* (a̤-krop'ō̤-lis). A general name for the citadel of an ancient Greek city. The name is especially appropriated to that of Athens, whose Acropolis is a precipitous rock that rises about 260 feet above the city, extends 1000 feet from E to W, and is 400 feet in its greatest width. It forms a natural citadel, and in earliest times was the site of ancient Athens itself, strongly fortified and containing the palace of the king. It was a center of worship from most ancient times. Here were the palaces of Cecrops and Erechtheus, and here Athena vied with Poseidon for control of the city.

The well of Clepsydra, below the northwest corner of the Acropolis and reached in ancient times by a covered stairway, supplied the citadel with water. Nearby was the cave where Apollo is said to have ravished Creusa, daughter of Erechtheus, and fathered Ion, ancestor of the Ionians. Traces of settlements of the Neolithic Age have been found on the slopes of the Acropolis. The first palace on its upper surface was erected between 1900 and 1600 B.C. Traces of structures of the age of Cecrops (traditional date, 1581 B.C.), Erechtheus, and other early kings include a palace, parts of Pelasgian walls, and the platform where the temple of Nike stands. Traces of a temple from the period 1100–750 B.C. also survive. Down to about the 7th century B.C. the Acropolis was a fortified citadel. After that time it came to be considered as a sacred area and private dwellings were removed from it, leaving a few temples and a simple propylaeum. The foundations of an ancient temple of Athena, lying between and partly under the sites where the *Erechtheum* and the *Parthenon* now stand, were recognized and studied by Dörpfeld in 1885. The Doric, peripteral temple, which measured 70 by 137 feet, went through three phases. The earliest part of it was raised on the foundations of a prehistoric Mycenaean palace about the time of Solon (c638–c559 B.C.), and was entirely dedicated to Athena Polias. Toward the end of the 6th century B.C. the Pisistratidae, seeking to equal the beautiful temple erected by their rivals the Alcmaeonidae at Delphi, transformed the naos of the temple and, 520–510 B.C., added 12 columns on the flanks, six columns on the façades, and painted marble pediments. The temple was destroyed by the Persians, 480 B.C., and was partly restored. In 454 B.C. the treasury of the Confederacy of Delos was brought from Delos and placed in the restored temple. On completion of the Parthenon the treasury was removed thither. After the completion of the Erechtheum (407 B.C.), the restored section of the ancient temple of Athena Polias fell into disuse. It was destroyed by fire in 406 B.C. and its foundations were covered over by a terrace. In the 6th century B.C. there was a temple on the present site of the Parthenon, and many smaller temples and treasuries as well on the Acropolis. In this century Pisistratus and Clisthenes made additions to the temples. All of these were completely destroyed when the Persians attacked, took the citadel and burned it, 480 B.C. After the successes of the Greeks at Salamis (480) and Plataea (479 B.C.), the Athenians returned to the city which they had abandoned when the Persians swept down on it. Themistocles, the successful commander at Salamis and the most influential man in Athens, immediately set about rebuilding the walls of the city and those on the north side of the Acropolis as well, using drums of the columns of the ancient temple of Athena and other marble fragments created by the Persian destruction as building materials. These fragments, set into the wall in a kind of pattern and plainly visible to all, were a constant reminder to the Athenians of the Persian vandalism. Cimon continued the work of Themistocles. He built walls on the east and south slopes and increased the top area by filling it in with the rubble that was strewn about the Acropolis. By the time

(obscured) errant, ardent, actor; ch, chip; g, go; th, thin; ₮н, then; y, you; (variable) ḍ as d or j, ṣ as s or sh, ṭ as t or ch, ẓ as z or zh.

of Pericles (c495–429 B.C.), the Acropolis had been shored up by walls and its area increased but its surface was a mass of ruins. Cleared of ancient structures of varying periods, it presented a site for a planned development of new buildings. Pericles seized this opportunity to create here a great religious center and artistic memorial to the victory of the Greeks over the Persians. Ictinus, Callicrates, and Phidias were given the responsiblity and authority to carry out his plan. The buildings and remains from this period (last half of the 5th century B.C.) make of the Acropolis a world-famous monument of the Classical period. The traveler Pausanias describes the Acropolis as it was in the 2nd century A.D. His description, the only complete contemporary account of any age, provides a full description of buildings, statues, and altars that have since disappeared, and also makes possible the identification of many objects that have remained.

In the Pelasgic period (1600–1100 B.C.) the Acropolis could be approached by a stairway cut into rock at the northeast corner. This led to the palace of the ancient kings. The natural entrance was on the west, through the *Enneapylon,* the nine gates that were added to the Acropolis perhaps in the 10th century B.C. By the time of Pausanias the main entrance was by a great gate, the *Propylaea* on the west. This vast, never-completed structure was designed by Mnesicles. His design, majestic and symmetrical, had to be altered when priests of Athena Nike and Brauronian Artemis refused to allow their ancient precincts to be invaded to make room for the south side of the proposed Propylaea. Work on the structure was begun in 438 B.C., but was halted 431 B.C. by the outbreak of the Peloponnesian Wars. The design was modified in succeeding centuries and additions were made to it. Among the last of these was that by Caligula in 40 A.D. The present approach to the Propylaea is by the *Beulé Gate,* so-called because it was uncovered by the French archaeologist Ernest Beulé in 1853. A western extension of the Propylaea, it was added perhaps in the 2nd century A.D., and was covered by the Turks when they used the Acropolis as a fortress. The Propylaea were transformed into an arch-bishop's palace (12th century), and were later used for administrative offices; about the middle of the 17th century the Turks who had occupied the Acropolis since 1394 stored

fat, fāte, fär, fåll, åsk, fåre; net, mē, hėr; pin, pīne; not, nōte, möve, nôr; up, lūte, pûll; oi, oil; ou out; (lightened) ĕlect, agǫny, ūnite;

gunpowder in it. This was ignited by a thunderbolt and exploded. Thus, part of the structure was destroyed (1640). It is now being restored. In ancient times a winding path was followed by the sacred processions to the Acropolis in the Panathenaic festival. This was replaced by a marble ramp that led to the Propylaea. On the south or right side of the Propylaea is the little temple of Athena Nike, goddess of Victory, built on a bastion that juts out to the west, on a site that was from ancient times a precinct of Athena. The ancient cult image was of wood, and depicted the goddess without wings, holding in one hand a pomegranate, symbol of peace and fertility, and in the other her war helmet. This edifice came to be known as the temple of *Nike Apteros* (Wingless Victory) perhaps from the ancient statue. Here, some say, Victory was presented as wingless so that she could never fly from Athens. The exquisite relief sculptures of the Victories, including the charming *Victory Loosing Her Sandal,* from the balustrade of the temple, are now in the museum on the Acropolis. On the site of the temple of Athena Nike, so legend says, Aegeus stood to look over the sea, watching for the ship whose sails would tell him the fate of Theseus. From here, when he saw the black sails of death, he hurled himself to the rocks below. The temple of Athena Nike, built 440 B.C., was pulled down by the Turks in 1687, and its material was used by them to build a rampart against the Venetians. It was carefully reconstructed from its original pieces in 1835, later found to be near a state of collapse, and in 1936–41 was rebuilt again, when remains of an older temple were found. To the left of the Propylaea was what Pausanias referred to as a building with pictures, the *Pinacotheca.* He mentions a number of pictures he saw there, all of which have since been lost. Inside the Propylaea, at the entrance to the Acropolis, was a figure of *Hermes of the Gateway.* Near it was a small stone on which Silenus was supposed to have sat and rested when he came in the train of Dionysus to Athens.

To the south center of the Acropolis is the Parthenon, a temple that for strength and simplicity, perfect proportions and harmonious relation to its site, has never been equalled. This was Athena's great temple, named from her epithet Athena Parthenos (Virgin). Pericles engaged Ictinus as architect and gave Phidias general charge of its construction and ornamentation. Periods in history when such a fortunate combination of geniuses lived at the same time have been rare. Work on the temple, which faces the east, was commenced in 447 and completed in 438 B.C. On its pediments were great sculptured scenes, skillfully designed to fit the awkward and constricted area of a thin elongated triangle with perfect grace. The scene at the birth of Athena was on the east pediment; the west pediment showed the contest of Athena and Poseidon. The building was richly decorated inside and out. Great artists worked on it; rich gifts were made to it in succeeding times, among them the golden shields presented by Alexander the Great after the battle of the Granicus, 334 B.C. In later times, when Christianity spread over the Mediterranean world and the Emperor Theodosius II destroyed many of the great monuments, the Parthenon was dedicated as a Christian church (630 A.D.). Later it was turned into a mosque and equipped with minarets by the Turks, who had occupied the Acropolis since 1394, and it was used by them as an arsenal in a war with the Venetians. During the siege a shot from the Hill of the Muses pierced the roof, ignited the gunpowder stored there, and blew the magnificent building apart (1687). This was the worst disaster that had ever befallen it. Afterward its monumental sculptures, statues, altars, and columns lay in broken heaps on the ground. In succeeding years some of the marble was carried away and used for building material. Early in the 19th century Lord Elgin, ambassador of Great Britain in Constantinople, received permission from the Sultan to gather up what he wished of the fallen and neglected marbles and to carry them off to England, where they were placed in the British Museum, 1816. Across from the Parthenon, to the north, rises the Erechtheum, built after 421 B.C., on the site of one of the oldest sanctuaries of the Acropolis. Here, according to tradition, Athena and Poseidon vied for control of Athens. Poseidon struck the rock with his trident, and a fountain of sea water gushed forth. Athena gave the olive tree as her gift to the city. It was voted the more useful to man and she was awarded the city and became its chief goddess. The Erechtheum housed the ancient shrines of the rivals. The cella in the east of the building was that of Athena. In it was the ancient olive-wood image of the goddess, said to have fallen from heaven in the

fat, fāte, fär, fåll, ȧsk, fãre; net, mē, hėr; pin, pīne; not, nōte, möve, nôr; up, lūte, půll; oi, oil; ou out; (lightened) ẹlect, agǫny, ụnite;

time of Cecrops. It was burned when the Persians destroyed the Acropolis, or, as some say, was saved by being taken aboard a Greek ship just before the battle of Salamis (480 B.C.). Behind the cella of Athena, to the west, was the cella of Poseidon-Erechtheus. Thus the two rival immortals, Athena and Poseidon, were united in one temple. In Poseidon's cella was enclosed the fountain of sea water, sometimes called the "Sea of Erechtheus," brought forth by Poseidon's trident, as well as the marks of his trident. It was said that when the south wind blew the cistern gave forth the sound of waves. There were also altars to Hephaestus, a god closely associated with Athena in the arts of civilization, and to Butes, an ancient priest of Athena and ancestor of the priestly family, the Butadae. Behind the cella of Poseidon was the *Pandroseum,* the sanctuary of Pandrosos, daughter of Cecrops and first priestess of Athena. In the enclosure was the sacred olive tree Athena planted as a gift to Athens. The tree was burned during the Persian Wars, but according to tradition it immediately put forth a new shoot. The famous *Porch of the Maidens* formed a south wing of the Erechtheum, and a north porch was a place of sacrifices to Zeus. The Erechtheum was converted into a church, probably in the 7th century A.D., and in the time of the Turkish occupation it housed the harem of the Turkish commander on the Acropolis. Many altars and statues were on the Acropolis, among them the statue of *Athena Lemnia* by Phidias, said by Pausanias to be his finest work. There were also numberless statues representing scenes from mythology, images of the gods, and of such mortals as Pericles, Xanthippus, and Anacreon of Teos, the poet. On the south slope of the Acropolis was the sanctuary of Asclepius, begun c420 B.C., an important healing center until its close in the 5th century A.D. To the east of the sanctuary of Asclepius are the remains of a theater of Dionysus built in the 4th century B.C. on the site of the ancient theater in which the plays of Aeschylus, Sophocles, and Euripides had been performed. At the southeast corner on the lower slopes was the *Odeum,* constructed about the same time as the Parthenon.

In 86 B.C. Sulla besieged Athens and destroyed many buildings on the south slope of the Acropolis. In Roman times additions were made to the Propylaea and buildings were added on the Acropolis. A circular shrine dedicated to

(obscured) errạnt, ardẹnt, actọr; ch, chip; g, go; th, thin; ͳH, then; y, you;
(variable) ḏ as d or j, ş as s or sh, ṭ as t or ch, ẓ as z or zh.

the goddess Roma and to the Emperor Augustus was erected 14 B.C. Hadrian made rich gifts and repaired buildings. Herodes Atticus, wealthy Athenian and generous donor of buildings, built the theater named for him on the south slope, in memory of his wife Regilla, c160 A.D. From the reign of Theodosius II (401–450 A.D.), the Acropolis ceased to be a center of worship. He caused the monuments to be mutilated or destroyed in a ruthless campaign of Christianization. As noted earlier, the Acropolis was occupied by the Turks for about 400 years. In 1833, following the liberation of the Greeks, the royal ensign of their first king, Otto I, was hoisted on the Acropolis. Almost immediately work was begun on the restoration of the monuments, among the most precious in the western world. Excavations have revealed successively earlier stages of development, before the time of Pericles. The site, crowned by the Parthenon, the Erechtheum whose more delicate outlines, façade, and famous Porch of the Maidens are in good state of preservation, and the temple of Athena Nike, is a center of artistic and cultural pilgrimage. Large marble fragments and the drums of columns of these and other structures remain where they fell, in the hope that means will be found to reassemble and raise them.

*Actium* (ak'shi-um, -ti-um) In ancient geography, a promontory on the NW coast of Acarnania, in Greece. The ancient *peribolos* or sacred enclosure, rectangular in plan and built in *opus reticulatum,* the seat of the famous Actian games of Augustus, still remains. Modern excavations have laid bare extensive ruins of several successive temples, one of the latest of which is that dedicated by Augustus after the victory of 31 B.C. A famous naval battle was fought (Sept. 2, 31 B.C.) near Actium by Octavian (the future Augustus) against Mark Antony and Cleopatra. It was decided by the flight of Cleopatra, Mark Antony's land forces thereupon surrendering to Octavian. The victory secured for Octavian supreme rule over the Roman dominion.

*Addua* (ad'ö-ạ). [Modern name, *Adda.*] River in N Italy, which rises in the Rhaetian Alps, traverses Lacus Larius (Lake Como), and joins the Po River about eight miles W of Cremona.

*Adige* (ä'dē-jä). See *Athesis.*

*Adramyttium* (ad-rạ-mit'i-um) or *Adramyti* (-i). [Modern name,

*Edremit.*] In ancient geography, a town in the Troad near the head of the Gulf of Adramyttium (Gulf of Edremit) NE of the island of Lesbos. It was one of the towns seized and sacked by Achilles during the Trojan War, according to legend.

**Adramyttium, Gulf of.** [Modern name, *Gulf of Edremit.*] In ancient geography, an arm of the Aegean Sea on the coast of Mysia. It separates the mainland from the island of Mytilene. Length, about 50 miles; width, about 15 miles.

**Adria** (ā′dri-ạ). In ancient geography, the sea now called the Adriatic, and also (about the 1st century A.D.) that part of the Mediterranean which lies between Crete and Sicily.

**Adriatic Sea** (ā-dri-at′ik, ad-ri-at′ik). [Italian *Mare Adriatico;* Latin, *Adria, Mare Adriaticum.*] That part of the Mediterranean Sea which lies between Italy on the W and NW, and Yugoslavia and Albania on the E, and is connected with the Ionian Sea by the Strait of Otranto. Its chief arms are the Gulfs of Manfredonia, Venice, Trieste, and Quarnero (Velik Kvarner), and its largest tributaries are the rivers Po and Adige. Length, about 500 miles; area, about 51,000 square miles; average depth, about 795 feet; greatest known depth, 4590 feet.

**Aegaleos** (ē-gā′lẹ-os), **Mount.** In ancient geography, a mountain in W Attica, W of Athens. It ended in a promontory (Amphiale), opposite the island of Salamis, from which Xerxes is said to have witnessed (480 B.C.) the defeat of his forces by the Greeks in the Battle of Salamis. Elevation, about 1534 feet.

**Aegates** (ẹ-gā′tēz) or **Aegadian** (ẹ-gā′di-ạn) **Isles.** [Modern name, *Egadi Islands.*] Group of small islands W of Sicily. The Romans defeated the Carthaginians in a naval battle near the islands in 241 B.C.

**Aegean Sea** (ē-jē′ạn). [Latin, *Mare Aegaeum.*] Name given to that part of the Mediterranean Sea which lies between Greece on the W and N, and Turkey on the E. It communicates with the Sea of Marmara (Propontis) and thence with the Black Sea (Pontus, Pontus Euxinus) by the strait of the Dardanelles (Hellespont). It contains many islands, of which the best known are Aegina, Euboea, the Cyclades, the Sporades, Samos, Chios, Lesbos, Samothrace, and Thasus. According to Greek legend, it received its name from the Athenian king Aegeus who threw himself into the sea believing that his son Theseus had been killed. The term *Aegean* has been used to designate the Bronze Age civilization of the Greek mainland, islands, and the mainland of Asia Minor, Thrace, and Macedonia. Length, about 400 miles; greatest width, over 200 miles; area, about 69,000 square miles; average depth, 1910 feet.

**Aegina** (ē-jī'na̯). An island in SE Greece, in the Saronic Gulf, or the Gulf of Aegina. According to legend it was to this island, once known as Oenone or Oenopia, that Zeus brought Aegina, the daughter of the river-god Asopus. The island was renamed Aegina by Aeacus, the son of Aegina and Zeus, who became king of the island. Hera was infuriated when she learned that the island had been named in honor of one of her rivals. She sent a plague which poisoned the waters, and a hot south wind to parch the fields and pastures; the land was infested by serpents; animals collapsed and died; hopeless men relapsed into licentious behavior. At the end of four months Aeacus appealed to Zeus: if indeed Zeus was his father he should either lift the plague or let Aeacus die with his people. Zeus answered his prayer and the plague was ended, but Aegina had been nearly depopulated. Once again Zeus heeded the prayers of Aeacus: hordes of ants climbing the trunk of a sacred oak tree were transformed into men who became known as Myrmidons.

Historically, Aegina was conquered and colonized in very ancient times by the Dorians, and it was an important Greek commercial state and center of art in the 6th and 5th centuries B.C. In 459 B.C. it was defeated for the first time by Athens, and some three decades later (431 B.C.) relegated to a position of comparative insignificance when the Athenians carried out a mass deportation of its population. The principal ancient remains are a late archaic (late 6th century B.C.) Doric temple of Aphaea, where the Aeginetan Marbles now in Munich were found, and scanty remains of a temple of Apollo. Aeginetan coins, bearing the image of a tortoise, were widely circulated in the Greek world and many Greek states adopted the Aeginetan standards of weights and measures.

**Aegina, Gulf of.** [Also: **Saronic Gulf;** Latin, **Saronicus Sinus.**] Arm of the Aegean Sea, lying SW of Attica and NE of Argolis, Greece. It contains the islands of Salamis and Aegina. Length, about 50 miles.

---

fat, fāte, fär, fâll, åsk, fāre; net, mē, hėr; pin, pīne; not, nōte, möve, nôr; up, lūte, pull; oi, oil; ou out; (lightened) ēlect, agǫny, ūnite;

*Aegospotami* (ē″gọs-pot′ạ-mī). [Also: *Aegospotamos.*] In ancient
geography, a small river and a town in that part of ancient
Thrace known as the Chersonesus Thracica (geographically
identical with what is now called the Gallipoli Peninsula of
Turkey in Europe). The area of the river's mouth is noted
as the scene of the decisive naval victory of the Spartans
under Lysander over the Athenians, in 405 B.C., which led
to the close of the Peloponnesian War. The Athenians maintained that they were not honorably beaten in battle but had
been betrayed by their commanders who they claimed had
been bribed by Lysander. This was all in fulfillment of two
oracles, they said. The oracles were:
> "And then on the Athenians will be laid grievous trou-
> bles
> By Zeus the high-thundered, whose might is the greatest,
> On the war-ships battle and fighting,
> As they are destroyed by treacherous tricks, through the
> baseness of the captains."

And this oracle from the writings, so it was said, of Musaeus:
> "For on the Athenians comes a wild rain
> Through the baseness of their leaders, but some consola-
> tion will there be
> For the defeat; they shall not escape the notice of the city,
> but shall pay the penalty."

Nevertheless, the Athenian fleet was destroyed and but for
the alert action of Conon, the commander in chief, against
whom incidentally there was no accustation of having accepted a bribe, Athens herself would have been threatened.
He knew that it was customary to remove the sails when the
ships went into battle. He therefore, having escaped,
swooped down on the Spartan ships and carried off their
sails, so that they could not pursue him nor sail immediately
against Athens.

*Aegusa* (ē-jö′sạ) or *Aethusa* (ē-thö′sạ). [Modern name, *Favi-
gnana.*]. Largest island of the Aegates, W of Sicily.

*Aeoliae Insulae* (ẹ-ō′li-ē in′sụ-lē). [Modern name, *Lipari Islands.*] Group of volcanic islands in the Tyrrhenian Sea, N
of Sicily. The chief islands are Lipara, Strongyle, Didyme,
Thermessa or Vulcania, and the small islands of Ericussa,
Phoenicussa, and Euonymus or Hicesia. According to Greek
legend, this was the island kingdom of Aeolus, keeper of the
winds, and his wife Enarete. Lipara was said to be a floating

island surrounded by a bronze wall. Its cliffs, rising sheer from the sea, confined the winds. When Aeolus, their master, wished to free one of the winds he pierced the side of the cliff and let it out; when he wishes to stop the wind he stopped up the hole in the side of the cliff.

*Aeolis* (ē'ọ-lis). [Also: *Aeolia*.] In ancient geography, originally the W coast of Asia Minor between the river Hermus and Lectum, settled by Aeolians. Later it extended along Troas (the Aegean coastal territory in the vicinity of the ancient city of Troy).

*Aepy* (ē'pi). In ancient geography, a town in Nestor's realm in Elis. According to Herodotus, it was one of six cities founded by the Minyans who had come to Laconia from the island of Lemnos but who fled to this region and settled, to escape the threats of the Laconians. Men of Aepy accompanied Nestor to the Trojan War. The town, which was also called Aepium, Epium, or Epeum, was ultimately taken over by the Eleans and demolished. Among its ruins are remains of a theater and several temples.

*Aesernia* (ē-sėr'ni-ạ). [Modern name, *Isernia*.] Town of SE Italy, situated on a tributary of the Volturnus River. It became a Roman colony in 265 B.C., and was conquered by Sulla in the Roman civil war (80 B.C.).

*Aesonis* (ē-sō'nis). A city of Magnesia, named for Aeson, the father of Jason. It was the name of Pelias.

*Aethalia* (ē-thal'i-ạ). [Modern name, *Elba*.] An island off the coast of northern Italy where the Argonauts stopped briefly on their roundabout journey home from Colchis.

*Aetolia* (ē-tō'li-ạ). [Also: *Aitolia*.] In ancient geography, a district of Greece, bounded by Epirus and Thessaly on the N, Doris on the NE, Locris on the E and SE, the Corinthian Gulf on the S, and Acarnania on the W. According to tradition, it was the land of the Curetes but was invaded from the Peloponnesus by Aetolus, a son of Endymion, and renamed for him.

*Africa* (af'ri-kạ). In ancient geography, the designation for either the entire continent, or for that portion of the northern coastal area along the Mediterranean comprising the Roman province of Africa, approximately coterminous with modern Tunisia. To the Greeks the continent was known as Libya. (JJ)

*Aganippe* (ag-ạ-nip'ē). In ancient geography, a fountain near Mount Helicon, in Boeotia, Greece, sacred to the Muses. It

fat, fāte, fär, fåll, àsk, fāre; net, mē, hėr; pin, pīne; not, nōte, möve, nôr; up, lūte, pûll; oi, oil; ou out; (lightened) ẹlect, agọny, ūnite;

was believed to inspire those who drank of it, and it gave the name "Aganippides" to the Muses.

*Agrae* (ā'grē). Suburb of ancient Athens extending E from opposite the temple of Olympian Zeus over the hills of the S bank of the Ilissus. In it lies the Panathenaic Stadium. In this area, southeast of the Acropolis on the Ilissus River, the Lesser Mysteries, established by Demeter in honor of Heracles, were celebrated.

*Agrigentum* (ag-ri-jen'tum). See *Acragas.*

*Aigai* (ī'gī). [Modern name, *Nimrud-Kalessi.*] In ancient geography, a town in Aeolia, Asia Minor. On its site are the ruins of various ancient structures.

*Alabanda* (al-a-ban'da). Ancient city of Caria, Asia Minor, on the site of the modern Arap Hissar. It is said to have been founded by Alabandus, who was later regarded by the inhabitants as a deity. (JJ)

*Alalcomenae* (al-al-kō-mē'nē). In ancient geography, a village of Boeotia, named, some say, for the aboriginal Alalcomeneus who brought up Athena; others say it was named for Alalcomenia, a daughter of the aboriginal Boeotian king Ogygus. Nearby was a stream named Triton near which the inhabitants claimed Athena was born. The temple of Athena in the village housed an ivory image of the goddess. When the Roman Sulla was raging through Greece in the 1st century B.C., he is said to have stolen the ivory image.

*Alba Fucentia* (al'ba fu-sen'shi-a) or *Alba Fucens* (fu'senz). [Modern name, *Alba Fucense, Albe.*] Village near Avezzano, in C Italy, in the province of Aquila. It contains an ancient amphitheater of the usual Roman elliptical plan, 114 by 305 feet, estimated to have seated 20,000 people. The arena measures 68 by 159 feet. The site also preserves extensive polygonal limestone fortification walls of c300 B.C., and in recent years excavations have revealed a forum of unusual archaeological interest.

*Alba Longa* (al'ba long'ga). In ancient geography, a town in Latium, Italy, about 15 miles SE of Rome, the ancient center of the Latin League. Its foundation is traditionally ascribed to Ascanius, son of Aeneas, and its destruction (665 B.C.) to Tullus Hostilius.

*Alban Hills* (al'ban). [Italian, *Monti Laziali, Monti Albani.*] Mountain group SE of Rome, near Albano Laziale. Its highest point is Monte Cavo.

*Albanus, Lacus* (al-bā'nus lā'kus). [Italian, *Lago (di) Albano,*

*Lago di Castello.*] Small lake in C Italy, noted for its picturesque scenery and occupying the crater of an extinct volcano. At the beginning of the 4th century B.C. the Romans were besieging the Etruscan city of Veii. According to the tale, in the course of the ten-year siege the waters of the Alban Lake, confined within their rocky walls, were observed to rise gently in an extremely dry summer. The waters rose steadily, overflowed the crater's rim and rushed down to flood the surrounding fields. News of this prodigy reached the enemy in Veii. An Etruscan soothsayer there laughed with glee when he heard of it. A Roman soldier who had become friendly with the soothsayer during the long siege lured him to the Roman camp, where he was imprisoned and compelled to interpret the prodigy concerning the waters of Albanus Lacus. He said there was an ancient oracle that Veii could never be captured until the waters of the Alban Lake overflowed and then were reconfined so that they did not mingle with the waters of the sea. The Roman Senate distrusted the enemy soothsayer, and sent to Delphi to inquire into the matter. The priestess told the Roman envoys that the Romans had neglected certain ceremonies in connection with the Latin feasts. She added that the waters must be confined; they must under no condition be allowed to flow to the sea. If the Romans could not force them back, they were instructed to dig ditches and canals to absorb the waters and thus prevent them from flowing to the sea. On receiving the instructions from Delphi the Roman priests offered sacrifices; the Romans set to work and dug canals and ditches to drain off the water. Shortly thereafter, under Camillus in 396 B.C., the Romans captured Veii. Another explanation for the construction of the canals and the channel bored through rock (still in existence) lies in the utilization of the water for purposes of irrigation.

*Alea* (ā′lē̬-a̬). In ancient geography, a city on the E border of Arcadia, near Argolis. According to tradition the city was founded by Aleus, grandson of Arcas and great-grandson of Zeus. The city was noted for its great sanctuaries of Ephesian Artemis and Athena Alea. A festival of Dionysus, the Scieria, was celebrated every other year here, at which time the women were flogged as the Spartan boys were flogged before the image of Artemis Orthia. Alea was abandoned

shortly after 371 B.C. when its inhabitants went to live in the
new city of Megalopolis.

*Alesia* (a̱-lē′zha̱). A city founded, according to legend, by Heracles on his journey into Iberia to seize the cattle of Geryon.
The name commemorated the wanderings of his companions and himself. The city remained free until Caesar took
it by storm, 52 B.C., from Vercingetorix. The site is occupied
by the modern village of Alise on the Côte d'Or in France.

*Alesium* (a̱-lē′zhi-um), *Mount.* Mountain in Arcadia, on the road
between Mantinea and Tegea. Its name, which means "wandering," was given to it because here Rhea wandered when
she was looking for a place to bear Zeus. On the mountain
was a grove sacred to Demeter. At the foot of the mountain
was a sanctuary of Poseidon Hippius, the original of which
was said to have been built by Agamedes and Trophonius.
It was forbidden to mortals to enter the sanctuary and across
its entrance the builders stretched no barrier but a thread of
wool. Inside the sanctuary, according to ancient legend, was
a fountain of sea water. Aepytus, king of Arcadia, disre-
garded the prohibition against entering the sanctuary, cut
the woolen thread and went in. As he did so a wave of sea
water swept into his face and blinded him. Centuries later
when the ancient sanctuary was in ruins, the Roman Emperor Hadrian commanded that a new sanctuary be built
over the ruins of the old one. Workmen detailed to complete
the task were forbidden either to look into the old sanctuary
or to move any of the ruins.

*Alexandretta* (al″ig-zan-dret′a̱). [Modern name, *Iskenderun* or
*Iskanderun.*] A seaport on the Gulf of Alexandretta (Issus,
Iskenderun) near Antioch, in the NE extremity of the Medi-
terranean Sea. The town was founded by Alexander the
Great in 333 B.C.

*Alexandria* (al-eg-zan′dri-a̱). Name given to a number of cities,
newly founded, reorganized by, or in the name of Alexander
the Great during his campaigns in Egypt and Asia (334–323
B.C.). Those of special historical interest are listed below.

*Alexandria.* [Arabic, *Al-Iskandariyah, Iskanderiyeh.*] Seaport in
NE Africa, in Egypt, founded (332 B.C.) by Alexander the
Great, from whom the city took its name. It is situated at the
NW extremity of the Nile delta on the strip of land which lies
between the Mediterranean Sea and Lake Mareotis, about
133 miles NW of Cairo. The modern city occupies what was

anciently the island of Pharos, together with the isthmus now connecting it with the mainland where the ancient city stood. According to Plutarch, Alexander chose the site of the ancient city because of a dream in which Homer appeared to him and mentioned Pharos. Surveying the location, Alexander remarked that Homer was a good architect. The lines of the city, which were laid out with flour, were devoured by flocks of many kinds of birds that swooped down. Alexander feared that the erasure of the lines by the birds was an unfavorable omen. However, seers convinced him that it meant not only that his city would be great but that it would become the nurse and feeder of many nations because there were so many kinds of birds in the flocks that fed on the flour. Ancient Alexandria was the capital of Egypt during the Ptolemaic period and became an important seat of Greek culture and learning. In 30 B.C. it was annexed by Rome and long ranked as the second city of the Roman empire.

*Alexandria Arachosiae* (ar-a̧-kō'si-ē). In ancient geography, a city of Arachosia, C Asia, founded by Alexander the Great, 329 B.C. The ancient site is now occupied by the city of Kandahar, SE Afghanistan.

*Alexandria Arian* or *Arion* (ār'i-a̧n, a-rī'o̧n). In ancient geography, a city of Aria, in C Asia, so named by Alexander the Great (330 B.C.) who made it the capital of his province of Aria. The site of the ancient city is now occupied by Herat in NW Afghanistan.

*Alexandria Eschata* (es-kā'ta̧). In ancient geography, a city on the Jaxartes River where it crossed the borders of Sogdiana in C Asia. The city was founded by Alexander the Great, c328 B.C., and was named Eschata *(Furthest)* to indicate that it marked the northeastern limit of his empire. The site of the ancient city is now occupied by Leninabad (formerly Khodjend) in the Tadzhik Soviet Socialist Republic, U.S.S.R.

*Allia* (al'i-a̧). [Also: *Alia;* modern name, *Aga.*] In ancient geography, a small river in Latium, Italy, joining the Tiber about ten miles N of Rome. On its banks in c390 B.C., the Gauls under Brennus defeated the Romans. The battle was followed by the capture and sack of Rome.

*Alope* (al'ō̧-pȩ̄). In ancient geography, a city of S Thessaly, near the Sinus Maliacus (Gulf of Lamia).

*Alpheus River* (al-fē′us, al′fę̄-us). [Also (for parts of its course): *Rouphia, Rufia, Ruphia;* Greek *Alpheios.*] River in Greece, in the Peloponnesus, flowing generally NW from S Greece into the Ionian Sea. The plain of Olympia touches its N bank, and its name is mentioned repeatedly in the legend and history of Greece. In more modern times, it occurs in English literature as the original of Coleridge's river Alph, mentioned in *Kubla Khan.* In Greek mythology, it was the river diverted by Heracles in order to clean the Augean stables. It flows at one point under the ground, and was for this reason believed by the ancient Greeks actually to flow under the sea to Sicily.

*Alps* (alps). [Latin, *Alpes.*] The most extensive mountain system in Europe, comprising a part of what is now SE France, most of Switzerland, a part of N Italy, a part of S Germany, and parts of Austria and Yugoslavia, and consisting of a number of ranges separated by deep valleys. The system was divided in ancient times into: 1) the Maritime Alps (Alpes Maritimae), including the Ligurian Alps, highest peak, Punta Argentera (10,184 feet) in NW Italy; 2) the Cottian Alps (Alpes Cottiae or Cottianus), highest peak, Monte Viso (Mons Vesulus) (12,605 feet) SW of Turin, NW Italy, near the French border; 3) the Graian Alps (Alpes Graiae), which include the Little St. Bernard Pass (7,177 feet) over which Hannibal is thought to have marched into Italy in 218 B.C., highest peaks, Gran Paradiso (13,324 feet) in NW Italy, and the Barre des Écrins (13,462 feet) in SE France; 4) the Pennine Alps (Alpes Penninae), the highest portion of the system, which includes the Great St. Bernard Pass (Mons Penninus) (8,111 feet) between Switzerland and N Italy and the summits Mont Blanc (15,781 feet) in SE France on the Italian border, Monte Rosa (15,217 feet) on the border between Switzerland and Italy, and Mont Cervin or the Matterhorn (14,780 feet) on the border between Switzerland and Italy; 5) Rhaetian Alps (Alpes Raeticae), including Saint Gotthard Pass (6,935 feet) and Finsteraarhorn (14,026 feet) in SC Switzerland, and Piz Bernina (13,295 feet) in the extreme SE corner of Switzerland; 6) the Noric Alps (Alpes Noricae), with Eisenhut (8,006 feet) and Gross Glockner (12,461 feet) in the Tirol, S Austria; 7) the Carnic Alps (Alpes Carnicae), with the summit Kellerwand (9,217 feet) on the border between Austria and Italy; 8) the Venetian

Alps (Alpes Venetae), also called the Dolomites, with the summit Marmolada (10,965 feet) in NE Italy; and 9) the Julian Alps (Alpes Juliae) in NW Yugoslavia with the summit Triglav (9,394 feet). Outlying ranges in Hungary and Yugoslavia are respectively: Karawanken (Caravanca Mons) and the Dinaric Alps (Alpes Dinaricae). The length of the range from the Pass of Giovi (N of Genoa) to Semmering Pass (SW of Wiener Neustadt, Austria) is over 600 miles, and its width is from 90 to 180 miles. The average height of the system is about 7,700 feet.

*Altilia* (äl-tē'lyạ). See *Saepinum*.

*Amanus* (ạmā'nus). [Modern name, *Alma Dagh* (or *Dăg*.] In ancient geography, a mountain group, a branch of the Taurus range on the borders of Cilicia and Syria.

*Amathus* (am'ạ-thus). In ancient geography, a city of Phoenician origin on the S coast of Cyprus near the site of the modern Limassol. It contained a sanctuary of Aphrodite. According to some accounts, when Theseus fled from Crete, having killed the Minotaur, his ship, bearing him and Ariadne, daughter of King Minos, was caught in a great storm. As they neared Cyprus Ariadne, who was suffering from seasickness, asked to be put ashore at Amathus. Theseus reboarded his ship which was caught up in a gale and driven to sea again, and he never returned for Ariadne. The women of Amathus were very kind to Ariadne and took good care of her as she was soon to bear Theseus' child. These accounts say she died giving birth to the child and that the people of Amathus gave her a splendid funeral. They say Ariadne's tomb is in Amathus in a grove sacred to her, and on Cyprus an annual festival of Ariadne was celebrated in which a youth groaned and writhed in imitation of a woman in labor. Because Amathus refused to join the other Cyprians in the revolt against Persia (c499 B.C.), Onesilus who had seized the throne of Cyprian Salamis laid siege to Amathus. While he was so occupied a Persian force landed and gave battle to Onesilus. The Cyprians were defeated and Onesilus was slain. Because he had besieged their city the people of Amathus cut off his head and set it up over their gates. The skull was eventually reduced to bone by the passage of time, and a swarm of bees settled in it and filled it with a honeycomb. The Amathusians observed the prodigy and consulted the oracle. The advice they received was to take down the head, bury it, and sacrifice to Onesilus as to a hero and their affairs would prosper. This they did, and they continued to sacrifice to Onesilus annually.

**Amber Islands** (am'bėr). [Also: *Electrides*.] In ancient geography, a name given by the Greeks in later times to the islands in the North Sea off what is now Denmark, Germany, and the Netherlands. See also *Glessariae*.

**Ambracia** (am-brā'shi-ạ). [Modern name, *Arta*.] In ancient geography, a city in NW Greece situated on the Arachthus River, N of the Ambracian Gulf. It was founded as a colony by the Cypselids of Corinth in the 7th century B.C., but following the death of Periander of Corinth (585 B.C.), Ambracia detached itself from the mother city and set up a democracy. In the Peloponnesian War the city appealed to Sparta for aid against Athens and her allies, the Amphilochians and Acarnanians. The Peloponnesians sent a force but in 426 B.C. betrayed the Ambracians by a secret agreement with the Athenian general Demosthenes, under which the Peloponnesians stole away without the knowledge of the Ambracian allies and left them to the mercy of Demosthenes. Demosthenes and the Amphilochians inflicted a stunning defeat on the Ambracians at Idomene. Of such magnitude was the disaster, according to Thucydides, that he did not record the number of the dead "because the amount stated seems so out of proportion to the size of the city as to be incredible." Following the defeat the Ambracians made a 100-year treaty with the Amphilochians and Acarnanians and withdrew from the war. Philip II of Macedon placed a garrison in the city after defeating the Greeks at Chaeronea (338 B.C.). This garrison was expelled after his death (336). Under Pyrrhus, the city became the capital of Epirus, 294 B.C.

**Ambracian Gulf** (am-brā'shi-an). [Also: *Gulf of Arta*.] Inlet of the Ionian Sea in W Greece. Length, about 25 miles, greatest breadth, about ten miles.

**Amestratus** (a-mes-trā'tus). [Modern name, *Mistretta*.] Town on the island of Sicily, situated near the N coast between Messana and Panormus.

**Amorgos** (ä-môr-gôs'). Island in the Aegean Sea, one of the Cyclades, about 16 miles SE of Naxos. It was the birthplace of the Greek poet Simonides. Area, about 50 square miles.

obscured) errạnt, ardẹnt, actọr; ch, chip; g, go; th, thin; ᴛʜ, then; y, you; variable) ḍ as d or j, ṣ as s or sh, ṭ as t or ch, ẓ as z or zh.

*Amphiale* (am-fī'a-lē). Promontory on Mount Aegaleos opposite the island of Salamis. From this spot Xerxes is said to have witnessed the Persian defeat at the Battle of Salamis (480 B.C.).

*Amphilochia* (am-fi-lō'ki-a). In ancient geography, a region on the eastern shore of the Ambracian Gulf, inhabited by a tribe from Epirus.

*Amphipolis* (am-fip'ō-lis). In ancient geography, a city in Macedonia, on the Strymon River, about three miles from the Aegean Sea. Originally a Thracian town, it was colonized by Athens c436 B.C., and was captured (424 B.C.) by Sparta. Near it the Spartans under Brasidas defeated (422 B.C.) the Athenians under Cleon. It later became a Macedonian and then a Roman possession.

*Amphissa* (am-fis'a). Town in Phocis, C Greece, N of the Gulf of Corinth, situated at the foot of the W slope of Mount Parnassus. In ancient times it was a Locrian city whose people claimed to be Aetolians, as they were ashamed to be thought of as Ozolian Locrians. According to tradition, it was named for Amphissa, beloved by Apollo. She was a daughter of Macareus and a descendant of Aeolus. On the citadel of the ancient city was a temple of Athena, in which was a bronze image said to have been brought from Troy. The Amphissians celebrated mysteries in honor of the Boy Kings, but no one could say who the Boy Kings were. Some said they were the Dioscuri, others that they were the Curetes, and still others claimed they were of the Cabiri. The Amphissians went to the aid of Delphi in the Sacred War of 356 B.C., but arrived too late and were repulsed by the Phocian general Philomelus. In 340 B.C., Amphissa was accused by Aeschines of Athens of cultivating the sacred plain of Crissa. The Amphictyonic League marched against Amphissa, imposed a fine on the city, but being unable to collect it, invited Philip of Macedon to come to the aid of the League. Philip captured and destroyed Amphissa. The rivalry and jealousy of the Greek city-states led some of them to invite Philip in; once in, they could not get him out Athens and Thebes, however, alarmed at his rapid progress into Greece banded together to oppose him. They were completely defeated at the battle of Chaeronea (338 B.C.)

*Ampsanctus, Lacus* (amp-sank' tus lā'kus) or *Amsanctus Lacu* (am-sank'tus). [Modern: *Amsancti.*] Small lake in a valley o the same name in Samnium (modern province of Avellino), SW Italy, E of Naples, noted for its sulfurous vapors and cave.

*Amyclae* (a̯-mī'klē). In ancient geography, a town on the Eurotas River in Laconia, Greece, about three miles S of Sparta. According to tradition, it was founded by Amyclas, a son of Lacedaemon, and it was the legendary seat of Tyndareus. The town was sacred to Apollo, and contained the most famous precinct of the god in Laconia. In it was a magnificient throne, made by the Magnesian sculptor Bathycles. The reliefs on the throne depicted a large number of figures of mythology as well as a band of dancers who represented the Magnesian assistants of Bathycles. The throne, as described by Pausanias, consisted of several seats, the center one of which was reserved for the image of the god. The Spartans used gold sent by Croesus to adorn the image and each year the women wove a tunic for it. The tomb of Hyacinthus, son of Amyclas, was under the throne. There was a sanctuary of Cassandra at Amyclae as well as what was supposed to be a tomb of Agamemnon. The Amyclaeans worshiped Dionysus as "Psilax," the Doric word for "wings," because wine uplifts men and lightens their spirits. Amyclae was laid waste by the Dorians and never recovered. According to a legend, the inhabitants of Amyclae had been so often alarmed by false reports of the hostile approach of the Spartans that all mention of the subject was forbidden; hence when they did come no one dared announce the fact and the town was captured. "Amyclaean silence" thus became a proverb.

*Anaphe* (ä-nä'fē). [Modern name, *Anafi* or *Anaphi*.] An island, seven miles long, in the SE Cyclades. Its name means "revealing" and was given to it for the following reasons: When the Argonauts were returning from Colchis with the Golden Fleece they were overtaken by a great storm and were lost in pitch darkness. Jason called on Apollo to save them and at once there was a flash of light from the silver bow of Apollo. The flash of light revealed the island; Ancaeus, helmsman of the *Argo,* was able to beach the ship there. The Argonauts landed and gave thanks to the god and named the island for the flash of revealing light which saved them.

*Anaurus* (a̯-nou'rus) *River.* In ancient geography, a small river of Thessaly.

(obscured) errant, ardent, actor; ch, chip; g, go; th, thin; ᴛʜ, then; y, you;
(variable) d̯ as d or j, s̯ as s or sh, t̯ as t or ch, z̯ as z or zh.

*Anchisia* (an-kī'si-ạ), *Mount.* Mountain in Arcadia. Some say that Anchises, father of Aeneas, died here on the way to Italy after leaving Troy, and that this mountain, where he was buried, was named for him.

*Andania* (an-dā'ni-ạ). Ancient city in C Messenia, founded, according to tradition, by Polycaon, the Lelegian who conquered the country. Polycaon and his wife Messene had their palace here, and to this place the mysteries of Demeter were first brought into the country. Generations later, when Cresphontes secured control of the country by guile, in the return of the Heraclidae, the king's palace was at Stenyclarus. Andania was the center of the revolt against the Spartans which was inspired by Aristomenes and led to the Second Messenian war. The Messenians moved from Andania to Mount Eira to continue their defense, and after their sufferings and defeat in the war never wanted to return to Andania. When the Messenians returned to their country, nearly three hundred years later, Epaminondas, the Theban, helped them to build a new city near Ithome, which was named Messene.

*Andros* (an'dros). Northernmost island of the Cyclades, E Greece, situated in the Aegean Sea, about six miles SE of Euboea. According to legend, the island was named for Andron, the son of Anius, priest of Apollo and king of Delos. Andron, who had the gift of prophecy, became king of the island and named it for himself. In the Persian War the people of Andros joined forces with Xerxes for the invasion of Greece. After the defeat of the Persians at Salamis the Greeks pursued their fleet as far as Andros. There they stopped and held a council to decide if they should sail to the Hellespont and destroy the bridges, the exit route of the Persian army. Having decided against this plan, they besieged Andros because the islanders refused to pay a tribute required of them by Themistocles. The Andrians said their gods were Poverty and Helplessness, and they did not have the money to pay, siege or no siege. Under the circumstances, the Greeks lifted the siege and sailed away. The island was anciently a possession successively of Athens, Macedon, Pergamum, and Rome. It is a mountainous island, about 25 miles long and ten miles wide in its greatest width.

*Anigrus* (ạ-nī'grus). River in Elis, in Greece, which gave off a very unpleasant odor and in whose waters no fish lived. It

fat, fāte, fär, fâll, àsk, fāre; net, mē, hėr; pin, pīne; not, nōte, möve, nôr; up, lūte, pùll; oi, oil; ou out; (lightened) ẹlect, agǫny, ụnite

is said that Chiron, when accidentally wounded by an arrow of Heracles, bathed his wound in its waters. The water of the river stank horribly ever after because of the Hydra's blood on the arrow. But others say the extremely disagreeable odor of the river was caused by Melampus, who cast into its waters the means by which he had purified the daughters of Proetus. In a cave nearby, persons suffering from certain diseases could go to pray to the nymphs of the river. They promised certain sacrifices, wiped the affected parts of their bodies, then swam in the river. The disease was left in the water and the sufferer emerged from it cleansed and healthy. Another cave nearby is said to have been sacred to the daughters of Atlas and was the site where Dardanus was born to Electra. In the *Iliad,* the Anigrus is called the Minyeius River.

*Anio* (än'yō). [Modern name, *Aniene,* and also, in its lower course, *Teverone.*] River in C Italy that flows into the Tiber just above Rome. It is the source of a famous waterfall, about 330 feet high, at a point just below Tivoli. It has been since ancient times a source of water for the city of Rome. Camillus, as general and dictator of the Romans, defeated the Gauls at the Anio, c366 B.C., when they marched against Rome a second time.

*Ansedonia* (an-sā-dō'nyạ). Promontory on the coast of Etruria, in Italy, south of the lagoon of Orbetello, on which in 273 B.C. was established the Latin colony of Cosa (q.v.), recently identified and in part excavated by an American mission. (JJ)

*Antalya* (än-täl-yä') *Gulf of.* [Former name, *Gulf of Adalia;* ancient name, *Pamphylian Gulf;* Latin, *Pamphylicus Sinus.*] Arm of the Mediterranean Sea, on the S coast of Turkey, on which the city of Antalya, founded by Attalus II of Pergamum, is located. Length, about 100 miles; width, about 40 miles.

*Antandrus* (an-tan'drus). In ancient geography, a city in the Troad, in Asia Minor. It was one of the cities attacked, taken, and sacked as an ally of Troy by Achilles in the Trojan War. In the time of Cambyses II it fell to Persia. Subsequently it belonged to Mytilene, and in the Peloponnesian Wars it was a battleground for the forces of Lesbos, Athens, and Sparta, falling now to one now to another. It was especially desirable because of its location near the Hellespont.

*Anthedon* (an'thȩ̄-don). In ancient geography, a harbor town of

(obscured) errạnt, ardẹnt, actọr; ch, chip; g, go; th, thin; ᴛн, then; y, you; (variable) ḍ as d or j, ṣ as s or sh, ṭ as t or ch, ẓ as z or zh.

Boeotia. There was a sanctuary and grove of the Cabiri at Anthedon, and a temple of Demeter and Core.

*Antheia* (an-thē'a̤). City in Messenia, near the Gulf of Messenia. Its name was later changed to Thuria and in the time of Augustus it was given to the Spartans because the inhabitants of the city lent aid to Antony.

*Anthela* (an-thē'la̤). In ancient geography, a place near the pass of Thermopylae, in Greece. It was the original seat of the Amphictyonic Council which was composed of representatives of the "dwellers around" the shrine of Demeter at Anthela. The meetings of the Council were held there, and later at Delphi also.

*Anticyra* (an-tis'i-ra̤). In ancient geography, a city in Locris, Greece, situated near Naupactus.

*Anticyra.* In ancient geography, a city in Phocis, Greece, situated on the Corinthian Gulf. It was noted for the medicinal plant hellebore (the ancient remedy for madness) obtained in its neighborhood.

*Anticyra.* In ancient geography, a city in Thessaly, Greece, situated on the Sperchius. Like Anticyra in Phocis, it was noted for hellebore, the ancient remedy for madness.

*Anticythera* (an-ti-si-thir'a̤). Small island in the Sea of Crete, NW of Crete. The *Ephebe of Anticythera* and other antiquities that had been lying at the bottom of the sea as a result of ancient shipwrecks were found near here by divers from Syme.

*Antiparos* (an-tip'a̤-ros). See *Oliarus.*

*Antiphellos* (an-ti-fel'os). In ancient geography, a town on the SW coast of Lycia, Asia Minor. Its site contains a Lycian necropolis of rock-cut tombs, which are architecturally important because the façades are in exact reproduction of a framed construction of square wooden beams, with doors and windows of paneled work, and ceilings of round poles laid closely together. These tombs evidently represent ancient dwellings, and the imitation is carried out in some of the interiors. There is also an ancient theater, the *cavea* of which is well preserved, with 26 tiers of seats.

*Antium* (an'shum, -shi-um). [Modern name, *Anzio.*] Town in C Italy, situated on the Tyrrhenian Sea, about 32 miles S of Rome, at one time part of the nearby community of Nettuno: a seaside resort already known to the Romans. In ancient times a Volscian stronghold, it was incorporated into Rome in 338 B.C. It was the birthplace of Nero and of Caligula who later patronized the town. The statue known as the Apollo Belvedere was discovered here in 1485.

*Aonia* (ā-ō′ni-ạ). In ancient geography, a district in Boeotia, Greece. The name is often used as synonymous with Boeotia.

*Aornum* (ā-ôr′num). A place in Thesprotia where there was said to be a passage to Hades. Some say Orpheus used this entrance when he descended to Hades in search of Eurydice.

*Apennines* (ap′ẹ-nīnz). [Latin, *Appenninus*.] Central mountain system of Italy. It forms the backbone of the peninsula and extends from the Ligurian Alps in the neighborhood of Savona SE to the extremity of the peninsula. The highest point is Monte Corno (9,585 feet), in the Gran Sasso d'Italia. Length, about 800 miles; average elevation, about 4,000 feet.

*Aphidna* (a-fid′nạ). In ancient geography, a city of Attica. According to legend, here Theseus hid Helen after abducting her from Sparta. He left her here (she was ten years old at the time) because he feared the Athenians disapproved of his deed.

*Aphrodisias* (af-rō-diz′iạs). In ancient geography, a town in Caria, Asia Minor, situated on the Maeander River (modern, Menderes) in what is now SW Turkey. The site contains the remains of an ancient hippodrome which coincide on one side with the city walls. Both ends are semicircular. The length is 919 feet, the breadth 270; the arena is 747 by 98 feet. There are 26 tiers of seats, divided into sections by flights of steps and bordered above by an arcaded gallery. There is also a comparatively well preserved Roman temple of Venus. It is Ionic, octastyle, pseudodipteral, with 15 columns on the flanks, in plan 60 by 119 feet. The peristyle columns are 35¾ feet high.

*Apollonia* (ap-ọ-lō′ni-ạ). [Modern name, *Marsa Susa*.] In ancient geography, the port of Cyrene, a Greek city in N Africa, in what is now E Libya.

*Apollonia*. In ancient geography, a city in Illyria, in what is now W Yugoslavia.

*Apollonia*. [Modern name, *Arsuf*.] In ancient geography, a town in Palestine, situated on the Mediterranean between Joppa (modern Jaffa) and Caesarea.

*Apollonia.* [Modern name, *Sozopol.*] In ancient geography, a city in Thrace, situated on the Euxine Sea. It is now only a small village in Bulgaria.

*Apulia* (ạ-pū′li-ạ). In ancient geography, a region of S Italy, lying S of the Frentani and E of Samnium. It was conquered by Rome in the 4th century B.C. Later it included the Messapian Peninsula. The ancient inhabitants were the Danui, Peucetii, and Salentini or Messapians. Throughout the centuries, Apulia was a place of entrance for Greek and Oriental influences. The region saw bitter fighting in the Punic Wars.

*Aquileia* (ä-kwi-lā′yạ). Town in NE Italy, situated at the head of the Adriatic Sea, near what is now Trieste. Founded by the Romans in 181 B.C., it became one of the chief market cities of the Empire, the strategic key to Italy on the NE. It was destroyed by Attila in 452 A.D., but rebuilt.

*Arabia Deserta* (ạ-rā′bi-ạ dẹ-zėr′tạ). [Eng. trans., "desert," or "uninhabited," Arabia.] In ancient geography, the N and C portions of Arabia.

*Arabia Felix* (fē′liks). [Eng. trans., "flourishing," or "happy," Arabia.] In ancient geography, the comparatively fertile region in the SE and S parts of Arabia, contrasted with the uninhabited and barren N and C portions.

*Arabia Petraea* (pẹ-trē′ạ). [Eng. trans., "stony" Arabia.] In ancient geography, the NW part of Arabia.

*Arabicus* (ạ-rab′i-kus), *Sinus.* Latin name of the *Red Sea.*

*Arachosia* (ar-ạ-kō′zhạ, -zhi-ạ). In ancient geography, a region in ancient Persia corresponding to part of modern Afghanistan.

*Arachthus* (ạ-rak′thus). River in NW Greece, in Epirus, which flows into the Ambracian Gulf about eight miles below Ambracia.

*Araethyrea* (a-rē-thē′rẹ-ạ). In ancient geography, the former name of Phlius. It was named for the daughter of the aboriginal king, Aras. Phlias changed the name to Phlius. The place was known as Araethyrea in the time of Homer, who listed it as one of the places that sent men to the Trojan War under the command of Agamemnon.

*Arbela* (är-bē′lạ). [Also: *Arbaïlu:* modern name, *Erbil.*] In ancient geography, a town in Assyria. It was an early seat of the worship of Ishtar, and a place of considerable importance. Sixty miles from here at Gaugamela, a Macedonian force said to have numbered 47,000 under Alexander the Great

fat, fāte, fär, fâll, àsk, fãre; net, mē, hėr; pin, pīne; not, nōte, möve, nôr; up, lūte, pùll; oi, oil; ou out; (lightened) ẹlect, agǫny, ūnite;

defeated a much larger Persian army (some estimates have run as high as one million) under Darius III, in 331 B.C. This battle, often called the Battle of Arbela, led to the final overthrow of the Persian empire.

*Arcadia* (är-kā′di-ạ). In ancient geography, a region in Greece, in the heart of the Peloponnesus, bounded by Achaea on the N, by Argolis on the E, by Laconia and Messenia on the S, and by Elis on the W. All but isolated by mountains and intersected by them, it was proverbial for its rural simplicity. It was the favorite haunt of the pastoral god Pan, who was born on Mount Maenalus within its borders and whose worship was especially strong throughout the region: caves, springs, blasted trees, mountains, etc., were sacred to him. The Arcadians also claimed that Athena was born in their country. They said that near Aliphera in western Arcadia is a stream called Tritonis and that near here Athena was born from the head of Zeus. For this reason they set up an altar of Zeus Lecheates *(In Childbed)* at Aliphera. The mountains and forests of Arcadia were a favorite hunting ground of Artemis, and Arcadia was one of the strongest centers of her worship. The mountains and woods also abounded in nymphs. The Arcadians are aboriginal to their region (they say they have lived in their land since before the birth of the moon), and they were never driven out, as were the inhabitants of the other states of the Peloponnesus. According to their own account, the first man in Arcadia was Pelasgus, a son of earth, who was the first king and who named the land Pelasgia after himself. When Arcas, son of Zeus and Callisto and a descendant of Pelasgus on his mother's side, ascended the throne he changed the name of the land to Arcadia, after himself, and this was the name by which it was known ever afterward. When the sons of Heracles under Hyllus attempted to return to the Peloponnesus, Echemus, king of Arcadia, accepted the challenge of Hyllus to decide the control of the Peloponnesus by single combat. Echemus killed Hyllus and the Heraclidae withdrew as they had agreed to do if Hyllus lost in the duel. In the second Dorian invasion by the sons of Aristomachus, the Arcadian king Cypselus gave his daughter to Cresphontes, son of Aristomachus, in marriage, and so made an ally of Cresphontes. For this reason the Arcadians were not disturbed nor dislodged from their country by the Dorian invasion.

(obscured) errant, ardent, actor; ch, chip; g, go; th, thin; ᵺ, then; y, you; (variable) ḍ as d or j, ş as s or sh, ṭ as t or ch, ẕ as z or zh.

The Arcadians played an active role in the Trojan War, to which they journeyed in ships loaned them by Agamemnon as they had no fleet of their own. In the wars between Messenia and Sparta the Arcadians allied themselves with the Messenians. Aechmis, king of Arcadia, and his countrymen fought openly on the side of Aristodemus, king of Messenia, in the First Messenian War. In the Second Messenian War the Arcadians were again allied with Messenia, and when they learned that their own leader Aristocrates had accepted bribes from the Lacedaemonians to betray their allies the Arcadians stoned him to death. Arcadians took part in the Persian War, especially at Thermopylae (480 B.C.) and Plataea (479 B.C.). Under compulsion, they joined with the Spartans to fight against Athens in the Peloponnesian Wars (431–404 B.C.). As Spartan allies, they were defeated at Leuctra (371 B.C.) by the Theban Epaminondas, and as their alliance with Sparta was an unwilling one, after this defeat the Arcadians broke away from their Spartan alliance. The cities of Arcadia, Tegea, Mantinea, and others, formed a confederation c370–360 B.C.

*Archipelago* (är-ki-pel′ạ-gō). [Also: *Greek Archipelago;* Turkish, *Jezairi-Bahri-Sefid.*] In ancient geography, a name for the various islands in the Aegean Sea, or for the sea itself.

*Arcton* (ärk′tọn). In ancient geography, a mountain ("Bear Mountain") near Cyzicus on the Pontus.

*Ardea* (är′dẹ-ạ). In ancient geography, a town in Latium, Italy, about 24 miles S of Rome. It was the chief town of the Rutulians, and later a Roman colony. In Republican times it served as a State prison. While Camillus, Roman tribune and dictator, was in voluntary exile here, the Gauls attacked, took, and sacked Rome (389 B.C.). Camillus, it is said, gathered a force of Ardeans and destroyed a part of the army of the Gauls that had encamped outside Ardea. From this victory he went on to free Rome. Ardea has the best example of early Italic fortifications of mounded earth, the agger, and interesting masonry fortifications in the volcanic stone known as tufa. Excavations have brought to light decorative architectural terra-cottas from several Italic temples of the 4th–2nd centuries B.C., and Swedish explorations have cleared the tufa foundations of a large temple and an early basilica. (JJ)

*Areopagus* (ar-ẹ-op′ạ-gus). [Eng. trans, "Hill of Ares."] Low rocky hill at Athens, Greece, continuing westward the line of the Acropolis, from which it is separated by a depression of ground. On the S side near the top there is a flight of 15 rock-cut steps, and portions of the summit are hewn smooth to form platforms, doubtless for altars. Upon this hill sat the famous court of the same name. Two unhewn stones were nearby. On one of them, the Stone of Outrage, the accuser stood during the trial; on the other, the Stone of Ruthlessness, stood the accused. This court, originally a Council of Elders, exercised supreme authority in all matters in ancient times. Under the developed Athenian constitution it lost many of its ancient powers but retained jurisdiction in cases of homicide (including wounding with intent, and arson) and in religious concerns, and exercised a general censorship. In ancient times murder and manslaughter had been avenged by the family of the slain person either by slaying the slayer or by accepting a payment in compensation. As the worship of the dead souls and of the gods of the Underworld developed, the principle arose that a murderer had offended them and must be purified of his offense in order to satisfy the avenging Erinyes or Furies. Furthermore, until purification had been achieved the wrath of the Erinyes fell not only on the murderer, but on the community of which he was a part as well. Hence purification was a matter concerning the state and one on which the community was compelled to act. It became the function of the Areopagus to adjudicate these matters. According to mythology, the very first trial for murder that took place was that of Ares for the murder of Halirrhothius, a son of Poseidon. Ares claimed he had resorted to murder to save his daughter Alcippe from being violated by Halirrhothius and was acquitted. Some say the hill and the Council was named Areopagus in commemoration of this trial, and some say the name comes from Athena's epithet "Areia," for in the second trial Orestes was acquitted of the murder of his mother when Athena cast the deciding vote in his favor. The trials of myth and legend reinforced a developing principle: the substitution of justice and law for the blind vengeance symbolized by the Erinyes or Furies. In historic times the Areopagus was constituted of all archons who, after their year of office, had successfully proved themselves guiltless of malfeasance, in accordance with the provisions of law.

(obscured) errạnt, ardẹnt, actọr; ch, chip; g, go; th, thin; ŦH, then; y, you; (variable) ḍ as d or j, ṣ as s or sh, ṭ as t or ch, ẓ as z or zh.

*Arganthonius* (är-gan-thō'ni-us). In ancient geography, a mountain ridge in Bithynia, Asia Minor, near the Propontis.

*Argillus* (är-ji'lus). In ancient geography, a colony of Andros in Macedonia. It revolted from Athens c424 B.C.

*Arginusae* (ạr-ji-nū'sē). In ancient geography, a group of small islands off the coast of Asia Minor, SE of Lesbos. Near here the Athenian fleet under Conon defeated (406 B.C.) the Spartans under Callicratidas.

*Argolis* (är'gọ-lis). In ancient geography, a division of the Peloponnesus, Greece, surrounded by Sicyonia, Corinthia, the Aegean (with the Saronic and Argolic gulfs), Laconia, and Arcadia, and containing the plain of Argos.

*Argoön* (är'gọ-on). A harbor on the island of Aethalia (Elba) into which, as legend would have it, the Argonauts put on their roundabout way home from Colchis. They gave it this name in honor of their ship, the *Argo*. The site is now occupied by Portoferraio, the chief city in the island of Elba.

*Argos* (är'gos, -gọs). Town in S Greece, in the district anciently called Argolis, in the Peloponnesus. It is situated about nine miles NW of Nauplia and the coast. According to legend, an ancient city was founded here by Phoroneus, son of Inachus, and his Pelasgian followers. He named it Phoronicum and sacrificed to Hera. Argus, a descendant of Phoroneus, changed the name of the city to Argos. It is regarded as the oldest city in Greece, and was one of the cities most beloved by Hera, who, the Argives claimed, was born in Argos. The region of Argolis fell under the domination of Danaus who fled hither from Egypt with his 50 daughters. He established his dynasty in Argolis and erected a temple to Lycian Apollo. His descendants Acrisius and Proetus partitioned the kingdom. Acrisius became ruler of the region around Argos. In a later generation Perseus, grandson of Acrisius, exchanged the kingdom of Argos for Tiryns. Argos was the home of Adrastus, father-in-law of Tydeus and Polynices and the leader of the expedition of the Seven against Thebes. By the time of the Trojan War Argos was under the influence of the ruler of Mycenae, of the dynasty of Pelops, and at the request of Agamemnon, its king, sent many Argives against Troy. They won great distinction under their leader Diomedes. The word "Argives" was habitually used by Homer in the *Iliad* to designate the Greeks. The great kingdom over which Agamemnon had ruled was diminished in the reign of

fat, fāte, fär, fåll, àsk, fãre; net, mē, hèr; pin, pīne; not, nōte, möve, nôr; up, lūte, pùll; oi, oil; ou out; (lightened) ẹlect, agọny, ụnite;

his grandson, Tisamenus, by the Dorian invasion, the so-called return of the Heraclidae, for the Dorians based their claim to Argos on ancient conquests by Heracles, who left it in trust for his descendants. The Heraclid Temenus became ruler of Argos, but such was the Argive love of liberty, according to some, that the king had but little power.

As a Dorian city Argos, thanks to its position in the plain (the name means "plain"), and its access to the sea, became the dominant city in this area of the Peloponnesus. Under the rule of King Pheidon, in the early 7th century B.C., Argos was the equal of any of the city-states of Greece. Pheidon coined the first Greek money in Aegina. Argos was a center of trade and in this period controlled Mycenae and Tiryns, destroyed Asine, and defeated the Spartans at Hysiae (669 B.C.). Pheidon captured Olympia from Elis and returned the management of the Olympic Games to Pisa. With the rise of Sparta the power of Argos declined, and she was unable to assist Pisa when Elis attacked and won back control of Olympia. In the 6th and early 5th centuries the power of Argos was reduced by Cleomenes I, king of Sparta, who defeated her at Sepeia (c494 B.C.) in her own territory. Six thousand Argives perished when Cleomenes set fire to the sacred grove in which they had taken refuge. The city itself would have fallen at this time if it had not been for the bravery of the poetess Telesilla. From that time forward, though remaining independent, a dangerous enemy or a valued friend, Argos was a second-rate power. Enmity toward Sparta caused the Argives to refuse to submit to Spartan leadership when Greece was threatened by the Persians and the city-state played no part in the Persian War. However, she could not prevent her former subject-cities of Mycenae and Tiryns from sending men to help the Greeks at Thermopylae and Plataea. After the Persians had been driven out of Greece, Argos attacked and destroyed Mycenae and Tiryns. Some say the attack was out of jealousy for the renown they had won in the Persian War. Others say it was because they had sheltered slaves escaped from Argos. Following the Persian Wars, Argos recovered some of her former power. A democratic constitution was adopted and an alliance with Athens against Sparta was concluded. With her allies, Athens, Corinth, and Mantinea, Argos was defeated by the Spartans at the first battle of Mantinea (418

B.C.). Argive hatred of the Spartans persisted and Argos took part on the side of Thebes in the defeat of Sparta at the second Battle of Mantinea (362 B.C.). In 229 Argos joined the Achaean League against Macedonia. The League was defeated (146 B.C.) by the Romans. Argos fell under Roman domination and enjoyed a new prosperity.

The citadel of Argos was on a rocky hill to the west, called Larissa. Cut into the flank of the hill are the remains of an ancient theater that seated 20,000 spectators. The upper tiers of seats of the cavea are rock-hewn; below these are tiers of masonry. Twenty tiers in all survive, the lowest consisting of thrones of honor. There are remains of a Roman stage and of several modifications of the Greek stage structure. An underground passage ran from behind the proscenium to the middle of the orchestra. Up the hill from the theater was a temple of Aphrodite. Near the summit was an ancient temple of Hera Acraea *(Of the Height)*. North of the city, near the summit of the hill called Aspis, was a sanctuary of Phythian Apollo and Athena. In the sanctuary was an oracle. Oracular responses were given in the following manner: each month a lamb was sacrificed in the night; a woman forbidden to cohabit with a man drank the blood of the lamb and then prophesied. In this sanctuary Diomedes is said to have dedicated an image of Athena Oxyderces *(Bright-eyed)* in gratitude to the goddess for clearing the mists from his eyes when he was wounded in the Trojan War. Near the citadel were buried the heads of the sons of Aegyptus, who were killed by their brides on their wedding night. Their bodies were buried at nearby Lerna. Argos was noted for its school of sculpture, in which Ageladas (late 6th century B.C.) and Polyclitus (5th century B.C.) were outstanding examples.

*Ariana* (ar-i-ā′nạ, ar-i-an′ạ). In ancient geography, a region in Asia, of vague boundaries, extending from Media on the W to the Indus River on the E, and from Hyrcania and Bactriana on the N to the Persian Gulf and Arabian Sea on the S.

*Aricia* (ạ-rish′ạ). [Modern, *Ariccia.*] An ancient Latin town, situated in the Alban Hills, 16 miles SE of Rome. There was a grove sacred to Diana (Artemis) to which Artemis brought Hippolytus after he had been restored to life by Asclepius. The grove surrounded a lake and was itself set off by steep cliffs. In the grove was an ancient oak tree, the branches of which were sacred. If a runaway slave, fled to the grove for sanctuary, chanced to break off one of the branches of the oak then the priest of the temple of Diana was compelled to fight him, and if he was killed in the fight the slave became priest. All the priests were drawn from runaway slaves, and each priest obtained his position by killing his predecessor. In later times the temple of Diana Nemorensis was one of the most famous and wealthy in Italy. The Romans also said that there was a nymph Aricia, the mother of a Virbius said to be the son of Hippolytus.

*Ariminum* (ä-rim′i-num). [Modern name, **Rimini.**] In ancient geography, a town of N Italy, situated on the Adriatic Sea. It was an Umbrian, then a Gallic settlement, and became a Roman colony in 268 B.C. It was the starting point of Julius Caesar in the civil war of 49 B.C. As the terminus of the Via Flaminia which, coming from Rome, here reached the Adriatic Sea, and of the Via Aemilia, it was of great military importance, and long dominated communications between Rome and upper Italy. Among the Roman antiquities are an amphitheater, triumphal arch, and the marble bridge of Augustus across the Marecchia River. The bridge is one of the most perfect of ancient bridges.

*Aristaeum* (ar-is-tē′um). In ancient geography, a city near Mount Haemus, in Thrace.

*Arno Valley* (är′nō). [Italian, **Val d'Arno.**] The fruitful valley of the upper Arno River, in N central Italy. See **Arnus.**

*Arnus* (är′nus). [Modern, **Arno.**] River in Tuscany, N central Italy, which rises in the Apennines, flows S, W, NW, and then W, and empties into the Mediterranean about six miles SW of Pisae. Pisae (Pisa) and Florentia (Florence) are situated on it.

*Arpinum* (är-pī′num). [Modern name, **Arpino.**] In ancient geography, a town of C Italy, situated near the Liris River, SE of Rome. The ancient town was first Volscian, then belonged to the Samnites, was taken by the Romans in the Second Samnite War, and was made a Roman ally with voting rights in 188 B.C. It was the birthplace of Marius and Cicero.

*Arretium* (a̦-rē′shum, -shi-um). [Modern name, **Arezzo.**] In ancient geography, a city in C Italy in Tuscany, situated in the Clanis valley, near the junction of the Arnus and Clanis rivers, about 38 miles SE of Florentia. An ancient Etruscan

(obscured) errạnt, ardẹnt, actọr; ch, chip; g, go; th, thin; ᴛʜ, then; y, you;
(variable) d̦ as d or j, ṣ as s or sh, ț as t or ch, ẓ as z or zh.

city, it was colonized by the Romans and became the terminus of the Via Flaminia. Arretium refused to take part in an Italian coalition against Rome (285–282 B.C.) and was besieged by the whole force of the confederacy, including paid hordes of Gallic Semones. Lucius Caecilius Metellus went to the relief of the city, but was defeated and slain, with seven military tribunes and 13,000 men, the rest of the army being made prisoners. The city contains many remains from the Etruscan and Roman periods. In the 1st century B.C. potters of Arretium perfected the production of a fine tableware known as *terra sigillata,* decorated in relief in imitation of embossed metal ware, with an excellent red glaze, which came to enjoy wide vogue in the Mediterranean and was widely imitated in western Europe. It appears in museums and excavation reports as Arretine Ware.

*Arsinoë* (är-sin′ọ̄-ē). In ancient geography, a city on the E coast of Cyprus near ancient Salamis. It was built by Ptolemy II of Egypt. The name of the city now on the same site is Famagusta.

*Artemisium* (är-tẹ-mish′i-um). A promontory in N Euboea, Greece, crowned by a temple of Artemis. Here where the sea runs in a narrow channel between the island of Sciathus and the mainland of Magnesia, the Greeks sent a fleet to engage the Persian fleet while their army was being engaged at the pass of Thermopylae. Alarmed over the fate of their country, now being invaded by the Persians, the people of Delphi consulted the oracle and were told to pray to the winds, for the winds would do Greece great service. When the Persian fleet assembled near Artemisium it was scattered by a great storm that lasted four days. The Athenians said Boreas sent the winds to help them, and raised a temple to Boreas on the Ilissus River. The Persians claimed that they brought the storm to an end by sacrificing to Thetis, for it was near where their fleet was anchored, Cape Sepias, that Peleus had seized Thetis, and the area was sacred to her. The Persians regrouped at Aphetae. The Greeks would have withdrawn, being greatly outnumbered, but some say Themistocles was bribed by the Euboeans to remain at Artemisium and risk a battle. The Persians thought to surround the small Greek fleet, and sent a fleet of 200 ships around Euboea to bottle up the Greeks in the strait. The Greeks, commanded by Eurybiades, were warned of the Persian plan by an Ionian who deserted from the Persians, and they resolved to sail against the Persian ships at Artemisium. The Persians thought they were mad when they saw the few Greek ships coming against them, and expected they would easily overcome them. The Greeks executed a maneuver: at a signal they brought the sterns of their ships together, the prows facing outward in a circle toward the enemy. At a second signal they attacked. They captured or sank 30 Persian ships. The battle was still raging when night fell. The Persians retired to Aphetae, the Greeks to Artemisium. During the night a crashing storm buffeted the Persian fleet at Aphetae and completely destroyed the 200 ships that were on their way around Euboea. After two more days of sea fights the Greek fleet withdrew, having inflicted heavy damage on the Persians but without reaching a decisive result. The battle at Artemisium took place at the same time as the nearby land battle at Thermopylae (480 B.C.). The two battles represented a desperate attempt to keep out the Persian invaders; neither of the battles succeeded in this aim.

In 1928, in the Straits of Artemisium, Greek sponge-divers located an ancient wreck containing fragments of classical sculpture, and further diving recovered the now famous Poseidon or Zeus of Artemisium, a bronze statue of the middle of the 5th century B.C. showing the god hurling his thunderbolt, and a Hellenistic group of a horse and diminutive jockey.

*Artemisius* (är-tẹ-miz′i-us), *Mount.* Mountain on the border of Arcadia and Argolis, near Mantinea. Here the Inachus River rises. On the mountain was a temple and image of Artemis, for whom the mountain was named.

*Ascalon* (as′kạ-lon). [Also: *Ashkelon, Askelon, Eshkalon;* Assyrian, *Isqualuna;* modern name, *Migdal Ashkalon.*] In ancient geography, one of the five chief cities of Philistia, situated on the Mediterranean about 39 miles SW of Jerusalem. According to Herodotus, it was the site of the most ancient of all the temples of Aphrodite, even antedating that at Cyprus, which was built in imitation of it. The temple was pillaged by Scythians when, having overrun Media, they were on their way to Egypt. As a punishment for their desecration of the temple Aphrodite caused these Scythians and many of their descendants to suffer from the "female sickness," that is, they were afflicted with a tendency to impotency. The temple to which Herodotus referred was later identified as the temple of Derceto, a Syrian goddess whose form was half-maiden and half-fish, and whose sacred lake was nearby. Ascalon is mentioned in Phoenician and Assyrian inscriptions; the names of four of its kings (Sidka, Sarludari, Rukibti, and Mitenti) appear in the annals of Sennacherib (705–681 B.C.) and Esarhaddon (680–668 B.C.). Herod I, whose birthplace it was, adorned the city with many edifices.

*Ascania* (as-kā′ni-ạ), *Lake*. [Modern Turkish, *Isnik* or *Iznik*.] In ancient geography, a lake in Bithynia, Asia Minor, draining finally into the Sea of Marmara. Nicaea was situated at its E extremity. Length, about 11 miles.

*Asculum Apulum* (as′kụ-lum ap′ụ-lum). [Modern name, *Ascoli Satriano*.] In ancient geography, a town of SW Italy, in the region of Apulia, on the slopes of the Apennines. The town was founded by the Romans. It was the scene of the costly victory (279 B.C.) of Pyrrhus over the Romans.

*Asculum Picenum* (pī-sē′num). [Modern name, *Ascoli Piceno*.] A town in the Abruzzi on the Adriatic slope of the Apennines, capital of the Picentes, which fought against Rome in the Social War and was destroyed by Pompey, but rapidly regained importance under the empire. It has many antiquities: fortification walls, a gate, the *Porta Romana*, remains of an aqueduct, a Roman bridge over the river Truentus (modern Tronto), still in use, a second Roman bridge whose arch fell recently, a well-preserved Roman temple of the 1st century A.D., now the church of S. Gregorio, and Romanesque churches and houses of exceptional interest. Ancient cemeteries in the vicinity have yielded evidence of early commerce via the Adriatic with central Europe and S Italy, the Aegean, and the Balkans. (JJ)

*Asea* (ạ-sē′ạ). Town in Arcadia, in the central Peloponnesus, with a fortified acropolis commanding the Asean Plain, celebrated for its springs which flow to the Alpheus, and capital of the short-lived Asean League. (JJ)

*Asia* (ā′zhạ). To the ancient Greeks, Asia meant the lands bordering the eastern end of the Mediterranean Sea. The name also embraced the few parts of Africa known to them, and it was only after the Nile began to be considered as a dividing river that the countries W of it were separated from Asia, while Egypt was still included in it. Moreover, the knowl-

fat, fāte, fär, fåll, åsk, fāre; net, mē, hėr; pin, pīne; not, nōte, mȯve, nȯr; up, lūte, ṗull; oi, oil; ou out; (lightened) ẹlect, agọny, ụnite;

edge of the ancients with regard to Asia did not reach far
beyond the boundaries of the Perso-Macedonian empire.
The parts S of the Himalaya range were called India, those
to the N Scythia. The west was termed Upper and Lower
Asia, the Tigris being the dividing line between them.

*Asia Minor* (mī'nor). Peninsula of W Asia which lies between
the Euxine Sea and the Propontis on the N, the Aegean Sea
on the W, and the Mediterranean Sea on the S; the E bound-
ary is vague. The chief divisions in ancient times were Mysia,
Lydia, Caria, Lycia, Pamphylia, Pisidia, Phrygia, Bithynia,
Paphlagonia, Galatia, Lycaonia, Cilicia, Cappadocia, and
Pontus. The surface is in the main a plateau, traversed by the
Taurus and other ranges. The chief rivers are the Sangarius,
Halys, Maeander, Sarus, and Hermus. It was the seat of
Troy, Lydia, and other ancient powers, and of the Ionian
Greek civilization; its possession has been disputed by
Persia, Macedonia, Syria, Rome, the Byzantine empire,
Parthia, the Saracens, the Seljuks, and the modern Turks.
According to Herodotus, there were 15 races or nations in
Asia Minor: in the S part the Cilicians, Pamphylians, Lycians,
and Caunians; W of the great central plateau, close to the
coast, the Carians, Lydians, Mysians, and Greeks; on the
shores of the Euxine, Thracians, Mariandynians, Paph-
lagonians, and Cappadocians; in the interior, the Phrygians,
Chalybes, and Matieni.

*Asinarus* (as-i-nā'rus). [Italian names, *Falconare, Fiume di
Noto.*] In ancient geography, a small river near Syracuse,
Sicily. To this stream came the Athenians under Nicias, after
their total defeat at Syracuse, 413 B.C. Tormented by thirst,
they rushed into the river. The Syracusans, with their Peloponnesian allies, manned the steep bank on the opposite
side of the river and shot them down ruthlessly as they
plunged into the water to drink. Nicias surrendered here to
stop the slaughter of his men. To celebrate the anniversary
of their great victory, the Syracusans established Asinarian
Games, named for the river where the total destruction of
the enemy took place.

*Asine* (a'si-nē). In ancient geography, a city of Argolis, on the
Gulf of Argolis. The people were Dryopes, who originally
came from Mount Parnassus. Men of Asine went to the
Trojan War under the command of Diomedes and his friend
Sthenelus. Asine was destroyed by Argos in the 7th century

B.C. Excavations have revealed substantial remains of a settlement of the bronze age.

*Asine.* City of the Peloponnesus, on the western shore of the Gulf of Messenia. It was given to people who had been driven out of Argos by the Spartans, after the First Messenian War, and the Argives occupied it ever after. At the end of the Second Messenian War, which resulted in the conquest of Messenia, Asine alone was left separate in the division of the land.

*Asopus* (a̯-sō'pus). A town in Laconia, on the eastern promontory of the Peloponnesus on the Gulf of Laconia. It was noted for a sanctuary of Asclepius, who was here given the epithet Philolaus, "Loved by the people." Athena here was named Cyparissia, "Cypress goddess."

*Asopus.* [Modern name, *Oropo.*] In ancient geography, a small river in Boeotia, Greece, flowing into the Euripus in N Attica.

*Asopus.* [Modern name, *Hagios Georgios.*] In ancient geography, a small river in Sicyonia, Greece, rising in Phliasia and flowing through Sicyonia to empty into the Corinthian Gulf about four miles NE of Sicyon. According to tradition, the water of the Asopus came under the sea from the Maeander River in Caria.

*Aspendos* (a̯s-pen'dos). [Also: *Aspendus.*] In ancient geography, a city in Pamphylia, Asia Minor, on the Eurymedon. It contains a Roman theater which is one of the best-preserved of all ancient structures of the kind. The cavea is quite intact. There is also a Roman aqueduct which crosses the valley by a long range of arches.

*Assus* (as'us). [Also: *Assos;* modern Turkish, *Behram* or *Behramköy.*] In ancient geography, a city situated on the Gulf of Adramyttium, Mysia. The site, in what is now W Turkey, was thoroughly explored and excavated (1881–82) by the Archaeological Institute of America, with the important result of illustrating the architectural and topographical development of a minor Greek city with a completeness comparable to the body of information supplied by Pompeii concerning Roman towns under somewhat similar conditions. The remains studied include very extensive fortifications of successive periods, and temples ranging from the archaic Doric to foundations of the Christian era, a theater, baths, porticoes, a gymnasium, private dwellings in great variety, a remarka-

ble and highly adorned street of tombs, and a Greek bridge.
*Assyria* (ạ-sir'i-ạ). [Greek, *Syria;* ancient name, *Assur, Asur,* or
*Ashur;* Persian, *Athura.*] Ancient Asiatic state which at the
period of its greatest power covered a territory of about
75,000 square miles, bounded by Armenia on the N, the
Lower Zab River on the S, the Zagros Mountains on the E,
and the Euphrates River on the W. The name was derived
from that of the national deity, Assur, and was first applied
to the city situated about 50 miles S of the modern Mosul.
The city of Assur is not mentioned in the Old Testament,
but it survived Nineveh, being still in existence in the time
of Cyrus of Persia (Cyrus the Great), the conqueror of Babylon. The name Assur, besides being given to the city (and
thence to the country), was also an element in the names of
many Assyrian rulers. The Persians called the city Athura.
The Greeks included under the name Assyria, or its short-
ened form Syria, the entire territory between Babylonia and
the Mediterranean, sometimes applying it even to Babylonia. The N and E portions of the country were mountainous
but the greater part was flat, being an extension of the
Babylonian plain. Its principal rivers were the Tigris, the
Upper and Lower Zab, the Kurnib, the Khoser, and the W
Khabur. It was a fertile country, and abounded in all sorts
of animals, among others the stag, roebuck, wild bull, and
lion. The hunting of the lion was the favorite sport of the
Assyrian kings. According to Genesis (x. 8–12, 22) the Assyrians were descendants of Shem and emigrants from Babylon. Their Semitic-Babylonian origin is fully attested by
their sculptures and inscriptions. Their langauge is, apart
from a few dialectical and orthographical variations, identical with Babylonian, and closely akin to Hebrew. Assyria
derived its civilization from Babylonia. Its religion was the
same as that of the mother-country, with the exception of
the national god Assur, who was placed by them at the head
of the pantheon. Assyrian architecture was a slavish copy of
that of Babylonia. Although stone abounded in Assyria,
bricks continued to be used in imitation of the practice in
Babylonia, where no stone existed. The Babylonian emigrants who founded Assyria have been dated by some scholars as leaving Babylonia c2000 B.C., although some recent
archaeological research indicates the probability of a settlement at an even earlier date. In the 15th century B.C., As-

(obscured) errạnt, ardẹnt, actọr; ch, chip; g, go; th, thin; ᴛʜ, then; y, you;
(variable) ḍ as d or j, ṣ as s or sh, ṭ as t or ch, ẓ as z or zh.

syria was involved in a war with Babylonia. War continued between the two countries for a long time with varying success. Finally, however, Assyria's glory was Tiglath-pileser I (c1120–1100 B.C.), who conquered the city of Babylon, other cities of Babylonia, and penetrated as far as the Mediterranean. His more important successors were Assurdan II (930–911 B.C.), Assurnazirpal (884–860 B.C.), Shalmaneser III (860–824 B.C.), who came in contact with Damascus and Israel, Tiglath-pileser III (Phul in the Old Testament), 745–727 B.C., whose power extended to the confines of Egypt and who put the crown of Babylon on his head, Sargon (722–705 B.C.), the conqueror of Samaria, who defeated the Egyptians of Raphia, Sennacherib (705–681 B.C.), and Esarhaddon (680–668 B.C.). These last two kings mark the height of Assyrian power, and Esarhaddon was enabled by his conquests to add to his name the title king of Upper and Lower Egypt and Ethiopia. Under Assurbanipal (the Sardanapalus of Greek writers), 668–626 B.C., the decline of the empire began. In some respects this reign was most properous and brilliant; it was the golden age of art and literature. Under this reign too, Susa was conquered and destroyed. But signs of the approaching disintegration were seen in the constant uprisings of the oppressed nations. The downward course was rapid. Once, c625 B.C., Assyria succeeded in repelling an attack of the Medes and Persians, but later, Cyaxares in union with Nabopolassar of Babylon repeated the attack (606 B.C.), Nineveh fell, and Assyrian power entirely disappeared.

*Astacus* (as'tạ-kus). ]Modern Turkish name, *Izmit*.] In ancient geography, a Greek colony in Bithynia, Asia Minor, near Nicomedia.

*Asterion* (as-tē'ri-ọn). In ancient geography, a river of Argolis, Greece. When Hera and Poseidon contended for control of Argos the river-god Asterion was one of the judges of the dispute. He awarded the land to Hera. In a rage at the decision, Poseidon dried up his waters. The stream Asterion flowed past the Argive shrine of Hera, called the Heraeum.

*Astypalaea* (as″ti-pạ-lē'ạ). [Also: *Astropalia;* Italian, *Stampalia*.] Greek island in the Aegean Sea, about 77 miles NW of Rhodes; one of the Dodecanese Islands. Length, about 13 miles.

*Atalanti* (at-ạ-lan'ti; Greek, ä-tä-län'dē), *Channel* (or *Gulf) of.*

[Also: ***Channel*** (or ***Gulf*) *of Atalante*** (or ***Talanti*).**] The NW
portion of the sea passage which separates Euboea from the
mainland of Greece.

***Athens*** (ath′ĕnz). [Greek, ***Athenai, Athinai;*** Latin, ***Athenae.***]
Capital of Greece, situated about five miles from its seaport
Piraeus (on the Saronic Gulf) between the Cephissus and
Ilissus rivers on the Attic peninsula. The city lies at 350 feet
above sea level on the Attic plain. Surrounding it are the
mountains Aegaleos, Parnes, Pentelikon, and Hymettus on
the W and E, which sometimes assume at dusk a delicate
lavender color and give to the city its epithet "violet-
crowned." Within the city limits stands the steep, rocky hill
of Lycabettus. The Acropolis, around which the ancient city
grew up, rises in the center of the city; it is the site of the
earliest settlement and a place of many historical remains.
In ancient times, on it were the royal palace and the dwellings of the Eupatrids. To the W is the Areopagus, or Hill of
Ares, the site of the most ancient court of Athens, and the
place where Saint Paul preached; farther W are the Hill of
the Muses, the Pnyx, and the Hill of the Nymphs. In the 5th
century B.C. long walls joined the city to its port. The city
was founded, according to the old account, by an Egyptian
colony led by Cecrops. It became the chief place in Attica,
with Athena as its especial divinity, and was ruled by kings,
among whom Erechtheus, Theseus, and Codrus are legendary and famous. Gradually the city spread to the lower
slopes around the Acropolis and to the banks of the Illisus
River. Thither the Eupatrids (nobles) moved and established the ancient aristocratic city described by Thucydides.
Besides the Eupatrid enclave, other groups of dwellings to
the north and northwest of the Acropolis formed the quarters occupied by artisians and tradesmen, such as the section
known as the Ceramicus, alongside the ancient agora which,
in the 7th and 6th centuries B.C. became the civic heart of
the city. According to tradition, it was Theseus who united
the twelve independent communities of Attica into a federal
union governed by delegates to Athens. He renamed the
Athenian Games the Panathenaea and invited all Attica to
share in them, and he united the suburbs mentioned above
to the city proper. Furthermore, he invited his fellow Greeks
to become Athenian citizens, and many came to Athens. He
is said to have divided the population thus enlarged into

(obscured) errạnt, ardẹnt, actọr; ch, chip; g, go; th, thin; ᴛʜ, then; y, you;
(variable) ḍ as d or j, ş as s or sh, ṭ as t or ch, ẓ as z or zh.

three classes: the Eupatrids, or nobles; the Georges, or farmers, and the Demiurges, or artisans. Lastly, he gave Athens a constitution, some say, and resigned his throne to further the democracy. After 1132 B.C., the legendary date of the death of Codrus, Athens was ruled by the Eupatrids, and had archons as magistrates, who were successively perpetual, decennial, and (after 683 B.C.) annual. Scholars have questioned the historical value of much of this legendary material. The laws of Draco were enacted in 621 B.C., and those of Solon in 594. Pisistratus became tyrant in 560 B.C. and his sons were expelled in 510. The reforms of Clisthenes (508 B.C.) made Athens (for its day) a pure democracy; popular assemblies of all its citizens (but not all, or even most, of its adult inhabitants were citizens) made the laws. The glorious period began with the Persian wars, in which Athens took a leading part, as at Marathon (490 B.C.) and Salamis (480). The city was temporarily held by the Persians (480 B.C.) who burned it and destroyed the buildings on the Acropolis. Athens became the head of the Delian League in c477 B.C., and for a short period had an extensive empire and was the first power in Greece. The Athenians in the "Age of Pericles" (c461–429 B.C.) at the onset of the Peloponnesian Wars are described by Thucydides. He puts the following speech into the mouth of the Corinthian envoy who addresses the Spartan assembly considering whether to declare war on Athens:

"You have never considered, O Lacedaemonians, what manner of men are these Athenians with whom you will have to fight, and how utterly unlike yourselves. They are revolutionary, equally quick in the conception and in the execution of every new plan; while you are conservative —careful only to keep what you have, originating nothing, and not acting even when action is most necessary. They are bold beyond their strength; they run risks which prudence would condemn; and in the midst of misfortune they are full of hope. Whereas it is your nature, though strong, to act feebly; when your plans are most prudent, to distrust them; and when calamities come upon you, to think that you will never be delivered from them. They are impetuous and you are dilatory; they are always abroad, and you are always at home. For they hope to gain something by leaving their homes; but you are afraid that any

fat, fāte, fär, fåll, àsk, fāre; net, mē, hèr; pin, pīne; not, nōte, mȯve, nôr; up, lūte, pṳll; oi, oil; ou out; (lightened) ĕlect, agȯny, ṵnite;

new enterprise may imperil what you have already. When conquerors, they pursue their victory to the utmost; when defeated, they fall back the least. Their bodies they devote to the country as though they belonged to other men; their true self is their mind, which is not truly their own when employed in her service. When they do not carry out an intention which they have formed, they seem to have sustained a personal bereavement; when an enterprise succeeds they have gained a mere installment of what is to come; but if they fail, they at once conceive new hopes and so fill up the void. With them alone to hope is to have, for they lose not a moment in the execution of an idea. This is the lifelong task, full of danger and toil, which they are always imposing upon themselves. None enjoy their good things less, because they are always seeking for more. To do their duty is their only holiday, and they deem the quiet of inaction to be as disagreeable as the most tiresome business. If a man should say of them, in a word, that they were born neither to have peace themselves nor to allow peace to other men, he would simply speak the truth."

In the short period from the victory over the Persians at Marathon (490 B.C.) and Salamis (480), to the defeat of Athens by Sparta (404 B.C.), the tremendous Athenian vitality described by Thucydides produced some of the world's greatest poetry, architecture, and sculpture. At the same time, Athenian commercial and maritime activity predominated in the Mediterranean. The Peloponnesian War (431–404 B.C.) resulted in the displacement of Athens by Sparta in the hegemony of Greece. Athens was defeated by Sparta in 404 B.C. and an aristocratic faction was put in power, but moderate democracy was restored a year later by Thrasybulus. Athens under the influence of Demosthenes resisted Macedonia, but was overthrown at the battle of Chaeronea (338 B.C.), and was generally after this under Macedonian influence. It was subjugated by Rome in 146 B.C., and pillaged by Sulla in 86 B.C.

The ancient architectural masterpieces are mostly on the Acropolis (q.v.), the chief ancient landmark. Other important structures are: the theater of Dionysus on the S slope of the Acropolis, where all the famous Greek dramas were produced. It was originally of wood, and was not completed

(obscured) errant, ardent, actor; ch, chip; g, go; th, thin; ᴛʜ, then; y, you;
(variable) ḏ as d or j, ş as s or sh, ṭ as t or ch, ẓ as z or zh.

in stone until the end of the 5th century B.C. The existing remains of the orchestra and stage structures are modifications of Roman date. East, and somewhat south of the Acropolis, are the remains of a temple of Olympian Zeus. According to legend, the first temple on the site was raised by Deucalion, in gratitude for his deliverance from the great flood. About 515 B.C. Pisistratus planned to raise a great temple on the site but the plan was not realized. In the 2nd century B.C., Antiochus IV, king of Syria, revived the plan of building a temple here, but work on it was suspended when he died. It was not until the Roman emperor Hadrian's time that the temple was completed (132 A.D.). Several columns with elaborate Corinthian capitals still stand. Also noteworthy are the Gate of the Oil Market, or New Agora, a gate built with gifts from Julius Caesar and Augustus; the Agora, to the north of the Acropolis and adjoining the quarter known as Ceramicus. This was the center of Athenian public life and after the Acropolis the heart of the city. Nearly in the center of the Agora was the altar of the Twelve Gods, from which distances from Athens were measured. Among other structures, there were temples of Apollo and of Ares, and an Odeum that held 1000 spectators. Many roads led to the Agora, which was not only the center of Athens but of all Attica. Here were such official buildings as the Bouleterium (Senate), the Tholos, and the Metroun. Here the votes for ostracism were cast. Here were colonnaded galleries for shops and meeting places, the Painted Portico, and various stoas. Public figures, artists, philosophers, and ordinary citizens gathered in the Agora. Religious activity was concentrated about its temples and altars, and through it wound the sacred Panathenaic procession on its way to the Acropolis. Excavations of the site have been carried on at intervals from the 19th century. Since 1931 the American School of Classical Studies has undertaken systematic excavations and restoration on a vast scale. Aided by large grants from John D. Rockefeller Junior and by Marshall Plan funds, and by a law authorizing the demolition of the structures which covered the ancient Agora, the site has been cleared and the excavations of the Agora have shed light on the entire history of Athens, from Neolithic times forward. By 1959 all but the northern side of the Agora had been cleared. The recent excavations had uncovered several 5th

fat, fāte, fär, fâll, ȧsk, fãre; net, mē, hėr; pin, pīne; not, nōte, möve, nôr; up, lūte, pˈull; oi, oil; ou out; (lightened) ĕlect, agǫny, ūnite;

century B.C. Ionic columns, remarkable for the good conditions of the paint on their capitals, and well-preserved sections of the Panathenaic Roadway, often used for religious
processions. In 1970 it was reported that the site of the
Royal Stoa, or Stoa of the Basileus, had been unearthed on
the Agora. Though completely in ruins, the stoa was estimated to have originally been about 60 feet long and 27
feet wide. It first had a series of Doric columns in front and
back, then in the 5th century B.C. further construction gave
it columned porches on either side of a large female statue,
of which the torso has been found. Named for the *archon
basileus* (archon king), this stoa was possibly the site of the
trial of Socrates, and stones from the north wall still have the
remains of stone benches where some of the judges may
have sat. In 1971 the discovery of a nine-foot-by-three-foot
limestone slab was reported. Originally placed on the steps
of the Royal Stoa, it was possibly the stone on which the nine
archons stood to take their oath of office. A museum built
on the site of the Agora holds the thousands of objects and
coins found in excavations there since 1931. On a slight rise
which gives a splendid panoramic view of the Agora stands
the well-preserved temple of Hephaestus commonly known
as the Theseum. The "Long Walls," traces of which have
now almost entirely disappeared, were two massive fortification walls extending from the ramparts of the city to those
of the Piraeus, at a distance apart, except near their diverg-
ing extremities, of about 550 feet. Built between 461 and
456 B.C., they made the port and the metropolis practically
one huge fortress, and assured Athenian supplies by sea
while rendering possible Athenian naval triumphs at times
when the Spartans held their land without the walls. They
were destroyed in 404 B.C. when Athens fell before Sparta
but were restored in 393 B.C. by Conon. The Long Walls
followed the crests of the group of hills SW of the Acropolis.
The arena of the Panathenaic stadium, a stadium still practically complete except for its sheathing of marble, measures
109 by 850 feet, and is bordered on its long sides and its
semicircular E end by the slopes which supported the spectators' seats (about 60 tiers). There were at intervals 29
flights of steps to give access to the seats. The original
stadium was begun about 330 B.C.; its stone tiers were covered with Pentelic marble through the generosity of Hero-

(obscured) errant, ardent, actor; ch, chip; g, go; th, thin; ᴛʜ, then; y, you;
(variable) ḍ as d or j, ṣ as s or sh, ṭ as t or ch, ẓ as z or zh.

dus Atticus c143 A.D. In 1895 money was given to restore the stadium in preparation for the Olympic Games of 1896; thus today it gleams with marble not even yet weathered to match other monuments. In 1958 the discovery of a Cave of Pan about 20 miles E of Athens was reported. Possibly an early place of worship of the Earth Goddess, it then fell into disuse until the Classical Greek period. Inside the cave were found fragments of pottery dating from about 3,500 B.C. to the 2nd century B.C. Roman period. All fragments have been sent to the National Museum in Athens to be studied.

*Athesis* (ath′ẹ-sis). [Modern name, *Adige*.] River in N Italy, rising in the Rhaetian Alps and flowing S through the Alps to the plain of the Padus (Po). It sends arms to the Padus, and flows into the Adriatic N of the mouths of the Padus. On it are Tridentum (Trent) and Verona.

*Athos* (ath′os). [Also: *Acte, Akte*.] Eastern-most peninsula of Chalcidice in Macedonia, NE Greece. It projects into the Aegean Sea and is connected with the mainland by a narrow isthmus. Length, about 30 miles. As part of his preparations for his invasion of Greece, Xerxes, the Persian king, caused a canal to be cut through the isthmus. The purpose of this canal, which was about a mile and a half long, was to save the Persian fleet from rounding the stormy headland of Mount Athos where a large part of the fleet of Mardonius, son-in-law of Darius, had been destroyed (492 B.C.) by storms. Once past this headland, the promontory would protect the fleet from the tempestuous north-east winds. In addition, the canal would allow the ships to keep contact with the army of Xerxes as it proceeded along the coast. The dry ditch which marks the course of Xerxes' canal can still be followed.

*Atlantis* (at-lan′tis). Legendary island in the Atlantic Ocean, NW of Africa, referred to by Plato and other ancient writers, which with its inhabitants (who had achieved, according to most accounts, a high degree of civilization) was said to have disappeared in a convulsion of nature. The belief in the possibility of such a place has continued to exist even into modern times and many writers (including Francis Bacon in his work *The New Atlantis*) have taken the name as an equivalent for a utopian state. A modern scholar has ingeniously suggested that the legend might have arisen from a prehistoric inundation of the bronze-age palace on the island

fat, fāte, fär, fåll, ȧsk, fãre; net, mē, hėr; pin, pīne; not, nōte, mȯve, nôr; up, lūte, pu̇ll; oi, oil; ou out; (lightened) ẹlect, agǫny, ūnite;

known as Gla (an Albanian name; the ancient name is not recorded, unless indeed it was Atlantis) in the Copaic Lake in Boeotia, which was subject to periodic flooding.

*Attica* (at'i-ka). In ancient geography, a division of C Greece, bounded by Boeotia (party separated by Cithaeron) on the NW, the Gulf of Euripus (separating it from Euboea) on the NE, the Aegean Sea on the E, the Saronic Gulf on the SW, and Megaris on the W. It contained several mountains (Cithaeron, Parnes, Pentelicus, and Hymettus) and the plain of Attica, watered by the Cephissus and Ilissus rivers. Its chief city was Athens, with whose history it is in general identified.

*Augusta Praetoria* (ô-gus'ta prē-tôr'i-a). [Modern name, *Aosta.*] Town in NW Italy at the foot of the Alps, situated on the Duria Major River. It was the ancient capital of the Gallic tribe of the Salassi, and became a Roman colony under Augustus. Roman walls, towers, gates, arches, and theaters are preserved.

*Augustodunum* (ô-gus-tǫ-dū'num). [Modern name, *Autun.*] Large town in Gaul, founded by Augustus in 12 B.C., supplanting the earlier Bibracte, with important Roman remains including fortifications and two town gates. (JJ)

*Aulis* (ô'lis). In ancient geography, a town on the E coast of Boeotia, Greece, said by some to have been named for a daughter of Ogygus. Twice the Greek fleet assembled here for the expeditions against Troy. The second time the fleet was held windbound through the will of Artemis. In accordance with instructions from a seer, Agamemnon made ready to sacrifice his daughter, Iphigenia, to appease Artemis and secure favorable winds. One tradition has it that Iphigenia was actually sacrificed. According to another account, as the sacrificial knife was at her throat, Artemis substituted in her place a hind, and took Iphigenia away to Tauris. In the temple of Artemis at Aulis were two white marble images of the goddess, one carrying a torch and the other showing the goddess in the act of shooting an arrow. Also in the temple was preserved the plane tree in which the eight nestlings and their mother were swallowed by a mottled serpent, just before the Greeks sailed to Troy, thus indicating that the war would last ten years. The traveler Pausanias, writing in the 2nd century A.D., says he saw the plane tree in the temple, and that he was also shown the bronze threshold of Agamemnon's tent at Aulis.

*Aventine Hill* (av'ẹn-tīn). [Latin, *Mons Aventinus;* Italian, *Monte Aventino.*] Name of the southernmost of the seven hills of ancient Rome, rising on the left bank of the Tiber, S of the Palatine. Below it to the N lay the Circus Maximus, and to the E the Baths of Caracalla. According to some accounts, the hill was named for Aventinus, a king of the ancient city of Alba Longa, who was buried on it.

*Avernus, Lacus* (ạ-vėr'nus, lā'kus). [Modern: *Lake Averno;* Italian, *Lago d'Averno.*] Small lake near Puteoli in Campania, Italy, about nine miles W of Neapolis, anciently believed to be the entrance to the infernal regions.

*Axine* (ak'sin). An early name for the Euxine (Black) Sea, meaning "Unfriendly."

*Axius* (ak'si-us). [Modern name, *Vardar.*] In ancient geography, a river of Paeonia, about 200 miles long. It flows south and empties into the Myrtoan Sea (Thermaic Gulf).

*Azani* (ạ-zā'nī). [Also: *Azanion, Aizani.*] In ancient geography, a city in Phrygia, Asia Minor.

# ───── B ─────

*Baalbek* (bäl'bek). See *Heliopolis.*

*Babylon* (bab'i-lon). [Possibly the Biblical *Babel;* ancient Persian, *Babirus.*] In ancient geography, a city in Mesopotamia, the capital of Babylonia, situated on both sides of the Euphrates River, above the modern city of Hilla, S central Iraq, about 50 miles S of Baghdad. The etymology of the name is, as ascertained by many passages in the cuneiform inscriptions, Bab-Ili (meaning "Gate of God"), from *bab* ("gate") and *ilu* ("god"). Babylon was one of the oldest cities of Mesopotamia, and was the undisputed capital of Babylonia at the time of the Elamite conquest, in the third millennium B.C. As capital of the country it shared in all its vicissitudes, and was the principal target of the Assyrian invasions. It was first conquered (c1270 B.C.) by the Assyrian king Tukulti-Adar, then (c1110 B.C.) by Tiglath-pileser I. Of Shalmaneser II (860–824 B.C.) and his son and grandson it is recorded that they victoriously entered Babylon and sacrificed there to the gods. It was customary with the Assyrian kings, in order to be recognized as fully legitimate kings, to go to Babylon and there perform the mysterious ceremony termed by them "seizing the hands of Bel." Sennacherib sacked it (690 B.C.), and completely razed it to the ground. His son and successor Esarhaddon undertook, 11 years later, the restoration of the city. But it was under Nabopolassar (625–604 B.C.), the founder of the new Babylonian empire, and especially under his successor Nebuchadnezzar (605–562 B.C.) that it became "Babylon the Great." The ruins, now covering both banks of the Euphrates, are those of the Babylon of these kings and their successors, and convey some idea of its former magnitude and splendor. Nebuchadnezzar, who took more pride in the buildings constructed under his auspices than in his victorious campaigns, concentrated all his care upon the adorning and beautifying of his residence. To this end he completed the fortification of the city begun by his father Nabopolassar. The city itself was adorned with numerous temples, chief among them Esagila ("the high-towering house"), temple of the city and of the national god Merodach (Babylonian, Marduk) with his spouse Zirpanit. In its neighborhood was the royal palace, the site of which was identified with the ruins of Al-Kasr. Sloping toward the river were the Hanging Gardens, one of the seven wonders of the ancient world, the location of which is in the N mound of ruins, Babil. The temple described by Herodotus is that of Nebo in Borsippa, not far from Babylon, which Herodotus included under Babylon, and which also in the cuneiform inscriptions is called "Babylon the second." This temple, which in the mound of Birs Nimrud represents the most imposing ruin of Babylonia, is termed in the inscriptions Ezida ("the eternal house"), an ancient sanctuary of Nebo (Assyrian, Nabu), and was restored with great splendor by Nebuchadnezzar. It represents in its construction a sort of pyramid built in seven stages, whence it is sometimes called "temple of the seven spheres of heaven and earth," and it has been assumed that the narrative of the Tower of Babel in Genesis xi. may have been connected with this temple. Concerning Babylon proper, Herodotus mentions that it had wide streets lined with houses of three and four stories. In the conquest (538 B.C.) of Cyrus of Persia, the city of Babylon was spared.

(obscured) errȧnt, ardȩnt, actọr; ch, chip; g, go; th, thin; ᵺн, then; y, you;
(variable) ḍ as d or j, ş as s or sh, ṭ as t or ch, ẓ as z or zh.

Darius the Great razed its walls and towers. Xerxes (486–465 B.C.) despoiled the temples of their golden statues and treasures. Alexander the Great wished to restore the city but was prevented by his early death. The decay of Babylon was hastened by the foundation (300 B.C.) in its neighborhood of Seleucia, which was built from the ruins of Babylon. The last who calls himself in an inscription "king of Babylon, restorer of Esagila and Ezida," was Antiochus the Great (223–187 B.C.). In the time of Pliny (23–79 A.D.) Babylon was a deserted and dismal place.

**Babylonia** (bab-i-lō′ni-ạ, -lōn′yạ). In ancient geography, a region and country of SW Asia. Its extent and boundaries are matters of divergence of opinion, some scholars considering it to have been coextensive with the whole, but others with the S part only, of Mesopotamia. Before the rise of Babylon to power, S Mesopotamia was known as Chaldea and as Sumer. A line running from the Euphrates near Hit to a little below Samarra on the Tigris has been suggested as an approximate boundary between Sumer to the south and Akkad to the north. Some, however, apply the name Sumer to the whole region; some also identify it with the Biblical Shinar (also spelled Shanhar, Shenar), which others differentiate from Sumer and apply only to N Mesopotamia.

*Culture.* The N part of the area between the Tigris and the Euphrates is an upland; the S part is an alluvial plain resulting from deposits of silt by the two rivers. This alluvial land advances into the Persian Gulf at the rate of about 115 feet a year. From this it is known that Eridu, anciently a seaport and now 130 miles inland, existed 6000 years ago. It is widely believed that man first attained civilization in this alluvial plain. The ruins of many cities and towns have been discovered, with artifacts of Stone Age and Bronze Age cultures. There is evidence that from an early age this was a region where many peoples met. The Sumerians drained swamps, built canals, practiced flood control, developed agriculture and trade, and developed skills in metal-working, pottery, and textiles. They had an advanced understanding of astronomy and also practiced astrology, and acquired such a reputation for magic that their other name, Chaldeans, was for ages a synonym for magicians. Their religion was polytheistic; different Semitic and non-Semitic deities were popular in different periods, and each city had its particular god or goddess. At Nippur, Bel was especially worshiped, but within the precincts of his temple there were shrines to 24 other deities. One of the great Sumerian achievements was the cuneiform alphabet, perhaps the first ever to take form. Systems of weights, measures, and accounting were also invented in Sumer and later highly developed in Babylon.

*History.* The Sumerians, a non-Semitic people, were conquered by the Akkadians, generally supposed to have been Semites, under Sargon I; the Akkad dynasty may be dated c2400–2200 B.C. At this time the city of Babylon began to dominate the entire region from the mountains E of the Tigris to the Arabian or Syrian Desert and from the Persian Gulf to the borders of what is now Armenia. Thus the ancient Babylonian empire occupied approximately the area now comprised in the kingdom of Iraq. From about 2200 B.C. it was ruled for some centuries by the Guti, a highland people; about 1850 B.C. it was conquered by the Amorites, who were probably Semites. The capture of Mari, chief city of the Amorites, by the Sumerian Hammurabi is now generally dated about 1700 B.C. Under Hammurabi the village of Babylon became a great city, and the laws were written down in the famous Hammurabian Code. Babylonia, however, was far from through with invasions, being conquered thereafter by Horites and Hittites and, about 1270 B.C., by the Assyrians. For centuries Assyria had been a vassal state of Babylonia, but now for more than 600 years the Assyrians were supreme. Under Nebuchadnezzar (605–562 B.C.) Babylonia enjoyed its greatest power and Babylon its peak of wealth and glory; but in 538 B.C. Cyrus of Persia put an end to Babylonian power. After the Persians, Babylonia was ruled by Alexander the Great, by the Seleucids, the Parthians, the Arabs, and the Turks. Throughout the later centuries the ancient system of drainage and irrigation was neglected, and the land became almost a wilderness, while ancient cities and towns were leveled by war or abandoned by their inhabitants.

**Bacchiglione** (bäk-kē-lyō′nä) *River.* See **Meduacus Minor.**

**Bactra** (bak′trạ). [Also known anciently as **Zariaspa;** modern, **Balkh.**] In ancient geography, a city in SW Asia, supposed by most authorities to have been the capital of the ancient country of Bactria. It was the center of Zoroastrianism, and

obscured) errạnt, ardẹnt, actọr; ch, chip; g, go; th, thin; ᴛʜ, then; y, you; variable) ḍ as d or j, ş as s or sh, ṭ as t or ch, ẓ as z or zh.

Zoroaster is said to have died there. Bactra, which its natives called "Mother of Cities," anciently rivaled Ecbatana, Nineveh, and Babylon. It was conquered by Cyrus the Great and by Alexander the Great.

**Bactria** (bak'tri-ạ). In ancient geography, a country in C Asia, N of the Paropanisus Mountains (now Hindu Kush) on the upper Oxus River (now the Amu Darya), nearly corresponding to the modern district of Balkh in Afghanistan. The ancient capital was Zariaspa, Baktry, or Bactra (now Balkh). Bactria was the cradle of the Persian religion which Zoroaster reformed c600 B.C. At a very early period it was the center of a powerful kingdom which was conquered first by the Medes, then (as part of the domain of the Medes) by the Persians, and finally by Alexander the Great, who took a Bactrian princess, Roxana, as one of his wives. It was a part of the kingdom of the Seleucidae (a dynasty of rulers in Asia that stemmed from one of Alexander's generals), and from 256 B.C. for about 100 years an independent Greco-Bactrian kingdom which extended to the Kábul and Indus rivers. Bactria belonged thereafter to the Sassanidae until c640 A.D., and has since been under Moslem rule. Bactria played in ancient times an important cultural role, acting as an intermediary between the civilizations of the Greek world, India, and China.

**Baetica** (bē'ti-kạ). In ancient geography, the southernmost division of Hispania (Spain). It was also known as *Hispania Ulterior.*

**Baiae** (bā'yē). [Modern name, *Baia.*] Seaport in SW Italy, in the Campania, near Cape Misenum on the Gulf of Puteoli, W of Neapolis. It was a great seaport and the leading Roman watering-place, especially in the times of Horace, Nero, and Hadrian. It was famous for its luxury, and contained the villas of many celebrated Romans. Among the antiquities of Baiae are: 1) A Temple of Diana, so-called, in reality part of a Roman bath. It is octagonal without, circular within, with a pointed dome 97 feet in diameter. The walls have four ornamental niches. The structure is in *opus incertum* cased in masonry of brick and stone. 2) A Temple of Mercury, so-called, in reality part of a Roman bath, three subdivisions of which survive. The chief of these is the *frigidarium,* or cold bath, a circular domed structure 144 feet in diameter, with a circular opening at the apex, as in the Pantheon at Rome.

fat, fāte, fär, fåll, åsk, fãre; net, mē, hėr; pin, pīne; not, nōte, möve nôr; up, lūte, pùll; oi, oil; ou out; (lightened) ẹlect, agǫny, ūnite.

The two others are rectangular and vaulted, the vault of one having excellent ornament in relief. 3) A Temple of Venus, so-called, in fact part of a Roman bath, an octagonal buttressed structure of *opus incertum* cased in brick, and *opus reticulatum*, circular within, 94 feet in diameter, and domed. It has eight windows above, four doors below, and had lateral chambers containing stairs.

**Balkh** (balch). See *Bactra.*

**Baltia** (bal'shi-ạ). In ancient geography, an unidentified island off the coast of Scythia, mentioned by Pliny and other writers. The name of the Baltic Sea is derived from it.

**Bantia** (ban'shi-ạ). In ancient geography, a town in S Italy, SE of Venusia and NE of the modern Potenza. The inhabitants spoke Oscan as evidenced by the *Tabula Bantina,* found in 1793 and now in the Naples Museum.

**Barathron** (bar'ạ-thron). Steep ravine on the W slope of the Hill of the Nymphs, at Athens, Greece, outside of the ancient walls, rendered more precipitous by ancient use of it as a quarry. In antiquity this was the "pit" into which the bodies of criminals were thrown after execution, or in some cases while still living.

**Barca** (bär'kạ). In ancient geography, a city in Cyrenaica, N Africa, situated near the coast: one of the cities of the Pentapolis.

**Basento** (bä-sen'tō). See *Casuentus.*

**Basilis** (bas'i-lis). In ancient geography, a town in Arcadia. It was the site of a sanctuary of Eleusinian Demeter.

**Bedriacum** (bẹ-drī'ạ-kum). [Also: *Bebriacum.*] In ancient geography, a village in N Italy, E of Cremona. The exact location is undetermined. Here the forces of Vitellius, under Cecina and Valens, defeated (April, 69 A.D.) the forces of Otho; later in the same year, the forces of Vespasian, under Antonius, defeated those of Vitellius.

**Behistun** (bä-his-tön'). [Also: *Bisitun, Bisutun;* ancient name, *Baghistan.*] In ancient geography, a place in C Asia, about 23 miles E of what is now the city of Kermanshah, Iran. It is the site of a monument of Darius the Great, called the "Rosetta Stone of Asia," consisting of bas-reliefs and trilingual inscriptions 500 feet up the face of a sheer cliff, 1700 feet high. The bas-reliefs include a sculpture showing Darius with his foot on the prostrate form of the False Smerdis (Gaumata). In front of Darius are nine of the rebel chiefs, their hands

(obscured) errạnt, ardẹnt, actọr; ch, chip; g, go; th, thin; ŦH, then; y, you; (variable) ḍ as d or j, ṣ as s or sh, ṭ as t or ch, ẓ as z or zh.

bound behind them and a rope around their necks. Over all is a winged figure of the god Ahura Mazda. The inscriptions are in three kinds of cuneiform writing (Old Persian, Elamite, and Accadian), and tell how he killed the False Smerdis after the death of Cambyses, won victory over the rebels, and "with the aid of his good horse and his good groom, got himself the kingdom of the Persians." The inscriptions, deciphered (c1846) by Sir Henry Rawlinson, provided the first key to the ancient Assyrian writings.

**Benacus, Lacus** (be-nā′kus, lā′kus). [Modern name, *Lake Garda;* Italian, *Lago di Garda.*] Large lake in N Italy, in Transpadane Gaul. The Mincius River carries its waters into the Padus. The lake is noted for storms.

**Beneventum** (ben-ẹ-ven′tum). [Modern name, *Benevento.*] In ancient geography, a city in S Italy, about 35 miles NE of Neapolis. It was an ancient Samnite town that became a Roman colony, with its name changed from Mal(e)ventum, in 268 B.C., after the victory of the Romans over Pyrrhus which took place there. The town was pillaged by Hannibal after his victory at Cannae in 216 B.C. Among the many Roman monuments that remain are the Arch of Trajan, built in 114 A.D. and some Roman bridges.

**Beroea** (bẹ-rē′ạ). In ancient geography, a town on the Haliacmon River, in Macedonia. It was taken and held briefly by Pyrrhus, king of Epirus, in 286 B.C. After that it remained a Macedonian town until the arrival of the Romans, 168 B.C., who came to fight Perseus, and to whom the town of Beroea was one of the first Macedonian towns to submit. Pompey spent the winter of 49–48 B.C. encamped here.

**Biancavilla** (byäng-kä-vēl′lä). See *Inessa.*

**Bibracte** (bi-brak′tē). In ancient geography, a hill-town in C Gaul, the capital of the Aeduṭ, about eight miles W of Autun, France, with which it was formerly identified. Near it Caesar defeated the Helvetii in 58 B.C.

**Bithynia** (bi-thin′i-ạ). In ancient geography, a division of Asia Minor, lying between the Propontis (Sea of Marmara), Bosporus, and Euxine (Black Sea) on the N, Mysia on the W, Phrygia and Galatia on the S, and Paphlagonia on the E. Its inhabitants were of Thracian origin. Nicomedes I became (c278 B.C.) its first independent king; and Nicomedes II bequeathed (74 B.C.) the kingdom to Rome. It was governed by Pliny the Younger. The chief cities were Chalcedon, Heraclea, Prusa, Nicaea, and Nicomedia.

**Black Sea.** See **Euxine Sea.**

**Blue Grotto.** Cavern on the shore of the island of Capreae.

**Boae** (bō′ē) or **Bavo** (bā′vō). [Modern, *Ciovo;* also: **Bua.**] Island off the Dalmatian coast, just W of Spalatum (now Split). It was a place of banishment under the Roman emperors.

**Boeae** (bē′ē). A city in Laconia, near the end of the southeastern promontory of the Peloponnesus.

**Boeotia** (bē-ō′shạ). In ancient times, a district in C Greece, bounded by Locris Opuntia on the N, Attica and the strait of Euripus on the E, Attica, Megaris, and the Gulf of Corinth on the S, and Phocis on the W. Its surface was generally level, forming a basin in which was Lake Copaïs, now drained. Through this region Cadmus was said to have driven a cow, as instructed to do by the oracle at Delphi, following it until it sank to the ground to rest. On that spot he built the city of Thebes. The area was named Boeotia to commemorate the journey of the cow through it, according to some accounts. The cities of Boeotia were loosely united into the Boeotian League, of which Thebes was the leading and dominant city. Plataea refused to join the League. This caused a war with Athens to whom the Plataeans turned for aid, in which the Boeotians were defeated (509 B.C.). Plataea maintained close ties with Athens thereafter. The Athenians took many Boeotians prisoners in the war and kept them in iron fetters until they were ransomed. Afterward the Athenians hung the fetters in their citadel, and with a tenth of the ransom they constructed a bronze chariot with four horses which they dedicated to Athena on the Acropolis with the following verses:

> When Chalcis and Boeotia dared her might,
> Athens subdued their pride in valorous fight;
> Gave bonds for insults; and, the ransom paid,
> From the full tenths these steeds for Pallas made.

When Xerxes invaded Greece (480 B.C.), the Boeotians, except those of Plataea and Thespiae, sent him earth and water as tokens of submission and agreed to march with him as allies against their fellow countrymen. The Greeks who had taken up arms to resist the Persians, swore an oath against those Greeks who "delivered themselves to the Persians without necessity." In the battle of Plataea (479 B.C.), the

Boeotians fought valiantly on the Persian side against the Athenians, but were defeated. The history of Boeotia after the Persian War is largely the history of Thebes, which took the commanding place among the Boeotian cities. According to ancient Greek tradition, the inhabitants of Boeotia were all extremely stupid (but this, like most other Greek traditions, has come down to us through Athenian sources, and the Athenians had little love for the people or cities of Boeotia, for obvious reasons); but some say that the worship of Dionysus and the art of writing were introduced into Greece through Boeotia, for they were brought there by Cadmus.

*Bola* (bō'la). A town of the Aequi in Latium.

*Bosporus* (bos'pō-rus). [Also: *Bosphorus;* Turkish, *Karadeniz Boğazi;* ancient name *Bosporus Thracius, Thracian Bosporus.*] Strait which connects the Euxine (Black) Sea and Propontis (Sea of Marmara) and separates Europe from Asia. On it are Byzantium (now Istanbul) and Chrysopolis (now Usküdar). The name means "Oxford": so named from the legend that Io, transformed into a heifer, swam across it. Length, about 20 miles; greatest width, about 2½ miles; narrowest, about 800 yards.

*Bovianum* (bō-vi-ā'num). In ancient geography, a city in Samnium, Italy.

*Branchidae* (brang'ki-dē). The site of a famous temple of Apollo and an oracle, situated in the territory of Miletus in Ionia near the port of Panormus. The oracle was frequently consulted by both the Ionians and Aeolians. Croesus, who made many rich offerings to the temple, sent to test the accuracy of this oracle when he was considering whether to attack the Persians. Evidently he was not satisfied with its accuracy, for he ultimately posed the question whether he should attack Persia to the oracle at Delphi, with disastrous results. Hecataeus, the historian and wise counselor, when he failed to dissuade the Milesians from their intention of revolting against the Persians, advised them at least to take the precaution of taking the treasures of the temple of Apollo at Branchidae, including a huge shield in gold which Croesus had dedicated there, and use them to build a fleet with which they could secure control of the sea. If the Milesians did not take the treasures, he said, the Persians would. His advice was ignored and the event turned out as he had

fat, fāte, fär, fåll, åsk, fåre; net, mē, hėr; pin, pīne; not, nōte, möv̇ nôr; up, lūte, púll; oi, oil; ou out; (lightened) ẹlect, agǒny, ūnit

foretold. When the Persians came to put down the revolt of the Milesians, the hereditary priests of the temple (who were also called Branchidae) surrendered the treasure to them (c494 B.C.). The Persians carried it off and burned the temple. Many of the men of Miletus were slain. Some of the women and children were sent up to Susa as slaves. Later Xerxes sent the Milesians who were considered responsible for the betrayal of the temple to Sogdiana, in C Asia, to save them from the vengeance of the Greeks. At Sogdiana these Greeks founded a small settlement in which they preserved their Greek customs, religion, and speech. When, over 150 years later (c327 B.C.), Alexander the Great came to their settlement in his march into Asia, the Branchidae of Sogdiana, so it is said, rushed to welcome him as a Greek and to give him their loyalty. Some say that Alexander could think of them only as the Greeks who had betrayed their trust concerning the temple of Apollo and had taken the side of the Persians against the Greeks. He submitted the case of the Branchidae to the men of Miletus in his army. These could not agree on a judgment against the descendants of the priests who had betrayed the temple. Alexander himself decided their fate, so some say. The settlement was seized and every one of its inhabitants was massacred to avenge the dastardly crime of their ancestors. Magnificent ruins of the Ionic temple of Apollo of Branchidae, near Miletus, and of the ancient port, remain.

**Brauron** (brô'ron). In ancient geography, a village on the east coast of Attica. It was to this place, some say, that Orestes and Iphigenia returned from Tauris, bearing the ancient wooden image of Taurian Artemis with them. The image was brought to this place on the instructions of Athena, and in obedience to her commands the temple of Artemis Tauropolus was raised to house the image. As part of the ritual in honor of Artemis Tauropolus, the throat of a man kneeling before the altar was pricked by a sword just enough to draw blood. This was in memory of the narrow escape Orestes had in Tauris, and was also a substitute for the human sacrifices that had been offered to Taurian Artemis. Iphigenia was the first priestess in the temple of Artemis at Brauron, and some say Artemis made her immortal and she became Hecate. Excavations carried out by the Greek Archaeological Society (1958) have revealed remains of an early 5th century B.C. Doric temple of Artemis at Brauron, on the site where, according to Euripides' *Iphigenia in Tauris*, Orestes and Iphigenia were commanded to raise the temple of Artemis. Further excavations and restoration, continuing until 1965, have revealed a colonnade, with double rows of Doric columns, and wide steps cut from the rock by the temple foundations, corresponding to the "holy stairs" mentioned by Euripides. A tomb located in a grotto behind the temple is thought by some to be that of Iphigenia. Votive offerings, statuettes, and inscriptions, found in the nearby marshes and now in the National Archeological Museum in Athens, confirm the ritual described above. The modern village of Vravron is near the site of ancient Brauron.

*Brindisi* (brēn′dē-zē). See *Brundisium.*

*Brisea* (brī-sē′ạ). A town in Laconia. See *Bryseae.*

*Brundisium* (brun-dizh′i-um). [Modern: *Brindisi.*] City in Apulia, in SE Italy, situated on a land tongue between two bays of the Adriatic Sea. The ancient town, occupied by the Romans c266 B.C., became a Roman colony (246) and a naval station (244 B.C.). It assumed great strategic importance as the terminus of the Appian Way and port of embarkation for Greece and the Levant.

*Bruttii* (brut′i-ī). [Also: *Bruttium, Bruthius; Bruttiorum Ager.*] In ancient geography, the southernmost division of Italy, corresponding to the modern provinces of Reggio di Calabria, Cosenza, and Catanzaro, and approximately coextensive with the modern region of Calabria.

*Bryseae* (brī-sē′ē). A town in Laconia, whose inhabitants sailed under Menelaus to the Trojan War. In the temple of Dionysus here, only women were permitted to see the sacred image, and the rites they performed in its presence were secret.

*Buphagus* (bū-fā′gus). In ancient geography, a river in Arcadia.

*Bura* (bū′rä). A city in Achaea, near the southern shore of the Gulf of Corinth. An oracle of Heracles there gave answers as the result of the throw of four dice. The city was destroyed by an earthquake in 373 B.C. It joined (275 B.C.) the Achaean League.

*Buthoë* (bū′thọ-ē). A city in Illyria, on Lake Lychnitis.

*Buthrotum* (bū-thrō′tum). [Modern name, *Butrinto, Vutrinto.*] In ancient geography, a seaport in Epirus, now in Albania. It is said to have been founded by Helenus, son of Priam

***Buxentum*** (buk-sen'tum). [Modern name, ***Policastro***.] Town of Greek origin in Lucania, situated on an arm of the Tyrrhenian Sea about 60 miles SE of Salernum. It was colonized by the Romans after the Second Punic War.

***Byblus*** (bib'lus). [Also: ***Byblos***; modern name, ***Jubeil***, also spelled ***Djebeil, Jebail, Jebeil, Jubayl***; in the Bible, ***Gebal***.] In ancient geography, a city in Phoenicia, situated on a hill close to the Mediterranean Sea, about 18 miles N of what is now Beirut. It was one of the earliest of the Phoenician settlements, and second in importance only to Tyre and Sidon. Its inhabitants, the Gebalites, are mentioned as skillful in hewing stones (1 Kings, v. 18) and in shipbuilding (Ezek. xxvii. 9). The word "Bible" comes (through Greek *biblion*, book) from the ancient name of the city, which exported papyrus. The city was most celebrated as the oldest seat of the cult of Adonis, to whom the city was sacred, and after whom the river it stood on was named. Gebal is mentioned as a kingdom paying tribute to Assyria in the annals of Tiglath-pileser II and Esarhaddon. It was taken by Alexander the Great. Excavations carried on there have unearthed numerous tombs and sarcophagi and the substructions of a large temple, perhaps that of Adonis.

***Byzantium*** (bi-zan'shi-um, -ti-). [Greek, ***Byzantion***.] In ancient geography, a Greek city built on the E part of the site of Constantinople (modern Istanbul), into which it was formally merged by the emperor Constantine I in 330 A.D. It was noted for the beauty of its location, for its strategic position controlling the entrance to the Euxine (Black) Sea, and for its control of the all-important grain trade between the Euxine region and Greece. It is said to have been founded by colonists from Megara under Byzas, for whom it was named, in 667 B.C. The Megarians had first founded Chalcedon, on the opposite shore of the Bosporus. When they returned to the oracle of Delphi, they were chided by the priestess for their blindness in overlooking the more advantageous spot to which they returned and where they founded Byzantium. In the reign of Darius the Great the city was destroyed. Pausanias, the Spartan victor at Plataea (479 B.C.), seized and recolonized it, 477, but was driven out by the Athenians, 476 B.C. The city became a member of the Athenian Confederacy, from which it revolted in 440 and 411 B.C. Alcibiades conquered it in 408 B.C. by means of a blockade and the treachery of the Athenian party inside the city. Lysander the Spartan took it in 403 B.C. and set a Spartan governor to rule it. The Athenians regained control in 390, and at last recognized it as independent in 354 B.C. In 340 B.C. it was besieged by Philip of Macedon and relieved by Phocion. During the reign of Alexander the Great it fell under Macedonian dominion, but with the disintegration of the Macedonian empire after Alexander's death it became a free city. It was allied to Rome, at first as a free city, then as a subject city, and was at length besieged by Severus (196 A.D.), who took it, destroyed its walls, and put the population to the sword. Constantine recognized the advantages of its location, rebuilt it, and transferred the government there, 330 A.D., and it became the capital of the long-lived Byzantine Empire.

**C**

*Cadmea* (kad-mē′ạ). In ancient times, the citadel or acropolis of Thebes in Boeotia, Greece, named from its mythical founder, the hero Cadmus. The remains of the ancient fortifications include a stretch of ruined Cyclopean wall on the north side, and fragments of more recent walls on the southeastern slope.

*Caelian Hill* (sē′li-ạn). [Latin, *Caelius Mons.*] Southeastern hill of the group of Seven Hills of ancient Rome, adjoining the Palatine, and between the Aventine and the Esquiline. The Lateran lies on its widely extending eastern slope. According to legend, the Caelian Hill was added to the growing city of Rome by Tullus Hostilius, third king of Rome (672–640 B.C.). He won dominion over Alba Longa, destroyed that city, and moved its inhabitants to Rome, where he settled them on the Caelian Hill.

*Caere* (sē′rē). [Earlier name, *Agylla.*] In ancient geography, a city in Etruria, Italy, situated about 25 miles NW of Rome. It was supposed to have been founded by a warlike tribe from Lydia. According to some accounts, when the Gauls took Rome (389 B.C.), the vestal virgins fled with the sacred

fire and their sacred vessels to Caere, and there performed
the rites. From this event, some say, the rites came to be
known as *ceremonies*, after Caere. The site of Caere is occupied by the modern village of Cerveteri (i.e., Caere
Vetere, "Old Caere," to distinguish it from the new town,
Cere Nuovo), noted for Etruscan ruins.

**Caesarea** (sē-za-rē'a). A name given to various cities of the
Roman empire in honor of an emperor.

**Caesarea Philippi** (fi-lip'ī, fil'i-pī). See **Paneas**.

**Caieta** (kā-yē'ta). [Also: **Portus Caieta**; modern name, **Gaeta**.]
In ancient geography, a town and port of Latium, stiuated
on a promontory between Rome and Naples. According to
legend, after he had visited his father in Hades and learned
from him what his future and the future of his race would
be, Aeneas coasted along the shores of Italy and put in at
this place. Here his old nurse, Caieta, died and was buried,
piously mourned by Aeneas. The town that grew up on this
spot was named for her. Historically, Caieta was a Greek
colony that ultimately became a Roman town.

**Caieta, Gulf of.** [Modern name, **Gulf of Gaeta**.] Indentation of
the Mediterranean Sea N of Neapolis, Italy.

**Caius Cestius** (kā'us, kī'us; ses'ti-us), **Pyramid of**. Massive sepul-
chral monument of brick and stone, at Rome, about 114 feet
high, encrusted with marble. Each side of the base measures
90 feet. The small burial chamber is painted with white
arabesques. The pyramid is of the time of Augustus.

**Calabria** (ka-lā'bri-a). See **Bruttii**.

**Calauria** (ka-lôr'i-a). [Modern name, **Poros**.] In ancient geography, a small island off Troezen on the E coast of the Peloponnesus. According to legend, it was given to Poseidon by
Apollo in exchange for the former's share of the oracle at
Delphi. A religious association of maritime towns—Athens,
Aegina, Epidaurus, Troezen, Hermione, Nauplia, Prasiae,
and Orchomenus in Boeotia—joined together to promote
the worship of Poseidon on the island; they built a stone
temple (7th century B.C.) for their god, and sailors of the
member towns propitiated him there with sacrifices. The
sanctuary was served by a maiden priestess, who retired in
favor of a younger one when she reached marriageable age.
Demosthenes, the Greek orator, was exiled to this island
after the unsuccessful uprising which he promoted against
the Macedonians. He was later recalled but banished a sec-

ond time. He returned to Calauria and committed suicide by taking poison in the temple of Poseidon (322 B.C.). His tomb is at Calauria, where he was especially honored.

*Callichorus* (ka̯-lik'ọ̄-rus). A river of Paphlagonia, the river of fair dances. It was so named because Dionysus, on his way back from India, held dances and revels in a cave nearby.

*Callipolis* (ka-lip'ọ̄-lis). [Modern name, *Gallipoli.*] Seaport on a rocky island in the Gulf of Tarentum, connected with the mainland by a bridge, founded by Dorian colonists from Tarentum. It submitted to Rome in 266 B.C., but supported the Carthaginians in 214; passed finally to the Romans in 213 B.C. It was known to the Romans as Anxa.

*Callipolis.* [Modern names, *Gelibolu, Gallipoli.*] Seaport in the Chersonesus Thracica, on the Hellespont.

*Calliste* (ka̯-lis'tē). The ancient name for the island of Thera, one of the Cyclades.

*Calpe* (kal'pē). A promontory on the southern coast of the Iberian peninsula, modern Gibraltar, opposite the ancient Abyla (the modern Jebel Musa at Ceuta). See *Pillars of Heracles.*

*Calydon* (kal'i-dọn). In ancient geography, a city of Aetolia, in C Greece, situated near the river Evenus. It is the legendary scene of the hunt of the Calydonian boar.

*Calymna* (ka̯-lim'na̯). [Also: *Kalymna;* modern name, *Kalimnos.*] Dodecanese island in the Aegean Sea SW of Asia Minor, between the islands of Lerus and Cos. According to tradition, some of the Greek heroes returning from the Trojan War were shipwrecked on its rocky coasts. Those who survived founded a settlement there. Sculptured tombs found there indicate that the island was settled from early times. Area, 49 square miles.

*Camares* (ka̯-mä'rēz). See *Kamares.*

*Camarina* (kam-a̯-rī'na̯). In ancient geography, a city on the S coast of Sicily, about 45 miles SW of Syracuse. It was founded by colonists from Syracuse (599 B.C.), was wrested from Syracuse by Hippocrates, tyrant of Gela (491 B.C.), razed to the ground and its inhabitants moved to Syracuse by Gelon of Syracuse (484), rebuilt, and then (405 B.C.) abandoned by its inhabitants at the instance of Dionysus the Elder, tyrant of Syracuse, who betrayed it to Carthage.

*Campagna di Roma* (käm-pä'nyä dē rō'mä). Large plain in C Italy, surrounding Rome, lying between the Mediterranean

fat, fāte, fär, fåll, åsk, fâre; net, mē, hėr; pin, pīne; not, nōte, möve, nôr; up, lūte, půll; oi, oil; ou out; (lightened) ẹlect, agọny, ụnite;

Sea and the Sabine and Alban mountains. It corresponds in great part to the ancient Latium. It is a volcanic formation, and has been for centuries noted for its malarial climate, though in antiquity it was covered with villas and towns and was brought to a high state of cultivation. It has been largely reclaimed.

*Campania* (kam-pā′ni-ạ). In ancient geography, a region in S Italy, lying between Latium on the NW, Samnium on the N and E, Lucania on the SE, and the Mediterranean Sea on the W. Its original inhabitants were probably of the Oscan or the Ausonian race; it was settled later by the Greeks, and submitted to Rome in 343 B.C. It contained the ancient cities of Cumae, Capua, Baiae, Puteoli, Herculaneum, and Pompeii. Ever since Roman times the region has contained numerous seaside resorts. Campania came to include Latium in early imperial times and the name was gradually restricted to Latium (see immediately preceding article).

*Campus Martius* (kam′pus mär′shus). [Italian, *Campo Marzio* (käm′pō mär′tsyō); Eng. trans., "Field of Mars."] Historic area in ancient Rome, lying between the Pincian, Quirinal, and Capitoline hills and the Tiber River. Throughout the early history of Rome this plain remained free of buildings, and was used for popular assemblies and military exercises. During the reign of Augustus it had become encroached upon from the S by the building up of the Flaminian Meadows, and from the E by public and other buildings on the Via Cata, corresponding closely to the later Corso. Under Augustus, however, a great extent of the plain still remained free, and served for chariot races and horse races, ballplaying, and other athletic sports; it was surrounded by the finest monuments of the city, and presented an imposing spectacle. It is now occupied by one of the most important quarters of modern Rome, including the Pantheon and the parliament buildings.

*Candia* (kan′di-ạ). See *Heracleum*.

*Cannae* (kan′ē). In ancient geography, a town in Apulia, Italy, situated S of the river Aufidus. Near here (and N of the river), Hannibal with a Carthaginian force of about 50,000 men virtually annihilated (216 B.C.) the Roman army of about 80,000–90,000 under Varro and Aemilius Paulus. It was one of the greatest military disasters ever suffered by the ancient Romans, and the site is still called locally the "Field

(obscured) errạnt, ardẹnt, actọr; ch, chip; g, go; th, thin; ₮H, then; y, you;
(variable) ḍ as d or j, ṣ as s or sh, ṭ as t or ch, ẓ as z or zh.

of Blood" (Italian, *Campo di Sangue*). The Battle of Cannae remains even to this day of interest to military historians from the fact that it provides (with the earlier victory at Lake Trasimenus) clear evidence of Hannibal's military genius. Carthaginian fortunes were at their peak after Cannae, but lack of support from Carthage made it impossible for Hannibal to press his advantage and led finally to the defeat (201 B.C.) of Carthage by Rome in the Second Punic War.

**Canopic Mouth of the Nile** (ka̱-nō'pik). In ancient geography, a branch of the Nile River, NE Africa, the westernmost of the important mouths.

**Canopus** (ka̱-nō'pus). [Also: *Canobus.*] In ancient geography, a seaport of Egypt, about 15 miles NE of Alexandria, on the Canopic Mouth of the Nile. It had considerable trade and wealth.

**Caphyae** (kaf'ĭ-ē). In ancient geography, a city in Arcadia.

**Capitolium** (kap-i-tō'li-um), **Capitol.** 1) At Rome, one of the traditional seven hills, Rome's inner citadel, with two summits, sometimes distinguished as *Arx et Capitolium*, the northern summit being the *arx* or citadel proper, the southern the *Capitolium*, dominating from the west the Forum Romanum. On the arx stood the temple of Juno Moneta, on the Capitolium the ancient triple-cella temple to the Capitoline Triad of Jupiter Optimus Maximus, Juno, and Minerva, focus of Roman state worship. With its religious, political, and military associations, it was regarded as the historic center of Rome, symbol of Rome's greatness. It is also referred to as *Mons Capitolinus* or Capitoline Hill. In modern Rome, the name has been corrupted to Campidoglio; the Piazza del Campidoglio, designed by Michelangelo, approached from the west by a monumental stairway, occupies the saddle between the two peaks; it contains the Museo Capitolino or Capitoline Museum, the Palazzo del Senatore, the Palazzo dei Conservatori, the fine bronze equestrian statue of Marcus Aurelius, other sculptures, milestones, etc.; near the site of the temple of Juno Moneta stands the church of S. Maria in Aracoeli; on the summit of the arx is the dazzling Victor Emmanuel Monument; on the southern summit, partly built over by the Palazzo Caffarelli, are the tufa foundations of the temple of Jupiter, Juno, and Minerva. 2) The term *Capitolium* was also applied to the triple cella temple to the Capitoline Triad, Jupiter Optimus

fat, fāte, fär, fâll, ȧsk, fãre; net, mē, hėr; pin, pīne; not, nōte, möve, nôr; up, lūte, pùll; oi, oil; ou out; (lightened) ḝlect, agǫny, ūnite;

Maximus, Juno, and Minerva, alternatively known as the temple of Jupiter Capitolinus, said to have been dedicated in the first year of the republic, 509 B.C., rebuilt after fires in 83 B.C., 69 A.D., and 80 A.D., repeatedly repaired and embellished, and systemically vandalized from the 5th century on. Only a few courses of the tufa foundations remain. 3) Outside of Rome, at first in Roman colonies and eventually elsewhere, the term *capitolium* was applied to a temple with three cellas, or with tripartite division indicated by chapels or niches, dedicated to the Capitoline Triad in emulation of Rome; examples at Ostia, Cosa, Minturnae, Pompeii, and elsewhere. (JJ)

*Cappadocia* (kap-a-dō′sha). In ancient geography, a country in the E part of Asia Minor, lying W of the Euphrates, N of Cilicia, and E of Phrygia; in a wider sense, the territory in Asia Minor between the lower Halys and Euphrates rivers, and the Taurus mountains and Euxine Sea; an elevated tableland intersected by mountain chains. The inhabitants of this region were called *Cappadocians* by the Persians and *Syrians* by the Greeks of Herodotus' time. Before the rise of Persia the area was subject to the Medes. It was invaded by Croesus and then came under the control of Persia under Cyrus. As warriors, the Cappadocians wore braided helmets, carried small shields, and fought with spears, javelins, and daggers. Under the Persians the area constituted two satrapies, afterward two independent kingdoms; they were Cappadocia on the Pontus, later called Pontus; and Cappadocia near the Taurus, called Great Cappadocia, the later Cappadocia in a narrower sense. In 17 A.D. Cappadocia became a Roman province. It had then only four cities, Mazaca, near Mount Argaeus, the residence of the Cappadocian kings, later called Eusebia, and by the Romans Caesarea, the episcopal see of Saint Basil (modern Kayseri); Tyana; Garsaura, later called Archelais; and Ariarathea. Of its other cities, Samosata (Samsat), Myssa, and Nazianzus, the birthplaces or seats of celebrated ecclesiastics, are noteworthy.

*Capreae* (kap′rē-ē). [Modern name, *Capri*.] Island off the coast of Campania, S Italy, situated about 19 miles S of Neapolis. It was famous in antiquity for the beauty of its scenery and its caves, especially the Blue Grotto. It was used as a resort by Augustus, and the emperor Tiberius spent his last ten years on Capreae, communicating by letter with the Senate at Rome. Area, five square miles.

*Capua* (kap'ū-ạ). Ancient city in Campania, Italy, about 17 miles N of Neapolis, famous for its wealth and luxury. It was founded by the Etruscans (c600 B.C.), was taken (c440 B.C.) by the Samnites, and came (c343 B.C.) under Roman rule. It opened (216 B.C.) its gates to Hannibal, whose army wintered there (216–215 B.C.). In 211 B.C. it was retaken by the Romans, and severely punished. It afterward flourished until sacked (456 A.D.) by Genseric. It was destroyed (840) by the Saracens, and its inhabitants colonized modern Capua. Its site is occupied by the village of Santa Maria di Capua Vetere. It contains the ruins of a triumphal arch and of a Roman amphitheater which dates from the early empire. The amphitheater was an imposing monument, much resembling the Roman Colosseum, and nearly as large. The axes of the outer ellipse are 557 and 458 feet; of the arena, 250 and 150 feet.

*Cardamyle* (kär-dam'i-lē). A city of Laconia on the Messenian Gulf. It had formerly belonged to Messenia.

*Cardia* (kär'di-ạ). In ancient geography, a city on the Thracian Chersonesus, founded by colonists from Miletus and Clazomenae.

*Caria* (kär'i-ạ). In ancient geography, a division of Asia Minor, lying between Lydia on the N, Phrygia and Lycia on the E, and the Aegean Sea on the S and W. The Maeander (modern Menderes), a noted river, flows through it. According to Herodotus, the Carians went to the mainland of Asia Minor from the islands, where they were formerly called Leleges and were subjects of King Minos of Crete. They were noted sailors and served brilliantly in the navies of Minos. They were the first to put crests on their helmets and devices on their shields, and they invented handles for shields, which were formerly worn suspended by straps around the necks of warriors. The Greeks borrowed these usages from the Carians. Herodotus says the Carians were driven from the islands by the Dorians and Ionians and settled on the mainland. The Ionians of the islands and of Asia Minor insisted that they were of pure stock, but in fact, says Herodotus, they were a mixture from the mainland of Greece. When they came among the Carians, they killed the men and forced marriage on the women; their descendants were thus

fat, fāte, fär, fâll, àsk, fāre; net, mē, hèr; pin, pīne; not, nōte, mȯve, nôr; up, lūte, pủll; oi, oil; ou out; (lightened) ḝlect, agǫny, ūnite;

inevitably of mixed race. The Carian women, compelled to marry the Ionians, vowed they would never sit at table with their husbands, or call them by name, because they had slain their fathers, sons and husbands, and they handed this practice down to their daughters. But the Carians themselves, according to Herodotus, say they were aboriginal to the mainland and never bore any other name. They claimed they were named for Car, and showed a temple of Carian Zeus in which the Mysians and Lydians, brother races of the Carians as the descendants of Mysus and Lydus, had the right to worship. In the Trojan War the Carians were allies of Troy. In the time of recorded history, Caria became subject to Croesus and later to Cyrus, falling to the Persian forces without much of a fight. Under Darius Caria was part of the first of the 20 satrapies into which Darius divided his empire, and paid a tribute to him of 400 talents of silver annually. In the Ionian revolt against Persian domination the Carians fought valiantly but were subdued. They furnished 70 ships to the Persian navy in the Persian Wars. The chief cities of Caria were Miletus, Myus, Halicarnassus, and Priene. The area fell to Alexander the Great and was later incorporated by the Romans into the province of Asia (129 B.C.).

*Carmania* (kär-māʹni-a̧). In ancient geography, a division of Ariana on the plateau of what is now Iran. It was a province of the Persian Empire, bounded on the N by Parthia, on the E by Drangiana and Gedrosia, on the S by what is now known as the Persian Gulf, and on the W by Persis and Media. Alexander the Great passed through it on his return from India (325 B.C.) and added it to his empire. Carmania occupied about the same area as the modern Iranian region of Kerman.

*Carpathus* (kärʹpa̧-thus). [Greek, *Karpathos;* Italian, *Scarpanto;* Turkish, *Kerpe.*] Island in the Aegean Sea, about 30 miles SW of Rhodes: one of the Dodecanese group. In ancient times the island was under the rule of Rhodes. Area, about 108 square miles; length, about 32 miles.

*Carrhae* (karʹē). [Also: *Charran;* modern name, *Haran.*] In ancient geography, a city of Mesopotamia, situated on the Bilichus River (Belikh), a small affluent of the Euphrates, about 23 miles SE of Urfa. It was the city named Haran in the Old Testament. Nearby was the scene of the defeat (53

(obscured) errạnt, ardẹnt, actọr; ch, chip; g, go; th, thin; ŦH, then; y, you;
(variable) ḑ as d or j, ş as s or sh, ţ as t or ch, z̧ as z or zh.

B.C.) of Crassus by the Parthians, who killed him shortly thereafter while he was engaged in an interview with one of their satraps.

**Carthage** (kär′thaj). [Latin, *Carthago;* Phoenician, *Karthadasht,* meaning "New Town."] Ancient city and state in N Africa, situated on the Mediterranean, a few miles NE of modern Tunis, and not far from the ancient city of Utica. It was founded by Phoenicians about the middle of the 9th century B.C. (According to tradition, Dido founded the city, having bought as much land as could be circumscribed by a buffalo hide; this she cut in strips with which, laid end to end, she encircled a sizable piece of ground and on it built the citadel called Byrsa, from the Greek word "hide.") It was a great commercial and colonizing center as early as the 6th century B.C., and was one of the largest cities of antiquity. It had two harbors, a naval and a mercantile. Its first treaty with Rome was made in 509 B.C. It was defeated at Himera in Sicily in 480 B.C., but overthrew Selinus and other Sicilian cities c400 B.C. It was the rival of Syracuse under Dionysius, Agathocles, and others. At the height of its power it had possessions in Sicily, Corsica, Sardinia, N Africa, and Spain. Its wars with Rome have the following dates: First Punic War, 264–241 B.C.; Second Punic War, 218–201 B.C.; Third Punic War, 149–146 B.C. It was recolonized as a Roman city by Caius Gracchus and successfully by Augustus c29 B.C., was taken by the Vandals in 439 A.D., and was retaken by Belisarius in 533. At present some cisterns, broken arches of an aqueduct, the Roman Catholic monastery of Saint Louis, and a museum mark the site of the former rival of Rome.

**Casilinum** (kas-i-lī′num). An ancient name of *Capua.*

**Casius** (kā′si-us). [Also: *Bargylus.*] Ancient name of the mountainous region in Asia Minor S of Antioch.

**Caspiae Portae** or *Pylae* (kas′pi-ē pôr′tē, pī′lē). [Also: *Albanian Gates; Caspian Gates;* Latin, *Albaniae Pylae; Caucasiae Portae.*] An old name of the defile of Derbent between the Caucasus and the Caspian Sea. It has long been a trade route.

**Caspium, Mare** (kas′pi-um, mā′rē). [Also: *Mare Hyrcanium;* modern, *Caspian Sea.*] Salt inland sea N of Media and Hyrcania. Length, 760 miles; greatest width, about 270 miles; area 169,330 square miles; elevation at surface, 85 feet below sea level.

**Cassandra** (kä-sän′drä). [Also: *Kassandra, Pallene.*] Western-

fat, fāte, fär, fåll, åsk, fāre; net, mē, hėr; pin, pīne; not, nōte, möve, nôr; up, lūte, půll; oi, oil; ou out; (lightened) ē̜lect, agọ̈ny, ūnite;

most peninsula of Chalcidice, NE Greece.

***Cassandra, Gulf of.*** See ***Toronaicus, Sinus.***

***Cassandrea*** (kas-an-drē′a). The name Cassander gave to Potidaea, a Macedonian city, when he rebuilt it after its destruction. See ***Potidaea.***

***Cassotis*** (kas′ō-tis). [Also: ***Kassotis.***] Spring at Delphi on the slopes of the hill above the theater. According to some accounts, it was named for a nymph of Mount Parnassus. The waters of the spring were said to sink into the ground and flow into the shrine of the priestesses of Apollo who, on drinking of them, were then inspired to prophecy.

***Castalia*** (kas-tā′li-a, -tāl′ya). A fountain at the eastern foot of the deep gorge that separates the rocks known as the Phaedriades, on the slopes of Mount Parnassus, Greece. The fountain was sacred to the Muses and to Apollo. Its waters were said to have the power of inspiring those who drank of them. The fountain was sealed off by earthquakes for centuries and its site was lost. Ensuing earthquakes opened it up and caused its waters to flow again. The basin, to the west on a slope above Castalia, where rites were performed before pilgrims approached the sanctuary of Apollo, may still be seen with streams from the fountain trickling into it.

***Casuentus*** (kas-ū-en′tus). [Modern: ***Basento*** or ***Basiento.***] River in S Italy which flows into the Gulf of Tarentum (now Taranto) near Metapontum about 27 miles SW of Tarentum.

***Catana*** (kat′a-na) or ***Catina*** (kat′i-na). [Greek, ***Katane;*** modern, ***Catania.***] City on the island of Sicily, situated on the Gulf of Catana on the E coast of the island. Founded by Greeks from Naxos in 729 B.C., the city lies in a very fertile plain at the foot of Mount Aetna, and because of its location and rich soil has often been contested. When the Athenians sent an expedition against Syracuse under the command of Alcibiades (415–413 B.C.), Catana was allied with Athens and served as a base for the Athenian fleet. In 404 B.C. Catana allied itself to the neighboring city of Leontini for protection against Dionysius the Elder, tyrant of Syracuse. However, the city fell into the hands of Dionysius by treachery. Traitors, bribed by Dionysius, opened the gates of the city to his forces (403 B.C.); he plundered the city, rounded up its inhabitants and sold them into slavery, and gave what remained of the city to his Italian allies, the Campanians. In

(obscured) errant, ardent, actor; ch, chip; g, go; th, thin; ᴛʜ, then; y, you;
(variable) ḏ as d or j, ṣ as s or sh, ṭ as t or ch, ẓ as z or zh.

the First Punic War (264–241 B.C.), Catana was one of the first Sicilian cities to be taken by the Romans (263 B.C.), and later, from the time of Augustus, it became one of the first cities of Sicily as an ally of Rome. Remains of a theater, odeum, and amphitheater of Roman times have been found at the site.

*Caucasus* (kô′kạ-sus) *Mountains.* Mountain system between the Black and Caspian seas. On a crag in these mountains, according to legend, Prometheus was chained at the command of Zeus, and eagles daily gnawed at his liver. Heracles at last freed Prometheus, with the consent of Zeus. The mountains extend SE and NW and are often taken as the conventional boundary between Europe and Asia. There are numerous passes, some of them reaching an elevation of 10,000–11,000 feet. The glaciers rival those of the Alps, but lakes are almost entirely lacking. The mountains have been extremely important historically as a barrier to migrations. Length of the system, about 800 miles; greatest width, about 120 miles.

*Caudine Forks* (kô′dīn). [Latin, *Furculae Caudinae.*] Two passes in the mountains of ancient Samnium, Italy, leading to an enclosed valley between Capua and Beneventum. Here the Romans under the consuls Spurius Postumius Albinus and T. Veturius were forced (321 B.C.) to surrender to the Samnites under Pontius. The Romans were forced to swear to a treaty of peace, and to give 600 Roman *equites* (knights) as hostages, while the whole Roman army was sent under the yoke (thus symbolizing their collective submission). Infuriated by this last humiliation, which was one of the worst ever accepted by a Roman military force, the Roman Senate refused to approve the treaty, and delivered the consuls to the Samnites, who refused to accept them.

*Caulonia* (kô-lō′ni-ạ). In ancient geography, a city in Bruttii, S Italy, situated on a rocky elevation near the Mediterranean Sea. The city was founded by Achaeans, perhaps from Croton or from Greece itself, in the 7th century B.C. It was captured by Dionysius the Elder, tyrant of Syracuse, in 389 B.C. He destroyed the city and gave its territory to the neighboring city of Locri. It was soon after restored, but was again taken by Pyrrhus, king of Epirus (c318–272 B.C.), and thereafter was almost abandoned. Excavations at the site have revealed remains dating from the 7th and 6th centuries B.C., and part of a temple of the 5th century B.C.

*Cavo* (kä′vō), *Monte*. [Also: *Monte* (or *Mount*) *Albano*.] Highest summit of the Alban Hills, situated about 13 miles SE of Rome. On it are the ruins of the temple of Jupiter Latiaris. Height, 3115 feet.

*Caÿster* (ka̧-is′tėr). [Also: *Caystrus* (ka-is′trus).] In ancient geography, a river in Lydia, Asia Minor, which flows into the Aegean Sea about 35 miles S by SE of Smyrna (Izmir); now called the Bayindir or, sometimes, the Little Menderes. The ancient city of Ephesus was near its mouth.

*Cecropia* (sē-krō′pi-a̧). An ancient name for Attica, from the ancient king Cecrops.

*Cefalù* (chä-fä-lö′). See *Cephaloedium.*

*Celaenae* (se-lē′nē). In ancient geography, an important and large city of Phrygia, situated at the source of both the Marsyas and Maeander rivers. Traditionally, Apollo flayed Marsyas here after he had beaten the latter in a musical contest. The city was the site of a royal residence in the time of Xerxes. The modern town on the ancient site is Dinar, Turkey.

*Cenaeum* (sȩ̄-nē′um). A promontory on the northwestern tip of Euboea. It was here that Heracles prepared to sacrifice to Zeus and donned the shirt poisoned with the blood of Nessus which led to his death.

*Cenchreae* (seng′krȩ̄-ē). In ancient geography, the harbor of Corinth, named for Cenchrias, a child of Poseidon and Pirene. Nearby was a temple of Artemis, and in the town, a temple and stone image of Aphrodite. The region was sacred to Poseidon, and a mole running out into the sea was crowned by a bronze image of him. Opposite Cenchreae was a stream of warm salt water that flowed from a rock into the sea and was known as *Helen's Bath.* Near Cenchreae was the common grave of the Argives who conquered the Lacedaemonians at Hysiae in the 7th century B.C. In 1963 it was reported that archaeologists at Cenchreae had found traces of three temples dating possibly from about 600 B.C. Most notable are the temple remains, now 10 feet below sea level, on a pier 330 feet long and 165 feet wide, located at the south end of the harbor.

*Centumcellae* (sen″tum-sel′ē). Also: [*Portus Trajani;* modern name, *Civitavecchia* or *Civita Vecchia*.] In ancient geography, an Etruscan town in C Italy, situated on the Mediter-

(obscured) errant, ardent, actor; ch, chip; g, go; th, thin; ŦH, then; y, you;
(variable) ḑ as d or j, ş as s or sh, ţ as t or ch, z̧ as z or zh.

ranean Sea, NW of Rome. The port was constructed in the time of the emperor Trajan.

*Centuripae* (sen-tū′ri-pē). [Also: *Centorbi;* modern name, *Centuripe.*] In ancient geography, a very old Sicel city in Sicily, in the eastern half of the island near Mount Aetna. It was allied with Athens against Syracuse in the Peloponnesian Wars, and was later allied to Dionysius the Elder, tyrant of Syracuse, in his wars against the Carthaginians. It was an independent city up to the time of the First Punic War (264–241 B.C.). It flourished under the Romans, and a number of antiquities of this period are preserved.

*Ceos* (sē′os). [Also: *Keos, Kea, Tzia, Zea, Zia.*] Island of the Cyclades in the Aegean Sea about 13 miles SE of Attica. According to legend, the island suffered a terrible scorching drought which afflicted it because the murderers of Icarius had taken refuge there. On learning from the oracle at Delphi that he would find honor there, Aristaeus went to Ceos, offered sacrifices to Zeus, and by killing the murderers of Icarius appeased the Dog-Star (the faithful hound of Icarius which had been translated to the heavens), which was causing the drought. From that time on cooling winds, the Etesian winds, now annually strike the islands for 40 days. Ceos formerly contained four cities, and was the birthplace of the poets Simonides and Bacchylides. In 1961 the discovery on Ceos of remains of a fortified city over 3,500 years old was reported. By 1963 excavations had revealed that the city, originally surrounded by a six-foot-thick fortification wall, had consisted of two- and three-story stone houses, the interiors of some covered with brightly painted stucco, lining three-foot-wide streets, with a rather sophisticated covered drainage system. Also found in the excavations of the city were the ruins of a temple, the earliest of its kind yet discovered in Greece, containing remains of three life-size statues dating from about 1200 B.C. Originally done in coarse and then fine clay over a wooden armature, the statues are now in fragments. Among these are two heads, one of which is that of a goddess, her headress and coiffure missing but her face very distinctive, with large round eyes, prominent cheekbones, a wide smile, and an unequivocal chin. Area of island, about 65 square miles.

*Cephallenia* (sef-ạ-lē′ni-ạ). [Modern *Cephalonia;* also: *Kefallinia, Kephallenia.*] The largest of the Ionian Islands, W of

fat, fāte, fär, fåll, àsk, fãre; net, mē, hėr; pin, pīne; not, nōte, möve, nôr; up, lūte, púll; oi, oil; ou out; (lightened) ẹlect, agǫny, ụnite;

Greece. Its surface is mountainous. Some say the island is the one called Same or Samos by Homer who, some think, meant this island as the center of the Kingdom of the Islands of which Odysseus was the ruler. There were four main cities there in ancient times: Cranii, Pale, Same, and Pronni. Remains of Cyclopean walls have been found at the sites of each of these cities. Tombs and graves of the Mycenaean period and the period of the Trojan War have revealed a rich store of vases and other objects that indicate a flourishing state of civilization from most ancient times. In later centuries, the 13th and 12th centuries B.C., rivals of Cephallenia—Mycenae, Thebes, Athens—waged war against her. At the outbreak of the Peloponnesian War (431 B.C.), Cephallenia was allied to Corinth, but was forced to change its allegiance to Athens. It became subject to Rome in 189 B.C. Length of the island, 30 miles; area, about 300 square miles.

*Cephaloedium* (sef-a-lē′di-um). [Modern name, *Cefalù*.] In ancient geography, a city on the N coast of the island of Sicily, situated at the foot of a headland over 1200 feet above sea level, from whence it derived its name (Greek, *kephale*, "head"). It was founded by the Sicels, one of the earliest tribes in the island and from whom the whole island ultimately took its name. The city was conquered by Dionysius the Elder, tyrant of Syracuse, c395 B.C., by the Romans in 254 B.C., and by the Saracens in 858 A.D. Among the ancient remains to be seen there are fortifications and a primitive sancturary known as the "Temple of Diana."

*Cephissus* (sē-fis′us). [Also: *Cephisus, Kephisos*.] In ancient geography, a river in Attica, Greece, flowing through the plain of Eleusis into the Gulf of Eleusis.

*Cephisus*. [Also: *Cephisus, Kephisos*.] In ancient geography, a river in Attica, Greece, flowing through the plain of Athens into the Saronic Gulf.

*Cephissus*. [Also: *Cephisus, Kephisos*.] In ancient geography, a river in Phocis and Boeotia, Greece, flowing into Lake Copaïs. This was the sacred river of the shrine of Delphi. Beside it was the shrine of Themis, where Deucalion and Pyrrha went after the great flood to pray to the gods, and where they learned how to repopulate the world.

*Ceraunii Montes* (sē-rô′ni-ī mon′tēz). [Also: *Ceraunian Mountains; Acroceraunia* or *Acroceraunian Mountains*.] In ancient

(obscured) errạnt, ardẹnt, actọr; ch, chip; g, go; th, thin; ℻H, then; y, you;
(variable) ḍ as d or j, ṣ as s or sh, ṭ as t or ch, ẓ as z or zh.

geography, a chain of mountains in NW Epirus, terminating in the promontory Acroceraunia.

*Ceraunian Mountains.* In ancient geography, a range of mountains in the E part of the Caucasus system, exact position undetermined.

*Cercinitis Lacus* (sėr-si-nī'tis lā'kus). [Also: *Cercinites, Kerkinitis, Limne Kerkinitis.*] In ancient geography, the lake or enlargement near the mouth of the river Strymon in Macedonia.

*Cerveteri* (cher-ve'tā-rē). See *Caere.*

*Cerynia* (ser-i-nī'a̯). In ancient geography, one of the 12 towns in Achaea occupied by the Achaeans after the Ionians had left the land. It was built on a high hill between the Cerynites River and Mount Cerynia, from which it took its name, according to some accounts. The sanctuary of the Eumenides in Cerynia was said to have been founded by Orestes. Of this sanctuary it was said that whoever entered it, guilty of murder or impiety, at once became insane with fright.

*Cerynitia* (ser-i-nish'a̯). Forested region in Arcadia where Heracles found the golden-horned, bronze-hoofed Cerynean stag (or hind) which he pursued for a year before capturing it alive as his third labor for Eurystheus.

*Chaeronea* (ker-ọ̄-nē'a̯). [Also: *Chaeroneia.*] In ancient geography, a town in W Boeotia, Greece. Chaeronea was the birthplace of Plutarch and it was here that he spent most of his life and did his work. It was a dependency of Orchomenus. Here Philip of Macedon defeated (388 B.C.) the Thebans, Athenians, and their allies. The Thebans gathered the bodies of those of the Sacred Battalion who had fallen in the battle and buried them in a common tomb. Over it the famous marble *Lion of Chaeronea* was raised as a memorial. The monument was broken apart by a chieftain who thought to find treasure there and it was not until 1818 that the lion was found lying in a field. In the early part of the 20th century it was restored and remounted on its ancient base. Nearby the lion a small theater was cut into the rocks of the hill called Petrachus. This hill was, some say, the place where Rhea deceived Cronus by handing him a stone wrapped in swaddling clothes in place of her new-born son Zeus. Chaeronea was the place where Sulla (86 B.C.) with 30,000–40,000 men defeated the army of Mithridates VI (about 110,000) under Archelaus. In ancient times the

Chaeroneans were noted for their skill in distilling unguents from the lily, rose, narcissus, and iris, that cured many human ills.

*Chalcedon* (kal′se̩-don, -do̩n; kal-se̱′do̩n). [Modern Turkish name, *Kadiköy*.] In ancient geography, a town in Bithynia, situated on the Bosporus opposite Byzantium. It was founded (c685 B.C.) by Megarian colonists.

*Chalcidice* (kal-sid′i-sē). [Also: *Chalkidike, Khalkidhiki, Khalkidike, Khalkidiki*.] In ancient geography, the chief peninsula of Macedonia, terminating in the three smaller peninsulas of Pallene, Sithonia, and Acte, projecting into the Aegean Sea. It was settled (c7th century B.C.) by Euboeans. Its chief cities were Olynthus and Potidaea.

*Chalcis* (kal′sis). [Also: *Chalkis, Egripo, Evripos, Negropont*.] City in C Greece, situated on the W coast of the island of Euboea on the Euripus strait about 34 miles N of Athens. It was the chief town in ancient Euboea, and sent out many colonial settlers. Cumae in Italy and Naxos in Sicily were colonized by Chalcidians, and the colonies of Chalcis in Italy and Sicily exceeded in number those of any other state. Chalcis was subdued (506 B.C.) by Athens, and was an important trading and colonizing center. Isaeus the orator and Lycophron the poet were born in Chalcis, and Aristotle died here in 322 B.C.

*Chelydorea* (kel″i-dō′rē̬-a̬). In ancient geography, a mountain in Arcadia, on the boundary between Pheneus in Arcadia and Pellene in Achaea. The inhabitants were mostly Achaeans. The mountain, near Mount Cyllene, the birthplace of Hermes, was said by some to be the place where Hermes found the tortoise from which he constructed the first lyre. The name Chelydorea means "Mountain of the flayed tortoise."

*Chemmis* (kem′is). [Also: *Panopolis;* modern *Akhmin*.] An ancient city on the right bank of the Nile, in Upper Egypt, between Asyut and Thebes. It was the seat of the cult of Ammon Chem. Chem was identified with Pan and the city was called Panopolis by the Greeks and Romans. According to legend, Perseus stopped in the city as he returned from Libya after securing the head of Medusa. There was a precinct sacred to Perseus in the city, and an image of him in the temple. The people of Chemmis declared, in the time of Herodotus, that Perseus often appeared to them. They said also that frequently a huge sandal belonging to Perseus was found, and on those occasions all Egypt prospered. The people of Chemmis claimed that Perseus himself had ordered them to establish the festival in his honor which they celebrated annually in the Greek manner with games and other contests. This honoring of Perseus was all the more unusual in that the Egyptians were decidedly averse to adopting the customs of other nations, and were especially hostile to Greek customs. It was accounted for by their belief that Perseus was of Egyptian origin through his ancestor Danaus, who was said to have been native to Chemmis before he fled with his daughters to Argos.

*Chersonesus* (kėr-sǫ-nē′sus). [Also: *Chersonese*.] Ancient Greek word for peninsula, specifically applied to the following: 1) Chersonesus Aurea, the modern Malay Peninsula. 2) Chersonesus Cimbrica, the modern peninsula of Jutland, Denmark. 3) Chersonesus Taurica or Scythica, the modern Crimea, U.S.S.R. 4) Chersonesus Thracica, the modern Gallipoli Peninsula, between the Hellespont and the Gulf of Saros.

*Chersonesus.* [Also: *Cherson, Chersonesus Heracleotica.*] Ancient city situated on the SW tip of the Crimean Peninsula, near what is now Sevastopol, founded by the Ionians at the beginning of the 5th century B.C. Because of its situation, it soon became an important trading city-state. Alliance with the kingdom of Cimmerian Bosporus was followed by subjection to the Roman Empire. It is archaeologically of interest, containing the remains of city walls and towers of the Byzantine era, foundations of some private dwellings, and foundations of basilicas, with mosaic floors and traces of frescoes. Many old Greek inscriptions were found here, and the necropolis contains numerous objects of the Greco-Roman and Byzantine periods. Some traces of a neolithic culture have been found here.

*Chios* (kī′os). [Also: *Khios;* Italian, *Scio;* Turkish, *Saki-Adasi, Saki-Adassi.*] Greek island in the Aegean Sea, situated W of Asia Minor. It is 30 miles long and has an area of 355 square miles. The surface is hilly and rocky. The island has been noted in ancient and modern times for wine and fruit. The inhabitants are mostly Greeks. In the 6th century B.C. it came under Persian rule and revolted against Persian rule at the beginning of the 5th century B.C. In 494 B.C. the

fat, fāte, fär, fâll, ȧsk, fāre; net, mē, hėr; pin, pīne; not, nōte, mŏve, nôr; up, lūte, pùll; oi, oil; ou out; (lightened) ę̄lect, agǫny, ūnite;

Chians, deserted by their Samian and Lesbian allies, fought with splendid valor against the Phoenician fleet that had come to the siege of Miletus, but were forced to withdraw, after inflicting great damage on the enemy ships and losing many of their own. After the Persian War Chios joined the Confederacy of Delos but revolted in 413 B.C. and was laid waste by the Athenians. Chios was noted in the ancient world as a center of art and literature, particularly for its school of epic poets.

**Chios.** [Also: *Kastro, Khios;* Italian, *Scio.*] Chief city of the island of Chios, E Greece, situated on the E coast. It is one of seven cities which claimed to be the birthplace of Homer.

**Chiusi** (kyö′sē). See *Clusium.*

**Chryse** (krī′sē). See *Comana.*

**Chrysopolis** (kri-sop′ō-lis). In ancient geography, a city on the Bosporus, opposite Byzantium. From ancient times it was important as a center of traffic from the Euxine Sea. In the last years of the Peloponnesian War Athens seized it and set up a toll-station there at which ships coming from the Euxine had to pay a percentage of the value of their cargoes.

**Cibyra** (sib′i-ra). [Called *Cibyra Magna* (mag′na).] In ancient geography, a town in Phrygia, Asia Minor, near the site of the Turkish village of Korzum, about 65 miles NW of Antalya. It was surnamed "Magna" to distinguish it from a smaller town of the same name in Pamphylia. Its ruins comprise an odeum, 175 feet in diameter, with 13 tiers of seats visible above ground. The front wall is noteworthy, and is practically complete; it has five arched doorways between two square ones. There are also an ancient theater of some size and considerable interest, and a stadium, in part excavated from a hillside. There are 21 tiers of seats in marble, which remain in place around the curved end. There was a monumental entrance, consisting of three lofty arches.

**Cilicia** (si-lish′a). In ancient geography, a province in SE Asia Minor, separated by the Taurus range from Lycaonia and Cappadocia on the N, and by the Amanus range from Syria on the E, and extending toward the sea. This describes the general area of Cilicia, but in fact the boundaries were subject to several shifts. During the Syrian period many Greeks and Jews settled in Cilicia. It was repeatedly invaded by the Assyrian kings, but was one of the few areas west of the Halys River that did not fall to Croesus, king of Lydia. It was conquered by the Persians and constituted the fourth of the 20 satrapies into which Darius divided his empire. The Cilicians paid a tribute to Darius of 360 white horses and 500 talents of silver annually. In the Persian Wars they furnished 100 ships. Cilicia later fell under Macedonian, Syrian, and Roman dominion. The dreaded Cilician pirates were subdued (67 B.C.) by Pompey.

*Cilician Gates* (si-lish'ạn). [Also: *Beilan Pass, Syrian Gates;* Latin, *Pylae Ciliciae.*] Pass between the Taurus mountains and the NE angle of the Mediterranean, about 25 miles N of Tarsus, leading from Cilicia to Syria. The pass has been in use for almost 3000 years as a passageway through the Taurus.

*Cimmeria* (si-mir'i-ạ). Country of the legendary Cimmerians of ancient Greek tales, fabled to be a place of perpetual darkness. Odysseus sailed to the edge of the world to the mist-enshrouded land of the Cimmerians where he made his descent to Tartarus, as instructed to do by Circe, when he was trying to get home to Ithaca after the Trojan War. The Cimmerians of legend are not to be confused with the historicial Cimmerians who lived near the Euxine Sea.

*Cimmerian Bosporus* (si-mir'i-ạn bos'pọ-rus). [Also: *Bosporus Cimmerius.*] In ancient geography, the name of a kingdom in S Sarmatia and also of the strait (modern Kerch Strait) between the Euxine Sea and the Palus Maeotis (now Sea of Azov). The Crimean side was colonized (c600 B.C.) by a Greek expedition from Miletus which founded Panticapaeum (now Kerch) there. It flourished until absorbed in the dominions of Mithridates VI of Pontus, and for some centuries afterward experienced alternating periods of hardship and prosperity. Close relations were early established with Athens, which sent oil, jewelry, and works of industrial art in return for Crimean wheat. The chief city was Panticapaeum, the center of the highly important archaeological discoveries which have been yielded by this region as well as by the territory around it. The first systematic excavations were made in 1816. After 1832 explorations were regularly conducted by the Russian imperial government, and their results, rich in Greek industrial antiquities, were placed in the Hermitage Museum at Leningrad. The architectural remains are scanty, perhaps the chief of them being the fine revetment, in quarry-faced ashlar with margin-draft, of the

fat, fāte, fär, fâll, àsk, fāre; net, mē, hèr; pin, pīne; not, nōte, möve, nôr; up, lūte, pùll; oi, oil; ou out; (lightened) ẹlect, agǫny, ụnite;

so-called Tumulus of the Czar at Kerch. The sculpture found, too, is scanty in quantity, late in date, and poor in style. The great archaeological wealth of the region lies in its abundant burial tumuli and catacombs. It was the practice of the ancient inhabitants to bury with their dead a large part of their possessions; hence the remarkable harvest of jewelry, vases, implements, and even textile fabrics and a pair of woman's leather boots, found in these graves. Little or nothing discovered is older than the 4th century B.C.; the finest specimens of jewelry and pottery are Athenian, and include some of the most beautiful work known in their classes. Many of the vases are decorated in brilliant polychrome; others have gilded ornament, and others bear figures in relief. Some of the tomb chambers bear interesting mural paintings.

*Circaeum* or *Circeium Promontorium* (sėr-sē'um prō″montôr'i-um). [Also: Latin, *Circeius Mons;* modern, *Monte Circeo*, *Circeio* or *Circello*.] Promontory or isolated rock on the W coast of Italy, near ancient Tarracina. It was a frequented resort in ancient times. It has some antiquities of the Roman town Circeii, and abounds in grottoes.

*Circeii* (sėr-sē'ī). In ancient geography, a town in Latium, Italy, situated on a former island now attached to the mainland by dune sand, about 57 miles SE of Rome. It belonged (340 B.C.) to the Latin League. Extensive fortifications of the 4th and 3rd centuries B.C. remain.

*Cirrha* (sir'a). In ancient geography, the seaport of Crisa (with which it is often confused) in Phocis, Greece. It was destroyed (c575 B.C.) in the First Sacred War, on account of sacrilege in interfering with pilgrims to Delphi.

*Civitavecchia* (chē″vē-tä-vek'kyä). See *Centumcellae*.

*Clarus* (klãr'us). Seat of an ancient oracle of Apollo near Colophon in Asia Minor. Seers at the oracle drank water from a secret well and gave their pronouncements in verse.

*Classis* (klas'is). In ancient geography, the harbor of Ravenna. Built up by Augustus, it served in Roman times as a port and arsenal.

*Clazomenae* (kla̤-zom'ẹ-nē). In ancient geography, an Ionian city in Asia Minor, situated about 20 miles SW of Smyrna (Izmir). It was colonized by Cleonaeans and Phliasians who had been driven out of their cities in the Peloponnesus by the Dorians. In its turn it sent colonists to Cardia in the

(obscured) errạnt, ardẹnt, actọr; ch, chip; g, go; th, thin; ₮ʜ, then; y, you; (variable) d̤ as d or j, ṣ as s or sh, ṭ as t or ch, z̤ as z or zh.

Thracian Chersonese. Clazomenae was conquered by Alyattes, king of Lydia and father of Croesus, and later fell under the dominion of Persia.

*Cleonae* (klē-ō'nē). In ancient geography, a city on the road between Corinth and Argos, in Greece.

*Clitor* (klī'tọr). In ancient geography, a city in Arcadia, Greece. The city was on a level spot surrounded by low hills. It had several temples, of Demeter, Asclepius, Ilithyia, and the Dioscuri, among others, and, according to Ovid, a fountain called the Clitorium, the water from which was said to destroy the desire for wine. The river Clitor flowed nearby. It was supposed to contain dappled fish that sang like thrushes.

*Clitumnus* (klī-tum'nus). [Modern name, *Clitumno*.] River in Umbria, Italy, an affluent of the Tinia. It is celebrated (especially through the descriptions of the younger Pliny) for its sanctity and beauty. He mentions especially the existence of shrines to the river deity (Clitumnus) at its source.

*Clusium* (klö'zi-um). One of the chief cities of Etruria, located in Tuscany between Sena (Siena) and Volsinii (Orvieto). In the *Aeneid*, it is named as an ally of Aeneas in his war with the Latins. The town, originally one of the 12 confederated ancient Etruscan cities, is now named Chiusi, and has a museum of Etruscan antiquities. In the neighborhood are notable Etruscan tombs.

*Cnidus* (nī'dus). Ancient city of Caria, Asia Minor, situated at the end of a narrow peninsula on the SW coast of what is now Turkey, between the islands of Rhodes and Cos. It was a Dorian city settled by the Lacedaemonians, and was a member of the Dorian Hexapolis of Asia Minor. Cnidus was a seat of worship of Aphrodite whom the Cnidians held in especially high honor. Their oldest sanctuary of the goddess was that of Aphrodite Doritis *(Bountiful);* others were the sanctuary of Aphrodite Acraea *(Of the Height),* and Aphrodite Euploia *(Fair Voyage)* or Cnidian Aphrodite. The famous statue of Aphrodite by Praxiteles was here. The Cnidians had a treasury at Delphi, and their Lesche, or Clubroom, at Delphi was decorated with paintings by the Thasian Polygnotus. One wall of the Lesche showed the taking of Troy and the Greeks sailing away, and contained figures of those who took part on both sides in the Trojan War. On another wall was depicted Odysseus visiting in Hades. At

Triopium in Cnidus was a famous temple in which only the peoples of the Dorian cities of Lindus, Ialysus, Camirus (Dorian cities of Rhodes), Cos, and Cnidus had the right to worship. These were the cities of the Dorian Hexapolis, which had formerly included Halicarnassus. The Cnidians, to escape conquest when the Persians were subduing Ionia in the reign of Cyrus, attempted to make their land an island by cutting a channel across the neck of the promontory on which their city was located. As the work progressed, it was hampered by an unusual number of accidents, many work-men were injured about the eyes by splintering rocks. The Cnidians sent to Delphi to inquire of the oracle why the work of making their country into an island was being impeded. The oracular response was:

"Fence not the isthmus off, nor dig it through—
Zeus would have made an island, had he wished."

On hearing this, the Cnidians at once abandoned the project of making an island, and when the Persians advanced against them they gave up without a struggle. Following the Persian War Cnidus was a member of the Athenian Confederacy, from which it revolted, c412 B.C., during the Peloponnesian Wars. In 394 B.C. a naval battle off its shores saw Conon, the Athenian leader, defeat the Spartans under Pisander. After-ward, Cnidus joined Ephesus, Samos, and Iasus, with Rhodes, in a federation to protect themselves against the Persians and the Spartans. The Federation issued their own coinage on which appeared a figure of the young Heracles strangling the snakes, in a possible allusion to their hope of crushing tyrants. On the site of Cnidus, known at the pre-sent time as Cape Crio, are, among other ruins, those of an ancient theater. The *cavea* is 400 feet in diameter, with 36 tiers of seats divided by two precinctions, and survives al-most perfect. There are considerable remains of the stage structure.

**Cnossus** or **Knossos** (nos'us). [Also: **Cnosus, Gnossus, Gnosus.**] In ancient geography, the capital of Crete, on the north coast and at the eastern end of the island. It was the site of a series of fabulous Minoan palaces. The site was discovered, 1886, by Heinrich Schliemann but he was unable to obtain the property at a price he considered fair, and abandoned his plan to excavate it. Sir Arthur Evans the English archaeolo-gist visited the island in 1894, subsequently acquired the site of Cnossus, and began his excavations in 1900. His finds there were equalled in importance only by the earlier discoveries of Schliemann at Mycenae. The area of the palaces constructed at Cnossus was a low hill, in the valley of the Caeratus River. The discovery of wooden and bone utensils of the Neolithic Age showed that the site had been occupied since c3000 B.C. In succeeding ages two great palaces were erected at the site, the second of which was rebuilt after being partially destroyed. The first great palace was built about 2000 B.C. It was destroyed, by unknown means, c1700 B.C. Immediately a new and grander palace was erected on the ruins. The second palace was badly damaged, c1600 B.C., and was reconstructed, on a less extensive scale, in succeeding years. When, c1400 B.C., this palace too was destroyed, perhaps by an earthquake or by a sudden enemy raid, the site was thereafter only sparsely occupied. The second Minoan palace is the one associated with King Minos, Pasiphaë, the Minotaur, and the exploits of Theseus. The palaces were built on several levels connected by stairways and without any particular plan. Around a large central court groups of separate buildings were clustered. As more buildings were added, light and air were admitted to them by secondary courts and porticoes. With the passage of time, the buildings were connected by corridors to link them all into the complex that formed the palace. The builders were less concerned with the outside symmetry of the palace than with the comfort within it, and added chambers, courts, and porticoes with their connecting corridors as they were required, with the result that the corridors linking various parts of the palace, the stairways by which different levels were approached, and the series of courts and porticoes, made it into a perfect maze. The double-ax, the word for which was *labrys,* was a symbol of power, as well as a religious symbol and a mason's mark. It appeared in many places throughout the palace marked on walls and vessels, and double-axes were found in the chamber that came to be known as the "Room of the Double-Axes." The ending *-nth,* not of Greek origin, means "place of." Hence the palace was called *Labyrinth,* "place of the double-ax," but because of its mazelike arrangement the word "labyrinth" came to be thought of in succeeding years as a "maze." It may well be, therefore, that the story of Theseus and the Minotaur refers

fat, fāte, fär, fåll, àsk, fãre; net, mē, hèr; pin, pīne; not, nōte, möve, nôr; up, lūte, pùll; oi, oil; ou out; (lightened) ĕlect, agǫny, ūnite;

to the success Theseus enjoyed in the sport of bull-leaping in the central court around which the Labyrinth, "place of the double-ax," was built. Captives were commonly trained to take part in this sport, which consisted in baiting a huge bull. At the moment when the animal lowered its head and charged, the performer seized both its horns, turned a somersault over its head, and landed on the animal's back or on the ground behind it. Engravings on gems and other representations of the sport form a vivid basis for the story of Theseus. A small frescoed panel gives a complete picture of the sport. One of the paved courts of the palace is called the dancing-floor that was built for Ariadne by Daedalus.

Rather than attempt an ordered description of the conglomeration of courts, offices, magazines, baths, royal quarters, domestic quarters, treasure chambers, services areas, etc., it must suffice to mention some of the outstanding features of the palaces that sprawled on the hill at Cnossus. The outer walls were of stone or stone facing. The inner walls were of plaster and were decorated with richly colored frescoes. The frescoes have given valuable knowledge of the dress, life, and ceremonials of the times. They have also given names to some of the areas of the palace. A long corridor on the west is called the "Corridor of the Procession," from the fresco showing slim-waisted men, clad in loin cloths, bearing sacred vessels on their heads, and marching in a trim line across the wall. Another fresco shows an audience, including women, watching the sport of bull-leaping; and still another portrays elegant, black-haired ladies of the royal court. Wooden pillars, tapering from the top down and painted a rich terra-cotta color with blue bands at the top, rested on stone bases and supported the roofs and floors of the different levels. Water was brought from the hills by a "siphon" system and distributed through the palace by terra-cotta pipes and stone ducts. The supply was augmented by collecting rain-water from the roofs in shafts and causeways. Light and air were provided by light wells, covered shafts with openings cut into the walls below the roofs. Light and air were also provided by using the roof of one level as a portico for the next one. The great central court, lying N-S on the hill, was the center about which the rest of the palace was clustered. Just off it, on the west side, is a small chamber that has been named the throne room

because in it, against the middle of one wall, a gypsum chair with rounded seat and high back was found. This is called the throne of Minos. On each side of it are stone benches for the royal visitors. The walls of the throne room were frescoed in strong colors with images of griffins and stylized vegetation. Opposite the throne is a sunken chamber, similar to others throughout the palace, that was probably used for purification rites. Its position so close to the throne indicates the close connection between the religious and temporal power of the king. To the east, the hill on which the palace stands drops away sharply. Here some of the underground rooms of the royal quarters have been preserved in their entirety, such as the Queen's Apartments, with blue-green dolphins leaping and playing on the frescoed walls. Four flights of the grand stairway that led down to the royal apartments have been preserved. This is a most noble and serenely proportioned structure. Short flights, carefully designed for dignified ascent and set at right angles to each other, rise up the stair well. Pillars set on stone balustrades form an outer rail and add to the beauty of the structure. Ranged throughout the palace, on varying levels, are magazines under the protection of the double ax, where oil and grain were stored. Huge earthenware storage jars still stand as they were left thousands of years ago. Some of the magazines were used for the storage of treasure, judging by the bits of gold leaf that were found in them. Others were used for the sacred vessels belonging to the snake-goddess. Workshops containing fine painted pottery, unfinished stone vases, and material for producing other objects, were located in the north end of the east wing of the palace. Gathered about the palace were luxurious private villas that shared such features of the palace as light-wells, plumbing, porches, and lively frescoes. To the south of the palace, across a little stream, there are the remains of an inn that housed distant visitors to the palace. Cnossus was the center of a network of roads that radiated out over the eastern end of the island. The palace was unfortified, attesting to the unchallenged supremacy of Minoan sea power, as the richness of the palace, its comfort, and the highly developed techniques that built and furnished it attest to the brilliance of the Minoan civilization. Sir Arthur Evans, to whom the world is indebted for the evidences of

fat, fāte, fär, fåll, ȧsk, fāre; net, mē, hėr; pin, pīne; not, nōte, möve, nôr; up, lūte, pull; oi, oil; ou out; (lightened) ĕlect, agǫny, ūnite;

this brilliant civilization, made a series of partial restorations of the palace. Following such clues as his excavations gave him he restored some of the frescoes, as that in the Corridor of the Procession (the original pieces of the fresco are in the Museum). Richly painted pillars were set up in certain places to restore porches and porticoes and more importantly, to replace the debris that was all that held up some of the upper floors. His restorations of porches, pillars, light-wells, and frescoes in several areas give a vivid impression of the style of architecture and decoration of the Minoan civilization, so different from those of the Classical Greek period. The tombs of many of the royal inhabitants of Cnossus were located on a hill about 10 miles southeast of the palace. Most of the tombs have long since been plundered, but in 1966 the discovery of an intact tomb was reported. The 3,250-year-old burial place of a queen, it had partially caved in but was kept from grave-robbers by a wall sealing it off from the other tombs. The burial chamber contained a terra-cotta sarcophagus, standing two-and-a-half feet high on legs and painted in a papyrus-leaf motif. About 120 gold objects, most of them dating from the Greek period in Crete after 1400 B.C., were found in the sarcophagus. Jewelry buried with the queen included a gold cylinder for her hair; eight necklaces, three of gold beads and five of semi-precious stones; and five gold rings. One of these rings, dating from before 1400 B.C., is delicately carved with a worship scene and is possibly the finest signet ring of this period ever found on Crete. Evidences of the burial ceremony included ceremonial vessels found in the tomb and the head of the queen's horse buried in the wall sealing the tomb.

*Colchis* (kol′kis). [Modern name, *Mingrelia.*] In ancient geography, a country in Asia, lying between the Caucasus on the N, Iberia on the E, Armenia on the S, Pontus on the SW, and the Euxine (Black) Sea on the W. It was watered by the Phasis River (the modern Rion in Georgia, U.S.S.R.). Herodotus claimed that the Colchians were of Egyptian origin, descended from an Egyptian king, Sesostris (the exploits attributed to this king by Herodotus probably represent the combined efforts of Senusret I, Senusret III, and Ramses II), who journeyed into the land and left settlers there. He allied the Colchians to the Egyptians because of the similarity of their languages, because the two peoples, from ancient times, followed the practice of circumcision, and because the linen for which the Colchians were famous was woven in a manner used only by the Egyptians of all other peoples. At the time when Phrixus, riding a golden-fleeced ram, fled to Colchis from Orchomenus, the Black Sea was known as the Axine, or "Unfriendly" Sea. The land about it was inhabited by wild people who, nevertheless, received Phrixus kindly. The ram was sacrificed and its fleece hung in a sacred grove guarded by a fabulous monster. Nearby was a magnificent palace of Helius. Jason and the Argonauts journeyed to Colchis to recover the Golden Fleece. With the aid of Medea Jason was successful and escaped with the Fleece and Medea from Colchis. According to Herodotus, the abduction of Medea by Jason at her own request was one of the ancient causes of enmity between Europe and Asia that culminated in the Persian Wars. The Colchians, known to the Greeks as a barbarous and unfriendly people, did not bury or burn their male dead. Only women were buried. The men were wrapped in ox hides and exposed on trees to be eaten by the birds. Outside the city of Aea, Aeëtes' home in Colchis, Jason and his companions passed by such a cemetery, sacred to Circe, on their way to recover the Golden Fleece.

*Colonna* (kô-lôn′nạ), *Cape.* See *Sunium.*

*Colonus* (kọ̄-lō′nus). [Also: *White Hill of Colonus; Kolonos Hippios.*] Site about one and a half miles NW of Athens, Greece, N of the Academy, on the banks of the Cephissus. It was the birthplace of Sophocles, and is immortalized by his description in the *Oedipus at Colonus.* It was a place sacred to the Furies in their later role of benign goddesses. Oedipus fled there with his daughter Antigone, and died there, comforted by the oracle. Upon the hill now stand the tombs of two noted archaeologists, the German Hellenist Karl Otfried Müller and the French Orientalist Charles Lenormant.

*Colophon* (kol′ọ̄-fon). In ancient geography, one of the 12 Ionian cities of Asia Minor, situated near the coast, N of Ephesus. According to the Colophonians, the first Greeks who came there were colonists from Crete, who landed under their leader Rhacius and drove out the native Carians. Rhacius later married Manto, daughter of the seer Tiresias, and was, some say, the father of the seer Mopsus. Rhacius

fat, fāte, fär, fâll, àsk, fāre; net, mē, hėr; pin, pīne; not, nōte, möve, nôr; up, lūte, pùll; oi, oil; ou out; (lightened) ẹlect, agǫny, ūnite;

allowed the Thebans who came to Colophon with Manto to settle there, and his son Mopsus drove out the last remaining Carians. After the Trojan War Calchas the seer went overland to Colophon, since he knew by his prophetic powers that heavy storms would assail the Greeks who sailed home from Troy. In Colophon he met Mopsus and, being defeated by him in a divining contest, died there and was buried at nearby Notium. In later years Ionians came to Colophon. They swore an oath of friendship with the Greeks already there and lived on equal terms with them. Some think that Gyges, the Lydian king, may have captured Colophon when he expanded his empire southward in the 7th century B.C., but he was forced to withdraw when the Cimmerians invaded his own country. The Colophonians took part in the Ionian revolt against Persia at the beginning of the 5th century B.C., and were subdued. Lysimachus, one of Alexander's bodyguards, completely destroyed the city (c302 B.C.), because its inhabitants fought against the Macedonians. At Clarus near Colophon was a famous oracle of Apollo.

**Colossae** (kọ-los′ē). In ancient geography, a city in SW Phrygia, Asia Minor, situated on the Lycus. It was the seat of the early Christian church to which Paul wrote the *Epistle to the Colossians*.

**Comana** (kọ-mā′nạ). [Also: *Chryse.*] In ancient geography, a city in Cappadocia, Asia Minor, situated on the river Sarus. It was noted for its great temple to Ma, the Cappadocian mother goddess, with its elaborate festivals and great retinue of temple prostitutes and attendants, said to have numbered in the thousands.

**Comana.** In ancient geography, a city in Pontus, Asia Minor. It was perhaps a colony of the Cappadocian city of the same name and it was sacred to the same goddess, Ma.

**Commagene** (kom-ạ-jē′nē). [Called *Kummuh* in the Assyrian cuneiform inscriptions.] In ancient geography, a district in N Syria, between the Euphrates on the E and Cilicia on the W. At one time tributary of the Assyrian empire, it fell to Alexander, then to the Seleucids after his death, and was an independent kingdom from 65 B.C. to 17 A.D.

**Copae** (kō′pē). In ancient geography, a town on the shore of Lake Copaïs, in Boeotia, Greece.

**Copaïs** (kọ-pā′is). In ancient geography, a lake in Boeotia, into which emptied the sacred river of Delphi, the Cephissus. Completely ringed by mountains, the Copaic Lake has no surface outlet, drainage in ancient times having been provided by natural tunnels ("katavothrae") in the limestone whose choking was often followed by disastrous floods. Efforts to channel the waters and promote drainage began as early as the Bronze Age. From the lake bed rises a low rocky hill crowned with the massive defenses of a late Bronze Age palace, now known by the Albanian name of Gla or Goulas, the ancient name being unknown. Finally drained at the end of the last century by a British engineering firm, Lake Copaïs has yielded to reclamation nearly 100 square miles of extremely fertile agricultural land. In antiquity, the lake was celebrated for its eels, pickled Copiac eels being a special delicacy. (JJ)

**Cora** (kō′rạ). [Modern name, *Cori*.] Town in C Italy, situated about 30 miles SE of Rome. It was a town of the Volsci in Latium. It contains many Roman antiquities, such as columns, walls, and a temple of Hercules.

**Corcyra** (kôr′sī-rạ). [Modern name, *Kerkyra, Corfu*.] The largest and most northern of the seven Ionian islands, separated from the coast of Epirus, Greece, by a broad channel. Odysseus was cast ashore here on his way home from the Trojan War and was graciously received by King Alcinous, a descendant of Corcyra and Poseidon. Hence, this island has been identified with *Scheria* and *Phaeacia* mentioned in the *Odyssey*.

The fertile soil and mild climate of Corcyra attracted settlers from an early time. Among the first to occupy it were the Eretrians. They were driven out when the island was colonized by Corinth, traditional date 734 B.C. The colony prospered and built up a strong fleet that dominated the surrounding waters. The Corcyraeans were said to take special pride in their fleet because they considered themselves to be descendants of the prime sailors of antiquity, the Phaeacians. As they increased in wealth and power, the Corcyraeans threw off their dependence on the mother city and defeated Corinth in a naval battle in the first half of the 7 century B.C. This was thought to be the first naval battle between two Greek powers. Subsequently, in their pride, the Corcyraeans denied Corinth the honors due a mother ci and took every opportunity to show their contempt. Cy

selus, tyrant of Corinth, brought them to heel and restored
the sovereignty of Corinth over her colony. Corcyra in-
curred the wrath of Periander, son of Cypselus, by sheltering his son Lycophron. Lycophron refused all his father's
pleas to return to Corinth while Periander was still there. At
last Periander agreed that he himself would go to Corcyra
and allow Lycophron to take his place as ruler of Corinth.
To keep Periander away, the Corcyraeans killed Lycophron,
to whom they had hitherto granted asylum. Periander punished Corcyra by seizing 300 Corcyraean boys and sending
them to Alyattes, king of Lydia, as eunuchs. On the way, the
Corinthian ship carrying the boys touched at Samos, and the
Samians, touched by the plight of the boys, and probably
also to annoy the Corinthians, freed them and told them to
seek sanctuary at the temple of Artemis in Samos. The Corinthians dared not violate the sanctuary, and attempted to
force the boys out by cutting off their food supply. The
Samians invented a festival in which Samian youths and
maidens daily carried cakes of sesame and honey to the
temple. The Corcyraean boys there in the sanctuary were
allowed to snatch the cakes and so kept themselves alive.
The festival continued to be observed long after the Corinthians, despairing of ever recapturing the boys, had given
up and departed. When the Persians were invading Greece,
480 B.C., the assembled defenders sent to Corcyra, urging
them to send help. The Corcyraeans readily promised to
give assistance for, they said, if Greece fell, Corcyra would
also fall. They manned 60 ships, but delayed putting them
to sea. When at last their fleet did sail, it went only to the
Peloponnesus and waited there to see how the war would
go. For they fully expected the Persians to overwhelm the
Greeks and wanted to be in a position to win Persian friendship when that result occurred. When the war was over, the
successful Greeks reproached the Corcyraeans, who replied
that they had indeed sent a fleet but that the Etesian winds
had prevented it from rounding Cape Malea and joining the
Greeks at Salamis.

Before the Persian War Corcyra had founded the colonies
of Epidamnus and Apollonia in Epirus (7th century B.C.).
Epidamnus was subsequently weakened by wars with her
neighbors and by internal strife, and appealed to Corcyra
for aid (436 B.C.). Corcyra rejected the plea. The Epidamni-

(obscured) err*a*nt, ard*e*nt, act*o*r; ch, chip; g, go; th, thin; ᴛʜ, then; y, you;
variable) ḍ as d or j, ṣ as s or sh, ṭ as t or ch, ẓ as z or zh.

ans next sought advice from the oracle at Delphi, and were told to put themselves under the protection of Corinth. The Epidamnians obeyed. Corinth sent an expedition to their relief. This infuriated the Corcyraeans. They commanded the Epidamnians to expel the Corinthian garrison, and when they refused, sent a fleet, besieged the city, and defeated the Corinthians at sea (435 B.C.). This was one of the precipitating causes of the Peloponnesian Wars, for the Corinthians drew Sparta to their side as allies and the Corcyraeans appealed to, and received the aid of Athens. In the long wars that followed, Corcyra was weakened by internal strife and finally destroyed by revolution. In the next century the island was taken by Sparta, and it ultimately fell to the Romans.

*Corfinium* (kôr-fin′i-um). In ancient geography, a town in C Italy, near the modern Sulmona. It was the capital of the Paeligni, and of the confederates in the Social War (90–88 B.C.).

*Corfu* (kôr-fö′, kôr′fū). See *Corcyra.*

*Cori* (kō′rē). See *Cora.*

*Corinth* (kôr′inth, kor′-). [Also: *Gortho;* Greek, *Korinthos;* Latin, *Corinthia, Corinthus;* ancient name: *Ephyra.*] City "in the corner of Argos" in the Peloponnesus, situated near the Isthmus and Gulf of Corinth. According to tradition, it was founded c1350 B.C., some say by Sisyphus. Poseidon and Helius contended for control of Corinthia, and Briareus acted as arbitrator of their dispute. He awarded the Isthmus and adjoining land to Poseidon, and the height above the city (the Acrocorinthus) to Helius. Thereafter, the Isthmus was sacred to Poseidon, who had a temple there in which were altars and images of various sea-deities. The body of Melicertes, son of Ino and Athamas, was washed ashore on the Isthmus and buried there, and Isthmian Games were established in his honor. The graves of Sisyphus and Neleus were on the Isthmus, but their exact whereabouts was a well-kept secret. The region was also the scene of some of the exploits of Theseus. Theseus, Poseidon, and Corinthus represent the original Ionian inhabitants of Corinthia. Sisyphus, Jason, and Neleus represent the Aeolians who immigrated there. Cenchreae was the east port and Lechaeum was the west port of the Isthmus. A coin of the time of the emperor Hadrian represents the two harbors as two nymphs

fat, fāte, fär, fåll, àsk, fâre; net, mē, hèr; pin, pīne; not, nōte, möve, nôr; up, lūte, pùll; oi, oil; ou out; (lightened) ēlect, agǫny, ūnite;

facing opposite ways with a rudder between them. In ancient
times, ships were sometimes placed on rollers and dragged
across the Isthmus, to save the long voyage around the
Peloponnesus. Periander, tyrant of Corinth (c625–585 B.C.),
planned to breach the Isthmus with a canal, but gave up the
idea. Much later, the emperor Nero began to cut a canal, but
he too abandoned the project. (The existing canal was completed in 1893). In the Persian Wars, the Peloponnesians,
under the leadership of Sparta, built a wall across the Isthmus as a fortification against the Persians. Some say the land
about the Asopus River, in the NE corner of the Peloponnesus, was divided by Helius between his son Aeëtes, to
whom he gave Ephyraea (ancient name for Corinthia), and
Aloeus to whom he gave Sicyonia. Aeëtes migrated to Colchis and left his kingdom in trust with Bunus, son of
Hermes. After the death of Bunus the kingdom fell successively to the rule of Epopeus, then to his son Marathon, and
then to his grandson Corinthus, for whom the name of the
city was changed from Ephyra to Corinth. Corinthus died
childless just at the time when Medea arrived from Colchis
with Jason. She claimed the throne for Jason. Some say that
when she was forced to flee from Corinth, she gave her
kingdom to Sisyphus. His descendants were ruling when the
Dorians invaded the Peloponnesus in the 11th century B.C.,
defeated the Corinthians, and expelled them. The Dorian
rulers were followed by Bacchis (926–891 B.C.) and his descendants, the Bacchiadae, who were overthrown by Cypselus c657 B.C. The city of Corinth was well supplied with
water. According to tradition, the river-god Asopus gave
Sisyphus the never-failing Pirene spring in return for information about the whereabouts of one of his daughters,
Aegina. It was at this spring that Athena bridled Pegasus for
Bellerophon. In memory of the event, a temple of Athena
Chalinitis *(Bridler)*, was raised. The well of Glauce at Corinth
was said to be the one in which Glauce, daughter of Creon,
flung herself to get relief from the burning poison of the
robe Medea had sent her. Nearby the well was the tomb of
Medea's children. Some say they were stoned to death by
the Corinthians in revenge for the death of Glauce. Afterward the Corinthians were punished until, at the command
of the oracle, they offered annual sacrifices in honor of the
dead children and set up a figure of Terror. As they were

subject to Argos and Mycenae, the Corinthians had no leader in the Trojan War, but took part in it under the command of Agamemnon.

Corinth was noted in ancient times as a center of commerce, literature, and art, and as one of the wealthiest and most powerful of the ancient Greek cities. It sent colonies to Corcyra (Corfu) and Syracuse in 734 B.C., and founded Potidaea in Chalcidice and Apollonia on the coast of Epirus. During the rule of Periander (c625–585 B.C.) son of Cypselus, Corinth had reached a peak of cultural and commercial prosperity. The rise of Athens following the Persian Wars threatened the commercial supremacy of Corinth. A struggle over the Corinthian city of Potidaea, which was a tributary ally of Athens, was one of the precipitating causes of the Peloponnesian Wars, in which Corinth sided with Sparta against Athens. The alliance with Sparta disintegrated after the defeat of Athens in the Peloponnesian Wars, and Corinth engaged (395–387 B.C.) in the "Corinthian War" against Sparta. It was defeated by Sparta in 394 B.C. It later fell to the Macedonians and was held by them until 243 B.C., when it joined the Achaean League of which it was the capital. In 146 B.C. it was captured, sacked, and burned by the Romans, under Mummius; it was rebuilt by Julius Caesar in 46 B.C. Pausanias visited the rebuilt city in the 2nd century A.D. and has left descriptions of the monuments of the restored city. He tells, for example, of an image of Dionysus in the market-place that was supposed to have been made from the tree from which Pentheus spied on the maenads as they celebrated their revels, and from which he was dragged to his death. He mentions a temple of Palaemon (the name by which Melicertes was known when he became a god), and of Aphrodite Melaenis (*Black*). Still to be seen are the ruins of an archaic temple of Apollo, a Roman theater, an odeum, the agora with basilicas, colonnades, a hostelry, fountains, and other public buildings, the Fountain of Pirene, and much besides, excavated since the 1890's by the American School of Classical Studies at Athens.

**Corinth, Gulf of.** [Also: *Gulf of Lepanto;* Latin, *Corinthiacus Sinus.*] Arm of the Mediterranean Sea, with which it is connected by the Gulf of Patras. It separates central Greece from the Peloponnesus.

*Corinth, Isthmus of.* Isthmus which connects the Peloponnesus with central Greece. It is now pierced by a canal. Width, 4–8 miles.

*Corinthia* (kō-rin'thi-ạ). [Also: *Corinth;* Greek, *Korinthos.*] In ancient geography, a division of Greece, lying between the Gulf of Corinth on the N, Megaris on the NE, the Saronic Gulf on the E, Argolis on the S, and Argolis and Sicyonia on the W.

*Coronea* (kor-ọ-nē'ạ). In ancient geography, a small town in Boeotia, Greece, situated W of Lake Copaïs. It was famous for two battles, in one of which (447 B.C.) the Boeotians defeated the Athenians, and in the other (394 B.C.) the Spartans under Agesilaus defeated the Thebans and other allied Greeks.

*Corsica* (kôr'si-kạ). [Greek, *Cyrnos.*] Mountainous island in the Mediterranean Sea, N of the island of Sardinia. Phoenicians, Tyrrhenians, Etruscans, Greeks, Carthaginians, and Romans invaded the island, no one group ever completely suppressing the others. After the beginning of the First Punic War the Romans took the island from the Carthaginians. Remains of the ancient invaders have been found there. The Roman philosopher Seneca the Younger was banished (41 A.D.) to Corsica by the emperor Claudius, and had some very unkind things to say of the inhabitants, namely: that their first law consisted in avenging themselves, the second in living by rapine, the third in lying, and the fourth in denying the gods—but it must be remembered that Seneca's stay among the Corsicans was involuntary. Strabo speaks admiringly of their refusal to act the slave for Roman masters, who found them so intractable that they soon regretted the little they had spent in buying them.

*Cortona* (kôr-tō'nä). An ancient city of C Italy, in Tuscany, situated above the Mucellia River, about 50 miles SE of what is now Florence. It was one of the 12 great Etruscan cities. Important Etruscan and Roman antiquities, as well as ancient walls and a temple, remain.

*Coryphasium* (kôr-i-fā'shi-um). Promontory in Messenia which became the site of Pylus, and which was afterward called Pylus.

*Cos* (kōs) or *Kos.* One of the Dodecanese islands in the Aegean Sea, near the coast of Asia Minor. According to Homer, Hera raised a great storm and shipwrecked Heracles on this

obscured) erränt, ärdent, actor; ch, chip; g, go; th, thin; ᴙH, then; y, you; variable) ḍ as d or j, ṣ as s or sh, ṭ as t or ch, ẓ as z or zh.

island. It is celebrated as the birthplace of the painter
Apelles, Ptolemy Philadelphus, and the physician Hippocrates, and also for its sanctuary of Asclepius, a large and
well-organized sanatorium and medical school established
and directed by Hippocrates. Area, about 111 square miles.

**Cosa** (kos′ạ). A settlement on the coast of Etruria, founded as
a Latin colony by Rome in 273 B.C. It stands on the hill of
Ansedonia, between the Laguna di Orbetello and the Lago
di Burano, some 85 miles northwest of Rome. Surface exploration combined with photographic reconnaissance from
the air revealed the city walls, gates, street plan, forum, arx,
Capitolium, and other buildings of the 3rd century B.C., and
excavations directed for the American Academy in Rome by
Frank E. Brown and Lawrence Richardson, beginning in
1948, have brought to light foundations of republican temples and public buildings, fragments of architectural decoration, and other finds. Air reconnaissance has also revealed
the now silted port of Cosa, engineering measures taken in
ancient times to prevent silting, and the secondary roads
which linked colony and port with the Via Aurelia. The type
of polygonal masonry represented by Cosa's massive limestone fortification walls was formerly assumed, on mistaken
analogies with early walls in Greece, to belong to a relatively
early period, the 6th century B.C. or earlier. This, plus its
name, referred to a hypothetical Etruscan Cusi, and its location led earlier generations of scholars to assume that Cosa's
walls were in fact of Etruscan construction and date, and
that excavation within them would reveal Etruscan buildings
and an Etruscan town plan. Professor Brown's demonstra-
tion that Cosa's walls actually date from the 3rd century, and
that no construction earlier than 273 B.C. can be identified
in the town, is a milestone in the unraveling of Etruscan and
Italic chronology. The community which grew up at the foot
of Ansedonia, around the port, appears to have been called
Succosa, i.e., Sub-Cosa. (JJ)

**Cossura** (kọ-sö′rạ) or **Cossyra** (kọ-sī′rạ). [Modern names, *Pantalaria* or *Pantelleria*.] Island in the Mediterranean Sea, off the
W tip of Sicily. The surface is rocky and volcanic. It was early
occupied by the Carthaginians, but was taken by the Romans
in 217 B.C. It was highly favored as a place to which members
of the imperial family and other prominent persons were
banished in the time of the Roman empire.

***Cranaë*** (kran'ā-ē). [Modern name, ***Marathonisi.***] A small island in the Gulf of Laconia, off the coast of Gythium. Here Paris and Helen are said to have made their first stop when they eloped from Sparta, and here Helen first yielded in love to Paris. A sanctuary of Aphrodite Migonitis *(Uniter)* on the mainland opposite the island, commemorated the event, and the fulfillment of Aphrodite's promise to Paris to give him the most beautiful woman in the world in return for his award to her of the Apple of Discord.

***Crannon*** (kran'ọn) or ***Cranon*** (krā'nọn). [Also: ***Ephyra.***] In ancient geography, a city in Thessaly, Greece, about ten miles SW of Larissa; its exact site is not known. Here, in 322 B.C., Antipater defeated the confederated Greeks.

***Cremera*** (krem'ẹ-rạ). In ancient geography, a small river in Etruria which joins the Tiber a few miles N of Rome. It is the traditional scene of the defeat of the Fabii in c477 B.C.

***Cremona*** (krẹ-mō'nạ; Italian, krä-mō'nä). City in NW Italy on the Po River. It was founded by the Gauls and became a Roman colony in 218 B.C. The old city, on the site of modern Cremona, was destroyed in 69 A.D. in a struggle between Vitellius and Vespasian.

***Crete*** (krēt). [Also: ***Candia;*** Greek, ***Kriti, Krete;*** French, ***Crète, Candie;*** Italian and Latin, ***Creta;*** Old Turkish, ***Kirid, Kirit.***] Island in the Mediterranean Sea, situated SE of Greece and SW of Asia Minor. It has an area of 3235 square miles, is 160 miles long, and 35 miles wide in its greatest width. Sharply rising mountain ridges separate the parts of the island from each other. The mountain slopes, once covered with cedar and cypress, are now largely bare. In the fertile plains and river valleys wheat, fruit, wool, olives, and wine are produced. According to legend, the inhabitants of Crete sprang from the soil. Their first king was Cres, for whom the island was named. Some say the Idaean Dactyls, who discovered the use of fire and metal-working, were born in Crete. The nine Curetes, either sprung from the earth or born of the Dactyls, originated in Crete, and the Titans, especially during the Golden Age of Cronus when men lived like gods, were associated with the island. In a cave on Mount Ida the Curetes protected the infant Zeus by clashing their shields to drown out his cries, while nymphs nourished him with milk and honey. To memorialize the contribution of the bees Zeus changed their color to copper that gleamed like gold in the sun, and made them impervious to changes in the weather, an important consideration in Crete. Athena was said by some to have been born from the head of Zeus at the source of the Triton River in Crete, where a temple was raised to her. The marriage of Zeus and Hera was also said by some to have taken place on the island. Cretans annually reënacted the ceremony at a temple that commemorated this event. Teucer, the ancestor of the Trojans, came from Crete, and Minos, Daedalus, Pasiphaë, the Minotaur, and many other figures of mythology and legend are associated with the island. Long before the Greeks on the mainland had developed their ideas of the great god Zeus, however, the Cretans had elaborated their own concepts of the gods. The chief figure in their worship was the Great Mother, who had power over life and death, who was the goddess of the forest and of wild beasts, and who occupied the central place in Cretan religion. Her attributes were the double ax, the *labrys,* a symbol of power, and the Horns of Consecration, which may have been connected with the bull, an animal that appears later in connection with the story of Europa. The Great Mother was a triple goddess, who ruled in heaven, on earth, and under the earth. The animals sacred to her came from each of her kingdoms—the dove from the air, the bull or lion from the earth, and the snakes from the underworld. Joined to the Great Mother was a male figure, a son-husband, he who was first named Zagreus by the Greeks and later developed by them into the great sky-god Zeus, whom the Cretans claimed was born on their island. They also claimed his tomb in the hill of Iuctas, the outline of which appears to be a giant lying on his back, pointing his great bearded profile at the sky. It was because the Cretans claimed to have the tomb of Zeus that the Greeks called them "liars," and gave them a bad reputation throughout the Greek world. Obviously, Zeus, being a god, could not have died and been placed in a tomb. Because Crete was subject to frequent earthquakes, there was a strong chthonic element to Cretan religion. The Cretans explained the earthquakes as the tossing of the earth on the great bull's horns, and propitiated him by offering him sacrifices of bulls.

The Cretans are thought to be of Libyan or Anatolian stock. Homer names them as Achaeans, Cydonians, Dori-

fat, fāte, fär, fâll, ȧsk, fāre; net, mē, hėr; pin, pīne; not, nōte, möve, nôr; up, lūte, pull; oi, oil; ou out; (lightened) ĕlect, agǫny, ūnite;

ans, Pelasgians, and Eteocretans, the last of whom are believed to be the original non-Hellenic inhabitants. But Homer wrote long after the greatest ages of Cretan civilization had passed away. Cretan civilization existed before 3000 B.C., and was in a continuous state of development thereafter, reaching its height in the period 3000–1400 B.C. The German archaeologist Heinrich Schliemann believed that Crete was the legendary isle of Atlantis. He thought Crete might be the origin of the highly developed art he had found in Greece. He discovered the site of the palace of Cnossus in 1886, but was unable to carry out his plan for excavating it. It remained for Sir Arthur Evans the British archaeologist, who had visited the island in 1894, to acquire the site and, in 1900, to begin his excavations. Other excavations in various parts of the island have been carried on by the Italians, by the French School, the English School, by Americans, and by the Greeks. Sir Arthur Evans classified the distinctive periods into which Cretan civilization falls according to ceramic development, as follows:

| | | |
|---|---|---|
| Early Minoan | I (E.M.I.) | 3400–2800 B.C. |
| " " | II (E.M.II) | 2800–2400 B.C. |
| " " | III (E.M.III) | 2400–2100 B.C. |
| Middle Minoan | I (M.M.I.) | 2100–1900 B.C. |
| " " | II (M.M.II) | 1900–1700 B.C. |
| " " | III (M.M.III) | 1700–1580 B.C. |
| Late Minoan | I (L.M.I.) | 1580–1450 B.C. |
| " " | II (L.M.II) | 1450–1375 B.C. |
| " " | III (L.M.III) | 1375–1100 B.C. |

The relatively strict dates for each period are possible because of close synchronization with Egyptian history, for Cretan external relations were oriented toward Egypt from an early date. Habitations have been discovered beneath the palaces of Cnossus (q.v.) and Phaestus that date from the Neolithic Age, before 3000 B.C. Wooden and bone utensils, and polished and incised pottery of this period have been found on these and other sites. In the period from 3000–2000 B.C. two great centers of civilization developed, that around the plain of Mesara, on the southern side of the island, and that at the eastern end of the island. In this period close commercial relations were held with the islands of the Cyclades, with Egypt, and with Asia Minor. This period saw the development of gray incised pottery, decorated

(obscured) errạnt, ardẹnt, actọr; ch, chip; g, go; th, thin; ᴛʜ, then; y, you;
(variable) ḍ as d or j, ş as s or sh, ţ as t or ch, ẓ as z or zh.

with simple figures—zig-zags, herring-bones, groups of parallel lines, and rows of dots (E.M.I); pottery decorated with red and black on a natural clay ground (E.M.II); and pottery painted in white on a black glazed ground on which new patterns were introduced (E.M.III). Also in this period, great progress was made in metal-working and in the art of carving stone vases, employing the natural strata of the stone as decoration. In the Middle Minoan periods the polychrome style, called "Kamares ware" (because first examples of it were found by the English in a cave at Kamares, on the south slope of Mount Ida) was developed, with white, red, and yellow decorations on a black glazed ground. By the Middle Minoan periods I and II (2100–1700 B.C.), a brilliant civilization had evolved. The first palaces were built at Cnossus and Phaestus; the polychrome Kamares ware had become highly decorative with stylized figures, such as the octopus motif; and the refinement developed in the techniques of the potter's wheel led to the production of "eggshell" vases, so named for their thinness with fluted bodies and rims of great delicacy. A system of hieroglyphic writing was in use; commercial relations in the Aegean were widened, continued with Egypt, and extended into Asia. At the end of this era of the fabulous development of a civilization far in advance of any that had developed on the Greek mainland at this time, some unknown catastrophe struck all the centers of Cretan civilization and destroyed them, about 1700 B.C. The interruption was temporary. Between 1700 and 1400 B.C. new and grander palaces were raised at Cnossus, Phaestus, and Mallia; comfortable private houses with oiled parchment for window panes were built around the palaces; new cities were founded; relations with Egypt and the Near East flourished; and Cretan colonies were sent out to the neighboring islands and to the Greek mainland. Cretan civilization and power was at its height. The age was characterized by the figure of King Minos, who had the largest and most powerful navy in existence and controlled the waters of the Mediterranean. Some say that the name "Minos" was a title similar to the Egyptian word "Pharaoh," and that it applied to at least two Cretan kings, and perhaps to a series of them. Palaces and houses were decorated inside and out with brilliantly colored frescoes that depicted naturalistic scenes, such as the human figure, sacrificial processions, and religious gatherings, thus recording much of the Cretan way of life. Sculptured stone vases, decorated pottery jars, some of great size, and golden cups worked in relief with consummate artistry, were in use in the palaces. Fragile vases and delicate figurines played a part in religious ceremonies or served for ornamentation. The king and others had exquisite seals cut in gems for sealing their documents. Seal engraving was developed to perfection in the Middle Minoan and following periods. Animals at rest and in action, birds in flight, human figures, were engraved with exquisite grace and fidelity on ivory, steatite, crystal, jasper, and other hard surfaces. From the miniature seal engravings of ceremonial scenes comes much of our knowledge of Minoan ritual. Relief decorations on cups and carving reached a peak of refinement. These are exemplified by the famous Vaphio cups (so-called because they were found at Vaphio, near Sparta, whither they had been carried from Crete), with their scenes of the bull hunt and of the bulls in pasture beautifully worked in repoussé, and by the extraordinary figure of the bull-leaper carved in ivory. Frescoes show large audiences, including women, watching the sport of bull-leaping, which differed from the bull-fight in that the performer must catch the horns of the bull as the animal charged, leap over its head, and land on his feet on its back. Many scenes and stories, as well as religious ceremonies, centered about the bull. Two styles of linear writing were in use in this period—the Linear Script A and Linear Script B —and indicated that the Cretans had an alphabet long before Cadmus introduced the Phoenician alphabet into Greece. The Linear Script B was deciphered, half a century after the first examples of it had been found, by the Englishman Michael Ventris, in 1952. In 1957 Prof. Cyrus H. Gordon of Brandeis University announced that an adaptation of Accadian was the language of the Linear Script A. In the houses and palaces of this era brilliant use of "light-wells" was made for ventilation and illumination; ingenious "siphon systems" brought water from the hills to the palaces, where it was then distributed by means of terra-cotta pipes and stone ducts. The household water supply was also augmented by rain water drained from the roofs. This period, so briefly described, was the era of Cretan supremacy, in commercial and maritime power, and in the refinement

(obscured) errant, ardent, actor; ch, chip; g, go; th, thin; ŦH, then; y, you; (variable) ḍ as d or j, ṣ as s or sh, ṭ as t or ch, ẓ as z or zh.

and brilliance of its civilization. About 1400 B.C. general catastrophe overcame the flourishing civilization and destroyed it, apparently at once. Some think it must have been a great natural disaster, as an earthquake, that put such a sudden end to the great palaces and Minoan cities. Others think it was perhaps a swooping raid by Achaeans from the mainland that utterly overthrew the Cretan civilization. The Athenian legend is that Theseus caused the overthrow of Cretan civilization, for when he fled with Ariadne, the Cretan fleet pursued him and in its absence the island was beset by enemies. Others say the island was exposed to raiders when King Minos sailed off in his fleet to recover Daedalus, who had escaped on waxen wings to the kingdom of Cocalus in Sicily. In the following centuries, 1400–1100 B.C., Crete was dominated by the Mycenaean culture. Its own became decadent, the palatial sites were not reoccupied to any great extent; the importance of Crete as a center of art, culture, and commerce declined completely. Homer mentions in the *Iliad* that Crete, "century-citied," sent soldiers against Troy under the leadership of Idomeneus and Meriones. In the *Odyssey* he describes the palace of Alcinous, with its gold and silver doors, and its decorations of blue enamel, and though some think the island home of Alcinous was Corcyra or Corfu, the description of the palace might equally well apply to the palaces of Crete. After the time of the Trojan War the "hundred cities" of Crete warred so among themselves that they became an easy prey for the Dorians, who invaded their island, c1100 B.C., and put a period to the Minoan civilization. At the beginning of the era that culminated in the Classical period, c750 B.C., Cretan culture enjoyed a renascence. Cretan archaic art and skilled craftsmanship, heirs of the master smith Daedalus, influenced developments on the Greek mainland. Independent cities coined their own money, and it was in this time that the famous Gortynian Code of Laws was promulgated—an extraordinary document that detailed all kinds of social and economic laws, and was engraved on the walls of a portico or arcade near Gortyna. Crete played no role in the Persian and Peloponnesian Wars. Its relations with the mainland were slight. By the height of the great Classical period its artistic developments had come to a halt. Its age of greatness was far in the past. In 66 B.C. the island fell, but not without difficulty, under the domination of the Romans. In 1963 it was reported that ruins of a palace destroyed about 1450 B.C. had been discovered at Kato Zakro, in the Sitea area of eastern Crete. Possibly the seat of a minor Minoan king, the palace occupies part of the site of an ancient city that may have served as a trading post and naval base for Cnossus. The palace, covering an area of about 25,000 square feet, was originally built to the height of two or three stories around a central courtyard. It held ceremonial and banquet halls as well as extensive royal apartments, including what may have been a gymnasium with a 17-foot swimming pool off the royal bedrooms. Excavations of the ruins yielded several major finds, including the only capital of a Minoan pillar ever found on Crete, twelve tablets in Linear Script A, and a ceremonial bronze double-ax of a type previously known only from depictions of ceremonial scenes. Other finds include food remains, household crockery and utensils, copper money, a wine press, a detachable table pedestal, a bronze mirror, and numerous painted and carved ceremonial and household vessels of ceramic and stone.

*Crimisus* (kri-mī′sus). [Also: *Crimissus*.] In ancient geography, a river in W Sicily, probably near Segesta. Here Timoleon with 11,000 men defeated (339 B.C.) 70,000 Carthaginians.

*Crisa* (krī′sa). [Also: *Crissa*.] In ancient geography, a city in Phocis, Greece, situated SW of Delphi. It was styled "the divine" by Homer. It is often confused with its port, Cirrha.

*Crommyon* (krom′i-on). In ancient geography, a place in the territory of Corinth, named, some say, for Cromus, a son of Poseidon. Here Phaea, the Crommyonian sow, was bred and was later slain by Theseus. Not far from here was an altar of Melicertes, for his body was brought ashore here by a dolphin. Sisyphus found the corpse, buried it on the Isthmus, and established the Isthmian Games in his honor.

*Cronus* (krō′nus) or *Cronius* (-ni-us), *Mount.* Low wooded hill N of the sacred precinct, the Altis, at Olympia.

*Croton* (krō′ton) or *Crotona* (krō-tō′na). [Modern name, *Crotone;* former name, *Cotrone*.] Town in S Italy, in Bruttii, situated on the Ionian Sea N of Catacium (Catanzaro). A Greek colony, one of the most important cities of Magna Graecia, it was noted for its devotion to athletics and as the seat of the Pythagorean school. There is a Greek temple of Hera Lacinia at the extremity of the nearby promonotory on the Ionian Sea. This famous shrine has been greatly damaged by vandalism and earthquakes, but its platform of masonry and the results of excavations have supplied data for a partial restoration. It was of the 5th century B.C., Doric, hexastyle, with 14 columns on the flanks, and an interior range of four columns before the pronaos. The Crotonians destroyed the rival town of Sybaris in 510 B.C. but were defeated by the Locrians at the Sagras River in 480 B.C.; later the city submitted to Syracuse. It was occupied by the Romans in 277 B.C. Hannibal embarked here on his return to Africa in 203 B.C. The Romans founded a colony here in 194 B.C. A castle now stands on the site of the ancient acropolis.

*Crustumerium* (krus-tū-mē'ri-um). In ancient geography, a city of the Sabines in Latium, Italy, situated a few miles NE of Rome.

*Cumae* (kū'mē). In ancient geography, a city on the coast of Campania, Italy, about ten miles W of what is now Naples. It was founded (c1000 B.C.) by Greek colonists from Cyme in Euboea, was one of the chief Greek cities in Italy until the 5th century B.C., and became (338 B.C.) a Roman *municipium* (a town whose citizens enjoyed certain of the rights of Roman citizenship). Located near the haunted lake Avernus, it was the home of the Cumaean sibyl, the most famous of these prophetesses of antiquity. She gave her prophesies from a cave, in the hill of Cumae, which had 100 approaches from which 100 voices issued. Nearby were temples of Zeus and Apollo and a grove of Diana. Among the remnants of antiquity remaining at Cumae is a Roman amphitheater, imperfectly excavated, but displaying 21 tiers of seats. The axes of the great ellipse are 315 and 255 feet, of the arena 240 and 180 feet. The inhabitants of Cumae founded Neapolis (now Naples) and Puteoli (now Pozzuoli). The Vergilian Society of America maintains a summer school of classical studies in a villa located among the ruins.

*Cunaxa* (kū-nak'sạ). In ancient geography, a place in Babylonia near the Euphrates, probably about 75 miles NW of Babylon. Here, in 401 B.C., a battle took place between Artaxerxes II, king of Persia (with 400,000–1,000,000 men), and his brother Cyrus the Younger (with 100,000 Asiatics aided by 13,000 Greeks). Cyrus was slain and his Asiatic forces fled; the Greek contingent, successful in the engagement, also succeeded in escaping eventually to the Euxine (Black)

Sea, as Xenophon, one of their leaders, relates in his *Anabasis.*

**Cures** (kū'rēz). In ancient geography, a city of the Sabines, about 24 miles NE of Rome. It was a legendary city of Numa Pompilius and Titus Tatius.

**Curium** (kū'ri-um). Ancient city in Cyprus, W of the river Lycus, said to have been founded by the Argives. Its ruins contain a Phoenician temple, remarkable especially for its crypt of four rock-hewn chambers, about 23 feet in diameter, connected by doors and a gallery. The objects in gold and silver constituting the "Treasure of Curium" in the Metropolitan Museum, New York, were found in these chambers.

**Cyclades** (sik'lạ-dēz). [Also: **Kikladhes, Kyklades, Kykladon Nesoi.**] Group of islands belonging to Greece, situated in the Aegean Sea. The name, from the Greek word for "circle," derived from the belief that they formed a ring about Delos. Among the major islands are Andros, Tenos, Ceos, Syrus, Naxos, Melos, and Paros.

**Cydnus** (sid'nus). In ancient geography, a river of Cilicia, Asia Minor, flowing into the Mediterranean Sea about 12 miles S of Tarsus.

**Cydonia** (sī-dō'ni-ạ). [Modern name, **Canea.**] City and seaport on the N coast of Crete. It was founded by Samians (6th century B.C.), who had been exiled from Samos. They sought to return to Samos with the help of Spartans, but failing in their attack on the island, they sailed to Crete and founded Cydonia. They prospered in Cydonia, and built many temples, among them a famous temple of Dictynna (Britomartis).

**Cyllene** (si-lē'nē), **Mount.** In ancient geography, a mountain in Arcadia, Greece, reputed to be the birthplace of Hermes. Elatus, son of Arcas, inherited the region about Mount Cyllene as his share of his father's kingdom and named it Cyllene after his son, Cyllen. The mountain was the highest in Arcadia, and was noted in classical times for the fact that the blackbirds indigenous to the mountain were white. Hermes had the name *Cyllenian* from his mountain birthplace, and a sanctuary of Cyllenian Hermes stood on it.

**Cyllene.** In ancient geography, the port of Elis, situated on the Ionian Sea, north of the promontory of Chelonatas (*Tortoise*

*Shell).* Among its public buildings were sanctuaries of Asclepius and of Aphrodite.

**Cyme** (sī'mē). Ancient Greek city in W Asia Minor, about 28 miles N of Smyrna (now Izmir), on a small coastal bay. It was founded in the early Greek colonization of Aeolis, and rose to prominence as the principal city of this region. In the 7th century B.C. Cyme was ruled by a king, but later it had oligarchic rule. It was involved in the intrigues between Athens and Sparta, and changed hands numerous times in the struggles between Greek and Persian empires. In 17 A.D. it was severely damaged by an earthquake. The site of Cyme is supposed to be at the small village of Namúrt Kjöi.

**Cyme.** In ancient geography, a city on the coast of Campania, settled by Greek colonists from Chalcis in Eretria, and Cyme in Euboea. This is said to have been the earliest (c1000 B.C.) Greek colony on the Italian peninsula. Euboeans from Cyme in Greece brought the alphabet with them to their colony in Italy, and thus introduced the fundamental tool for the creation of the great civilization that developed in Italy. They also brought their Greek religion, gods, and heroes. These were adopted by the Italians so universally and from such an early date that they came to be considered as native Italian divinities. Among the colonists of Cyme were some Graeans from Euboea. In Italy all the colonists, from peoples who had hitherto been variously called Achaeans, Danaans, Argives, and other names according to locality, came to be named Graeci after these Graeans, and from them the word Greece, a name unknown to Homer, is derived. Cyme appears in Latin as Cumae, and was the seat of the famous prophetess of Apollo, the Cumaean sibyl. See also **Cumae.**

**Cynaetha** (sin-ē'tha). In ancient geography, a city in N Arcadia, Greece.

**Cynoscephalae** (sin-o-sef'a-lē). Heights in Thessaly, Greece, between about 10 and 20 miles SE of Larissa. Here the Thebans under Pelopidas defeated (364 B.C.) Alexander of Pherae, and the Romans under Flamininus defeated (197 B.C.) Philip V of Macedon.

**Cynosuria** (sī-no-shö'ri-a). See **Cynuria.**

**Cynthus** (sin'thus), *Mount.* An eminence, conspicuous from the sea (height 370 feet) and commanding a fine view of the Cyclades, on the small Aegean island of Delos, where, according to early legend, Leto bore Zeus' twin children

fat, fāte, fär, fâll, àsk, fāre; net, mē, hėr; pin, pīne; not, nōte, möve, nôr; up, lūte, púll; oi, oil; ou out; (lightened) ēlect, agǫny, ūnite;

Apollo and Artemis. On the western slope of Mount Cynthus are the remains of a primitive rock sanctuary, the Grotto of Apollo, and on the summit was once a shrine of Zeus and Athena. From this Apollo received the epithet Cynthius, and Artemis, Cynthia. (JJ)

**Cynuria** (sī-nū′ri-a̱). [Also: **Cynosuria**.] In ancient geography, a district in Greece in the E part of the Peloponnesus, situated on the Gulf of Argolis.

**Cyparissia** (sip-a̱-ris′i-a̱), or **Cyparissiae** (sip-a̱-ris′i-ē). [Modern name, **Kyparissia** or **Kiparissia**.] In ancient geography, a city of Messenia, situated on the Ionian Sea. Men of the city accompanied Nestor against Troy. The city fell into ruin but was rebuilt by Epaminondas as the port for the new city of Messene, which he built after the battle of Leuctra (371 B.C.). Among the landmarks of the city was a spring that Dionysus caused to gush forth by striking the earth with his thyrsus. Nearby, remains of an ancient temple of Apollo have been found.

**Cyphanta** (sī-fan′ta̱). A city of Laconia, on the Myrtoan Sea. Here a fountain of clear cold water springs from the rock. It was said that Atalanta, hot and tired from hunting, came to this spot and, being thirsty, struck the rock with her spear; the fountain immediately gushed forth. Nearby was a cave sacred to Asclepius, containing a stone image.

**Cyprus** (sī′prus). [French, **Chypre;** German, **Cypern;** Greek, **Kypros;** Italian, **Cipros;** Turkish, **Kibris**.] One of the largest islands of the Mediterranean, situated in its E corner, about 40 miles S of Turkey and about 240 miles N of Egypt, with the mountain range of the Lebanon on the mainland to the E and that of Taurus to the N. Its name is supposed to be derived from its rich mines of copper (Greek *kypros*). Cyprus has limestone mountains averaging about 2000 feet in elevation along its N coast, and a higher and more extensive range occupies the S and W parts of the island, culminating in Mount Olympus, or Troodos (6000 feet). Between these ranges lies a fertile plain. Cyprus was celebrated in antiquity as the birthplace and favorite abode of Aphrodite, and was famous for its beauty and wealth, but also for its licentiousness. It was early settled by Phoenicians, who were followed by Greeks. Its principal cities were Paphos (still known by that name) on the W coast (a center of the cult of Aphrodite), Salamis (near modern Famagusta) on the E, Kittim, or

(obscured)  errant, ardent, actor; ch, chip; g, go; th, thin; ᴛʜ, then; y, you;
(variable)  ḏ as d or j,  ṣ as s or sh,  ṭ as t or ch,  ẕ as z or zh.

Citium (on the site of modern Larnaca) on the SE, and Amathus (near modern Limassol) on the S. In the center of the island were the Phoenician mining cities Tamassus and Idalium (modern Dali), with the celebrated grove of Aphrodite. For a time Cyprus was tributary to Assyria. Its name in the cuneiform inscriptions is Yatnan, and the Assyrian king Sargon relates that seven kings from this island (probably chiefs of the Phoenician colonies) brought him costly gifts and "kissed his feet," i.e., acknowledged his sovereignty. He in turn presented them with a marble stele containing a full-length sculptured portrait of himself, and an inscription commemorating his principal deeds. This monument was found in 1846, well preserved, near Larnaca (the ancient Kittim or Citium), and was acquired by the Royal Museum of Berlin. Cyprus was in succession subject to Persia, Macedon, and Egypt, and in 57 B.C. became a Roman province.

*Cyrenaica* (sir-ē-nā′i-ka̧). [Also: *Pentapolis.*] In ancient geography, a country in N Africa, lying between the Mediterranean on the N, Marmarica on the E, the desert on the S, and the Syrtis Major (modern Gulf of Sidra) on the W. It corresponded closely to the modern territory of the same name, in NE Libya, and was noted for its fertility. It was settled (c631 B.C.) by Theraeans, was subject to Egypt from 321 B.C., and formed (67 B.C.) with Crete a Roman province.

*Cyrene* (sī-rē′nē). [Also: *Cirene.*] In ancient geography, the principal city of Cyrenaica in Africa, situated about ten miles from the Mediterranean coast. It was founded (c631 B.C.) by Theraeans under Battus. According to Herodotus, Aristoteles, the son of Phronima of Crete and Polymnestus of Thera, was afflicted by a stammer. He went to the oracle at Delphi to inquire about his speech, and was ordered by the priestess, who addressed him as Battus, or "king," to establish a colony in Libya. Henceforth called Battus, he returned to Thera, and shortly all sorts of evils descended on the island. The inhabitants, unaware of what the priestess had told Battus, sent to Delphi and now learned that if Battus would found a colony at Cyrene in Libya, everything would go well with them. After a false start Battus and the Theraeans arrived on the coast of Libya, but were soon persuaded to move by the natives. The Libyans promised them a better site for a colony and undertook to lead them to it. They craftily arranged the journey so that all the most delightful

fat, fāte, fär, fåll, àsk, fāre; net, mē, hèr; pin, pīne; not, nōte, mŏve, nôr; up, lūte, pùll; oi, oil; ou out; (lightened) ḝlect, agǫny, ūnite

and suitable places were passed during the night. At last the
Libyans brought Battus and his companions to a place
where there was a spring called Apollo's Fountain. Here, on
two hills overlooking a plain, Battus founded Cyrene. Battus
ruled 40 years, and was followed by his son Arcesilaus (for
generations, the names of the Cyrenaean kings were alter-
nately Battus and Arcesilaus), who reigned for 16 years. In
the reign of the second Battus, who followed Arcesilaus,
Greeks from many areas began to flock to Cyrene and the
colony prospered mightily. The Libyans found themselves
pushed back and appealed to Apries, king of Egypt, for aid
against the Cyrenaeans. Apries sent an army against them
which was utterly defeated. This led to the downfall of
Apries. He was succeeded by Amasis II, who made a treaty
of friendship and alliance with the Cyrenaeans, and married
Ladice, daughter of their king. He was so delighted by her
that he honored Cyrene by sending a statue of Athena,
overlaid with plates of gold, to the city. In a later generation,
the ruler of Cyrene (an Arcesilaus) quarreled with his brothers and they withdrew to another site in Libya and founded
Barca. When Cambyses II conquered Egypt, the Cyrenaeans
offered to submit to him, and afterward paid tribute to
Darius. Cyrene was the only Greek colony in Africa to become strong and wealthy. It was a center of Greek learning
and culture. One of her sons, Eugammon the poet, wrote a
continuation of the *Odyssey*, the *Telegony*. In this work Odysseus was connected with the line of Cyrenaean kings. The
Cyrenaeans also claimed Aristaeus as their ancestor, for it
was to this spot that Apollo brought Cyrene, for whom the
city was named, and it was here that she bore Aristaeus to
the god. The Cyrenaeans were celebrated in ancient times
as physicians. This was perhaps owing to their connection
with Apollo, but it is more likely that it was on account of
a medicinal herb that grew in their land, called silphion,
which through its export brought wealth to the king. The
modern town on the site of Cyrene contains many antiquities. It was the birthplace of Aristippus, Eratosthenes, and
other famous men.

**Cyrnos** (sir'nos, kür'nos). Greek name of *Corsica*.

**Cyrrhestica** (sī-res'ti-ka̲) or **Cyrrhus** (sir'us). In ancient geography, a region in N Syria, W of the Euphrates and S of Commagene.

**Cythera** (si-thir′a̱). [Also: **Cerigo, Cerigotto;** Greek, **Kithira, Kythera, Kytherion.**] One of the Ionian Islands in S. Greece, situated between 8 and 10 miles S of Laconia. It was near this island that Aphrodite was said to have arisen from the foam of the sea, whence her epithet "Cytherea." But some say the worship of Aphrodite was brought to the island by the Phoenicians. The sanctuary of Aphrodite Urania *(Heavenly)* on the island is the oldest of all the sanctuaries of Aphrodite among the Greeks. A wooden image of the goddess, armed, stood in it. In ancient times the island was known as the "Purple Island" because the shellfish of the region yielded such a fine dye. The island, once an Argive possession, came into the hands of the Spartans, but was wrested from them by the Athenians, 424 B.C., and became a base from which Athens attacked Sparta. This fulfilled the warning made generations earlier by the sage Chilon, that Sparta would gain if Cythera were sunk to the bottom of the sea, for he saw it, by its location, as a dagger pointed at the heart of Sparta. Area of the island, about 110 square miles.

**Cyzicus** (siz′i-kus). [Also: **Cyzicum.**] In ancient geography, the peninsula projecting from Mysia, Asia Minor, into the Propontis (Sea of Marmara); also, the Greek town on its isthmus, named, according to legend, for Cyzicus, king of the Doliones. Jason and the Argonauts stopped there on their way to Colchis in the quest for the Golden Fleece. Among its ruins are a Roman amphitheater, a temple of Hadrian, and an ancient theater. The Roman amphitheater dates from the 2nd century A.D. The ruins still rise to a height of 65 feet, built of rubble faced with rusticated masonry in granite. There are 32 arched entrances in the lower story. The longer axis of the ellipse is 325 feet. The temple of Hadrian, dedicated in 167 A.D., was greatly admired in antiquity. It was a Corinthian *peripteros* (building surrounded by a row of columns) of six by 15 columns, of white marble. The cella, or main chamber, was small, without *pronaos* (vestibule) or *opisthodomos* (rear chamber); there were four interior rows of columns in front and two behind. The temple measured 112 by 301 feet; the cella 70 by 140 feet. The columns were seven feet in base-diameter and 70 feet high (the highest of any classical temple). The pediments and the cella were richly adorned. The ancient theater, apparently contemporaneous with the amphitheater, was in part built up of rough masonry and faced with marble. The diameter is 328 feet.

***Dacia*** (dā′shạ). In ancient geography, a province of the Roman Empire, lying between the Carpathian Mountains on the N, the Tissus or Tisia (Tisza) on the W, the Ister (Danube) on the S, and the Tyras or Danastris (Dniester) on the E. It corresponded approximately to modern Rumania, including Transylvania. The inhabitants were the Getae or Daci. It was invaded by Alexander the Great in 335 B.C., by Lysimachus c292 B.C., and its people defeated the generals of Domitian in 86–90 A.D. It was conquered by Trajan in 101 and succeeding years, and made a Roman province. It was abandoned by the Romans in the reign of Aurelian (270–275), but not before the Romans, during some 200 years of occupation, had left their imprint on the region by establishing the language that has developed into modern Rumanian.

***Daphne*** (daf′nē). In ancient geography, a famous grove and sanctuary of Apollo, situated about five miles SW of Antioch, in ancient Syria. It was established by Seleucus Nicator.

***Dardanelles*** (där-dạ-nelz′). See ***Hellespont.***

***Dardania*** (där-dā′ni-ạ). [Also: ***Dardanice.***] In ancient geography, a territory in Mysia, with uncertain boundaries. It is mentioned, indefinitely, in the *Iliad.*

***Dardanus*** (där′dạ-nus). [Also: ***Dardanum.***] In ancient geography, a city in Mysia, Asia Minor, situated on the Hellespont, about nine miles SW of Abydos.

***Daulis*** (dô′lis). In ancient geography, a city in Phocis, Greece, situated about 12 miles E of Delphi.

***Daunia*** (dâ′ni-ạ). In ancient geography, a kingdom in Apulia, in Italy.

***Decelea*** (des-ẹ-lē′ạ). In ancient geography, a city and mountain citadel in Attica, Greece, situated about 14 miles from Athens and commanding the Attic plain and the routes to

Euboea and Boeotia. On the advice of Alcibiades, Athenian general who fled to Sparta to escape trial for impiety, the Spartans under King Agis seized and fortified Decelea in the course of the Peloponnesian War, 413 B.C. This was a crushing blow for Athens. Hitherto the Spartans made raids into Attica and then withdrew, so that it was still possible for Athens to be supplied from the surrounding farms and from Euboea. With the continued occupation of Decelea the Spartans effectively cut off the farmlands as a source of supply, for they continually patrolled the area from the fortress, and cut off supplies from Euboea. This compelled Athens to import supplies by sea and caused great hardship. The Spartans held Decelea until the end of the Peloponnesian War, 404 B.C.

*Delium* (dē'li-um). In ancient geography, a place in Boeotia, Greece, situated on the coast about 24 miles N of Athens. Here during the Peloponnesian War the Boeotians defeated (424 B.C.) the Athenians. Socrates took part in the battle. During the retreat as he made his way with others through the enemy, Alcibiades came along on horseback and protected him from the attacks of the enemy and saved his life.

*Delos* (dē'los). [Also: *Mikra Dilos;* ancient names, *Asteria, Ortygia.*] Smallest island of the Cyclades, Greece, situated in the narrow passage between the islands of Myconus and Rhenia. Area, two square miles. Here, according to some accounts, Asteria, daughter of the Titans Coeus and Phoebe, leaped into the sea to escape the embraces of Zeus and was transformed into a quail. A city was named Asteria for her, but afterward renamed Delos. Delos was also known, in her memory, as Ortygia, "quail." Leto, about to bear her children by Zeus, was pursued all over the world by a serpent sent to harass her by jealous Hera. As the time for her confinement neared, no place on earth would receive her out of fear of the anger of Hera. At last she came to Delos, at that time a floating island, and there she was welcomed and kindly received. Some say her children, Artemis and Apollo, were both born on the tiny island, but others say Artemis was born on neighboring Rhenia, and as soon as she was born, helped her mother across to Delos. The birth of Apollo took place in the shadow of the Hill of Cynthus where the stream of the Inopus issues from the hill. The palm tree there, that Leto clasped when she bore Apollo, was one of the sights of antiquity from the time of Homer to that of Pliny. In its joy at being the birthplace of the god, the island covered itself with golden blossoms. Some say four pillars rose from the sea after the birth of the twin gods and moored the island, so that henceforth it ceased to float. Others say Apollo himself anchored the island, to reward it for receiving his mother. From earliest times, Delos was connected with the Hyperboreans. When Apollo and Artemis were born, some say, two Hyperborean maidens, Arge and Opis, came to Delos to help the birth goddess deliver the children of Leto. The Hyperborean damsels died on Delos and were entombed behind the temple of Artemis. Ever after they were honored by the Delian women from whom the rest of the islanders learned to honor them also. Later two more Hyperborean maidens, Hyperoche and Laodice, came to Delos, accompanied by several men. They brought offerings wrapped in wheaten straw. These maidens also died on Delos and were entombed. In their honor the maidens of Delos cut off a lock of their hair before their wedding day and laid it upon the graves of the Hyperborean damsels. The youths also made offerings of their hair on their tombs. When the Hyperboreans saw that their envoys did not return, they ceased to send them to Delos. Instead they sent their offerings to Scythia, from where they were conveyed in relays to Delos.

Delos became the seat of a great sanctuary in honor of Apollo, one of the most famous religious foundations of antiquity. From the time of Solon, Athens sent an annual embassy to the Delian festival, in which the "tunic-trailing Ionians" honored Apollo with boxing, dancing, and song. When Pisistratus regained control of Athens for the third time, he purified Delos, on the advice of an oracle, by having all the bodies that were buried within sight of the temple dug up and reburied in another part of the island. Only the tomb of the two Hyperborean maidens who came to assist at the birth of Apollo and Artemis were left untouched. This spot was sacred and was not disturbed. In the Persian War, Datis assembled the Persian fleet off Delos. The Delians fled from their island and refused to return, even though Datis assured them that he would do no harm to the land that was the birthplace of two gods. On the contrary, he landed and made an offering of 300 talents' weight of frankincense on the altar at Delos and then sailed away. After he left, Delos was shaken by an earthquake. This was the first time such a thing had occurred and was taken as a warning of evils to come to Greece, and as a fulfillment of the oracle that had predicted:

"Delos self will I shake, which never yet has been shaken."

But Datis himself so much respected the sacred place that on his way back to Asia, after Marathon, he stopped at Delos and left a golden image of Apollo that had been stolen by some of his Phoenician allies and hidden on their ship. He asked the Delians to return it to the temple from which it had been stolen. Twenty years later, in obedience to an oracle, the Delians did so.

After the Persian War, Delos was the center of the Delian League, formed (c477 B.C.) to resist Persian aggression. In 454 B.C. the sacred treasure of Delos, contributed by the members of the League, was removed to the Athenian Acropolis. In 426 B.C., Delos was purified again; all the dead who had been buried on the island were removed. Thenceforth no one was permitted to be born on the island, and no corpses could be buried there. The seriously ill were removed to some other place so as not to desecrate the island by dying there. Expectant mothers were taken off well before their time came so that no mortal children should first see the light of day in the island where Apollo was born. Games in honor of Apollo were restored, and a few years later all the inhabitants of the island were removed and it became purely a sacred place. The island was an Athenian dependency down to the Macedonian period, when it became semi-independent, and in the 2nd century B.C. it again became subject to Athens. The city of Delos was made a free port by the Romans and developed into a great commercial mart. It was raided in 88 B.C. by the forces of Mithridates VI and soon fell to the status of an almost uninhabited place. Now it is uninhabited. The sanctuary of Apollo was excavated by the French School at Athens, beginning in 1873. The work ranks as one of the chief achievements of its kind. The buildings disclosed lie for the most part within the enclosure or temenos of Apollo, which is of trapeziform shape, and about 650 feet to a side. Mosaic floors, bathing rooms, large underground drainage wells, and the floor plans of many buildings have been uncovered. In 1960 it was

reported that ruins of a section of an ancient town had been
discovered on the western slopes of the Hill of Cynthus. The
finds there include the foundations of a large building with
remains of a mosaic pavement worked in geometric designs.
In addition to the interesting finds of architecture and sculpture, epigraphical discoveries of the highest importance
have been made, bearing upon history and particularly upon
the ceremonial and administration of the sanctuary.

*Delphi* (del'fī). [Also: *Delphoi*.] In ancient geography, a town in
Phocis, Greece; the seat of the world-renowned oracle of
Pythian Apollo, the most famous oracle of antiquity. It lies
at an altitude of about 2000 feet, on the slopes of Mount
Parnassus, whose peak rises to a height of more than 8000
feet to the NE. Towering 800 feet immediately above the
sanctuary, on the N and E, are two great bare gray rocks, the
Phaedriades or "shining ones." The Phaedriades are separated by a deep gorge at whose eastern foot is the sacred
spring of Castalia. To the S, the ground falls away swiftly to
the ravine cut by the Plistus River as it flows into the Gulf
of Corinth at the ancient port of Cirrha (Itea), six miles
away. The area is subject to earthquakes and the menace of
rock slides. Fissures opened up in the ground, and closed
again by tremors, exhaled vapors said to inspire the priestesses who inhaled them to prophesy. In its location alone,
Delphi is majestic and dramatic, the "wild and rocky glen"
described by the poets.

From remote ages this was the seat of an oracle. Because
it was subject to violent earthquakes, the earliest oracle belonged to the chthonian gods, those who hold sway under
the earth. The most ancient oracle belonged to Gaea
(Earth). Some say Poseidon, "the earth-shaker," shared the
oracle with her. Through her prophetess Daphnis, a nymph
of Mount Parnassus, Gaea gave her oracles. Poseidon uttered his through priests called Pyrcones. Gaea set the serpent Pytho to guard the chasm whence the prophetic vapors
emanated. Her priestesses were called Pythia. Some say
Gaea gave her share of the oracle to Themis, but Pytho
continued to guard it. This was the situation until Apollo
arrived, a relative newcomer to an ancient oracle. Some say
he took the form of a dolphin (hence his epithet *Delphian
Apollo*), and swam with a Cretan ship to the port of Cirrha.
Arrived there, he resumed his divine form and commanded

the Cretans to become his priests. When they protested that no one would come to worship at such a remote spot, he promised that so many would bring offerings that the sacrificial axes would never be idle. Having reassured them, he went to the chasm and slew the dragon that guarded the oracle. Some say the place was first named Pytho, "the place of the rotting," because he left the bones of the dragon to rot there, and that it was later named Delphi because Apollo had come to the nearby shores in the shape of a dolphin. But some say it was named Delphi in honor of Delphus, a son or a descendant of Apollo. Apollo received Poseidon's share in the oracle in exchange for a place near Troezen, in the Peloponnesus, and became sole master at Delphi. Having killed Pytho, Apollo was compelled to seek purification, and was away doing penance for eight years. The penance and purification of Apollo were commemorated in a sacred drama that was enacted at Delphi, at first, every eight years. The epithet *Pythian* was given to Apollo because he slew the dragon; his priestesses were called Pythia, or sometimes, Pythonesses. Others say, and the two legends existed side by side, that Apollo came from the land of the Hyperboreans at the back of the north wind, and seized the oracle. These say that his first prophet, the only man who ever served in this capacity, was Olen, a Hyperborean. But most say that Phemenoë was his first prophetess, and that she pronounced her oracles in hexameter verse. At first the priestess was available for consultation only once a year, on Apollo's birthday. In later times she prophesied once a month, or every day, if the omens were favorable. Those who sought advice from the oracle came as suppliants, wearing laurel wreaths and fillets of wool; they purified themselves, sacrificed a victim, and inquired whether it was worth their while to ask a question. If the response to this query was favorable, they approached the priestess in her shrine. Three priestesses served in turn. The priestess was purified, drank the waters of the spring of Cassotis, chewed laurel leaves, and seated herself on a tripod over the chasm from which the vapors issued and which stimulated prophetic utterance. Only a priest was present when the priestess gave her responses. His function was to interpret the utterances, which were often obscure or, at the least, capable of two interpretations. Heracles, seeking information from the ora-

fat, fāte, fär, fåll, åsk, fåre; net, mē, hėr; pin, pīne; not, nōte, mȯve, nôr; up, lūte, pủll; oi, oil; ou out; (lightened) ḙlect, agǫny, ṵnite;

cle, was denied by the priestess because of his impurity. Enraged, Heracles attempted to seize the sacred tripod and threatened to set up his own oracle. Apollo came to protect his shrine and the two struggled until Zeus parted them by a thunderbolt and forced them to compose their differences. The priestess gave Heracles a response, and the sanctuary remained firmly in Apollo's hands. Some say that the myth of the fight between Heracles and Apollo symbolizes the Dorian invasion of Greece (c1100 B.C.). Most of the Dorians went on into the Peloponnesus, but some remained in Doris and continued to have great influence over the sanctuary. After the Dorian invasion the influence and power of the sanctuary flourished, and in the succeeding period of more than a thousand years was felt from the shores of Asia to Rome. Other gods came to share the sacred spot with Apollo. Athena Pronoea *(Fore-thought)* had her place. Her sanctuary was on a slope below the temple of Apollo. (The temples in her precinct fell into ruin and the spot became known as the *Marmaria,* roughly, "the marble quarry," from the many fragments there.) Dionysus, an oracular god who prophesied during the winter, when Apollo was off with the Hyperboreans, was consulted. He was considered a god who died and was reborn annually, and his tomb at Delphi was the scene of rites held by women. Delphi also possessed the "omphalos" *(navel),* a stone that represented the exact center of the world. The myth was that Zeus sent out two eagles in opposite directions to make a circuit of the universe. They met at Delphi, and established it as the center. Another stone, or possibly it was the same one, was also called "omphalos," and was the stone given by Rhea to Cronus in place of her new-born son Zeus. A sacred city grew up around the oracle and these cult objects. According to tradition the first temple erected on the site was a hut of branches of laurel, a tree sacred to Apollo. This was replaced by a temple made by the bees, of beeswax and feathers, and sent to Delphi by the Hyperboreans. The third temple was of wood, covered with bronze plates and was made, some say, by Hephaestus. Of these three temples no trace has ever been found. The fourth temple was of stone. Trophonius and Agamedes, according to tradition, were the builders.

Delphi was at first under the control of Crissa, in Phocis, whose territory included the port of Cirrha. Pilgrims, making their way to the sanctuary, were subject to all sorts of dues and exactions by the Crissaeans. The priests of Delphi complained to the Amphictyonic Council, a group of representatives from 12 Greek cities (mostly Thessalian and Dorian), that had its seat at Anthela. The members were pledged to aid each other. The Amphictyons acted against Crissa. Solon of Athens and Clisthenes, tyrant of Sicyon, lent their assistance in the Sacred War (c600–c590 B.C.). Crissa was destroyed, its territory was dedicated to Apollo and henceforth the tilling of the Crissaean plain was forbidden, and Delphi became autonomous. The management of the sanctuary was left in the hands of the Amphictyonic Council. The Pythian Games, descended from the old religious drama representing the purification of Apollo (the *Stepteria*), and with the addition of musical and athletic contests, also came under the supervision of the Council. Thereafter, from 586 B.C., the Games were held every four years. The end of the Sacred War marked the beginning of a period of great prosperity for Delphi. The treasuries of Corinth and Sicyon were dedicated. Cypselus, tyrant of Corinth (c655–625 B.C.), was said to have dedicated the former, and Clisthenes the latter. These treasuries, the earliest of many, were small temple-like structures erected and dedicated by individual city-states. In them sacred, and often precious, vessels for religious ceremonies were kept. Rich offerings were made to them, and they also served as meeting places for pilgrims and officials from the cities that had dedicated them. The Lydian kings, Gyges (c685–653 B.C.), and Croesus (6th century king who reigned from 560–546 B.C.), made rich gifts to the sanctuary in gratitude for favorable oracles. Amasis II (fl. c569–525 B.C.), of Egypt was also a contributor. In 548 B.C. the temple built by Trophonius and Agamedes was destroyed by fire. The Alcmaeonidae, aristocrats who had been exiled from Athens, raised a great sum to rebuild it. Croesus and Amasis II again made large contributions for this cause. Spintharus of Corinth was the architect. At their own expense, it was said, the Alcmaeonidae had the temple faced with Parian marble instead of the limestone that was called for by the plan. The treasury of the Siphnians, one of the richest of them all was dedicated c524 B.C. (Large fragments of its pediments and friezes, depicting the Greeks and the Trojans in combat, War of the

Giants, the Judgment of Paris, and the exploits of Heracles, are preserved in the museum at Delphi.) The Cnidians raised their *Lesche,* a kind of club house, in the first half of the 5th century B.C. Its walls were decorated with paintings by the Thasian artist Polygnotus.

Croesus, who had made such rich gifts to Delphi in return for favorable responses, was later one of the most ill-fated victims of its obscure pronouncements. Having made every provision to secure the most reliable oracle, he sent to Delphi to ask if he should wage war on Cyrus. He learned that if he crossed the Halys River and marched against the Persians, he would destroy a great empire. Greatly encouraged, he attacked Cyrus and destroyed a great empire—his own. When he reproached the priestess, he was told that he had misinterpreted the oracle, which had been duly fulfilled. Croesus humbly acknowledged his error, so it is said. Not all the answers, however, were equivocal. In a later time the question was put: who was the wisest man in the world? The priestess replied with the flat statement that there was no man in the world wiser than Socrates.

When the Persians invaded Europe in 490 B.C., Delphi feared to be destroyed if it resisted, and "medized," that is, it was favorable to the Persians. But the priests were able to gloss over this period of weakness, and the Athenians dedicated the treasury of Athens at Delphi with the spoils taken from the Persians at Marathon. The walls of their treasury were covered with inscriptions, many of which record the gratitude of freed slaves. Among the inscriptions is also a hymn to Apollo bearing the only recorded musical notations ever found in Greece. (The rebuilt treasury of Athens can still be seen at Delphi. The fitting together of its scattered and broken walls was greatly facilitated by matching the inscriptions.) Ten years after Marathon the Persians returned. When Xerxes had taken the pass at Thermopylae, he sent an army into Phocis to plunder the sanctuary of Delphi, of whose treasures, according to Herodotus, he knew more than those in his own palace; he had heard so much about them. The Delphians were stricken with terror and asked the oracle if they should bury the treasures or remove them to another place. The god replied, through his priestess, that he was well able without their help to protect his own. On receiving the response the Delphians concentrated on saving themselves and their goods. They retired, some across the Gulf of Corinth and some to the heights of Parnassus. Only 60 men and a prophet remained in the sanctuary. When the Persians approached, the prophet saw the sacred armor divinely removed from the shrine. The Persians advanced to the shrine of Athena Pronoea. Suddenly there was a crack of thunder. Two immense crags split off from Mount Parnassus and rolled down on the Persians, crushing a great number of them, while from the temple of Athena were heard a war-cry and a shout of victory. The Persians, terrified by the portents, fled in confusion. The Delphians, seeing how the god protected his own, fell on the Persians and slaughtered them wholesale. Those who escaped were pursued into Boeotia by two gigantic armed warriors, heroes who had sacred precincts at Delphi. Herodotus, who tells this tale, saw the huge stones that had crushed the Persians in the precinct of Athena Pronoea. Before this miraculous event, the Athenians had sent envoys to consult the oracle as to their defense against the Persians. The priestess replied:

"Wretches, why sit ye here? Fly, fly to the ends of creation,
   Quitting your homes, and the crags which your city crowns with her circlet.
All—all ruined and lost. Since fire, and impetuous Ares,
   Speeding along in a Syrian chariot, hastes to destroy her."

The envoys refused to return to Athens with such a gloomy reply. They returned to the shrine as suppliants and vowed to die in the sanctuary rather than leave without some more encouraging word. It would be the greatest impiety if any died in the shrine. The priestess grudgingly and obscurely uttered the following:

"Safe shall the wooden wall continue for thee and thy children."

Themistocles interpreted the "wooden wall" to mean the fleet, worked to build it up, and went on to defeat the Persians at Salamis. The temporizing of Delphi was forgotten when the Persians were driven out. Rich offerings of trophies, statues, and tripods were made for the victories of Salamis, Plataea, and Mycale. The offering for Plataea was a golden tripod set upon a pillar of three bronze intertwined serpents. On its base were inscribed the names of the Greek peoples who dedicated it.

fat, fāte, fär, fȧll, ȧsk, fãre; net, mē, hèr; pin, pīne; not, nōte, mȯve, nôr; up, lūte, pu̇ll; oi, oil; ou out; (lightened) ḙlect, agǫny, ūnite;

Following the Persian War, Delphi became embroiled in the disputes between the various city-states, and lost some of its credit, because it seemed to take sides and because the charge of bribery leveled against it was never satisfactorily cleared. In the Second Sacred War (c448 B.C.), Pericles returned control of Delphi to the Phocians, but it regained its autonomy by the Peace of Nicias (421 B.C.), according to the terms of which the common temples of Greece were to be free to all. As a great sanctuary, it continued to receive gifts and offerings from the rival city-states and from foreign rulers as well. In 373 B.C. the temple was destroyed by an earthquake. Funds were raised by international subscription, and construction of a new temple was begun which was finished c330 B.C. Before its completion, a Third Sacred War broke out (357–346 B.C.) when the Phocians cultivated the sacred plain of Crissa and were punished by the Amphictyonic Council. Philomelus, the Phocian general, pillaged the rich treasures of the sanctuary to build a fortress. Philip of Macedon intervened, crushed the Phocians and imposed a heavy fine on them. Peace was short-lived. The city of Amphissa committed impiety against Delphi (339 B.C.), and brought on the Fourth Sacred War. Philip of Macedon, who had taken the place of the Phocians in the Amphictyonic League, interfered to "restore order." The Athenians and Thebans, fearing his growing power in Greece, resisted him, and he overwhelmingly defeated them at Chaeronea, 338 B.C. In 279 B.C., the Gauls, under Brennus, attacked Delphi and were driven off, so it was said, by the direct intervention of the god, who sent earthquakes, snow, and bitter cold to repulse them. After 189 B.C., Delphi came under the dominion of the Romans. In 91 B.C. the temple was burned by Thracians. In 86 B.C. Sulla pillaged the sanctuary. The story is that the priests, to deter Sulla from his purpose, set a harpist to playing in a concealed place and warned Sulla that the god was playing to forbid him to violate his temple. Sulla turned their remark by saying that the god was playing to show that he welcomed a friend, and proceeded to carry off what he wished. Later, the Emperor Nero carried off over 500 statues from the sacred city, but 3000 or so were still left there. Even so, Delphi retained great wealth. But it had lost its place as the center of the universe, and enjoyed only a short revival as a religious center under Hadrian. In the reigns of Constantine and Theodosius many of its treasures were stolen to adorn other capitals, including the golden tripod of Plataea, which Constantine set up in the city named for him. Theodosius II, a Christian emperor, delivered the final blow to Delphi when he silenced the oracle, destroyed (390 A.D.) the temple, and systematically mutilated the statues and images.

The influence of Delphi was felt throughout the Mediterranean world for a period of centuries. It received pilgrims and envoys from all quarters, and became a great clearing house for receiving and spreading information. No colonizing force set out from Greece before consulting the oracle. Political decisions were based on its responses. It was the arbiter in education, art, and literature, as well as in religion. It was an enlightening and elevating force, emphasizing as it did on many occasions, a rule of law rather than of vengeance, moral purity rather than purifying rites. With the Pythian Games it brought the Greeks together, in athletics, musical contests, and literary competitions, and stressed the tendencies that unified the Greeks rather than those which divided them. In addition, as the recipient of rich gifts from city-states, generals, heroes, kings, victors in athletic contests, grateful individuals, and even beautiful women, Delphi was the art center of Greece. Images and statues by the finest sculptors over the course of centuries adorned the sanctuary and its environs. Among them was the famous bronze *Charioteer* on view in the museum at Delphi today. The site was occupied by a great temple of Apollo, to which pilgrims ascended by a winding sacred way that was lined with treasuries and votive offerings. All around the temple were other shrines and buildings, as well as uncounted hundreds of statues. In the flanks of the hill that rises sharply behind Apollo's temple was a theater, near the fountain of Cassotis whose waters flowed underground into the shrine and were drunk by the priestesses. Above the theater was a stadium where certain of the contests were held. The stadium, remains of which can still be seen, replaced an earlier one on the plain around Crissa. The sacred monuments and temples were carried off or destroyed, early in the Christian era. Earthquakes and landslides covered the site. A village, Castri, grew up over the buried remains. In 1892, the entire village having been removed to a new site, French

---

fat, fāte, fär, fåll, ȧsk, fâre; net, mē, hėr; pin, pīne; not, nōte, mōv̇e, nôr; up, lūte, pu̇ll; oi, oil; ou out; (lightened) ḙlect, agǫny, ūnit

excavators began work there. In succeeding years, many remains of the ancient site have been uncovered, including the temple of Apollo, the theater, bases of votive offerings and sites of treasuries, so that today it is possible not only to admire the imposing majesty of the physical scene, but to recreate, with the help of some imagination, the profusion and richness of the site as it existed in an earlier time.

*Dendera* (den'dẽr-ạ). See *Tentyra.*

*Dia* (dī'ạ). An island in the Aegean Sea, one of the Cyclades. It was one of the homes of Dionysus, and was also the island on which Theseus abandoned Ariadne on his return from Crete after escaping the Minotaur. Here Dionysus found Ariadne and married her. This island is better known by its name Naxos.

*Dicaeopolis* (dī-sẽ-op'ọ̄-lis). See *Segesta.*

*Dicte* (dik'tē). A cave in the mountains of Lassithion, in E Crete. It was one of many caves where, according to legend, Zeus was born. In the Minoan and Archaic eras it was used as a cult site. It has two chambers; one held an altar and was a place for making sacrifices; the other, approached by a stairway, was a place where votive offerings were deposited.

*Didyme* (did'i-mē). Ancient name for one of the Lipari islands, now called *Salina.*

*Dinaric Alps* (di-nar'ik alps). [Latin, *Alpae Dinaricae.*] Mountain ranges in Illyria (now Yugoslavia), which are a continuation of the main Alpine system. They run parallel to the Adriatic Sea coast.

*Dindymus* (din'di-mus). [Also: *Dindymum.*] A mountain in Phrygia, sacred to Cybele.

*Dine* (dī'nē). In ancient geography, a place in Argolis, on the seacoast, where a fountain of fresh water rises out of the sea. The name means "whirlpool." The Argives used to cast bridled horses into this fountain of fresh water as offerings to Poseidon.

*Dium* or *Deium* (dī'um). Place in Macedonia near the Hebrus River. According to the legend, Orpheus withdrew to this spot after his final parting from Eurydice and played and sang for birds, beasts, and trees only, refusing to have anything more to do with women. Here he was set upon, according to some accounts, by maenads who were sent by Dionysus to punish him for denying his cult; according to others, it was the women of the Cicones who attacked him for keeping apart from the society of women. In any case, the women tore him limb from limb and cast his severed head into the Hebrus River. Afterward the women were transformed into oak trees.

*Dodecanese* (dō-dek-ạ-nēz′, nēs′). [Greek, *Dodekanesos*, meaning "Twelve Islands."] Group of Greek islands in the SE part of the Aegean Sea near the SW coast of Turkey. There are 12 main islands: Astypalea, Chalce, Calymna, Carpathus, Casus, Cos, Lerus, Nisyrus, Patmos, Rhodes, Syme, and Telus. In addition, there are many small ones.

*Dodona* (dō-dō′nạ). An ancient town in Epirus, probably situated on or near Mount Tomarus, SW of modern Ioannina. It was the seat of the oldest Greek oracle, dedicated to Zeus Naios in an oak grove hung with vessels of brass, by which the god's voice was thought to be made audible.

*Doris* (dō′ris, dôr′is). In ancient geography, a territory in C Greece, surrounded by Phocis, Locris, Aetolia, and Malis; a valley between Oeta and Parnassus. It was occupied by the Dorians, perhaps c1100 B.C. Although they moved on through Greece, conquered the Peloponnesus, made forays into Crete and the Aegean islands, founded many cities in Greece and Asia Minor, the small area of Doris was ever after considered as the motherland of the Dorians. This was its most important role in Greek history.

*Doris.* In ancient geography, a part of the coast of Caria, Asia Minor.

*Dorium* (dō-rī′um). In ancient geography, a town in Nestor's realm, in N Messenia. Here, some say, Thamyris engaged in a contest with the Muses. He lost in the contest and was struck blind and lost his art of singing.

*Drabescus* (drạ-bes′kus). [Modern name, *Drama.*] In ancient geography, town in N Greece, situated between the Strymon and Nestus rivers, about 78 miles NE of Thessalonica.

*Drama* (drä′mạ). See *Drabescus.*

*Drangiana* (dran-ji-ā′nạ). [Also: *Drangiane;* modern name, *Seistan.*] In ancient geography, a region in C Asia, bounded on the N by Areia, on the E by Arachosia, on the S by Gedrosia, and on the W by Carmania. It was a province of the ancient Persian empire, and was conquered by Alexander the Great, who brought it into his empire. The area lies in what is now SW Afghanistan and E Iran.

*Drepana* (drep′an-ạ). The island of the Phaeacians, later known as Corcyra (Corfu). The name Drepana means sickle and was given to this island either because it was formed from the sickle which Cronus threw into the sea after mutilating Uranus, or because Demeter, whose symbol is the sickle, once lived on the island. Still another explanation is that the outline of the island, as seen on a map, suggests the shape of a sickle.

***Drepanum*** (drep′a̯-num). [Modern name, ***Trapani***.] A cape and town on the west coast of Sicily. It was near the cape that Cronus threw the mutilated genitals of Uranus, along with the sickle that performed the emasculation, into the sea, according to some accounts. The discarded sickle gave the cape its name. In the First Punic War the city was one of the strongholds of the Carthaginians, was fortified by Hamilcar Barca, and was close to the scene of the great Carthaginian naval victory (249 B.C.) by Adherbal over the Roman fleet under Publius Claudius. It fell to the Romans only after a protracted siege in 241 B.C.

***Dulichium*** (dū-lik′i-um). In ancient geography, an island in the Ionian Sea, near Ithaca. According to legend, it was a part of the island kingdom of Odysseus, and the home of some of the suitors of Penelope.

***Dyme*** (dī′mē). In ancient geography, a city of Achaea in the Peloponnesus, situated on the Gulf of Calydon (Gulf of Patras). It was founded by the Epeans. It was the westernmost of the 12 Ionian cities of Achaea.

***Dyspontium*** (dis-pon′ti-um). Town near the Alpheus River, in Elis. It was a vassal community of Elis, and was destroyed in the 6th century B.C. when it joined Pisa in a revolt against Elis.

# —E—

***Eburum*** (eb′ū̯-rum). [Modern name, ***Eboli***.] Town in Campania, S Italy, situated near the Silarus River, about 45 miles SE of Naples. The ruins of ancient Paestum, including beautiful Greek temples, are nearby.

***Ecbatana*** (ek-bat′a̯-na̯). In ancient geography, the capital of

(obscured) errant, ardent, actor; ch, chip; g, go; th, thin; ᴛʜ, then; y, you;
(variable) ḍ as d or j, ṣ as s or sh, ṭ as t or ch, ẓ as z or zh.

Media. According to the Greeks it was built by order of Deïoces in the first half of the 7th century B.C. The ancient city, on a hill, was surrounded by seven encircling walls which were coated, beginning with the outer one, in white, black, scarlet, blue, and orange colors, with the two innermost walls coated respectively with silver and gold. Ecbatana was taken from the Median king Astyages by Cyrus the Great (550 B.C.), and became the summer palace of the Persian and Parthian kings. Alexander the Great captured it in 330 B.C. When Alexander returned from India he stopped at Ecbatana for several months and held great feasts and celebrations. Here, 324 B.C., his friend Hephaestion died. Modern Hamadan, in W Iran, occupies the ancient site of Ecbatana, and is, according to tradition, the site of the tombs of Biblical Mordecai and Esther.

*Echinades* (ē-kin′a-dēz). In ancient geography, a group of islands W of Acarnania in Greece, formed in and near the mouth of the Achelous River and now reunited, in part, to the mainland. According to Greek mythology, the islands were once naiads. These five naiads forgot to sacrifice to Artemis when they sacrificed to all the other rural deities at a festival. In her anger Artemis flooded the area where they were dancing, split it up into five parts and washed it into the sea where the land and the naiads became the islands known as the Echinades.

*Ecnomus* (ek′nō-mus). Hill near the modern town of Licata, on the S coast of Sicily. Here the Carthaginians defeated (311 B.C.) the Syracusan tyrant Agathocles. Near here the Roman fleet defeated (256 B.C.) the Carthaginians.

*Egypt* (ē′jipt). [Biblical name, *Mizraim;* Latin, *Aegyptus;* Arabic, *Misr.*] Country in NE Africa, famous for the great antiquity and former splendor of its civilization. It is bounded by the Mediterranean Sea on the N, and extends S, including the delta and the valley of the Nile River, to the second cataract of the Nile and the border of the Sudan. On the E it is bounded by Israel, the Gulf of Aqaba, and the Red Sea, and on the W by Libya. It includes the Sinai Peninsula, between the gulfs of Suez and Aqaba. The usual geographical divisions are the Nile valley region from Cairo south, called Upper Egypt, and the delta region, called Lower Egypt. To the ancient Greeks Egypt consisted of the delta and the land lying along the Nile, and was for this reason called, "The

fat, fāte, fär, fåll, åsk, fāre; net, mē, hėr; pin, pīne; not, nōte, möve, nôr; up, lūte, púll; oi, oil; ou out; (lightened) ẹlect, agǫny, ụnite;

Gift of the River." According to them, the regions to the west and the interior of Africa were Libya (of indefinite boundaries), and those to the east and south were Aethiopia. Trade between Egypt and Crete began at least as early as the 16th century B.C. and probably from much earlier times. The Egyptians called the Cretans *Keftiu,* and evidence of commerce between the Keftiu kings and the Egyptian rulers exists from the XVIIIth Dynasty.

A history of ancient Egypt for Greek consumption was compiled in the 3rd century B.C. by the priest Manetho, who listed the kings in 31 dynasties. The dynasties are grouped thus by Breasted: the Old Kingdom (c3400–c2475 B.C.), Dynasties I-VI; the Middle Kingdom (c2445-1580 B.C.), Dynasties IX-XVII; the New Kingdom or Empire (1580–1090 B.C.), Dynasties XVIII-XX. The First Dynasty was founded by Menes c3400 B.C. During the early dynasties Memphis was the leading city, and in the time of the IVth Dynasty occurred the building of the Pyramids (c2900–2800 B.C.). The construction of Lake Moeris and the labyrinth are assigned to the XIIth Dynasty. Thebes now became the center, and later the invasion of the Hyksos occurred (in the XVth Dynasty). After a period of confusion and obscurity Egypt was united under the great Theban XVIIIth Dynasty, and under this and the XIXth Dynasty reached its highest point in extent and in the grandeur of its monuments. Among the great sovereigns were Thutmose III, Seti I, and Rameses II. The "Pharaoh" of the Exodus has frequently been identified with Merneptal or Meneptah of the XIXth Dynasty, and the date stated approximately at c1300 B.C., but he is now dated at 1225–1215 B.C. With the next dynasty began the decline of the country's power. There were some revivals of power, and in the 7th and 6th centuries Greek settlements began, but in 525 B.C. Egypt was conquered by Cambyses, and this Persian dynasty ranks as the XXVIIth. From 406 B.C. native rulers again held power, but in 340 B.C. a short-lived Persian dynasty (the XXXIst and the last of Manetho) began; this was overthrown in 332 B.C. by Alexander the Great. After his death Egypt was ruled by his general Ptolemy and Ptolemy's successors down to the death of the famous Cleopatra (Cleopatra VII or VI) in 30 B.C., when Augustus seized it as the private province of the emperor.

(obscured) errạnt, ardẹnt, actọr; ch, chip; g, go; th, thin; ᴛн, then; y, you;
(variable) ḍ as d or j, ṣ as s or sh, ṭ as t or ch, ẓ as z or zh.

**Elam** (ē'lăm). [Also: **Susiana;** ancient Greek, **Elymaïs.**] Ancient country and empire E of the lower Tigris, S of Media, and N of the Persian Gulf. It is a region of fertile and picturesque mountains, valleys, and ravines, the only flat tract being on the shores of the Persian Gulf; and was in very high antiquity the seat of a mighty empire of which Susa was the capital. The oldest historical information about Elam is that it subjugated Babylonia in the period c2300–2076 B.C. The Elamite dynasty is identical with the Median of Berosus, which ruled over Babylonia, c2300–2076 B.C. Among these Elamite kings is also very probably to be counted Chedorlaomer (Kudur-Lagamaru) of Gen. xiv. The next historical notice is that Elam was subdued by Nebuchadnezzar I, king of Babylonia, c1130 B.C. From the 8th century B.C. on, Elam was connected with the rivalry between Assyria and Babylonia supporting the latter against the former. Elam was defeated by Sargon in 721 and 710 B.C., and by Sennacherib in several campaigns, especially in a decisive battle on the Tigris c691 B.C. In 645 B.C. Assurbanipal destroyed Susa. Soon after this catastrophe Elam is met with under the dominion of Theispes. In union with Media and Persia it helped to bring about the fall of Assyria and Babylonia. It shared thenceforth the fate of the other Assyrian provinces, and had no history of its own. The ancient Elamites were not Semites. This is ascertained by the names of their kings, which are alien to all of the Semitic dialects, and by their representations on the monuments, which exhibit a type widely different from the Semitic. The enumeration of Elam among the sons of Shem in Gen. x. 22 may perhaps be accounted for by the fact that the Elamite valley was early settled by the Semites, who predominated over the non-Semitic element of the population, and also by the fact that the Elamites had for more than two centuries the upper hand in Semitic Babylonia. The name Elymaïs was used either as an equivalent of Elam or for a part of it.

**Elea** (ē'lē-à). See **Velia.**

**Eleia** (ē-lī'a). See **Elis.**

**Eleusis** (ē-lö'sis). A little town about 14 miles W of Athens, in Attica, situated near the bay and opposite the island of Salamis. Eleusis *(Advent)* was one of the oldest of the parishes of Attica, the seat of a very ancient cult of Demeter, and of the famous Eleusinian mysteries. It was annexed to Athens in the 7th century B.C., but kept control of the mysteries, in the celebration of which the Athenians, as well as Greeks from all other states, annually came for initiation into and celebration of the rites. The observation of the mysteries of Demeter and Kore (Persephone) continued down to the end of the 4th century A.D. Politically, Eleusis played no role in the development of Greece, but its religious significance was of paramount importance. The most important monuments lay within the sacred enclosure at Eleusis, which consisted of a spacious terrace on the E slope of an acropolis, surrounded by a massive wall and towers. The earliest sanctuary antedated the 7th century B.C., and was reconstructed and enlarged in the 6th century B.C. by the Pisistratidae. In succeeding years it was further enlarged as the importance of the mysteries increased. During the Persian Wars it was burned, but was restored by Cimon and Pericles. Entrance to the sanctuary of the Great Goddesses (Demeter and Kore) was forbidden, on pain of death, to the uninitiated. Those who had been initiated, like the traveler Pausanias, never described the buildings within the wall, only ruins of which now remain. Before the sacred enclosure was a large paved court, constructed in Roman times, and nearby an ancient spring where pilgrims purified themselves. Also in the area was a large altar and a ditch where victims, sacrifices to the gods of the Underworld, were burned. A sacred way led to the sanctuary. On the right of the sacred way a grotto cut into the flank of the hill was the precinct of Pluto and represented the entrance to the Underworld by which Hades (Pluto) carried off Persephone. The sacred precinct was entered through two propylaea (of Roman construction) in succession, and its chief building was the Telesterion, where the rites of initiation took place, rites surrounded by a secrecy that was never entirely violated. The remains of the Telesterion date from the 6th century B.C., with additions made in the time of the Roman emperors, and replace much earlier buildings. The Telesterion was a huge, nearly square, roofed hall, on the four sides of which rows of seats, some of which were cut into the rock, were constructed for the *mystae* (initiated), who sat on them and observed the rites of initiation as they took place. The seats accommodated about 3000 spectators. The unique architecture of the Telesterion and its successive transformations, as well as remains of the entire precinct, were revealed by the excavations of the Archaeological Society of Athens and others, carried out at intervals since 1882.

*Elis* (ē'lis). [Also:*Eleia.*] In ancient geography, a country in the W part of the Peloponnesus, Greece, lying between Achaea on the N, Arcadia on the E, Messenia on the S, and the Ionian Sea on the W. It comprised three parts: Elis proper or Hollow Elis, Pisatis, and Triphylia. Olympia, the site of the Olympic Games and the temple of Olympian Zeus, is in Elis; Elis, Pisa (later known as Olympia), Pylus, Lepreum, Letrini, and Hyrmine were some of the cities of Elis. According to tradition, the people of Elis came into the Peloponnesus from Calydon and Aetolia. According to the *Iliad,* the Eleans sent 40 ships to accompany the Greek forces in the war against Troy.

Historically, the Eleans played their part in the Persian Wars. Later they reluctantly joined with Sparta (420 B.C.) in the invasion of Attica, but soon abandoned the alliance with their ancient enemy, which enmity had survived since Pisans of Elis aided the Messenians in their war with Sparta, and drove the Spartans (401–399 B.C.) out of the sacred precinct at Olympia. In 398 B.C. they submitted to Sparta and were compelled to allow the Spartans to take part in the Olympic Games, from which they had banned them. For a time they were unwilling allies of Philip II of Macedon, but after the death of Alexander they fought on the side of the Peloponnesians against Antipater and the Macedonians and were defeated with their allies.

*Elysian Fields* (ē-lizh'an). Name given to a region near the ancient town of Baiae (modern Baia), Italy, which is particularly fertile and delightful, and is, therefore, supposed to resemble the Elysium or Elysian Fields of Greek mythology.

*Emathia* (ē-mā'thi-a). An ancient name for Macedonia, or a region in Macedonia. The name was also sometimes applied to Thessaly and Pharsalia.

*Engyum* (en'ji-um) or *Enguium* (eng'gwi-um). In ancient geography, a city of Sicily, supposed to have been situated in the mountains N of Enna on a site near the modern town of Gangi. It possessed a celebrated temple of the Great Mother of the Gods.

*Enipeus* (ē-nī'pē-us). A river of Thessaly which flows into the Peneus (also sometimes called the Alpheus) River.

---

fat, fāte, fär, fåll, åsk, fāre; net, mē, hėr; pin, pīne; not, nōte, möve, nôr; up, lūte, pùll; oi, oil; ou out; (lightened) ēlect, agǫny, ūnite;

*Enna* (en′ạ) or *Henna* (hen′ạ). [Former name, *Castro Gio-vanni.*] City of Sicily, situated in a mountainous region in the center of the island. In ancient times, Enna was the seat of the cult of the goddess Demeter, whose temple was here; Enna, more specifically the nearby Lake of Pergusa, was supposed to be the location at which the rape of Perse-phone, Demeter's daughter, occurred. The city was called the navel of Sicily, because of its position in the center of the island. It belonged to the Carthaginians, and fell into the hands of the Romans in the First Punic War. It was a head-quarters of the slaves in the First Servile War, resisting the Roman armies for two years.

*Epeiros* (ancient, ẹ-pī′rọs; modern, ē′pē-rôs). See *Epirus.*

*Ephesus* (ef′ẹ-sus). In ancient geography, one of the 12 Ionian cities in Asia Minor, in Lydia, situated on the Caÿster River near its mouth, S of Smyrna. According to legend, it was founded by Ephesus, a son of the river-god Caÿster, and by Coresus. The first inhabitants were Leleges and Lydians, and Amazons dwelt nearby. Later, Androclus, a son of Co-drus, the legendary king of Athens, drove out the natives and settled there with Ionian colonists. They identified the nature-goddess who was worshiped there from very ancient times with their Artemis, and allowed the natives who dwelt near the ancient temple to remain, and exchanged oaths of friendship with them. Androclus died in battle and was buried at Ephesus. Through its trade and its importance as a port, the city flourished mightily. In later times the tyrant of Ephesus married a daughter of Alyattes, king of Lydia and father of Croesus, and the city became part of the kingdom of Croesus when he succeeded his father. Subsequently the city fell to the Persians, but continued to thrive. Alexander the Great established (334 B.C.) a democratic constitution there. While he was in the city the artist Apelles painted a portrait of him, holding the lightning in his hands, that was set up in the temple of Artemis. In 133 B.C. Ephesus was taken by the Romans but still remained great and powerful. Through ancient times Ephesus, the city of Artemis, was celebrated for its temple of Artemis, and as a great commer-cial city whose wealth was proverbial. It was sacked by the Goths (262 A.D.), the temple was destroyed, the harbor silted up and destroyed the importance of the city as a port, and small villages and ruins covered the site. Among its ruins are a theater, an odeum, a stadium, and the temple of Artemis. The great theater is mentioned in Acts, xix. 23. It is Greek in plan, with Roman modifications. The *cavea* (auditorium), 495 feet in diameter, has two precinctions (landings between tiers of seats), with 11 *cunei* (blocks of seats) in the two lower ranges, and 22 in the highest, which is skirted by a colonnaded gallery. The orchestra is 110 feet in diameter, and the proscenium 22 feet wide. The odeum (a type of small theater) is ascribed to the 2nd century A.D. In plan it is a half-circle 153 feet in diameter. There is one precinction, with five cunei below and ten above it, and a rich Corinthian gallery around the top. The orchestra is 30 feet in diameter; the stage has five doors and Corinthian columns. The stadium, ascribed to the time of Augustus, is 850 feet long and 200 feet wide. The N side and semicircular E end are supported on vaulted substructions, the S side on the rock of the hillside. A double colonnade was carried along its entire length, and communicated with the upper gallery of the stadium by a series of stairways. The temple of Artemis (Diana of the Ephesians) was a famous and ancient sanctuary celebrated as one of the Seven Wonders of the Ancient World. It was burned in the 4th century B.C. and rebuilt. The temple was Ionic, dipteral, octastyle, with 21 columns on the flanks, and measured 164 by 342 feet. The base-diameter of the columns was 6 feet, their height 55 feet. The base-drums of 36 columns of the front and rear were beautifully sculptured with figures in relief. Croesus dedicated the golden heifers at the temple, and gave most of the columns, on the bases of which fragments of the words "Dedicated by Croesus," can be seen. The cella had interior ranges of columns, Ionic in the lower tier, Corinthian above. Xenophon, author of the *Anabasis,* deposited ransom money received for captives taken during the retreat of the 10,000 in the temple at Ephesus. The money was subsequently restored to him, and he used it to build (c370 B.C.) a small replica of the temple of Artemis at Ephesus at Scillus, in Elis, and for an annual festival of the goddess.

*Epidaurum* (ep-i-dô′rum). In ancient geography, a maritime town in Illyricum. It was destroyed sometime after the reign of Justinian, and was replaced by Ragusa, now Dubrovnik, Yugoslavia. It was a Roman colony.

*Epidaurus* (ep-i-dô′rus). Ancient town on the E coast of the

Peloponnesus, in the district called Argolis. The land was especially sacred to Asclepius, for the Epidaurians said that when Phlegyas, the Lapith king, came to the Peloponnesus to spy out the land and learn whether its people were warlike, he brought his daughter Coronis with him, unaware that she was about to bear Apollo's child. When her child, Asclepius, was born, she exposed him on a mountain, formerly called Myrtium but subsequently named Nipple. A she-goat pastured on the mountain slopes nursed him, and the watch-dog of the flock stood guard over him. The shepherd of the flock remarked that one she-goat and the watch-dog were missing. He looked about for them and found them behind a bush, guarding an infant. As he approached to take up the infant, lightning flashed from the child's body. The shepherd concluded that it was a divine child and so left it to divine protection. From the beginning Asclepius was a god, and his fame as a healer spread throughout the land. The most famous of his sanctuaries had their origin in Epidaurus. Throughout the flourishing period of Greek history Epidaurus was an independent state, possessing a small territory, bounded on the W by Argeia, on the N by Corinthia, on the S by Troezenia, and on the E by the Saronic Gulf. It was the most celebrated seat of the ancient cult of Asclepius. The sanctuary occupied a valley among hills, at some distance from the city. The sacred grove was enclosed and contained a temple of Asclepius, in which lived tame sacred serpents, the architecturally important *tholos* (round building) of Polyclitus, extensive porticoes which served as hospitals to the sick who came to seek the aid of the god and his priests, and many votive offerings. As at Delos, no birth or death could take place in the sacred enclosure, and all offerings must be consumed within it. In the temple was an ivory and gold image of the god, representing him seated, holding a staff in one hand, and the other hand held above the head of a serpent. A dog stretched out at the side of the image. Originally, suppliants at the temple slept in the open air, but in the time of the Romans shelters were built for them. On slabs about the precinct were inscribed the names of the people who had been cured by Asclepius and the diseases from which he had freed them. Pausanias tells of a very old slab on which it was recorded that Hippolytus dedicated 20 horses to the god, because Asclepius had raised

(obscured) errant, ardent, actor; ch, chip; g, go; th, thin; ᴛʜ, then; y, you;
(variable) ḍ as d or j, ş as s or sh, ṭ as t or ch, ẓ as z or zh.

him from the dead. Outside of the sacred enclosure were the stadium, a gymnasium, propylaea, and other buildings, the arrangements for the collection and distribution of water being especially noteworthy. The theater at Epidaurus built probably by Polyclitus the Younger, was, and still is, unrivaled in its acoustical perfection. Extensive excavations conducted by the Archaeological Society of Athens (1881, *et seq.*) have greatly added to our knowledge of the sanctuary of Epidaurus.

*Epidaurus Limera* (lī-mē′rạ). In ancient geography, a town on the E coast of Laconia, Greece, about 22 miles NW of Cape Malea. According to tradition, some Epidaurians who were on their way to Cos, touched here and were warned by dreams to remain here. A snake they were bringing from Epidaurus escaped from their ship and disappeared into the ground near the shore. This event confirmed the dreams which instructed the Epidaurians to remain. On the spot where the snake disappeared into the ground they built altars of Asclepius and planted olive trees around them, and founded a city.

*Epirus* or *Epeiros* (ẹ-pī′rus). In ancient geography, the part of N Greece lying between Illyria on the N, Macedonia and Thessaly on the E, Aetolia, Acarnania, and the Ambracian Gulf on the S, and the Ionian Sea on the W (to the Acroceraunian promontory). In earlier times the name was given to the entire W coast S to the Corinthian Gulf. The kingdom of Epirus was at its height under Pyrrhus (295–272 B.C.). It was ravaged by Aemilius Paulus in 167 B.C., and was a part of the Roman Empire from 146 B.C. to 1204 A.D. In 1961 the discovery and excavation of the remains of a necromanteion (oracle of the dead) near the Acheron River in Epirus was reported. Dating from the 3rd century B.C., the structure, about 200 feet long and 145 feet wide, is thought to have been built on the site of an earlier oracle, possibly the one described by Homer as the "gateway to the underworld." The necromanteion consisted of a long corridor, in which offerings were burnt, leading to the inner sanctuary. Enclosed in an 11-foot-thick stone wall, which remains to the height of 10 feet, the inner sanctuary had six square rooms, probably used for storing food offerings, flanking the Hall of Hades, where the audiences took place. Directly beneath the Hall of Hades, and of the same dimensions, was

fat, fāte, fär, fâll, ȧsk, fāre; net, mē, hėr; pin, pīne; not, nōte, möve, nôr; up, lūte, pu̇ll; oi, oil; ou out; (lightened) ẹlect, agǫny, ūnite;

an underground chamber, its curved ceiling supported on arches; it is speculated that this room was used in some way by the priests during the ceremony of talking with the dead. Finds in the ruins include ceremonial vessels, statuettes of Persephone and Cerberus, and remains of honey in jars in the storage rooms. The N part of Epirus is now in Albania, the remainder in Greece.

*Epium* (ē'pi-um). See *Aepy.*

*Ercta* (ėrk'tạ) or *Ercte* (ėrk'tē). [Modern name, *Monte Pellegrino.*] Isolated mountain peak just N of Panormus (Palermo), in Sicily, overlooking the city and harbor. It was occupied by Hamilcar in the First Punic War. Elevation, about 1900 feet.

*Eretria* (e-rē'tri-ạ). In ancient geography, a city on the island of Euboea, Greece, about 29 miles N of Athens. It was a rival of Chalcis, was destroyed (490 B.C.) by the Persians, and was afterward rebuilt. An ancient theater has been excavated on its site by the American School at Athens. The *cavea* (auditorium) is supported on an artificial embankment. It was divided by radial stairways into 11 *cunei* (blocks of seats), and is 266 feet in diameter. The orchestra, 81½ feet in diameter, presents a highly important feature, here first recognized, in an underground passage leading from its center to the interior of the stage structure.

*Erginus* (er-jī'nus). A river of Thrace.

*Eridanus* (ē-rid'ạ-nus). A large mythical river in northern Europe, later identified with the Rhone, or, usually, with the Po. According to legend, it has its source in the Elysian Fields of the Underworld. Its waters still steam from receiving blazing Phaëthon, a youth who fell into them when he failed successfully to drive the chariot of Helius across the sky and was felled by a thunderbolt of Zeus to save the world from burning up. Along its banks the Heliades, sisters of Phaëthon, were turned into poplar trees as they grieved for their fallen brother.                                    .

*Erymanthus* (er-i-man'thus). [Also: *Olonos.*] Mountain peak on the border of Arcadia and Achaea, Greece. It was named after a son of Apollo who was blinded by Aphrodite because he saw the goddess bathing. It was the haunt of the Erymanthian Boar. The mountain was sacred to Artemis.

*Erythrae* (er'i-thrē). In ancient geography, an Ionian city in Asia Minor, situated opposite the island of Chios. According to legend, it was founded by Erythrus, son of Rhadamanthys of Crete, and named for him. Lycians and Carians joined the Cretan settlers, and soon their city was further enlarged by the arrival of some Pamphylians who had wandered there with Calchas the seer after the fall of Troy. Some time later Cleopus, son of Codrus, the legendary king of Athens, attacked the city with a band of Euboean and Boeotian colonists and secured control of it. There was a famous sanctuary of Heracles at Erythrae. According to some accounts, an image of Heracles, riding on a wooden raft, floated to a cape midway between Erythrae and Chios. The men of both places were most anxious to obtain the image, and strove mightily to pull it ashore but to no avail; they couldn't move it. A blind fisherman, one Phormio, had a vision that if the women of Erythrae would cut off their hair and make a rope of it the raft bearing the image could be pulled ashore. The women of Erythrae refused to cut off their hair, but the Thracian women who were in the city, both free and slave, volunteered to give their hair. The rope was made and the raft was then easily drawn ashore. A sanctuary of Heracles was raised in which the image was set, but only Thracian women were admitted to it. The rope of hair was also put in the sanctuary, and, it is said, that Phormio recovered his sight. Erythrae was called "The Crimson City" because of the purple dye obtained there by Tyrian traders.

*Erythraean Sea* (er-i-thrē′an). [Latin, *Mare Erythraeum,* also *Mare Rubrum,* meaning "Red Sea."] In ancient geography, a name given to the Arabian Sea, or to the Indian Ocean including the Red Sea and Persian Gulf.

*Eryx* (e′riks). A mountain on the NW coast of Sicily.

*Eryx.* [Modern name, *Erice;* formerly, *Monte San Giuliano.*] Town on the island of Sicily, situated on a mountain 2465 feet high, overlooking the Tyrrhenian Sea. It was colonized by Phoenicians, later occupied by Greeks, captured (278 B.C.) by Pyrrhus, and was the base of the Carthaginian army under Hamilcar Barca in the First Punic War. The central seat of the cult of the goddess Venus (Greek, Aphrodite), it had a temple of which the ruins may still be seen. Fortification walls, some having Phoenician inscriptions, are also preserved.

*Esquiline Hill* (es′kwi-līn, -lin). [Latin, *Mons Esquilinus.*] Central

hill of the three which form the E side of the group of Seven
Hills of ancient Rome. It lies between the Viminal on the N
and the Caelian on the S, and E of the Palatine. It is divided
from E to W by a depression. On the part to the N, called
the Mons Cespius, stands the Church of Santa Maria Maggiore; on that to the S, the Mons Oppius, rise the Church
of San Pietro in Vincoli and the Baths of Titus. Here, too,
were the houses of Horace, Vergil, and Propertius. Between
the Esquiline and the Palatine stands the Flavian Amphitheater ("Colosseum").

*Ethiopia* (ē-thi-ō′pi-ạ). [Also: *Aethiopia, Axumite Kingdom*.] In
ancient geography, a country S of Egypt, corresponding to
the kingdom of Meroe, from the neighborhood of Khartoum
N to Egypt. In a more extended sense it comprised Nubia,
the N part of modern Ethiopia, Sennar, and Kordofan. It was
closely connected with Egypt. Conquered by Egyptian kings
of the XIIth Dynasty, lost in the period of the Hyksos, and
reconquered under the XVIIIth Dynasty, it remained with
Egypt until after the XXth Dynasty. An Ethiopian founded
the XXVth Egyptian Dynasty. The Greeks visited the country in the middle 7th century B.C. and gradually extended
their relations with the inhabitants. In the 1st century A.D.
a powerful Ethiopian state, with Axum as its capital, arose
and remained powerful until far into the Byzantine era.

*Etna* (et′nạ). [Italian, *Monte Etna*, (Sicilian) *Mongibello*.] Chief
mountain in Sicily, and the highest volcano in Europe, situated in the E part of the island. Elevation, about 10,758 feet.

*Etruria* (ē-trö′ri-ạ). In ancient geography, a division of Italy
which extended along the Mediterranean, and was separated from Umbria, the Sabine territory, and Latium by the
Tiber, and from Liguria by the Apennines. It nearly corresponds to modern Tuscany. It contained a confederation of
12 cities. The Etruscans developed as a great naval power,
influential in N and C Italy, and had possessions on the Po
and in Campania. Etruscan kings ruled at an early time at
Rome (probably until c500 B.C.). The Etruscans were defeated by Syracuse in a naval battle in 474 B.C., and suffered
from the invasion of the Gauls c400 B.C. Veii was lost to
Rome in 396 B.C. Defeat by Rome at the Vadimonian Lake
in 283 B.C. was followed by the fall of Tarquinii and the
other Etrurian cities.

*Euboea* (ū-bē′ạ). [Modern Greek, *Evvoia;* Italian, *Negroponte;*

Turkish, *Egripo;* sometimes in English, *Negropont.*] Largest island belonging to Greece, in the Aegean Sea. It lies E of Phocis, Boeotia, and Attica, from which it is separated by the strait of Euripus. It is traversed by mountains, Delphi reaching the height of 5725 feet. The chief towns in ancient times were Chalcis and Eretria. It was subdued by Athens after the Persian wars. Length, about 98 miles; greatest width, about 30 miles.

*Euboea.* In ancient geography, a Greek city of Sicily, situated on the coast N of Syracuse. The city was abandoned after most of its inhabitants were moved to Syracuse by the tyrant Gelon (485 B.C.), and its exact location is now uncertain.

*Euganean Hills* (ū-gā'nē-an). [Italian, *Colli Euganei.*] Chain of volcanic hills in NE Italy, SW of Padua. Highest point, 1800 feet.

*Euphrates* (ū-frā'tēz). [Arabic, *Al Furat;* Armenian, *Yeprad;* Assyrian, *Purattu;* Hebrew, *Perath;* Turkish, *Frat;* Old Persian, *Ufrates.*] Great Mesopotamian river which has its origin in the Armenian mountains in NE Turkey. It is formed from the East Euphrates (Murad-Su), which rises NE of Erzurum, and a branch rising NW of Lake Van. The united river then makes a wide circuit W, breaks through the mountain chain of the Taurus, enters the terrace region at Birecik, and turns in a meandering course toward the Tigris. In the neighborhood of Baghdad these two rivers approach one another, and there the Babylonian canal system begins. In its lower course, below the site of Babylon, the Euphrates has changed its bed, shifting more and more westward. According to notices in classical authors, confirmed by the inscriptions, it came in ancient times nearer Sippara (Sepharvaim, modern Abu-Habba) and Erech (modern Warka) than now; and it did not empty into the sea, united with the Tigris, through the Shatt el-Arab, as at present. As late as the time of Sennacherib (705–681 B.C.) and his successors, the twin rivers flowed separately into the Persian Gulf, which extended then at least as far as the ancient city of Eridu, known to have been a seaport. Babylon has been rightly termed "the gift of Euphrates and Tigris." The soil is formed from the alluvial deposits of these rivers, and this formation still continues. During the winter months the Euphrates has but little water in its bed; but in the spring, and especially toward the summer solstice, it swells by the melting of the snow of the mountains, which often causes disastrous floods.

*Euripus* (ū-rī′pus) or *Euripos* (-pos.). Narrowest portion of the channel between the island of Euboea and the mainland of Greece. It was near here, at Aulis, that Agamemnon's fleet en route to Troy was stormbound and Iphigenia was sacrificed. The strait is remarkable for the force of its current and its frequent changes of direction in response to the tides. Its width at the narrowest part (opposite Chalcis) is about 120 feet.

*Europus* (ū-rọ̄′pus). Name of a city in Macedonia, in honor of which several cities founded by the Seleucids in Asia were named. (JJ)

*Europus (Dura)*, often called *Dura-Europus.* A town founded c300 B.C., probably by Seleucus I, on the right bank of the middle Euphrates, as a military colony. It became an agricultural market and district administrative center of local importance, prospered, and was heavily fortified, to be held in turn by the Parthians and the Romans, and taken by siege and destroyed by the Sassanian king Sapor c256 A.D. Identified in 1921, it was excavated by the Belgian scholar Franz Cumont in 1922–23 and by a Yale University expedition, 1928–1937. The remarkable fortifications belong probably to the second century B.C. The planning is in regular rectangular blocks, entire blocks being devoted to temples, market, or private houses. The Temple of the Palmyrene Gods, built into a corner of the fortification walls, preserved mural paintings of extraordinary interest. In the dryness of the soil, wood, leather, wool, felt, paper, cordage, and other substances usually considered perishable are preserved, and Dura-Europus has yielded important and unique documents on parchment, vellum, and papyrus, including contracts and legal codes in Greek and the military records of the 3rd century A.D. Roman garrison, in Latin. Dura-Europus has also yielded hundreds of inscriptions in Greek, Latin, and dialects of Semitic, of which a gratifyingly large number contain exact dates; a horoscope scratched on a house wall, with other evidence, made possible the reconstruction of the *enneadecateris* or nineteen-year lunisolar calendar cycle adopted by the Seleucids and widely employed in Asia. The nomenclature of the parchments, papyri, and inscriptions indicates a mixed population descended from the

Macedonian and Greek troops of the garrison and the native community. Dura-Europus has also provided a very early Christian chapel, with wall paintings illustrating scenes from the New Testament, an unprecedented synagogue with wall paintings from the Old Testament, a shrine of the soldiers' god Mithras, and many other places of cult. The reconstruction of the events of the final siege by Sapor, not recorded in the literary sources, is a masterwork of archaeological exploration and deduction. (JJ)

**Eurotas** (ū-rō′tạs). [Modern name, *Iri, Iris.*] In ancient geography, a river in Laconia, Greece, flowing into the Mediterranean about 25 miles SE of Sparta.

**Eurymedon** (ū-rim′ẹ-don). [Modern Turkish name, *Köprü,* formerly also *Capri-Su.*] In ancient geography, a river in Pisidia and Pamphylia, Asia Minor, flowing from the Taurus Mountains generally S into the Mediterranean about 25 miles E of what is now Antalya, Turkey. Near its mouth, in 466 or 465 B.C., the Greeks under the Athenian general Cimon defeated the Persian fleet and army.

**Euxine** (ūk′sīn) *Sea.* The Black Sea, in Latin, *Pontus Euxinus.* Inland sea between SE Europe and W Asia, bordered on the N and E by Scythia, on the S by Cappadocia, Paphlagonia, and Bithynia, and on the W by Thrace, communicating with the Mediterranean by the Bosporus, the Propontis (Sea of Marmora), and the Hellespont (Dardanelles). The word means "hospitable, friendly to strangers." It had also been called the Axine ("unfriendly"), presumably in reference to the hostile tribes living on its shores, or to its frequent savage storms; but this may have resulted from the operation of folk etymology on a non-Greek term. A late writer says that it was Heracles who changed the name, from Axine to Euxine, because he was hospitably received by the tribes who dwelt there. According to legend, the voyage of the Argonauts (13th century B.C.?) was the first Greek exploration of the Euxine. Scholars, seeking for the Trojan War a more cogent issue than the abduction of Helen, have suggested that the war was fought to end Troy's control and taxation of commercial traffic between the Euxine and the Aegean via the Hellespont. Between 800 and 600 B.C. Ionian Greeks explored the entire coastline and established numerous colonies. In the 6th and 4th centuries B.C. the Crimea, under Scythian domination, produced surplus wheat which was shipped in substantial quantities to the Aegean, particularly to Athens. In Roman times it was still regarded as frontier country; as a punishment only slightly preferable to death, Ovid was ordered to exile at Tomis, modern Constanza. The establishment at Constantinople of the eastern capital of the Roman empire intensified commerce throughout the lands bordering the Euxine, accelerating the advance of civilization and urbanization. Length, about 740 miles; greatest width, about 390 miles; estimated area, 168,500 square miles. (JJ)

*Evenus* (ē-vē′nus). [Modern name, *Fidaris, Fidhari.*] In ancient geography, a river in Aetolia, Greece, flowing into the Gulf of Patras (or Calydon) about seven miles SE of what is now Missolonghi.

*Evripos* (ev′rē-pôs). See *Euripus* and *Chalcis.*

*Faesulae* (fē′sū-lē). [Modern name, *Fiesole.*] An ancient Etruscan town in C Italy, about three miles NE of Florence. It became an ally of Rome, to which it adhered during the campaigns of Hannibal. Stilicho defeated an army of Gothic invaders here in 406 A.D. Beautifully located on a hill above Florence, it is one of the oldest bishoprics in Tuscany, rich in monuments from ancient times, the Middle Ages, and the Renaissance period. It has Etruscan and Roman remains, among them baths and an amphitheater.

*Falerii* (fạ-lir′i-ī). [Also: *Falerium Vetus;* modern name, *Cività Castellana.*] Town in Latium, about 27 miles N of Rome. The town belonged to the Etruscan Confederation and was destroyed (241 B.C.) by the Romans.

*Falerium Novum.* Town in Latium, three miles NW of Falerium Vetus (Falerii), established by the Romans c240 B.C., where the inhabitants of Falerium Vetus were resettled after the destruction of their city by the Romans in 241 B.C. It has interesting and well-preserved fortifications in ashlar tufa, with arched gates ("Porta di Giove" and "Porta del Bove"), and remains of a theater and amphitheater. In medieval times, the inhabitants abandoned Falerium Novum and moved back to Falerium Vetus, now Città Castellana. (JJ)

*Falernus Ager* (fạ-lêr'nus ā'jèr). In ancient geography, a fertile territory in Campania, Italy, situated N of the Volturnus, from 20 to 25 miles N of Naples. It was celebrated for its wines.

*Famagusta* (fä-mä-gös'tä). [Also: *Famagosta;* Latin, *Fama Augusta.*] See *Arsinoë,* city of Cyprus.

*Fanum Fortunae* (fā'num fôr-tū'nē). [Modern name, *Fano.*] In ancient geography, a town of C Italy, situated on the Adriatic Sea near the mouth of the Metaurus River. There was a temple of Fortune there, from which the town took its name. There was also a temple of Jupiter and one of Augustus. The town was held by Julius Caesar in 49 B.C.; Augustus later sent a colony there and built a wall around the town. The architect Vitruvius describes a basilica which he said was built at Fanum from his designs. Parts of the wall and a triumphal arch dedicated to Augustus remain.

*Ferentinum* (fe-ren-tī'num). [Modern name, *Ferentino.*] In ancient geography, an important town of the Hernici, situated about 48 miles SE of Rome. It was captured by the Romans in 364 B.C., and its inhabitants were given the citizenship after 195 B.C. The town was located on a hill and was strongly fortified. The powerful walls, polygonal masonry repaired in ashlar, survive in almost their entire extent, as do several gates, including the famous Porta Sanguinaria, or Bloody Gate, an arched postern gate, and an interesting corbelled sally port.

*Ferentum* (fe-ren'tum). [Modern name, *Ferento.*] Ruined city in C Italy, about 5½ miles N of Viterbo. It contains extensive Etruscan, Roman, and medieval remains which have been excavated. The ancient theater is of particular interest. Ferentum was the birthplace of the emperor Otho.

*Fescennia* (fe-sen'i-ạ). A Tuscan city on the Tiber.

*Fidenae* (fi-dē'nē). In ancient geography, a town of the Sabines in Latium, situated on the Tiber River about five miles NE of Rome.

*Fidentia* (fī-den'shi-ạ, -shạ). [Modern name, *Fidenza;* formerly *Borgo San Donnino.*] In ancient geography, a town on the Via Aemilia, in N Italy, about 14 miles NW of the city of Parma. It was the site of a victory of Metellus Pius over Carbo, the leader of the Marian faction, in 82 B.C.

***Firmum*** (fėr'mum). [Modern name, ***Fermo.***] In ancient geography, a town of C Italy, situated on a hill overlooking the Adriatic Sea. It was founded as a Roman colony, 264 B.C. Remains of a Roman amphitheater and of the ancient walls may be seen.

***Florence*** (flor'ents). [Latin, ***Florentia;*** Italian, ***Fiorenza,*** now ***Firenze.***] Ancient town in Tuscany, on the banks of the river Arnus (Arno), probably established in the 1st century B.C. as a Roman colony, traces of whose checkerboard plan and a few streets have survived. In the Middle Ages and Renaissance it was a center of intense creative activity. Driven by Dante, Boccaccio, Petrarch, Macchiavelli, and Galileo, and the artists Cimabue, Giotto, the della Robbias, Donatello, Botticelli, da Vinci, Michelangelo, Raphael, Cellini, and their hardly less distinguished pupils, Florence became the intellectual capital of Italy and the artistic capital of Europe. The Galleria degli Uffizi contains, in addition to splendid Florentine paintings, a major collection of Greek and Roman sculptures, and the archaeological museum holds important Etruscan, Greek, and Roman ceramics, bronzes, and some sculptures. (JJ)

***Formiae*** (fôr'mi-ē). [Modern name, ***Formia;*** formerly ***Mola di Gaeta.***] Town in Latium, C Italy, situated on the Gulf of Caieta, about 44 miles NW of Neapolis (Naples). An ancient town of the Volsci, on the Appian Way, it became a Roman city with limited rights of citizenship in 322 B.C., and with full rights in 188 B.C. It was a summer resort of rich Romans from the time of the late republic; Cicero had a villa here. Remains of ancient Roman structures are still standing.

***Frigidus*** (frij'i-dus). [Also: ***Frigidus Fluvius.***] In ancient geography, a small river in what is now NW Yugoslavia: noted for its coldness. In its valley Theodosius defeated the forces of Eugenius and Arbogast in 394 A.D.

***Frusino*** (frö'sē-nō). [Modern name, ***Frosinone.***] In ancient geography, a town of the Hernici, in C Italy, about 53 miles SE of Rome. Conquered by the Romans in 304 B.C., it later became a colony of Rome.

***Fundi*** (fun'dī). [Modern name, ***Fondi.***] In ancient geography, a town of the Volsci, situated on the Appian Way, near the Gulf of Tarracina between Rome and Naples, Italy. Because the inhabitants granted the Romans safe passage through their territory they were given limited citizenship by the

Romans (c388 B.C.). In 188 B.C. they received full citizenship. Parts of the ancient walls and gates remain.

*Furculae Caudinae* (fér'kŭ-lē kô-dī'nē). Latin name of the *Caudine Forks*.

# —G—

*Gabii* (gā'bi-ī). In ancient geography, a city in Latium, Italy, situated about halfway between Rome and Praeneste at the foot of the Alban Hills; one of the oldest of the cities belonging to the Latin federation. It was a nameless site at the time when Aeneas visited his father in the Underworld. According to Roman legend it was conquered by Tarquinius Superbus in the following manner: His youngest son, Sextus, presented himself before Gabii in the guise of a fugitive from his father's tyranny, and was received by the Gabines as their leader, whereupon Sextus sent to Rome for further instructions. The messenger found Tarquin in his garden. Without saying a word, the king knocked off the heads of the tallest poppies. The messenger returned to Sextus, who saw the meaning of the parable, and cut off the heads of the chief men of Gabii, which was then surrendered to Tarquin. The most notable remains of antiquity is the barnlike shell of a temple cella in the local tufa, dating most plausibly from the 2nd century B.C., perhaps of the temple of Juno of Gabii. Gabine tufa, *lapis Gabinus,* was quarried in substantial quantities for new construction at Rome.

*Gadara* (gad'a̱-ra̱). In ancient geography, a city of the Decapolis in Syria, situated about seven miles SE of the Sea of Galilee, probably the capital of Peraea; the modern village of Umm Qeis (Um Keis). It was rebuilt by Pompey. There are remains of a large Roman theater, not excavated in a hill but entirely built up of masonry on vaulted substructions and in good preservation, and of a smaller theater on the same site. Orthography has led the place to be associated with the parable of the Gadarene swine (the herd of swine into which demons were cast from two men and which then perished. Matt. viii. 28; Mark, v. 1; Luke, viii. 26). The textual variants (Gadarenes, Gerasenes, Gergesenes) in the several books have led some to believe that the miracle occurred either at Gadara or at Gerasa (modern Jerash, in Jordan), but modern scholarship identifies the scene with Kersa, a town on the E shore of the Sea of Galilee on the Wadi Samak, where the physical setting is more in consonance with the Biblical description than it is at either Gadara or Gerasa.

*Gades* (gā'dēz). [Phoenician, *Gadir;* Greek, *Gadeira* or *Gadira.*] In ancient geography, the remotest colony of the Phoenicians in the west. It was founded c1100 B.C. beyond Gibraltar at the NW extremity of an island, about 12 miles long, which lies off the W coast of Spain, and occupied almost exactly the same site as the modern city of Cádiz. It was the headquarters of the western commerce of the Phoenicians, and contained various temples of the Phoenician gods. The Carthaginians used Gades as a base for their conquest of Spain. It fell to the Romans in 206 B.C.

*Gaeta* (gä-ē'tä). See *Caieta.*

*Gaeta, Gulf of.* See *Caieta, Gulf of.*

*Gaetulia* (jē-tū'li-a̧). In ancient geography, the land of the Gaetuli, mentioned in the *Aeneid* as a warlike tribe that threatened Dido and Carthage. It was a region in N Africa, S of Mauretania and Numidia, extending from the land of the Garamantes W to the Atlantic. The Gaetulians were subjected to Roman rule about the time of Christ.

*Galatia* (ga̧-lā'sha̧). In ancient geography, a division of Asia Minor, lying between Bithynia and Paphlagonia on the N, Pontus on the E, Cappadocia and Lycaonia on the S, and Phrygia on the W; originally a part of Phrygia and Cappadocia. It was conquered and settled by a Celtic people which crossed the Hellespont in 278 B.C. It was made a Roman province in 25 B.C. Theodosius subdivided it into Galatia Prima and Galatia Secunda. See also under *Gaul.*

*Gallipoli Peninsula* (gal-ip'ō̧-lē). Modern name of the ancient Chersonesus Thracica, a long tongue of land between the Hellespont and the Gulf of Saros.

*Ganges* (gan'jēz). [Hindi, *Ganga;* also, in its upper course, *Bhagirathi.*] It rises (under the name of the Bhagirathi) in the Himalyas, near the Tibetan border, and is called the Ganges after its junction with the Alakanada. In its upper course it flows through gorges and mountain valleys, emerg-

(obscured) errant, ardent, actor; ch, chip; g, go; th, thin; ᴛн, then; y, you; (variable) ḑ as d or j, ş as s or sh, ţ as t or ch, z̧ as z or zh.

ing into its extensive plain at Hardwar. It flows SE across the largest and most densely peopled plain of India, finally energing upon its great delta of 17,000 square miles where the main stream now enters the Meghna estuary of the Bay of Bengal. At various times it has followed numerous different courses in the delta region, which is traversed by many branching distributaries. Its chief tributaries are the Jumna, Ramganga, Gumti, Gogra, Gandak, Kosi, Atrai, Son, and Jamuna (the main stream of the Brahmaputra). The length of the main stream is 1557 miles. It was formerly navigable from Hardwar, and from Allahabad for larger vessels. It is no longer navigable because of the large amounts of water taken out for irrigation. On it are situated Calcutta, Patna, and many holy places, such as Benares, Allahabad, Hardwar, and Gangotri.

*Garganus* (gär-gā'nus). A mountain in Apulia. The region, a mountainous peninsula projecting into the Adriatic Sea, was later known as Monte Gargano; the highest point is Monte Calvo (3460 feet).

*Gargaron* (gär'ga̱-ron), *Mount.* [Also: *Mount Gargarus.*] In ancient geography, the highest summit of Mount Ida, Mysia, in what is now NW Turkey.

*Gate of Italy* (it'a̱-li). Gorge in the Italian Tyrol, in the valley of the Adige River near Rovereto, N Italy.

*Gaugamela* (gô-ga̱-mē'la̱). In ancient geography, a place in Assyria, near the modern Mosul, the scene of Alexander's victory (331 B.C.) over Darius III of Persia (called the battle of Arbela).

*Gaul* (gôl). [French, *Gaule;* German, *Gallien;* Italian, Latin, and Portuguese, *Gallia;* Spanish, *Galia.*] In ancient geography, the country of the Gauls; in an inexact use, France. It was divided into Cisalpine Gaul and Transalpine Gaul, and is often taken as equivalent to Transalpine Gaul. The name Galatia was also sometimes used, specifically Celtic or Roman Galatia. In the later Roman Empire Gaul comprised the dioceses of Spain, Gaul, and Britain, and corresponded to Spain, Portugal, a small strip of Morocco, France, Belgium, Switzerland, the Netherlands and Germany to the Rhine, England, Wales, and the S part of Scotland.

*Gaul, Cisalpine.* [Latin, *Gallia Cisalpina, Gallia Citerior.*] In ancient history, that part of Gaul lying on the S side of the Alps. It extended from the Alps S and E. A Roman colony

fat, fāte, fär, fåll, a̱sk, fåre; net, mē, hėr; pin, pīne; not, nōte, mӧve, nôr; up, lūte, pu̇ll; oi, oil; ou out; (lightened) e̱lect, ago̱ny, u̱nite;

was founded (282 B.C.) at Sena Gallica. Part of the country was reduced between the First and Second Punic Wars, Mediolanum (Milan) and Comum (Como) being captured, and the conquest was completed in 201–191 B.C. It was made a Roman province, and was incorporated (42 B.C.) with Italy.

*Gaul, Cispadane.* [Latin, *Gallia Cispadana.*] In ancient geography, the part of Cisalpine Gaul S of the Padus (Po) River.

*Gaul, Transalpine.* [Latin, *Gallia Transalpina.*] In ancient geography, that part of Gaul which lay beyond the Alps (that is, N and NW of the Alps from Rome). It comprised in the Roman period Narbonensis, Aquitania, Lugdunensis, and Belgica. Its ancient inhabitants were Gauls, Iberians, and Germans. Many remains of early inhabitants have been discovered, especially in the center of Gaul (Auvergne, and elsewhere). The Gallic antiquities are especially numerous in the N (Brittany). Some Greek colonies were planted in early times in the S. The Roman settlements were made first in the SE in the end of the 2nd century B.C. Gaul was thoroughly conquered (58–51 B.C.) by Julius Caesar. Augustus divided it into four provinces.

*Gaul, Transpadane.* [Latin, *Gallia Transpadana.*] In ancient geography, the part of Cisalpine Gaul N of the Padus (Po) River.

*Gaurus* (gô′rus). [Modern name, *Monte Barbaro*] In ancient geography, a mountain in Italy, about seven miles W of Neapolis (Naples). Here, c342 B.C., the Romans under Valerius Corvus defeated the Samnites.

*Gaza* (gä′za). [Also: *Ghazze, Ghazzeh.*] Seaport and important trading place in SW Palestine, near the Mediterranean coast, about 50 miles SW of Jerusalem: one of the five chief cities of the ancient Philistines. The town was taken by Alexander the Great in 332 B.C. after a two-months' siege.

*Gedrosia* (jē-drō′zhạ). In ancient geography, a country in Asia, corresponding nearly to the modern Baluchistan and SE Iran. It was bounded on the N by Drangiana and Arachosia, on the E by India, on the S by the Indian Ocean, and on the W by Carmania. It was a province of the Persian Empire, and voluntarily submitted to Alexander the Great when he passed the winter at nearby Seistan (330–329 B.C.). He made it a satrapy with its capital at Pura. On his return journey from India (325 B.C.), Alexander elected to march through

(obscured) errạnt, ardẹnt, actọr; ch, chip; g, go; th, thin; ŦH, then; y, you;
(variable) ḍ as d or j, ş as s or sh, ṭ as t or ch, ẓ as z or zh.

the trackless deserts of coastal Gedrosia, to parallel the voyage of Nearchus along the coast. With little water and failing supplies, parched by the heat and exhausted by the shifting sands through which they marched, the army suffered great losses in the wastelands of Gedrosia. Some say the force was reduced to one-quarter its size; others say Alexander lost more men in the desert of Gedrosia to heat, thirst, and exhaustion, than he lost in all his campaigns.

*Gela* (je′lä). [Former name, *Terranova di Sicilia.*] City on the S coast of the island of Sicily. Ancient Gela, on whose site the modern town is built, was founded (689 B.C.) by colonists from Crete under the leadership of Entimus, and by colonists from Rhodes under the leadership of Antiphemus, the two groups having united to found the city. The city, on a hill between the sea and a plain, was named for the nearby Gelas River, called "its own wild river." The Rhodians called the fortified citadel of the new city Lindii, after their own city of Lindus in Rhodes. The colonists adopted Dorian institutions in their new home. About 100 years after the founding of Gela, colonists from the city founded Acragas (Agrigentum), which became the second most important city of ancient Sicily. Under the tyrant Hippocrates (died 491 B.C.), Gela flourished and extended its power over Naxos, Zancle, Camarina, and other Greek cities of Sicily. Gelon, who succeeded Hippocrates as tyrant, won control over Syracuse. He moved his court and half the inhabitants of Gela to Syracuse, leaving his brother Hieron in charge of a greatly reduced Gela. Henceforth, Gela which had been the most powerful Greek city in Sicily, gave place to Syracuse. In 405 B.C. the Carthaginians attacked and laid siege to Gela. The inhabitants defended their walls courageously. They appealed to Dionysius the Elder, tyrant of Syracuse for aid, and he did indeed march out with the apparent intention of helping them to drive off the Carthaginians. However, he seems to have betrayed them, and instead of helping them, he persuaded them to march out under cover of darkness and abandon their city. By the terms of a peace he afterward negotiated with Carthage, Gela fell to the Carthaginians, who destroyed it. Some of the inhabitants afterward moved back and rebuilt it, and it was fortified again by Timoleon in 338 B.C. In 312 B.C. Agathocles, tyrant of Syracuse, massacred 4000 of the inhabitants in the course of a war with Carthage, and it was finally destroyed in 282 B.C.

fat, fāte, fär, fåll, ȧsk, fāre; net, mē, hėr; pin, pīne; not, nōte, möve, nôr; up, lūte, pùll; oi, oil; ou out; (lightened) ḙlect, agǫny, ūnite.

by the Mamertines, after which the few remaining inhabitants were transferred to a neighboring town. Remains of temples of the 6th and 5th centuries B.C. have been found at the site, and recent excavations have uncovered long stretches of the 4th century B.C. city walls, with superstructure of mud brick on a socle of carefully fitted ashlar stone masonry, a discovery of extraordinary importance for the history of military architecture. Smaller finds are tastefully displayed in the new museum.

*Gerasa* (jĕr'a̧-sa̧). [Modern name, *Jerash.*] In ancient geography, a city of the Decapolis, in Palestine, about 56 miles NE of Jerusalem. The site contains many antiquities. The forum, which is oval and 300 feet long, is surrounded by a range of Ionic columns, many of which still stand with their entablature. From it extends a great colonnaded street, intersecting the entire city, and crossed at right angles by another. More than 100 columns still stand along the street. They seem to have formed a series of porticoes with galleries above. Among the remains are those of a great temple, the cella of which (66 by 78 feet) is in great part standing, together with many columns of the peristyle. A theater has 28 tiers of seats still remaining above ground, with one precinction (landing), to which vaulted passages give access. In the back wall of the precinction there are small chambers, perhaps boxes. A gallery surrounds the top of the cavea. A smaller theater on the same site is equally perfect and interesting. Gerasa was important in the early Christian period, and the early churches, incorporated in pagan temples and other structures, are important for understanding the development of church architecture and the history of the early church.

*Gergovia* (jĕr-gō'vi-a̧). In ancient geography, a Gallic town, situated in the region known today as the Plateau de Gergovie, S of what is now Clermont-Ferrand, France. Caesar besieged it (52 B.C.), and was defeated here by Vercingetorix. There are some relics on the site.

*Germania* (jĕr-mā'ni-a̧). In ancient geography, the region included between the Mare Germanicum (North Sea), Mare Suevicum (Baltic Sea), Vistula River, Ister (Danube) River, and Rhenus (Rhine) River (from near Mainz to near Emmerich); often extended to include certain territories W of the Rhenus. In the first sense it was never a part of the Roman Empire.

**Gerrha** (jer′a̯). [Also: **Gerra.**] In ancient geography, a city of Arabia Felix, situated on the Persian Gulf. It was important in the 7th and 6th centuries B.C., under the Assyrians Babylonians, and Persians.

**Glessariae** (gle̯-sā′ri-ē). In ancient geography, a chain of islands stretching from the Rhenus (Rhine) to the estuary of the Albis (Elbe), noted for the abundance of amber found there They were sometimes called the Electrides after the islands in Greek legend, and also the Amber Islands.

**Gnossus** or **Gnosus** (nos′us). See **Cnossus.**

**Golden Horn.** Inlet of the Bosporus, in European Turkey forming the harbor of Istanbul, and separating Pera and Galata from the main part of Istanbul. Length, about five miles.

**Golden Mount, The.** Name applied to the Janiculan Hill of Rome with reference to its yellow sand composition.

**Gordium** (gôr′di-um). In ancient geography, a town in N Galatia, Asia Minor, near the river Sangarius (Sakarya). It is noted as the capital of the Phrygian kingdom of the 8th and 7th centuries B.C. In the neighborhood are many large burial mounds, one of which, recently excavated by a University of Pennsylvania expedition, proved to contain an intact royal burial, one of the most important post-war archaeological discoveries. Also exhibited at Gordium was the intricate Gordian Knot, which Alexander solved by cutting through it with his sword. (JJ)

**Gortyna** (gôr-tī′na̯). [Also: **Gortyn.**] In ancient geography, an important Dorian city in S central Crete, near Mount Ida According to legend, Zeus, in the form of a white bull landed near here after swimming the sea with Europa on his back. Traditionally founded by Gortys, son of Rhadamanthys, Gortyna was an important center of Cretan civilization, second only to Cnossus. After the Roman conquest Gortyna replaced Cnossus as the leading city of Crete. It became the capital of the Roman province of Crete and Cyrenaica when the island was subdued by the Romans in 66 B.C. The famous Gortynian Code was discovered here in 1862 and 1884. Nearby are the remains of a temple of Pythian Apollo, the earliest parts of which date from the 7th century B.C., and a temple of Isis from the era of Greco-Roman civilization. Attached to the latter is a small crypt that seems to have played some part in the rites of initiation into the mysteries of Isis. Also at Gortyna are the remains

fat, fāte, fär, fåll, ȧsk, fȧre; net, mē, hėr; pin, pīne; not, nōte, mȯve nôr; up, lūte, pull; oi, oil; ou out; (lightened) e̯lect, agȯny, ūnite

of a basilica of St. Titus, companion of St. Paul, who brought Christianity to the island and became the first bishop of Gortyna. Nearby is a spot said to contain his grave.

*Gournia* (gôr'ni-ạ). In ancient geography, a town on the E end of the island of Crete. Remains uncovered on the site present the only extensive picture of a Minoan village, with private houses and a small palace, to be found on Crete.

*Graecia* (grē'shạ), *Magna.* See *Magna Graecia.*

*Granicus* (grạ-nī'kus). A small river in Mysia, Asia Minor, flowing into the Propontis (the modern Sea of Marmara or Marmora). On its banks Alexander the Great won (334 B.C.) his first victory over the Persians.

*Greece* (grēs). [Modern Greek, *Ellas;* ancient Greek, *Hellas;* Latin, *Graecia.*] In the widest sense the ancient name includes the Greek Colonies in Asia Minor, Sicily, Africa, and elsewhere; in its restricted and more usual meaning it is the peninsula S of the Cambunian Mountains, with the neighboring islands. Peninsular Greece comprised Thessaly, Epirus, Central Greece (including Acarnania, Aetolia, Doris, Western Locris, Eastern Locris, Phocis, Boeotia, Attica, and Megaris), and the Peloponnesus (including Corinthia, Sicyonia, Phliasia, Achaea, Elis, Arcadia, Argolis, Laconia, and Messenia). The chief islands were Crete, Rhodes, Cos, Samos, Chios, Lesbos, Tenedos, Imbrus, Samothrace, Thasus, Lemnos, Scyrus, Euboea, Salamis, Aegina, the Cyclades, Thera, Cythera, and the Ionian Islands (including Zakynthos [Zante], Cephalonia, Ithaca, Leukas, Corcyra [Corfu], and others). Cyprus was sometimes included, and in later times Macedonia and Thrace. The following are some of the more important facts and incidents of ancient Greek history: Dorian invasion of the Peloponnesus (c1100 B.C.); commencement of the hegemony of Sparta (6th century B.C.); Persian wars (500 to c449 B.C.); hegemony transferred to Athens (c477 B.C.); Peloponnesian War (431–404 B.C.); hegemony of Sparta (404–371 B.C.); of Thebes (371–362 B.C.); hegemony of Macedon commenced 338 B.C.; rise of Aetolian League and renewal of Achaean League (c280 B.C.); independence of Greece proclaimed by Flamininus (196 B.C.); final subjection of Greece to Rome (146 B.C.); Greece made (in great part) into the Roman province of Achaea (27 B.C.). Later, Greece formed part of the Byzantine Empire.

*Grumentum* (grö-men'tum). In ancient geography, a town in

Lucania, S Italy, situated on the Aciris (now Agri) River near the modern Grumento Nova.

**Gryneum** (grī-nē′um) or **Grynea** (grī-nē′ą). In ancient geography, a small Aeolian city in Mysia, on the shore of the Aegean Sea. It was noted for a sanctuary and ancient oracle of Apollo, as well as for a white marble temple, and a grove sacred to Apollo.

**Gythium** (jith′i-um, ji-thī′um). [Modern name, **Gytheion.**] In ancient geography, a seaport in Laconia, Greece, situated on the Gulf of Laconia. According to tradition, when Heracles asked the priestess at Delphi how he could be cured of a sickness afflicting him she refused to answer. He seized the tripod from her and threatened to set up his own oracle. Apollo came to the rescue of his priestess and strove with Heracles. Zeus parted them and compelled them to compose their quarrel. After this Apollo and Heracles together founded the city of Gythium, where images of Apollo, Heracles, and Dionysus stood side by side in the market-place. Near Gythium is a stone on which Orestes is said to have sat to rest when he had been driven to madness by the Furies. As he sat on the stone his madness left him. Off the coast of Gythium is the island of Cranaë, where Helen first yielded in love to Paris after he had carried her off from Sparta. On the mainland opposite the island was a sanctuary of Aphrodite Migonitis (*Uniter*), but afterward Menelaus set up near the sanctuary an image of Thetis and the goddesses Praxidicae (*Extracters of Justice*).

# —H—

**Haemonia** (hē-mō′ni-ą). An ancient name for Thessaly.

**Hagios Elias** (ä′yôs ē-lē′äs). [Also: **Hagios Ilias, Mount Saint Elias.**] Mountain summit in Greece, in the Taÿgetus range about 11 miles S of Sparta. It is the highest point in the Peloponnesus. Elevation, about 7903 feet.

**Haliacmon** (hal-i-ak′mon). [Modern name, **Vistritsa.**] In ancient geography, a river of Macedonia which empties into the Myrtoan Sea (Thermaic Gulf).

fat, fāte, fär, fâll, ȧsk, fāre; net, mē, hèr; pin, pīne; not, nōte, möve, nôr; up, lūte, pùll; oi, oil; ou out; (lightened) ẹlect, agǫny, ụnite;

*Haliartus* (hal-i-ạr'tus). In ancient geography, a city of Boeotia, Greece, situated on the S shore of Lake Copaïs, about 14 miles NW of Thebes, and under the shadow of Mount Tilphusius. Nearby it ran the Lophis River. Haliartus was important because of its location on the main route between N and S Greece. In the Persian War the inhabitants threw in their lot with the Greeks. The Persians overran the town and burned it (480 B.C.). In 395 B.C. the Spartan general Lysander was defeated and killed at Haliartus by the Thebans. The city was completely destroyed in 171 B.C. by the Romans, because it had favored the cause of Perseus, king of Macedonia.

*Halicarnassus* (hal″i-kär-nas'us). In ancient geography, a city in Caria, Asia Minor, situated on the island of Zephyria close to a promontory of the mainland. The island was eventually united to the mainland and the city extended to include both. It was colonized by Dorians from Troezen and perhaps Argos who came to the region, according to tradition, under the leadership of Anthes. The city was a member of the Dorian Hexapolis for a time, but was later excluded from the religious rites when the Halicarnassian Agasicles, in defiance of the laws, carried off to his own house the bronze tripod he had won at the games for Apollo. In the time of the Persian War it was ruled over by Artemisia, queen of Caria, who commanded her own ship in the Persian fleet that was defeated by the Greeks at Salamis (480 B.C.). Following the Persian War it was for a time a member of the Delian Confederacy. Later, by the Peace of Antalcidas (the "King's Peace"), it fell to Persia and was governed by satraps as part of Caria. Among these satraps was Mausolus, whose wife Artemisia built (352 B.C.) his tomb, the famous Mausoleum, celebrated as one of the seven wonders of the ancient world. Scopas and other renowned sculptors of the time cooperated in the building of the tomb. It consisted of a quadrangular peristyle of Ionic columns on a high basement, above which rose a pyramid of 24 steps, supporting a *quadriga* (a chariot drawn by four horses), in which stood a huge statue of Mausolus. Important remains of the sculptured decoration are in the British Museum. In 334 B.C. Alexander the Great besieged the city, took it, and sacked it, and it never recovered its former importance. The city is famous also as the birthplace of the historians Herodotus and Dionysius. The site is now occupied by the Turkish town of Budrum.

*Halicyae* (hal-is′i-ē). [Modern name, *Salemi.*] Town on the island of Sicily, about 40 miles SW of Panormus. It was a Greek town originally, then came under Carthaginian influence, and submitted to the Romans in 262 B.C.

*Halys* (hā′lis). A river of Paphlagonia, about 800 miles long (the modern Kizil Irmak), the longest river in Asia Minor Phineus directed the course of the Argonauts past it. It i famous for the defeat of Croesus, king of Lydia, brough about by his misinterpretation of the ambiguous oracle given him by the priestess of Delphi: "If Croesus passes over the Halys he will destroy a great empire."

*Harma* (här′ma). In ancient geography, a city of Boeotia Greece, The name means *Chariot,* and was given to the city some say, because here the chariot bearing Amphiaraus wa swallowed up when the earth opened as he fled from Thebes.

*Hebrus* (hē′brus). [Modern name, *Maritsa.*] A river of Thrace about 300 miles long, that flows into the NE Aegean Sea The maenads who attacked and dismembered Orpheu flung his head and his lyre into this river. There they miracu lously floated, the lyre playing a plaintive air and the head murmuring sadly, and crossed the sea to the island of Lem nos.

*Hecatompylon* (hek-a-tom′pi-lon). A name from Thebes i Egypt, meaning "100-gated," a city said to have bee founded by Heracles as he passed through Egypt on his wa to the west to fetch the cattle of Geryon.

*Helena* (hel′e-na). Island off the coast of Attica, between Cap Sunium and the island of Ceos. Helen is said to have lande there first on her return with Menelaus from Troy, and th island was named for her.

*Helice* (hel′i-sē). In ancient geography, a city of Achaea, on th south coast of the Gulf of Corinth. According to some ac counts, it was founded by Ion, son of Apollo and Creus and named for his wife Helice, daughter of King Selinus c Aegialus. Men of Helice went to the Trojan War under th command of Agamemnon. Poseidon had a temple there. I 373 B.C., according to Pausanias, some suppliants who ha fled to his temple and taken refuge in his famous sanctuar were dragged away from the altars by the Achaeans. T

---

fat, fāte, fär, fâll, àsk, fãre; net, mē, hèr; pin, pīne; not, nōte, mōv nôr; up, lūte, pùll; oi, oil; ou out; (lightened) ēlect, agǫny, ūni

punish them for this impiety Poseidon sent an earthquake against the Achaeans. Helice was shaken to the ground and was then swallowed up in the sea by a tidal wave; none of its inhabitants was left alive.

*Helicon* (hel'i-kon, -kon). [Also: *Elikon, Helikon, Zagora.*] Mountain range in S central Greece, on the N shore of the Gulf of Corinth, about 50 miles NW of Athens. According to legend Helicon and Cithaeron were brothers. Cithaeron was fierce and brutal. He murdered his father and attempted to hurl gentle Helicon from a rock, whereupon the brothers were transformed by the gods into the mountains which bear their names. Helicon became the home of Apollo and the Muses. Wild Cithaeron became a mountain on which unwanted infants were often exposed to die. Helicon contained the fountains of Aganippe and Hippocrene. Peak elevation, about 5868 feet.

*Heliopolis* (hē-li-op'ō-lis). [Ancient Egyptian, *An* or *On;* modern name, *Matarieh, Matariya;* known as the *"City of the Sun-God."*] In ancient geography, a city in Lower Egypt, on the Pelusiac branch of the Nile. According to legend, it was founded by Actis, a son of Helius and Rhode, who named it for his father. It was situated on the edge of the desert, about four miles E of the apex of the Nile delta. It was a seat of learning ("the university of Egypt") and of the worship of the sun-god Ra. Its site is about six miles N of Cairo.

*Heliopolis.* [Modern name, *Baalbek, Baalbec,* or *Ba'albek.*] Ancient city of Syria, situated on the slope of the Anti-Libanus mountains, about 34 miles NW of Damascus; now a small town in E Lebanon. Famous in modern times chiefly for its ruins, it was a center of the worship of Baal as sun-god, whence both the original and Greek names. The city was a Roman colony (Colonia Julia Augusta Felix) under Augustus, and was adorned, especially with the great temple of Jupiter which he began, by Antoninus Pius. There are also remains of temples to Bacchus and Venus. Its decline began with its capture by the Arabs, and it was totally destroyed by an earthquake in 1759. The site is famous for the ruins of the great temples on its acropolis. The older portions of the acropolis wall, made of huge stones, are of Phoenician or kindred origin, and date from the time when the worship of Baal was still supreme. Aside from these sections of the wall, all the structures now remaining are Roman or later in time, and are interesting for their grouping, their great size, and the beauty of the materials. The site has been known to Europeans since the 16th century, and its monuments have been studied and sketched by many explorers.

*Hellas* (hel'as). In ancient geography, originally a town and small district in Phthiotis, Thessaly, later extended to denote the lands inhabited by the Hellenes, modern Greek Ellas. The terms Greek and Greece were never applied by the Greeks to themselves, being used by Italians first to designate the Hellenes of S Italy (Magna Graecia) and subsequently extended to include the Hellenes of the mainland. (JJ)

*Hellespont* (hel'es-pont). [Modern name, *Dardanelles.*] Strait connecting the Propontis (Sea of Marmara) with the Aegean Sea, and separating the Chersonesus Thracica (Gallipoli peninsula) from Asia Minor. It was named for Helle, the sister of Phrixus. As she and her brother were escaping from Orchomenus on the back of a golden-fleeced ram, Helle lost her hold and fell into this strait, which ever after bore her name. It was celebrated in the legend of Hero and Leander. It was crossed by Xerxes in 480 B.C., and by Alexander the Great in 334 B.C. Length, about 45 miles; average width, 3 to 4 miles; narrowest point, about 1¼ miles.

*Helos* (hē'los). In ancient geography, a town in Laconia, situated near the sea, about 25 miles SE of Sparta. It was said to have been founded by Helius, the youngest son of Perseus. The Dorians reduced it by siege and reduced the inhabitants to slavery and carried them off to Sparta.

*Heptanesus* (hep-ta-nē'sus). The seven principal inhabited islands of the Ionian Sea: Corcyra, Paxos, Leucas, Ithaca, Cephallenia, Zacynthus, and Cythera. (JJ)

*Heraclea* (her-a-klē'a). In ancient geography, a city of Magna Graecia, situated near the Gulf of Tarentum, in what is now Lucania, S Italy, near the modern village of Policoro. It was established as a colony of Tarentum, and was the scene of a victory of Pyrrhus, king of Epirus, over the Romans in 280 B.C. It was this victory and that of Asculum in the following year, in which Pyrrhus lost heavily, which gave rise to the saying "a Pyrrhic victory," meaning a gain made at great cost to the victor.

*Heraclea Minoa* (mi-nō'a). [Also: *Heraclea.*] In ancient geogra-

phy, a city on the S coast of Sicily, about 18 miles NW of
Acragas.

*Heraclea Perinthus* (her-ạ-klē'ạ pẹ-rin'thus). See *Perinthus.*

*Heraclea Pontica* (pon'ti-kạ). [Also: *Heraclea;* modern Turkish
name, *Ereğli.*] In ancient geography, a city in Bithynia, Asia
Minor, situated on the Euxine Sea about 100 miles E of what
is now Istanbul, Turkey. According to legend, it was
founded by the Mariandyni and named for Heracles in gratitude to him for repelling the Bebryces and restoring the
land to the Mariandyni. According to some accounts, it was
near here that Heracles came up from the Underworld with
Cerberus, and as the three-headed dog of Hades emerged
into the light foam fell from his jaws. From this foam sprang
the poisonous aconite plant, which flourished in this region
thereafter. Colonists from Megara later settled at Heraclea
(c560 B.C.) in obedience to the advice of an oracle to settle
on land that had been dedicated to Heracles.

*Heraclea Sintica* (sin'ti-kạ). In ancient geography, a town in
Macedonia, situated about 40 miles NE of Therma (now
Salonika); the modern Zeruokhori.

*Heraclea Trachinia* (trạ-kin'i-ạ). [Called *Heraclea.*] In ancient
geography, a town in Malis, C Greece, about six miles W of
Thermopylae; a Spartan colony founded in 426 B.C.

*Heracleum* (her-ạ-klē'um). [Also: *Candia, Heraklion, Heraklei-
on, Iraklion, Megalokastron.*] City on the N coast of the island
of Crete, near the site of ancient Cnossus.

*Heraea* (hẹ-rē'ạ). In ancient geography, a city in W Arcadia, on
the Alpheus River; according to tradition, it was founded by
Heraeus, son of Lycaon. Among the temples were those of
Pan and of Hera, and of Dionysus Citizen and Dionysus
Giver of Increase.

*Herculaneum* (hèr-kū-lā'nẹ-um). Ancient city in Campania, S
Italy, near the coast, about six miles SE of Naples, directly
at the W foot of Mount Vesuvius. Like Pompeii it was overwhelmed in the eruption of 79 A.D. The city was buried deep
under heavy volcanic ash which solidified to a form of tufa.
The ancient town was forgotten, and modern Resina grew
up over its ruins. In 1709 an inhabitant of Resina sank a well
which reached the ancient theater, and brought to light
sculptures and marble facings. Further search was made,
solely for the marbles and works of art, and subsequent
excavations were undertaken by the Italian government, but

were very unscientifically and irregularly conducted, and the galleries pierced were in great part filled again. Under the French rule (1806–15) systematic explorations were instituted; a little was done between 1828 and 1837; then nothing until Victor Emmanuel caused (1869) the resumption of the work. The most important remains are the theater, basilica, prison, some interesting private dwellings, and portions of several streets paved with lava. In Herculaneum were found a number of carbonized manuscripts on papyrus, some of which have been deciphered, and some of the best-known statues in the Naples Museum, including the Agrippina, Sleeping Faun, Aristides, and busts of Plato and Demosthenes.

*Hercynian Forest* (hėr-sin'i-an). [Latin, *Hercynia Silva;* Greek, *Herkynia Hule.*] In ancient geography, a mountain range forming the N boundary of what was then known as Europe, and seemingly identified by Aristotle with the Alpine mass. Caesar described it as a nine days' journey wide and a 60 days' journey long, apparently including all the mountains and forests in S and C Germany. It has been variously represented as in C Germany, and as identical with the Böhmerwald, the Thüringerwald, and others.

*Hermione* (hėr-mī'ọ̄-nē). In ancient geography, a city on the E coast of the Peloponnesus, near Troezen. According to tradition, it was founded by Hermione, a grandson of Phoroneus, but some say the Hermionians were Dryopes who had been driven out of Doris by Heracles. Hermione was noted for having its own private entrance to Hades. Consequently, the thrifty Hermionians considered it unnecessary to put a coin under the tongue of a corpse to pay Charon to ferry it across the Styx. By this entrance, the Hermionians claimed that Heracles dragged Cerberus, the Hound of Hell, up to the light, and Hades, they said, carried Persephone to his realm through this chasm. In the Trojan War men of Hermione joined the Greeks before Troy under the leadership of Diomedes. When the Dorians invaded the Peloponnesus, Dorians from Argos settled in Hermione. In the Persian War Hermione sent three ships to join the Greek fleet at Salamis (480 B.C.), and its name was inscribed on the trophy dedicated at Delphi as having taken part in the victory of Plataea (479 B.C.).

*Hermonthis* (hėr-mon'this). [Modern name, *Armant, Erment.*]

In ancient geography, a town in the Thebaid, Egypt, situated on the Nile about eight miles SW of Thebes. It was a seat of ancient worship, and important ruins remain, notably those of a temple built in the time of Cleopatra.

*Hermus* (hėr′mus). [Modern name, *Gediz*.] In ancient geography, a river of Asia Minor, said to have gold-bearing sands in its channel. On it was located Sardis, the Lydian capital of King Croesus. The river was also called Sarabat.

*Hesperia* (hes-pir′i-ạ). According to the ancient Greeks, the region of the west, especially Italy, and sometimes, according to the poets, the Iberian peninsula.

*Hetruria* (hẹ-trö′ri-ạ). See *Etruria.*

*Hierapolis* (hī-ėr-ap′ọ-lis). [Eng. trans., "Sacred City."] Ancient city in Phrygia, Asia Minor, near Laodicea. It was held sacred on account of its hot springs and cave called "Plutonium," and was the birthplace of Epictetus.

*Hierapolis.* Ancient city in Syria, about 50 miles NE of Beroea (Aleppo); the Greek Bambyce, and the modern Membij.

*Himera* (him′ẹ-rạ). In ancient geography, a town on the N coast of Sicily, about 30 miles E of Panormus (Palermo). Famous warm springs, sacred to the nymphs, were located here. The city was founded, 648 B.C., by Greek colonists from Euboea. Here (480 B.C.) Gelon of Syracuse defeated the Carthaginians under Hamilcar. By a trick, the forces of Gelon secured entrance to Hamilcar's camp and slaughtered him as he stood by a great altar of Poseidon. Hamilcar's grandson Hannibal (d. 406 B.C.) conquered Himera (408 B.C.), sacrificed 3000 men on the spot where his grandfather had been killed to appease his shade, and completely destroyed the city to avenge his grandfather's defeat and death. No city was ever again raised on the spot. Afterward Thermae Himerenses (the modern Termini Imerese) was the chief town in the vicinity. Himera is also known as the birthplace of Stesichorus.

*Himera.* Ancient name of two rivers in Sicily, one (the modern Salso) flowing S, and the other (the modern Grande) flowing N past the ancient town of Himera.

*Hippocrene* (hip′ọ-krēn, hip-ọ-krē′nẹ). Fountain on Mount Helicon, in Boeotia, sacred to the Muses. Traditionally it sprang up from a hoof mark of Pegasus, and is alluded to as a source of poetic inspiration.

*Hire* (hī′rẹ) or *Hira* (hī′rạ). See *Ire.*

*Hissarlik* (hi-sär-lik'). See *Troy*.

*Histiaea* (his-ti-ē'a̧) or *Hestiaea* (hes-). In ancient geography, a city on the NW coast of Euboea, Greece, opposite Thessaly, colonized by Thessalians. In the Trojan War Greeks from "vine-clad" Histiaea fought under the command of Elephenor, captain of the Abantes. In 447–446 B.C. it was conquered by Athens under Pericles and Tolmides. Its inhabitants were driven out and fled for refuge to Macedonia; the territory was annexed by Athens, and nearby the deserted city the Athenians sent colonists to found the city of Oreus. After the defeat of Athens in the Peloponnesian Wars, Oreus fell under the dominion of Sparta. The Athenian colonists were expelled, the ancient name Histiaea was restored. In 207 B.C. Attalus II conquered the city, lost it to the Romans, and reconquered it, 200 B.C.

*Hybla* (hī'bla̧). [Also: *Hybla Magna, Hybla Geleatis, Hybla Major.*] In ancient geography, a city in Sicily, on the S slope of Mount Aetna, about 11 miles NW of Catana (Catania); believed to have been at or near the modern Paternò.

*Hybla Heraea* (he-rē'a̧). In ancient geography, a town of S Sicily, W of Syracuse. It was an ancient Sicel town. Hippocrates, tyrant of Gela, besieged the town, 491 B.C., and was killed while attempting to breach its walls. The modern city of Ragusa lies on the slopes of the hill where ancient Hybla Heraea stood.

*Hybla Minor* (mī'nor). [Also: *Megara Hyblaea.*] In ancient geography, a city on the E coast of Sicily about 12 miles N of Syracuse. The celebrated Hyblaean honey, mentioned frequently by ancient poets, may have been produced in the vicinity. It is often confused with Hybla on Mount Aetna, sometimes called Hybla Major.

*Hydaspes* (hi-das'pēz). Ancient name of the Jhelum River, a river in the Punjab, West Pakistan, rising in Kashmir and joining the Chenab about 80 miles NE of Multan; in its upper valley is the Vale of Kashmir. On its banks Alexander the Great defeated Porus in 326 B.C.

*Hydrus* (hī'drus). [Modern name, *Otranto.*] In ancient geography, a seaport of Apulia, SE Italy, called by the Romans Hydruntum, situated about 45 miles SE of Brundisium. It was founded by colonists from the Dorian city of Tarentum and retained its Greek language and culture until the 11th century.

fat, fāte, fär, fåll, ȧsk, fāre; net, mē, hėr; pin, pīne; not, nōte, möve, nôr; up, lūte, pull; oi, oil; ou out; (lightened) ȩlect, ago̧ny, ūnite;

*Hyettus* (hī-et′us). In ancient geography, a village of Boeotia, Greece, near Lake Copaïs.

*Hymettus* (hī-met′us). A mountain ridge in Attica, Greece, lying SE of Athens. For a few minutes just before dusk it sometimes glows with a soft violet color, and from this Athens has the epithet "violet-crowned." In ancient times the mountain was celebrated for its honey, and also for its bluish-gray marble. Elevation, about 3368 feet.

*Hyrcania* (hėr-kā′ni-ạ). In ancient geography, a region in W Asia, around the S end of the Hyrcanum Mare (Caspian Sea); now part of N Iran.

*Hysiae* (hī′si-ē). In ancient geography, a city in Argolis, Greece, situated in the mountains west of Lerna. Here Argos defeated the Spartans in battle (traditional date, 669 B.C.).

*Hysiae.* Village of Boeotia, Greece, situated on the lower slopes of Mount Cithaeron, on the border between Attica and Boeotia. There was a temple of Apollo here, and a sacred well, from which oracles could be obtained by drinking the waters at night. The village, once part of Boeotia, fell under Athenian control following a war between Athens and Boeotia (509 B.C.), in which the Boeotians were defeated. In the Persian War, the Persians and Greeks faced each other across the Asopus River near here (479 B.C.). The Greeks, instructed by an oracle to fight on the plain of Eleusinian Demeter, found at Hysiae, thanks to the intervention of Zeus, a very ancient sanctuary of Eleusinian Demeter, and in the battle of Plataea nearby they thoroughly defeated the Persians. The Persian general Mardonius was slain, and some say his tomb was at Hysiae.

**I**

*Ialysus* (ī-al′i-sus). Ancient city in N Rhodes, on the NW coast of the island about six miles SW of the modern city of Rhodes. It was a Dorian city, and a member of the Hexapolis (League of Six Cities); it flourished c1000 B.C. About the 4th century B.C. it was surpassed by the city of Rhodes, and declined.

*Iapygia* (ī-a̯-pij′i-a̯). In ancient geography, a name used vaguely by the Greeks for a region approximating what is now the SE part of Italy.

*Iardanus* (ī-är′da̯-nus). [Also: *Jardan, Jardanus;* modern name, *Iardhonos.*] In ancient geography, a river of Elis, Greece, that had the same name as the Phoenician river, the Jordan. Homer mentions it in the *Iliad* as the place where Nestor and the Pylians fought against the Arcadians in his youth and where he slew Ereuthalion.

*Iberia* (ī-bir′i-a̯). [Latin, *Hispania.*] In ancient geography, the peninsula of SW Europe, now known as the Iberian Peninsula.

*Iberia.* In ancient geography, the region bounded by the Caucasus Mountains on the N, (ancient) Albania on the E, Armenia on the S, and Colchis on the W; now largely the E portion of the Georgian Soviet Socialist Republic.

*Icaria* (ī-kär′i-a̯). [Also: *Ikaria, Nicaria, Nikaria, Kariot.*] Island in the Aegean Sea, situated about 13 miles W of Samos. According to legend, it was to this island that Daedalus brought the body of his son Icarus after the latter, flying so close to the sun as to melt the wax holding his wings together, fell into the sea and was drowned. Daedalus buried his son here and named the island after him. Area, about 99 square miles; length, about 25 miles.

*Icaria.* Site in the Rapedosa valley, Attica, Greece, N of Mount Pentelicus, excavated and identified (1888) by an expedition from the American School at Athens. Here, according to the legend, wine-making and the Dionysiac cult were introduced into Attica by Dionysus himself, and here was born Thespis, who, by the changes he introduced into the old dithyrambic songs, became the originator of tragic drama, with Icaria as the theater.

*Icarian Sea* (ī-kär′i-an). [Latin, *Mare Icarium.*] In ancient geography, part of the Aegean Sea surrounding Samos and the neighboring small island of Icaria, along the coast of Asia Minor. In Greek legend it is the scene of the drowning of Icarus, son of Daedalus, and was named for him.

*Ichnousa* or *Ichnusa* (ik-nö′sa̯). Greek name for the island of Sardinia. The name means "footprint," and was given to the island because of its shape. It was also called Sandaliotis, from its resemblance to a sandal.

---

fat, fāte, fär, fåll, a̯sk, fãre; net, mē, hėr; pin, pīne; not, nōte, möve, nôr; up, lūte, pu̇ll; oi, oil; ou out; (lightened) e̯lect, agǫny, ūnite

*Icos* (ī'kos). An island in the Aegean Sea, near the coast of Thessaly and Euboea.

*Ida* (ī'dạ), *Mount*. [Modern name, *Psiloriti; Latin, Ida Mons*.] Mountain in C Crete, the highest peak of the island. According to Greek mythology, the infant Zeus was raised on Mount Ida by Amalthea. Elevation, about 8,195 feet.

*Ida, Mount*. A mountain in the range of the same name in Phrygia and Mysia, Asia Minor. At the base of it was the Troad, whose capital was Troy. The mountain, described in the *Iliad* as "many-fountained," was a seat of Zeus and had a grove sacred to him and an altar to him. It was from here that Zeus directed the Trojan War on many occasions and watched the progress and weighed the fates of his favorites. Mount Ida was also known as the place from which Zeus carried off Ganymede, as the site of the Judgment of Paris, and as a seat of worship of Cybele. The highest peak of the mountain was also known as Gargarus or Gargaron (5749 feet).

*Idalium* (ī-dā'li-um). [Also: *Idalia;* modern village name, *Dali*.] In ancient geography, a town and promontory on the coast of Cyprus, with a temple to Aphrodite, who was sometimes called Idalia.

*Ilion, Ilios, Ilium* (il'i-ọn, -os, -um). Names for Troy, meaning the city founded by Ilus. See *Troy.*

*Ilissus* (i-lis'us). [Modern Greek name, *Ilissos* or *Eilissos*.] In ancient geography, a small river in Attica, Greece, flowing just S of Athens.

*Ilium* (il'i-um). See *Troy.*

*Illyria* (i-lir'i-ạ). [Greek, *Illyris, Illyria*.] In ancient geography, a region in the W part of the Balkan peninsula, N of Greece. Its boundaries are vague. In the second millennium B.C. this region was occupied by tribes speaking an Indo-European language and collectively known as Illyrians. The S part of Illyria came early under Greek influence. According to some legendary accounts, Cadmus fled to this region with his wife after the death of his grandson Pentheus, who had denied the divinity of Dionysus. He settled among the Encheleans who defeated the Illyrians in war and made Cadmus their king. In his old age Cadmus had a son, Illyrius, for whom the Illyrians were named. Historically, the Greeks, apparently attracted by the mines in the interior, began colonizing the coast in the 6th century B.C. and continued for a number of centuries thereafter. The kingdom of Illyria, with Scodra as its capital, was important in the 3rd century B.C., and was overthrown (168 B.C.) by Rome. The region formerly known as Illyria is now occupied principally by Yugoslavia and Albania.

*Imbrus* (im'brus). [Also: *Imbros.*] An island in the NE Aegean, situated just W of the Hellespont. Near here, according to the *Iliad,* was a deep chasm under the sea where Poseidon stabled his horses while he went to observe the Trojan War and to help the Achaeans. The island was won for Athens by Miltiades just before the outbreak of the Persian War. Like its neighbor Samothrace, it was a center for the worship of the Cabiri.

*Inachus* (in'a̯-kus). [Modern Greek name, *Inakhos* or *Inachos.*] In ancient geography, a river in Argolis, flowing into the Gulf of Argolis SE of Argos.

*Indus* (in'dus). [Also: *Sind;* Sanskrit, *Sindhu.*] Chief river of Pakistan. It rises among the Himalayas of W Tibet, and flows NW through gorges in Tibet and Kashmir. Near the N part of Kashmir it turns S and flows SW through Pakistan (Punjab and Sind) into the Arabian Sea. It has formed an extensive delta. Its chief tributaries are the combined rivers of the Punjab (Jhelum, Beas, Chenab, Ravi, and Sutlej, entering through the Panjnad) and the Kabul. By means of the Sukkur Barrage, in Sind, the Indus irrigates several million acres of land. The volume of water in the Indus varies greatly, with floods in the spring and summer, and low water in winter; because of this extreme variability and silt deposition, it is not much used for navigation. Alexander the Great returned from India (325 B.C.) by the Indus valley, proceeding to Patala.

*Inessa* (in-es'a̯). [Modern name, *Biancavilla.*] Town on the island of Sicily, S of Mount Aetna and about nine miles NW of Catana. It was a Greek settlement.

*Iolcus* (i-ol'kus) [Modern name, *Volos.*] In ancient geography, a city of Thessaly, in NE Greece, situated on the Gulf of Pagasae. The site of Iolcus was inhabited from ancient times; the ancient city occupied a height that rose abruptly above the shore. Iolcus, or nearby Pagasae, is, according to tradition, the point from which the Argonauts set forth on their expedition to recover the Golden Fleece. In 1958 it was reported that, on a site near this traditional rendezvous

fat, fāte, fär, fȧll, ȧsk, fãre; net, mē, hėr; pin, pīne; not, nōte, möve, nôr; up, lūte, půll; oi, oil; ou out; (lightened) ḝlect, agǭny, ūnite;

point, ruins of an ancient palace had been discovered. The palace was built in the late Mycenaean period, about 1400 B.C., to replace an earlier structure, the floor of which lies underneath the palace. Destroyed by fire about 1200 B.C., the palace had a white stucco floor and walls reinforced with crisscrossing wooden beams. Excavations of the site have yielded Mycenaean pottery in a continuous series dating from about 1600 B.C. to 1200 B.C. Most notable among these pieces are numerous tall-stemmed ceramic cups. Other remains of the Mycenaean and Geometric periods have also been found in the area.

*Ionia* (ī-ō′ni-ạ). In ancient geography, a maritime region on the W coast of Asia Minor, including Chios, Samos, and the adjacent islands. It included the mainland cities of Phocaea, Clazomenae, Erythrae, Teos, Lebedus, Colophon, Ephesus, Priene, Myus, Miletus, and later Smyrna. According to tradition, it was colonized about the 11th century B.C. by Ionian refugees fleeing from the Greek mainland before the invading Dorians. Conquered by Croesus in the middle of the 6th century B.C., it passed later to Persia, was the scene of an unsuccessful revolt, 500–494 B.C., became, on the close of the Persian War, a dependent ally of Athens, but passed again to Persia in 387, and to Macedonia in 334 B.C. Later it fell to Pergamum and Rome. Ionia was noted for its wealth, and for the early development of art, music, philosophy, and literature.

*Ionian Islands* (ī-ō′ni-ạn). In ancient geography, the islands lying in the Ionian Sea W of Greece, and including Corcyra or Kerkyra (Corfù), Paxos, Leucas (Levkas), Ithaca (Ithaki or Thiaki), Cephallenia (Kephalonia), Zacynthus (Zante) and many smaller islands. Cythera, off the southern coast of the Peloponnesus, is sometimes counted among the Ionian Islands. The seven principal islands may be referred to as the Heptanesus. (JJ)

*Ionian Sea.* [Italian, *Mar Ionio;* Latin, *Mare Ionium.*] Part of the Mediterranean between Greece on the E and S Italy and Sicily on the W.

*Ios* (ī′os). [Also: *Nio.*] Island in the Aegean Sea, one of the Cyclades, about 12 miles SW of Naxos. Length, about 11 miles; area, about 46 square miles.

*Ipsus* (ip′sus). In ancient geography, a town in W central Asia Minor, in Phrygia. Here in 301 B.C., Lysimachus and Seleu-

(obscured) errạnt, ardẹnt, actọr; ch, chip; g, go; th, thin; ꝥн, then; y, you; (variable) ḏ as d or j, ṣ as s or sh, ṭ as t or ch, ẓ as z or zh.

cus defeated and slew Antigonus, and brought to an end the wars carried on by the successors of Alexander the Great.

*Ire* (ī'rē) or *Ira* (-rā). Ancient town in Messenia, on the eastern shore of the Gulf of Messenia.

*Isauria* (ī-sô'ri-ā). In ancient geography, a district in Asia Minor on the northern side of the Taurus range, bounded by Phrygia on the N, Lycaonia on the E, Cilicia on the S, and Pisidia on the W. The surface was rugged. The inhabitants were famous in guerrilla warfare. They were defeated by Servilius in 76 B.C., and by Pompey, but continued unsubdued.

*Ischia* (ēs'kyā). [Ancient names, *Aenaria, Pithecusa.*] Volcanic island in the Tyrrhenian Sea, situated about 16 miles W of Naples. It was early colonized by Greeks from Eretria and Chalcidice, but was abandoned by them because of the volcanic eruptions of Monte Epomeo. Hieron I, tyrant of Syracuse, sent a garrison there (c470 B.C.) but they refused to stay when the volcano erupted again. The island has many hot springs and was known as a spa from Roman times. In ancient times it was known as Pithecusa (q.v.).

*Isernia* (ī-sèr'ni-ā). See *Aesernia.*

*Ismenium* (is-mē'ni-um). Place in Boeotia where there was an oracle of Apollo. Oracles were given as a result of the inspection of entrails of victims.

*Issus* (is'us). In ancient geography, a town in Cilicia, SE Asia Minor, situated near the head of the Gulf of Issus, about 45 miles E of what is now Adana, Turkey. Here Alexander the Great defeated (333 B.C.) the Persians under Darius III; Septimius Severus defeated (194 A.D.) his rival Pescennius Niger; and Heraclius defeated (622) a Persian army.

*Ister* (is'tèr). An ancient name for the Danube River.

*Istria* (is'tri-ā). [Also: *Ister, Istropolis.*] In ancient geography, a colony of the Milesians, founded about the time of the Cimmerian invasion of Asia Minor (7th century B.C.), near the mouth of the Ister (the modern Danube). It was a trading center for the lower Danube basin for many centuries.

*Italica* (i-tal'i-kā). Ancient Roman town in Spain, near Seville; founded by Scipio Africanus in 206 B.C. It has ruins of an amphitheater, and is said to have been the birthplace of three emperors: Trajan, Hadrian, and Theodosius I.

*Ithaca* (ith'-ā-kā). [Modern Greek, *Ithake, Thiaki.*] One of the Ionian Islands, about two miles NE of Cephallenia. Accord-

---

fat, fāte, fär, fâll, àsk, fāre; net, mē, hèr; pin, pīne; not, nōte, möve; nôr; up, lūte, půll; oi, oil; ou out; (lightened) ēlect, agǫny, ūnite;

ing to tradition, it was the center of the island kingdom of Odysseus, which comprised in addition, the islands of Dulichium, Same, and Zacynthus, and was the site of his palace. As described in the *Odyssey*, it has no plains suitable for agriculture or the rearing of horses, but has a topography well adapted for goats. The location of Ithaca, commanding the routes to Corcyra, Elis and Triphylia, and the western entrance to the Gulf of Corinth, could have given it the maritime importance it had as Odysseus' kingdom. From this island he sailed with 12 ships to accompany the Greeks to Troy. Some say that the topographical descriptions given by Homer in the *Odyssey* fit the island Leukas more accurately than Ithaca. And other scholars, in consideration of the topographical details, point out that Homer was writing poetry, and his descriptions are not necessarily to be taken as a geographical guide, although in fact they have been so taken, successfully in some cases. Excavations by archaeologists have not been able to support either claim; the question remains an open one.

*Ithome* (i-thō′mē). A strong, natural fortress west of the Pamisus River in the western mountains of Messenia. To it the Messenians withdrew in the First Messenian War with Sparta (8th century B.C.), and walled it. In the Second Messenian War (7th century B.C.), under the command of Aristomenes, they were again defeated after a long struggle, but were permitted to withdraw from their fortress on Mount Eira unharmed on condition that they never return to the Peloponnesus. Before he left, Aristomenes returned to Ithome and in a remote spot buried the mysteries that had been brought to Messenia by Caucon. Nearly 300 years later, the mysteries were recovered, owing to a dream had by Epaminondas, the Theban conqueror of the Spartans at Leuctra (371 B.C.). His dream instructed him to restore the Messenians to the land where the mysteries were found. He recalled them from their exile all over the Greek world, and to the music of flutes helped them to lay out a new city, which bore the name Messene. Ithome formed the citadel of the new city, and one side of its boundaries.

*Itius Portus* (ish′i-us pôr′tus). In ancient geography, the place from which Caesar sailed for Britain; generally identified with Boulogne or Ushant (Ile d'Ouessant).

(obscured) errạnt, ardẹnt, actọr; ch, chip; g, go; th, thin; ŦH, then; y, you;
(variable) ḍ as d or j, ş as s or sh, ţ as t or ch, ẓ as z or zh.

# ——J——

*Janiculum* (jạ-nik′ụ-lum). [Also: *Mons Janiculus, Mons Aureus;* Italian, *Monte Gianicolo.*] Long ridge or hill in Rome, on the W bank of the Tiber, extending S from the Vatican, and opposite the Capitoline and Aventine hills. It is the highest of the seven hills of Rome, attaining an elevation of about 276 feet. At its highest point, guarding the Via Aurelia which here crosses the Janiculum, was an early blockhouse. Where the 3rd-century wall of Aurelian (270–275 A.D.) crosses the Via Aurelia was the Porta Aurelia, dismantled in 1643 and replaced by the modern Porta San Pancrazio. Nearby are the buildings of the American Academy. (JJ)

*Jaxartes* (jak-sär′tēz). In ancient geography, a river (modern Syr Darya) of Scythia, in C Asia. Alexander the Great crossed the river (328 B.C.) and penetrated Scythia. Returning, he founded a city on the banks of the Jaxartes where it crossed the borders of Sogdiana. He named the new city Alexandria Eschata *(Furthest)*, because it was intended to mark the northeastern limit of his empire. In succeeding centuries, the name of the city was changed to Khodjend. It is now Leninabad, in the Tadzhik Soviet Socialist Republic, U.S.S.R.

# ——K——

*Kalamai* (kä-lä′mē). An unimportant ancient village at the foot of Mount Taÿgetus in Messenia, S Greece, now known as Kalámi. The name has been transferred to the modern port city of Kalamai or Kalamata, near the mouth of the Nedon river, which stands on the site of Pherae (Pharae) of Homeric legend. (JJ)

*Kalamai* or *Kalamata* (kä-lä-mä′tä). The modern port city

which stands on the site of the Homeric Pherae or Pharae
in S Messenia. The name *Kalamai* is borrowed from an ancient village (now Kalámi) which stood several miles further
inland. See *Pherae.* (JJ)

*Kalamata* (kä-lä-mä′tä). See *Kalamai.*

*Kamares* or *Camares* (ka̞-mä′res). A cave on the S slope of
Mount Ida in Crete. In it the British School of Archaeology
found important remains of the Middle Minoan civilization;
particularly the polychrome vases painted in white, red, and
yellow on a black glazed ground that came to be known as
"Kamares ware."

*Kanish* (kä′nish). [Modern name, *Kultepe.*] In ancient geography, a town in C Asia Minor, in the Anatolian plateau, about
100 miles N of what is now Adana, Turkey. Silver was mined
here for Assyria c1900 B.C.; it was a Hittite center.

*Kea* (ke′ä), or *Keos* (ke′ôs). See *Ceos.*

*Kephallenia* (ke″fä-lē-nē′ä). See *Cephallenia.*

*Kephisos* (kē-fē-sôs′). See *Cephissus.*

*Khios* (kē′ôs). See *Chios.*

*Knossos* (nos′os). See *Cnossus.*

*Kolonos Hippios* (ko̞-lō′no̞s hip′i-o̞s). See *Colonus.*

*Korinthos* (kô′rēn-thôs). See *Corinth* and *Corinthia.*

*Kos* (kos). See *Cos.*

*Kyklades* (kē-klä′thes) or *Kykladon Nesoi* ka̞-klä′thôn nē′sē). See
*Cyclades.*

*Kythera* (kē′thē-rä) or *Kytherion* (kē-thē′rē-ôn). See *Cythera.*

——L——

*Lacedaemon.* See *Laconia* and *Sparta,* both in ancient Greece.

*Laconia* (la̞-kō′ni-a̞). [Also: *Lacedaemon, Laconica.*] In ancient
geography, the SE division of the Peloponnesus, Greece,
lying S of Argolis and Arcadia, and E of Messenia. It was
traversed by the Eurotas River. Chief city, Sparta.

*Laconia, Gulf of.* [Modern Greek, *Lakonikos Kolpos;* Latin,
*Laconicus Sinus.*] Arm of the Mediterranean S of Laconia,
Greece.

*Lade* (lä′dē). In ancient geography, a small island in the

Aegean Sea near Miletus. Near it, in 494 B.C., the Persian
fleet defeated the Ionian Greeks.

*Ladon* (lā′dọn). In ancient geography, a river in Arcadia,
Greece. Rising in the mountains near Pheneüs, it is, according to Pausanias, the most lovely river in Greece. The river-
god of the Ladon was, according to some accounts, the
father of Daphne beloved by Leucippus and Apollo. The
nymph Syrinx fled to the Ladon, pursued by Pan, and on its
banks she was transformed into a reed. Pan, not knowing
which reed was Syrinx, cut the reeds he found in the place
where she was last seen and made them into a musical instrument called the syrinx, or Pan's pipes.

*Lamia* (lā′mi-ạ). Town in C Greece, near the head of the Gulf
of Lamia (an arm of the Aegean Sea). It was an ancient city
of Malis, where Antipater was besieged in 323 B.C.

*Lamia, Gulf of.* [Also: *Malian Gulf;* Latin, *Maliacus Sinus.*] Arm
of the Aegean Sea, S of Thessaly, Greece.

*Lampsacus* (lamp′sạ-kus). [Modern village name, *Lapseki.*] In
ancient geography, a city in Mysia, Asia Minor, on the E
shore of the Hellespont. It was colonized by Ionian Greeks
from Phocaea, fell to Persia following the Ionian revolt (499
B.C.), allied itself to Athens at the end of the Persian Wars
(479 B.C.) and paid Athens a large tribute. Its location on the
Hellespont made it important to Athens as one of the cities
that controlled the grain route. When Lampsacus revolted
against Athens (411 B.C.), the revolt was put down. The
Spartan Lysander besieged and took the city (405), but with
the signing of the King's Peace (387), it fell again to Persia.
It was occupied for Alexander the Great by his general Par-
menio (335), and ultimately, c196 B.C., became an ally of
Rome. Ancient Lampsacus was a center of worship of the
nature-god Priapus, a god of fertility.

*Lanuvium* (lạ-nū′vi-um). [Modern village name, *Lanuvio,* formerly *Città Lavinia.*] In ancient geography, a town in
Latium, Italy, about 20 miles SE of Rome. It was a center of
the worship of Juno Sospita, the succoring goddess.

*Laodicea* (lā-od-i-sē′ạ, lā″ọ-di-sē′ạ). [Full Latin name, *Laodicea
ad Lycum.*] Ancient city in Phrygia, Asia Minor, in the valley
of the Lycus, a tributary river of the Maeander (modern
Menderes), about 50 miles N of Aradus. It was founded
under the Seleucids, by Antiochus II (c250 B.C.) and named
after his wife, Laodice. It was an important early Christian

fat, fāte, fär, fâll, ȧsk, fãre; net, mē, hėr; pin, pīne; not, nōte, mȯve,
nôr; up, lūte, pull; oi, oil; ou out; (lightened) ẹlect, agọny, ụnite;

center, and in the Apocalypse is one of the congregations to which an epistle is addressed. Its great heap of ruins still attest to it former splendor.

*Laodicea.* [Full Latin name, *Laodicea ad Mare.*] Ancient city on the coast of Syria about 50 miles S of Antioch. It was known for its commerce in wine and fruit from the surrounding country, and in modern times has given its name to *Latakia* tobacco. (AH)

*Laphystius* (la-fis'ti-us), *Mount.* A mountain near Orchomenus, in Boeotia. Athamas had his palace at the foot of this mountain. It was on its summit that he was preparing to sacrifice his son Phrixus when the latter was rescued and carried off on the back of a miraculous winged ram with fleece of pure gold.

*Larissa* (la̱-ris'a̱). [Also: *Larisa.*] A city in Thessaly, NE Greece, situated on the Peneus River. Larissa became the seat of the Aleuadae, a Thessalian family prominent in organizing the Thessalian Confederacy in the 6th century B.C. The Aleuadae welcomed artists and writers from southern Greece to their court. In the Persian War Larissa was allied to Xerxes. The Aleuadae Dynasty was overthrown toward the end of the 5th century B.C. Philip II of Macedon brought Larissa under his control, c344 B.C. In 196 B.C. it became the capital of the Thessalian Confederacy organized by the Romans.

*Larissa Cremaste* (krē-mas'tē). In ancient geography, a town in Phthia, SE Thessaly, Greece, situated near the coast opposite the northern tip of Euboea. According to some accounts, this was the site of Achilles' city. The ancient citadel was taken by Demetrius Poliorcetes, 302 B.C.

*Larius, Lacus* (lā'ri-us, lā'kus). [Modern name, *Lake Como.*] Lake in N Italy, traversed by the Addua River and famous for its scenery.

*Las* (läs). An ancient town in Laconia, on the Gulf of Laconia.

*Lassithi* (lä-sē'thē). [Also: *Dhikti.*] Modern name of a mountain in Crete. The ancient name of the mountain was Dicte, where the cave in which some say Zeus was born is located.

*Latium* (lā'shi-um). In ancient geography, the part of C Italy lying along the Mediterranean SE of Etruria and NW of Campania. The name was originally restricted to the land of the Latini or Latins, chiefly comprised in the Roman Campagna. Its chief cities formed the Latin League, which was at war with Rome, 340–338 B.C., and was incorporated with

Rome after 338 B.C. In an extended sense Latium (also Latium Adjectum or Novum) was the region from the Tiber to the Liris or to Mount Massicus, including the territories of the Latini, Hernicans, Volscians, and Auruncans, and (in part) of the Aequians.

**Latmus** (lat′mus). In ancient geography, a mountain range in Caria, Asia Minor, E of Miletus. There was a sanctuary to Endymion here because it was on this mountain, according to legend, that Endymion slept forever while Selene, the moon-goddess, came to gaze on his ever-youthful beauty.

**Laurentum** (lô-ren′tum). In ancient geography, a city in Latium, Italy, situated near the coast between Ostia and Lavinium, about 16 miles S of Rome: the capital of ancient Latium. According to the *Aeneid*, it was founded by the Laurentes, men who colonized Latium under Latinus. They got their name from the sacred laurel tree which was found in the spot where the city was built.

**Laurium** (lô′ri-um). [Also: *Laurion;* modern name, *Lavrion*.] Low hills at the SE extremity of Attica, Greece. They were celebrated in ancient times as the site of silver mines that helped Athens to arrive at commercial greatness. Shafts of these mines, galleries of which remain, went down as much as 400 feet. From the silver mined here the Athenians minted coins that circulated throughout the world, and enjoyed such a high reputation that it was considered unwise to change the design. For this reason, lest a newer design be looked upon with suspicion in the remote parts to which Athenian traders ventured, the ancient coins, with the head of Athena on one side and her owl on the other, retained their original archaic design. In the time of the traveler Pausanias (2nd century A.D.), who described the shafts and galleries of the mines, the silver ore had been exhausted. Centuries later the mines were reopened, and produced lead and zinc. Near Laurium is the modern seaport of Lavrion.

**Lavinium** (la̯-vin′i-um). In ancient geography, a city in Latium, Italy, about 17 miles S of Rome. According to the *Aeneid*, it was built by Aeneas and named after his Latin wife, Lavinia.

**Lebadia** (le-bä′di-a̯) or **Lebadea** (le-ba̯-dā′a̯). A town in Boeotia, Greece, famous for its oracle of Trophonius. The town was said to have been named for Lebadus, an Athenian who settled there. The oracle was on the slope of a mountain

fat, fāte, fär, fâll, ȧsk, fãre; net, mē, hėr; pin, pīne; not, nōte, möve, nôr; up, lūte, pṳll; oi, oil; ou out; (lightened) e̯lect, ago͟ny, ūnite;

across the Hercyna River and beyond a sacred grove in
which there were many sanctuaries. According to tradition,
for a long time the Boeotians were ignorant of the oracle of
Trophonius within their borders. Once, during a drought,
they sent to the oracle at Delphi to learn how the drought
might be broken. The priestess instructed them to go to
Trophonius. They were at a loss where he could be found,
and Saon, a Boeotian, searched in vain. At last he saw a
swarm of bees and decided to follow them. Where the bees
disappeared into the ground, he found the oracle of Trophonius, and it was he, they say, who established the rites
to be observed there. The procedure for appealing to the
oracle was most involved. After elaborate purification ceremonies, the suppliant ate the flesh of a ram that had been
sacrificed to the shade of Agamedes, brother of Trophonius.
He was then led to the Hercyna River by two boys 13 years
of age. They bathed and anointed him. He then drank from
a spring, called the Water of Lethe, to make him forget the
past. Then he drank from another spring called the Water
of Memory, so that he would recall whatever he was told by
the oracle. Dressed in a prescribed costume and wearing
fillets on his head like a sacrificial victim, he was led to the
cave where the oracle was housed. Holding barley and
honey cakes in his hands he descended a ladder into a pit,
until he reached a narrow opening. There unseen hands
pulled him through and he received a stunning blow on the
head. While he was still unconscious from the blow, a voice
spoke and prophesied. As soon as the prophetic voice
ceased the suppliant was returned, feet first, through the
opening, hauled up the ladder, and seated on the chair of
Memory, where he repeated all that the voice had said while
he was unconscious. When he recovered consciousness, the
suppliant found that he no longer had the barley and honey
cakes: they were taken from him while he was in the second
cavern, before the prophetic voice spoke. The ceremonies
for consulting the oracle were so shattering that a long time
passed before the suppliant recovered his ability to laugh;
and especially solemn people were said to "have been to
Trophonius." The oracle of Trophonius was one of many
consulted by Croesus, King of Lydia, before he decided to
make war on Cyrus, King of the Persians. Trophonius is one
of the chthonian deities, the worship of whom is in sharp

contrast to that of the Olympian gods.

*Lebedos* (leb'ẹ-dos). In ancient geography, an Ionian seaport in Lydia, Asia Minor, about 25 miles NW of Ephesus. It was one of the 12 Ionian cities of Asia, and according to tradition, was colonized by Andraemon, son of Codrus, legendary king of Attica, as leader of an expedition of Ionians and Boeotians.

*Lechaeum* (le-kē'um). One of the harbors of Corinth. According to tradition, it was named for Leches, child of Poseidon and Pirene. There were a sanctuary and a bronze image of Poseidon there.

*Leibethra* (lī-bē'thrạ). See *Libethra.*

*Lemnos* (lem'nos). [Also: *Limni, Limno, Limnos.*] Island in the NE Aegean Sea. The surface is hilly and fertile, and in antiquity produced considerable grain crops. It has hot springs and a harbor on the S coast at modern Moudhros. It was sacred to Hephaestus in ancient times because, when he was hurled out of heaven by Zeus, he landed on the island, and the islanders who found him took care of him. According to legend, the Lemnian women, under their queen Hypsipyle, murdered all the men of the island for cohabiting with their Thracian female captives. Afterward, the island was purified every year of the guilt of this mass murder, which included the slaying of all male children as well as their fathers. Ceremonies of purification lasting nine days were held, during which time all fires on the island were put out. At the end of the nine days and after sacrifices had been offered to the dead, new fire was brought from Delos. The Argonauts stopped at Lemnos for supplies soon after they began their voyage to Colchis to secure the Golden Fleece. They found the island populated only by women. They were hospitably greeted and stayed for some time, Jason fathering the twin sons of Hypsipyle, their queen, and the other Argonauts leaving an island soon repopulated with a race called, for their fathers, the Minyans. Students see in the myth evidence of a former gynocracy (rule by women). Both Aeschylus and Sophocles wrote plays, now lost, on the story. Lemnos was conquered in the reign of Darius I by the Persians. It was gained for Athens by Miltiades c500 B.C., and remained a possession of Athens, except for a 10-year period of Spartan control, until Greece was conquered by the Macedonians. Lemnos was noted throughout antiquity, and

fat, fāte, fär, fâll, àsk, fãre; net, mē, hėr; pin, pīne; not, nōte, mŏve, nôr; up, lūte, půll; oi, oil; ou out; (lightened) ẹlect, agǫny, ụnite;

into modern times, for a product called "Lemnian earth" which was supposed to have unusual medicinal properties. To modern times it has been used as a cure for certain wounds and infections, and in ancient times it was also highly regarded as a cure for snake bite. On a fixed day each year a priestess went to the bare hill where the earth was dug, performed certain rituals, and supervised the digging of a prescribed amount of the earth. The earth was prepared in blocks, each of which was stamped with a head of Artemis and with the word "Lemnos," whence the name. In modern times the ceremony of digging the Lemnian earth was carried out on Aug. 6th; the blocks were stamped, and then distributed for sale by apothecaries. The island of Lemnos is about 20 miles long, and has an area of about 180 square miles.

*Lentini* (len-tē′nē). See *Leontini.*

*Leontini* (lē-on-tī′ni). [Modern name, *Lentini.*] In ancient geography, a city of Sicily, situated on a plain between two hills, about 21 miles NW of Syracuse. It was founded by Chalcidian Greeks from Sicilian Naxos, 729 B.C. Hippocrates of Gela took it, 498 B.C., and to it Hiero of Syracuse removed the inhabitants of Catana and Naxos. In 433 B.C. Leontini entered into an alliance with Athens to counteract the growing power of the Corinthian city of Syracuse, and in 427 B.C. an Athenian expedition was sent out to Sicily, largely owing to the urging of Gorgias of Leontini, but the expedition accomplished little. In 423 B.C. the city was taken by Syracuse. The restoration of Leontini was one of the objects of the second expedition undertaken by Athens against Sicily, 415 B.C. The expedition failed signally to accomplish its objects and brought diaster to Athens. After being devastated by the Carthaginians, 406 B.C., the independence of Leontini was restored briefly by a treaty of peace between Dionysius the Elder, tyrant of Syracuse, and the Carthaginians, but in 404 B.C. the city surrendered to Dionysius rather than risk annihilation at his hands. In the Second Punic War it was besieged and taken by the Romans under Marcellus, 214 B.C.

*Lepini* (lā-pē′nē), *Monti.* Italian name of the Volscian Mountains.

*Lepontine Alps* (lē-pon′tin, -tīn). [Italian, *Alpi Lepontine.*] That part of the Alps which extends from the Simplon Pass E to the Splügen Pass. It comprises the St. Gotthard, Ticino, and Adula Alps. Highest peak, Monte Leone (about 11,655 feet).

*Lepreum* (lep'rē-um). City of Elis on the coast of the Cyparissian Gulf. Some say that the city was founded by Minyans who had come from the island of Lemnos and settled there. They say the city was named for Lepreus, who challenged Heracles to a series of contests and was killed. Others say the city got its name from the disease that afflicted the inhabitants. The disease was called leprosy but was not the same as the modern disease of that name. It was a skin affection in which the skin became whitish in color, rough, and scaly. The people of Lepreum wished to be thought Arcadians, but they were in fact Eleans, and when they won in the Olympic Games, were announced as Eleans from Lepreum.

*Leptis Magna* (lep'tis mag'na). [Also: *Leptis, Neapolis;* modern name, *Lebda.*] In ancient geography, a seaport in N Africa, on the Libyan coast just E of the present town of Homs, said to have been founded by Sidonians. After the Second Punic War it was conquered by the Numidians, but in the wars waged by Jugurtha for control of Numidia, it appealed to Rome for protection and became an ally. It was the birthplace of Septimius Severus, Emperor of Rome 193–211 A.D., who embellished it with handsome buildings and extensive public works, including Septimius' great arch. Beginning in the 4th century it was repeatedly raided from the desert and its population dwindled; its ruins remain today, however, the most imposing of Roman Africa. The most recent explorations have indicated the presence of a Punic settlement underlying the imperial city.

*Lerna* (lėr'na). In ancient geography, a marshy region and town in Argolis, Greece, S of Argos, and situated on the Gulf of Argolis. It is said that out of love for Amymone, daughter of Danaus, Poseidon caused a never-failing spring to gush forth here, which became the source of the never-dry river of Lerna. Some say the marsh of Lerna was the home of the Nereids. On the banks of the river the many-headed Lernaean Hydra was born under a plane tree. It lived in the marsh and was so devastating that the name Lerna became synonymous with evil in the saying, "A Lerna of evils." To the marsh came Heracles, who sought out the monster, and with the aid of Iolaus slew it. In the marsh was the bottomless

Alcyonean Lake that once the Emperor Nero tried, and
failed, to sound. Some say this lake was an entrance to
Hades. Into it, they say, Dionysus plunged when he went to
Hades to seek his mother. His descent to Hades was remembered annually with secret rites on the banks of the lake at
night. Vine-wreathed trumpets pealed forth to summon the
god up from the depths.

*Lerus* (lē′rus) or *Leros* (lē′ros). [Also: *Lero.*] Small, rocky island
in the Aegean Sea, about 32 miles S of Samos and lying N
of Calymna. In the course of the Ionian revolt against Persia,
which began 499 B.C., Aristagoras, one of the chief instiga-
tors, was forced to flee from Miletus to Myrcinus in Macedonia by the successes of the Persians. Hecataeus the
historian proposed to the Ionians that they retire to Lerus
with its deep and well-protected harbors, fortify it, and pre-
pare to resist the Persians from there, or make it a base for
a later return to Miletus. His advice was not taken. Area of
the island, about 28 square miles.

*Lesbos* (lez′bos). [Also: *Lesvos, Mytilene, Mitylene, Mytilini;* Italian, *Metelino;* Turkish *Midillü.*] Mountainous and fertile island in the N Aegean Sea, lying just off the coast of Asia
Minor opposite ancient Mysia. It was to this island, according to legend, that the dismembered head of Orpheus
floated after it had been tossed into the Hebrus River by the
maenads. His lyre also landed here and remained until, at
the request of Apollo and the Muses, it was translated to the
heavens as the constellation Lyra. In the Trojan War, Lesbos belonged to Priam's realm and was assaulted and taken
by the forces of Achilles. In later times the noble families of
Lesbos claimed descent from Agamemnon. The island was
colonized by Aeolians and was one of the strongest Aeolian
centers. In the late 7th and early 6th centuries B.C. Pittacus,
known as one of the Seven Sages of Greece, became tyrant
and put an end to the internecine wars that divided the
island. Later in the 6th century B.C. Polycrates, tyrant of
Samos, defeated the Lesbians in a sea fight when they came
out against him to aid Miletus. The Lesbians he captured in
the battle were put in chains and compelled to build the
moat around the castle at Samos. The island came under the
dominion of the Persians and revolted, along with the
Ionian cities, in 499 B.C., through hatred of the satrap Coes
set over them by Darius. They furnished men and ships to

Histiaeus, a leader of the revolt. However, in the battle of
Lade (494 B.C.) for the relief of Miletus to which the Lesbians sent 70 ships, the Lesbians sailed away without joining
the battle, and the following year Lesbos again fell to the
Persians. After the Persian War Lesbos joined the Confederacy of Delos, under Athenian leadership, as an ally that
contributed ships and was not required to pay tribute. In
428 B.C. Lesbos, a free ally, revolted against Athens. The
Athenians sent a fleet, besieged Mytilene, which had now
become the chief seat of resistance as well as the center of
affairs of the island, and compelled its surrender. The
Athenians voted in assembly to put the entire adult male
population of Mytilene to death and to sell the women and
children into slavery. A ship was sent to Mytilene bearing
the order, but the day after the vote was taken in Athens
reaction set in, the vote was rescinded, and a second ship,
whose crew was promised large rewards if the first ship was
overtaken, set out for Lesbos to countermand the first terrible order. The second ship arrived at Mytilene almost at the
same time as the first ship, whose commander had not been
in a hurry to deliver his fatal message. The ringleaders of the
revolt were executed, the Lesbian fleet was taken over by
Athens, and the walls of Mytilene were pulled down, but the
population of Mytilene was spared. A second revolt, 412
B.C., was also put down. In the last years of the Peloponnesian War the island was frequently attacked by the Spartans
and their allies and parts of it were taken. Most of it was won
back for Athens by Thrasybulus. It joined the second
Athenian Confederacy in 377 B.C. and remained loyal. Later
in the 4th century B.C. it fell to Macedonia. It was taken by
Mithridates of Pontus (88 B.C.), and when he was defeated
by the Romans, it became part of the Roman province of
Asia. The five chief cities of ancient Lesbos were Mytilene,
Methymna, Antissa, Eresus, and Pyrrha. The island was celebrated in ancient times as a seat of literature. In the 7th
century B.C. it produced the musician Terpander, the Cyclic
poet Lesches, and the poet Arion of Methymna who was
credited with inventing the dithyramb, or cyclic chorus. The
lyric poets Sappho and Alcaeus were contemporaries of Pittacus in the 6th century B.C. The philosophers Theophras-
tus (c372–c287 B.C.) and Cratippus (1st century B.C.) were

also natives of Lesbos. Area of the island, about 630 square miles.

*Letrini* (let-rī'ni). [Modern name, *Pirgos* or *Pyrgos.*] Town in Elis.

*Leucas* (lö'kạs). [Also: *Leucadia, Leukados, Levkas;* Italian, *Santa Maura.*] One of the Ionian Islands, W of Aetolia and Acarnania in Greece. The island is separated from the mainland by only a narrow channel, and the ancients considered it as a peninsula which had been artificially made into an island by a man-made channel. Some say the island was named for Leucadius, a brother of Penelope, who was a king in Acarnania. And some say Leucas is the island described in the *Odyssey* as Ithaca, the center of the island kingdom of Odysseus. Those who hold this view claim that Homer's description fits Leucas and profess to recognize the site of Odysseus' palace at Nidri on the east coast. The great bay of Ithaca described by Homer is identified with the bay of Vlikhon. Other spots specifically described in the *Odyssey* have been identified by those who hold the view that Leucas was the home of Odysseus. The surface of the island is hilly and mountainous. Near the ancient temple of Apollo on the promontory in the SW part of the island is a steep cliff, known as Sappho's Leap, from which the poetess Sappho is said to have thrown herself into the sea. The ancient city of Leucas was founded by colonists from Corinth in the 7th century B.C. These colonists are said to have made Leucas into an island by cutting a canal across the isthmus. The canal later was silted up, for in 425 B.C. the Peloponnesian fleet was hauled across the Isthmus. In the time of Augustus the canal was cleared and the channel deepened. Bronze-age tombs and pottery found on the island indicate that it was occupied in Mycenaean times.

*Leuce* (lö'sē). In ancient geography, a wooded island off the mouth of the Ister river (Danube) in the Euxine Sea. According to some accounts in Greek mythology, Poseidon, at the request of Thetis, gave this island to Achilles and to it he retired after he was slain at Troy. His shade was joined by his companions Patroclus, Antilochus, the two Ajaxes, and Helen. There was a temple of Achilles there that contained an image of him and one of Helen. According to tradition, seamen were permitted to land and make sacrifices, but had to leave the island before sunset. No one could live on the island and women were absolutely forbidden to set foot on it. Achilles and his companions made merry there, and mariners sailing nearby claimed they could hear the voices of Achilles and his friends singing the verses of Homer, and sometimes the clashing of shields and the sound of horses stamping their hoofs were said to be wafted over the waves.

**Leucerae, Lacus** (lö-sėr'ē lā'kus). [Modern name, *Lake Lecco*.] Southeastern arm of Lacus Larius (Lake Como), NW Italy. Length, about 13 miles.

**Leucopetra** (lö-kop'ẹ-trạ). [Modern Italian name, *Capo dell' Armi*.] In ancient geography, a promontory at the SW extremity of Italy.

**Leucopetra.** In ancient geography, a village on the Isthmus of Corinth. Here (146 B.C.) the Romans under Mummius defeated the Achaean League under Diaeus.

**Leucophrys** (lū-kō'fris). An ancient name for the island of Tenedos.

**Leuctra** (lök'trạ) or **Leuctrum** (-trum). A city on the eastern coast of the Gulf of Messenia.

**Leuctra.** In ancient geography, a locality in Boeotia, Greece, about seven miles SW of Thebes. It is celebrated for the victory (371 B.C.) gained here by the Thebans under Epaminondas over the Spartans under Cleombrotus. The battle is significant as the decisive end of Spartan military supremacy in Greece and as a tactical turning point in military history, Epaminondas's victory being the result of his concentration of overwhelming force at a single point in the enemy line. He did this by strengthening the left wing of his phalanx to a depth of 50 men and by having it advance ahead of the other wing.

**Levadia** (le-vä'thyä), or **Levadhia, Levadeia, Livadia.** See **Lebadia.**

**Libethra** (lī-bē'thrạ). In ancient geography, a place at the foot of Mount Olympus where the remains of Orpheus, gathered by the Muses, were said to have been buried; the nightingales were said to sing more sweetly here than anywhere else in the world.

**Liburnia** (lī-bėr'ni-ạ). 1) In ancient geography, a country in Illyria, along the Adriatic Sea, corresponding to the W part of modern Croatia, Yugoslavia. The inhabitants were celebrated as navigators and pirates. 2) A fast, light cutter developed by the inhabitants of Liburnia, originally for piracy, the

fat, fāte, fär, fåll, ȧsk, fāre; net, mē, hėr; pin, pīne; not, nōte, mȯve, nôr; up, lūte, pu̇ll; oi, oil; ou out; (lightened) ẹlect, agọny, ūnite;

*liburna* or *liburnica*. The Romans adopted it and it became an indispensable part of the imperial fleet.

**Liburnum** (lī-bėr′num) or **Liburni Portus** (lī-bėr′nī pōr′tus). [Modern name, *Livorno;* English, *Leghorn.*] Seaport of C Italy, on the Ligurian Sea.

**Libya** (lib′i-ạ). In ancient geography, a name of varying signification, denoting Africa, or Africa excluding Egypt, or Africa excluding Egypt and Ethiopia.

**Libyan Desert** (lib′i-ạn). [In Egypt, *Western Desert.*] In ancient times, the Sahara; now restricted to an extremely barren and partly sandy desert region extending from the W side of the Nile Valley to E central Libya. Area, about 750,000 square miles.

**Libyan Sea.** [Latin, *Libycum Mare.*] In ancient geography, that part of the Mediterranean which extends from what is now Tunisia E to Egypt.

**Licata** (lē-kä′tä). See *Phintias.*

**Liguria** (li-gū′ri-ạ). In ancient geography, the country of the Ligurians, in NW Italy and SE France. At the time of Augustus it was included between the Mediterranean and the rivers Varus, Padus, Trebia, and Magra. Originally it extended beyond these limits. It was at war with Rome from c200 B.C. to c120 B.C., and was finally subjugated in 14 B.C.

**Ligurian Sea.** [Italian, *Mar Ligure;* French, *Mer Ligurienne;* Latin, *Mare Ligusticum.*] The part of the Mediterranean Sea which lies between Liguria and Corsica.

**Lilybaeum** (lil-i-bē′um). [Modern name, *Marsala.*] In ancient geography, a city on the W coast of Sicily. It was founded in 396 B.C. by the Carthaginian general Himilco to take the place of the Carthaginian stronghold of Motya, which had been destroyed (398 B.C.) by Dionysius the Elder of Syracuse and recaptured by Himilco (397 B.C.). Lilybaeum became the chief stronghold of the Carthaginians in Sicily; it resisted Dionysius and Pyrrhus (368 B.C. and 276 B.C. respectively) and the Romans during the First Punic War (264–241 B.C.), who occupied it only at the end of the war. It was used as the place of Scipio's embarkation for Africa in the Second Punic War (218–201 B.C.).

**Limnae** (lim′nē). In ancient geography, a section of Athens, Greece, important as the seat of the earliest cult of Dionysus and the first rudimentary dramatic performances at Athens.

*Limni* (lēm′nē) or *Limno* (lēm′nô) or *Limnos* (lēm′nôs). See
*Lemnos.*

*Lindus* (lin′dus). In ancient geography, a city on the southeast
coast of the island of Rhodes, situated on a commanding
and readily defended height. Prehistorically colonized by
settlers from Crete, it was a Dorian city from about 1000
B.C., and was a member of the Dorian Hexapolis—six Dorian
cities on or near the coast of Asia Minor. In the centuries
preceding the Persian Wars it was an important port of over
100,000 inhabitants, owing to its strategic location and wide
commerce throughout the Mediterranean. It was also the
mother city of many colonies on the neighboring islands and
on the coast of Asia Minor. Cleobulus, one of the Seven
Sages of Greece, was tyrant of Lindus in the 6th century B.C.
A lofty promontory, rising abruptly from the sea, formed the
acropolis of the city, and was crowned with a Doric temple
of Athena Lindia. Remains of the temple, of majestic
propylaea, and of a theater, may still be seen. Lindus was the
capital of the island of Rhodes until 408 B.C., when the three
principal cities of the island—Lindus, Camirus, and Ialysus
—jointly founded the city of Rhodes and made it the capital.
With the growth of the city of Rhodes as a religious, political, and commercial center, Lindus lost its commanding
importance in the ancient world. Modern Lindos, a village
of about 1000 inhabitants, occupies the site of the ancient
city at the base of the acropolis.

*Lipari Islands* (lip′ạ-ri; Italian, lē′pä-rē). Group of islands in the
Tyrrhenian Sea, N of Sicily. The chief islands are Lipari
(Lipara), Stromboli (Strongyle), Salina (Didyme), Vulcano
(Thermessa or Vulcania), and the small islands of Alicuri
(Ericussa), Filicuri (Phoenicussa), and Panarea (Euonymus
or Hicesia). See *Aeoliae Insulae.*

*Liternum* (li-tèr′num). In ancient geography, a town in Cam-
pania, Italy, situated on the W coast about 14 miles NW of
Naples, between Cumae and the mouth of the Volturnus
River. It was noted principally as the place to which Scipio
Africanus the Elder withdrew towards the end of his life. He
died at Liternum and his tomb was there.

*Locri* (lō′krī or lok′rī) or *Locri Epizephyrii* (ep″i-ze-fir′i-ī).
[Modern name, *Gerace.*] In ancient geography, a city on the
SE coast of what is now Calabria, founded before 680 B.C.
by colonists from Opuntian and Ozolian Locri in Greece

and probably also by Lacedaemonians. The severe law code prepared for the city by the famous lawgiver Zaleucus, about 650 B.C., appears to have been the first written legal code in Europe, widely copied in Magna Graecia. At one time closely allied with Syracuse, it survived the usual wars with its Greek neighbors, the Bruttians, Pyrrhus, Rome, and the Carthaginians without fatal injury, and was well-known to Polybius. Excavations have revealed a Doric temple of about 500 B.C. and traces also of an Ionic temple of the 5th century B.C., built over the foundations of a predecessor. (JJ)

*Locris* (lō'kris, lok'ris). In ancient geography, name applied to a division of C Greece, occupied by the Locri Epicnemidii, the Locri Opuntii, and by the Locri Ozolae.

*Luca* (lö'ka̩). [Modern name, *Lucca.*] City in N Italy, NE of Pisae. Presumably established in Etruscan times, but its first certain appearance in history is in 56 B.C., when Caesar summoned Pompey and Crassus to Luca and there organized with them the First Triumvirate. Later, perhaps in Augustus' time, a veteran colony was sent there. Careful study has recovered the plan of the central city and traces of the forum and buildings: theater, amphitheater, temple, and aqueduct; and the churches of S. Giovanni, S. Frediano, and S. Alessandro incorporate shafts and capitals of ancient columns removed from other Roman structures. (JJ)

*Lucania* (lö-kā'ni-a̩). In ancient geography, a division of S Italy. It was bounded by Campania, Samnium, and Apulia on the N and NE, the Gulf of Tarentum on the E, Bruttii on the S, and the Tyrrhenian Sea on the SW. The surface is mountainous. The inhabitants were Lucanians (a branch of the Samnites) and, on the coast, Greeks. It was reduced by Rome in the 3rd century B.C.

*Luceria* (lö-sē'ri-a̩). [Modern name, *Lucera.*] In ancient geography, a town in Apulia, SE Italy. In the wars between the Romans and the Samnites (321 B.C.) Luceria took the side of Rome. It was later colonized by the Latins.

*Lucrinus, Lacus* (lö-krī'nus, lā'kus). [Modern name, *Lake Lucrine.*] In ancient geography, a small salt-water lake in Campania, Italy, about nine miles NW of Neapolis.

*Lugdunensis* ((lug-dū-nen'sis). [Also: *Gallia Lugdunensis.*] In ancient geography, a province of the Roman Empire, situated in Gaul. It extended from Lugdunum (modern Lyons) N to the line of the lower Seine (including Paris), and NW

through Brittany to the ocean, including the upper course
of the Seine and nearly the entire course of the Loire. It was
conquered (58–51 B.C.) by Julius Caesar.

*Luna* (lö′nạ). [Modern site name, *Luni*.] In ancient geography,
a city in Italy, on the coast E of what is now La Spezia. It was
founded by the Etruscans and became a Roman town in the
2nd century B.C.

*Lusitania* (lö-si-tā′ni-ạ). In ancient geography, the country of
the Lusitanians, comprising the modern Portugal N to the
river Durius (Douro), and adjoining parts of W Spain. In a
later, more extended use, it was one of the Roman provinces
into which Hispania was divided by Augustus.

*Lusius* (lö′si-us). In ancient geography, a river in Arcadia. The
name means "Bathing-river," and was given to it because
Zeus was bathed in its waters after his birth. The river flows
through the city of Gortys. At some distance away from its
source it is called the Gortynius River, and it is noted for the
coldness of its waters.

*Lycabettus* (lik-ạ-bet′us, lī-kạ-) or *Lykabettos* (-os). Rocky hill
rising in the E part of Athens to a height of about 910 feet
above the sea. According to legend, it was originally a huge
stone. When Athena, who was carrying it to fortify the
Acropolis, heard of the death of Agraulos and her daughters
by leaping from the Acropolis, in grief at their deaths she
dropped the stone and formed Mount Lycabettus. It is a very
conspicuous object in the landscape, presenting from most
points of the city the general form of an abrupt, slightly
concave cone; there is, however, beyond a slight depression,
a long ridge N of it. Upon the top stands today a small chapel
of Saint George. On the S slope is the large reservoir built
by Hadrian and Antoninus Pius which still supplies the city.

*Lycaeus* (lī-sē′us) or *Lycaeum* (-um). Mountain in S Arcadia.
Some Arcadians called it Olympus and others called it Sacred Peak, because, they say, there is a place on the mountain called Cretea, and here, where no living creature cast a
shadow, Zeus was born to Rhea and was reared by the
nymphs Thisoa, Neda, and Hagno. Here was a course where
the Lycaean Games were held. On the spot where Zeus was
born was a precinct sacred to Lycaean Zeus forbidden to
mortals. Whoever ignored the rule and entered was des-
tined to die within a year. On the summit of the mountain,
from which a view over the whole Peloponnesus was possi-

SCALE OF MILES

0    50    100

N

Mediolanum

Cremona
Placentia

Patavium

Ravenna

Nicaea

Pisae

Ariminum

Volaterrae
Arretium
Cortona
Clusium
Perusia

CORSICA

Volsinii

Asculum Picenum

Tarquinii

Veii
Rome
Tusculum

Reate

Corfinium

Ostia
Antium

Tarracina
Minturnae
Cumae
Herculaneum

Arpinum

Turris
Libisonis

Capua
Beneventum
Neapolis

SARDINIA

Posidonia
(Paestum)
Velia
Heraclea

Metapontum

Brundisium

Tarentum

Tyrrhenian Sea

Buxentum

Siris
Sybaris

Hydrus
Callipolis

Thurii

Croton

AEOLIAE
INSULAE

Caulonia

Eryx
Motya

Panormus

Mylae

Zancle

Locri

Rhegium

Segesta
Lilybaeum
Selinus

Himera

Naxos

Heraclea Minoa

SICILY

Catana

Utica
Carthage

Acragas
Gela
Camarina

Leontini

Acrae

Hybla Minor
Syracuse

Mediterranean Sea

Adriatic Sea

ITALY
WITH
CITIES OF MAGNA GRAECIA
AND THE EARLY ROMAN REPUBLIC

THE GREEK WORLD
5TH CENTURY B.C.

MACEDONIA

• Pella    Amphipolis

Stagira

Methone •    CHALCIDICE

Olynthus •
Mt. Olympus +    Potidaea
Mende
Scione

Mt. Ossa +
Larissa •

CORCYRA    • Dodona

Ionian Sea    THESSALY    + Mt. Pelion

Pagasae

• Ambracia

Ambracian    Lamia •    + Artem
Gulf    Histiaea
LEUCAS    AETOLIA    Thermopylae    EUBOE
LOCRIS

• Olympia

• Sparta

SEE SEPARATE DETAILED MAP

Cyd

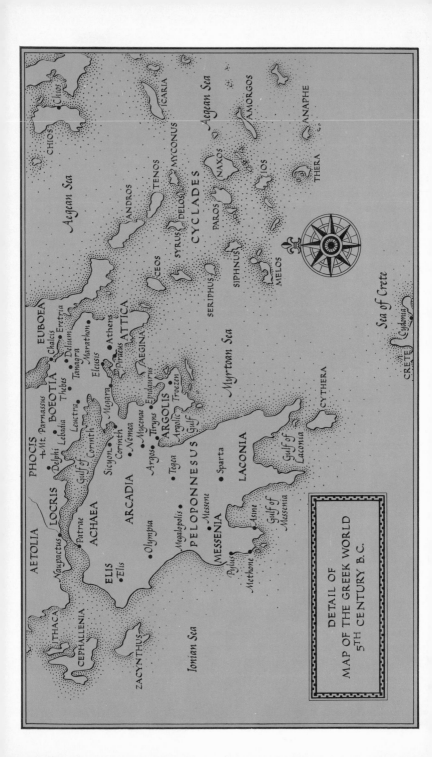

DETAIL OF
MAP OF THE GREEK WORLD
5TH CENTURY B.C.

ble, was an altar of Lycaean Zeus, on which sacrifices to the god were made in secret. On the east side of the mountain was a sanctuary of Apollo, at which an annual festival was held in his honor. As part of the festival sacrifices that were made in the market-place were carried to this sanctuary to the music of flutes. The mountain was also a center of the worship of Pan, who had a sanctuary there.

*Lycaonia* (lik-ā-ō'ni-ạ, lī-kā-). In ancient geography, a province in S central Asia Minor. It was bounded by Galatia on the N, Cappadocia on the E, Cilicia on the S, Pisidia on the SW, and Phrygia on the W. Sometimes it included Isauria, and sometimes it was included in Cappadocia. Chief city, Iconium.

*Lychnidus* (lik'ni-dus) or *Lychnitis* (lik-nī'tis). In ancient geography, a lake in Illyria. The modern name of the lake (on the border of Albania and Yugoslavia) is Ohrid.

*Lycia* (lish'ạ). In ancient geography, a division of SW Asia Minor, bordering on the Mediterranean and on Caria, Phrygia, Pisidia, and Pamphylia. The Lycians were one of the peoples of Asia Minor who invaded Egypt in the time of Ramses II and Merneptah. Its 23 cities formed the Lycian League. According to legend, Apollo had his winter palace in Lycia. Leto, his mother, was forced to flee from Delos after giving birth to her children, on account of the wrath of Hera. She wandered to Lycia and, being thirsty and worn, stopped at a pond to drink. Peasants who were gathering reeds at the edge of the pond tried to prevent her from drinking or from giving water to her children. They would not yield to her pleas and when she tried to drink, they muddied the water so that it was unfit to drink. To punish them for their malice Leto prayed that they might live in the pond forever, and the gods answered her prayer by changing them into frogs.

*Lycosura* (lī-kọ-sū'rạ). In ancient geography, a city in S Arcadia, near the border of Messenia. Pausanias says it was the oldest city in the world, that from it the rest of mankind learned how to build cities, and that a sacred deer about whose neck was a collar, on which was written, "I was a fawn when captured at the time when Agapenor went to Troy, lived in Lycosura, weakened by great age."

*Lydia* (lid'i-ạ). [Early name, *Maeonia*.] Ancient country, later a Roman province, on the W coast of Asia Minor, bordering on the Aegean Sea and on Mysia, Phrygia, and Caria. The earliest known inhabitants were Phrygians. Later it was invaded by Semites, who gave it the name of Lydia (compare the Old Testament Lud, descendants of Shem, Gen. x. 22). The name Maeonia was afterward confined to the E part of the country near the upper Hermus River, and Lydia to the W. About 700 B.C. a revolution overthrew the Semitic reign, and brought the native dynasty of the Mermnadae to the throne, with Gyges as first king. Under them Lydia rose to the position of a mighty kingdom extending from the coast to the river Halys (modern Kizil Irmak), with Sardis as capital. The prosperous Greek cities were brought either to subjection or alliance. But under the fifth and best-known of the dynasties, Croesus, the Lydian empire was brought to a sudden end by the Persian conqueror Cyrus, who in 546 B.C. captured Sardis and the king himself. From the Persians Lydia passed over, through Alexander the Great, to Syria, and later to Eumenes of Pergamum. During the Roman period Lydia formed a separate province, with Sardis as capital.

*Lykabettos* (lik-a-bet′os). See *Lycabettus.*

# M

*Macedonia* (mas-e-dō′ni-a). [Also: *Macedon.*] In ancient geography, a country in SE Europe, of varying limits. It lay N of the Aegean Sea and Thessaly, E of Illyria, and W of Thrace, separated from Illyria by the Scardus Mountains. The chief rivers were the Axius (Vardar) and Strymon; the chief cities, Edessa, Pella, and Thessalonica. Macedonia was not originally a part of Hellas. It first became powerful under Philip II, who united the country and made the Macedonian army the best-trained army of his time. Philip, who became the master of Greece, was succeeded by his son Alexander the Great, the conqueror of the entire geographical area that came to be known as the near East, making Macedonia the motherland of one of the greatest empires of history. After his death, its possession was contested by Alexander's successors, and was finally won (c278 B.C.) by Antigonus II (Antigonus Gonatas). The Macedonians were defeated by Rome at Cynoscephalae in 197 B.C., and finally at Pydna in 168 B.C., and Macedonia was made a Roman province in 146 B.C. Parts of it are now in Yugoslavia, Bulgaria, and Greece.

*Maddaloni* (mäd-dä-lō′nē), *Monte di.* See *Tifata.*

*Maeander* (mē-an′dėr). [Modern Turkish, *Menderes.*] In ancient geography, a river of W Asia Minor flowing, with many windings, generally SW and W through Phrygia and Ionia to the Aegean Sea. The name is the origin of the word "meander." According to legend, Maeander, son of Cercaphus and Anaxibia, was at war in Phrygia. He vowed to the goddess Cybele that if he was victorious, he would sacrifice the first person who congratulated him on his return. He was victorious, and on his return he was met and congratulated by his son, his mother, and his sister. In fulfillment of his vow he sacrificed them. He then hurled himself into the river which afterward bore his name.

*Maenalus* (men′a̱-lus, mē′na̱). A mountain in Arcadia, sacred to Pan.

*Maeonia* (mē-ō′ni-a̱). An ancient name of Lydia, the country on the W coast of Asia Minor. According to Herodotus, Tyrrhenians from Maeonia, who left their country to escape a famine, became colonizers and the ancestors of the Etruscans in Italy.

*Maeotis* (mē-ō′tis), *Palus.* Ancient name of *Azov, Sea of,* the shallow gulf opening from the north shore of the Euxine Sea, in the Chersonesus Taurica (Crimea).

*Maggiore* (mäd-jō′rä), *Lago.* See *Verbanus, Lacus.*

*Magna Graecia* (mag′na̱ grē′sha̱). [Eng. trans., "Great Greece."] In ancient geography, the name given to the part of S Italy colonized by Greeks. Among the leading cities were Cumae, Croton, Sybaris, Metapontum, Locri, Rhegium, Tarentum, Thurii, Heraclea, and Neapolis. Colonization began in the 8th century B.C. and the most flourishing period was the 7th and 6th centuries B.C.

*Magnesia* (mag-nē′zha̱, -sha̱). In ancient geography, the easternmost district of Thessaly, Greece, bordering on the Aegean Sea and the Pagasean Gulf.

*Magnesia.* [Sometimes called *Magnesia ad Maeandrum.*] In ancient geography, a city in Ionia, W Asia Minor, about 14 miles SE of Ephesus. The temple of Artemis Leucophryne, the remains of which still exist, was one of the most magnificent of ancient monuments, rebuilt c300 B.C. The frieze, now in the Louvre, bears reliefs of combats between Greeks and Amazons. There are also remains of a theater of the 4th century B.C., with later modifications, and of a large stadium.

*Magnesia* or *Magnesia ad Sipylum* (ad sip′i-lum). [Modern name, *Manisa* or *Manissa.*] In ancient geography, a city of Lydia, situated on the Hermus River. Here in 190 B.C. the Romans under Lucius Scipio, who had his famous brother Scipio Africanus the Elder as one of his lieutenants, defeated a vastly superior force under Antiochus the Great, king of Syria. Antiochus fled, sued for peace, and by the terms of it was compelled to withdraw behind the Taurus Mountains.

*Malea* (ma̧-lē′a̧). Easternmost of the three southern promontories of the Peloponnesus. Ships rounding this cape often encountered wind squalls and rough seas. Prudent masters, who preferred the Corinth isthmus portage to the risk of disaster off Cape Malea, contributed to the profits which made the wealth of Corinth proverbial. (JJ)

*Malea.* In ancient geography, the southernmost point of the island of Lesbos.

*Maliacus Sinus* (ma-lī′a̧-kus sī′nus). Latin name of *Lamia, Gulf of.*

*Malian Gulf* (mā′li-an). See *Lamia, Gulf of.*

*Malis* (mā′lis). In ancient geography, a district of Greece, S of Thessaly, N of Doris, and W of Locris. Lamia and Heraclea were the chief cities.

*Mallia* (mä′li-a̧). In ancient geography, a city on the N coast of Crete, E of Cnossus. Remains of a palace, built in the same period as the first palaces of Cnossus and Phaestus but on a smaller scale, have been found there.

*Maniae* (mā′ni-ē). In ancient geography, a place, near Megalopolis in Arcadia, where there was a sanctuary called Maniae *(Madnesses).* Here, they say, Orestes was overtaken by the Furies, who caused him to go mad for the slaying of his mother.

*Mantinea* (man-ti-nē′a̧). [Also: *Mantineia.*] In ancient geography, a city in Arcadia, Greece, SW of Corinth. The original city of this name, some say, was founded by Mantineus, son of Lycaon, on another spot. In obedience to an oracle Antinoë, daughter of Cepheus of Tegea, led the inhabitants to a new location. She was guided to the new site by a serpent, for which reason the river flowing beside the city was named Ophis *(Snake)*. Men of Mantinea went to the Trojan War under the leadership of Agapenor, son of Ancaeus the Argonaut. In the Persian War they were among the allies of Leonidas at Thermopylae and at the battle of Salamis (480 B.C.). In the Peloponnesian Wars Mantinea joined Elis to fight against Sparta and was defeated (418 B.C.). In 385 B.C. the Mantineans were defeated again by Sparta and their city was taken. Pausanias says the Spartans took the city by diverting the waters of the Ophis River against the walls made of unbaked brick. The bricks crumbled, and the Spartans rushed in and razed the city to the ground. It was restored by the Thebans, under Epaminondas, after 371 B.C., but the Mantineans treacherously negotiated with the Spartans to make a separate peace and betrayed their benefactors. Later they fought with the Spartans against the Thebans at Mantinea (362 B.C.) and were defeated. In honor of Alexander the Great's general, Antigonus, the Mantineans changed the name of their city to Antigonea, but its ancient name was restored during the reign of the emperor Hadrian.

*Mantua* (man′tū-ạ). [Italian, *Mantova*.] An ancient Etruscan town situated on a lake formed by the river Mincius. The town was further developed by the Romans and has long been known as the birthplace of the poet Vergil.

*Maracanda* (mar-ạ-kan′dạ). Ancient name of Samarkand, city in ancient Sogdiana, C Asia. Alexander the Great stopped here (327 B.C.) for some time on his expedition into India, and destroyed the ancient city. It was at Maracanda that Clitus, a friend of Alexander's, during a long evening of drinking, expressed resentment of the influence of the Orientals over Alexander. Rash words and insults were flung out; Alexander seized a spear and ran Clitus through.

*Marathon* (mar′ạ-thon). A plain in Attica, Greece, near the modern village of Vrana, about 18 miles NE of Athens, between Mount Pentelicus and the sea. Pisistratus landed there when he returned from exile in Eretria, prepared his assault on Athens there, and from there made his successful march on Athens when he became tyrant for the third time (c546 B.C.). The plain is celebrated as the site of the battle of September, 490 B.C., between the Greeks (10,000 Athenians and 1000 Plataeans) under Miltiades, and 30,000 or more Persians under Datis and Artaphernes. Hippias, son of

Pisistratus, who had been expelled from Athens, led the Persians to the plain because it was considered ideal terrain for the Persian cavalry. The Athenians, having learned of the approach of the Persians at Marathon, marched their forces thither under ten generals. The Athenians sent Phidippides (or Philippides) to Sparta with an urgent request for aid, but for religious reasons the Spartans could not march out of Sparta until the moon was full. In the meantime the Athenians drew up their battle lines in a precinct of Heracles, and were joined by the Plataeans. Five of the Athenian generals advised against risking a battle because they were so greatly outnumbered. The other five, including Miltiades, son of Cimon, wanted to engage the enemy at once. Miltiades feared that in case of an even division, those who favored withdrawal would prevail. For this reason he persuaded Callimachus, the *polemarch* (war-archon) to vote for the attack and break the tie. Under Miltiades as commander the battle array was set; sacrificial victims gave favorable omens. The Athenians made a running charge out onto the plain against the Persians. According to some accounts, a fully-armed image of Theseus led the Athenians in their rush against the Persians. The latter thought that the few Greeks running against them without horses or archers were mad, and prepared to receive them. The Greeks fought gloriously in close array, and it was some time before the Persians crashed through the center of their line, the weakest part, and were victorious in that sector. But the Athenians on the right wing and the Plataeans on the left wing were victorious. They permitted the Persians they had overcome to flee, while they reformed their line and fell upon the Persians who, thinking they had won, were pursuing the Greeks of the center of the line. With their reformed line the Athenians and Plataeans overcame the Persians. (Ever after this day, it was the custom of the Athenians, in the sacrifices and festivals they held every fifth year at Athens, for the heralds to call down the blessing of the gods on the Plataeans equally with the Athenians.) The Greeks purused the Persians to the shore, cutting down many, and seized seven of their ships, but the remainder of their fleet escaped. The Persian fleet made a feint at Athens at Phalerum, the harbor of the city, and then sailed away to Asia. Athens was safe. In the Battle of Marathon the Persians lost, according to Herodotus, 6400 men,

and the Athenians lost 192. After the full of the moon 2000
Spartans hurried up, so eager to lend their aid that they had
made the march from Sparta in three days. They found the
battle was over. However, they were anxious to see what the
Persians looked like and went to the plain of Marathon and
examined the slain. They praised the skill and bravery of the
Athenians, then turned around and went home again. This
victory ended Darius' attempt against Greece and is classed
among the decisive battles of the world. The *soros,* a conical
mound 40 feet high and 200 in diameter, which covers the
Athenian dead, marks the central point of the famous battle.
All doubt as to its identification was set at rest by an excavation made by the Archaeological Society of Athens, which
disclosed ashes, charred remnants of the funeral pyre, and
fragments of pottery dating from the beginning of the 5th
century B.C. The modern marathon race is run over a distance approximating that run by the messenger carrying
news of the victory in battle to Athens, a distance of 26
miles, 385 yards.

*Maritime Alps* (alps). [French, *Alpes Maritimes;* Italian, *Alpi
Marittime.*] Division of the Alps which lies on the border of
France and Italy, between the Ligurian Apennines and the
Cottian Alps. Peak elevation, about 10,817 feet; length,
about 120 miles.

*Marmara* (mär′mạ-rạ). See *Proconnesus.*

*Marmara, Sea of.* See *Propontis.*

*Marmore* (mär′mō-rā), *Cascate delle.* [English, *Falls of Terni.*]
Series of cascades in Umbria, C Italy, SE of Interamna Na-
hars (Terni), in the Velinus River near its mouth. The spot
has been celebrated for its beauty. Height of the falls, about
65 feet, 330 feet, and 190 feet, respectively.

*Marsala* (mär-sä′lä). See *Lilybaeum.*

*Marsian Hills.* A name for the Apennines.

*Massicus* (mas′i-kus), *Mons.* [Modern Italian name, *Monte Mas-
sico.*] In ancient geography, a range of hills on the border of
Campania and Latium, Italy. It was famous for its wines.

*Massilia* (mạ-sil′i-ạ). [Greek, *Massalia;* now, *Marseilles.*] An ancient Greek colony in southern France. It was founded by
Phocaeans c600 B.C., and, according to legend, was visited
by Heracles when he went to fetch the cattle of Geryon.

*Matera* (mä-te′rä). Town in S Italy, situated above a steep
ravine about 37 miles W of Tarentum. It was of strategic

importance because of its location, and was occupied by Hannibal and then by the Romans. In the vicinity are found numerous prehistoric remains and caves.

*Mauretania* (mô-rẹ-tā′ni-ạ). [Also: *Mauritania*.] In ancient geography, the NW part of Africa, corresponding to the N parts of Morocco and of W and C Algeria. Juba II of Numidia was confirmed (25 B.C.) king of Mauretania by Augustus. It was annexed (42 A.D.) to the Roman Empire by Claudius, and was divided into the provinces Mauretania Tingitana in the W and Mauretania Caesariensis in the E.

*Media* (mē′di-ạ). Ancient country comprising the NW part of the Iranian highland, extending from the Caspian Sea to the Araxes (modern Aras). It was bounded on the NE by Hyrcania, on the E by Parthia, on the S by Susiana and Persis, and on the W by Assyria. It nearly corresponded to the modern Iranian regions of Azerbaijan, Ardilan, and Iraq Ajemi. Later the SE part of the country was called Great Media, and the NW, or Atropatene, Little Media. The Medes (Hebrew and Assyrian, *Madai;* Old Persian, *Mada*) are enumerated in Gen. x. 2 as among the descendants of Japheth; and they, together with the Persians, constituted the most important and powerful Indo-European population in W Asia. It is assumed that the country was originally settled by another (perhaps Turanian) tribe, and that the Medes gradually advanced from the NE to the W and SW. Media came into contact with Assyria at least as early as the end of the 9th century B.C., when it is mentioned as a conquered and tributary land. Tiglath-pileser III was the first Assyrian king who annexed Median territory; and Sargon II transplanted Israelitish war captives to Median cities, and claims in his annals of 713 B.C. to have received tribute from 45 Median chiefs. Sennacherib also received tribute from the Medes. Under Esarhaddon the Medes entered into alliance with the Mineans and the Cimmerians against Assyria, apparently without success. But from that time the Medes grew more united and more powerful against tyrannical Assyria. The Assyrians had held Upper Asia from 1229–709 B.C. when the Medes successfully revolted, shook off Assyrian rule, and became self-governing. But their land was torn by robbery and lawlessness. According to Herodotus, Deïoces (c709–656 B.C.) made himself king of the Medes by following such a course of scrupulous justice in settling

fat, fāte, fär, fâll, ȧsk, fāre; net, mē, hėr; pin, pīne; not, nōte, möve, nôr; up, lūte, pl̇ull; oi, oil; ou out; (lightened) ẹlect, agǫny, ụnite;

disputes and punishing the lawless that his name spread from his own village throughout the area, and he was requested by the Medes to become their king and restore law and order. Deïoces accepted the throne, demanded a palace for himself and a personal bodyguard, and caused the strongly fortified city of Ecbatana (or Agbatana) to be built. To widen the distance between himself and ordinary men and to increase the respect in which he was held, he made himself inaccessible to those who sought his favor or counsel, organized an elaborate ceremony for his audiences, and, having secured his power, ruled justly and consolidated the Medes into a nation. At his death he was succeeded by his son Phraortes (reigned 647–625 B.C. or, as some think, 678–625 B.C.). Phraortes attacked the Persians and brought them under his sway. He extended his conquests over lesser neighboring tribes, and at last attacked Assyria, but died in the expedition after a reign of 22 years (or, as some think, 53 years). He was succeeded by his son Cyaxares (625–584 B.C.), who was even more warlike than his predecessors and organized his confused forces into systematic companies. Cyaxares marched against Nineveh to complete the attack his father had begun, but was diverted from the expedition when Media was attacked and overrun by the Scythians. For 28 years thereafter the Scythians dominated Asia. At the end of that time Cyaxares regained control, expelled the Scythians, and recovered his empire. After the Scythians had been driven out, the Medes, in alliance with the Babylonian Nabopolassar, advanced once more against Nineveh, and brought about its downfall (612 B.C.). In the division of the Assyrian Empire, Assyria proper and Mesopotamia as far as Haran fell to Media, which, however, could not develop into a dominant power on account of the rise of the new Babylonian Empire under Nabopolassar and Nebuchadnezzar. Under Cyaxares the Medes made war on Alyattes, king of the Lydians, because the Lydians refused to give up some Scythians who had fled as suppliants to the Lydians from the Medes. The war went on for five years, with neither side gaining an overall victory, although each side had won individual battles. One day (May 28, 585 B.C.) in the midst of the fighting, the sun was suddenly darkened; day became night. Alarmed by this omen (an eclipse of the sun, which had been foretold by Thales of Miletus), both sides sought peace. The matter was handed over to outside mediators and peace was arranged. To seal the peace, the daughter of Alyattes was given in marriage to Astyages, the son of Cyaxares. After a reign of 40 years Cyaxares died and was succeeded by his son. Astyages became the grandfather of Cyrus and was overthrown by him (550 B.C.), after which the fate of Media was bound up in that of Persia. Still it seemed to have preserved a kind of independence or particularism while united to Persia. Thus, the Old Testament writings speak of an empire of "the Persians and Medes." Only the Book of Daniel seems to assume the existence of a Median empire between the last Babylonian king, Nabonidus (Belshazzar), and Cyrus. After the destruction of the Persian Empire and in the division of Alexander's conquered territories Media fell to Seleucus, the founder of the Syrian monarchy, and later to the Parthian Empire. The old Medes were, according to the classical writers, a warlike people; in Isa. xiii. they are described as hard and cruel. The religion of the Medes was, according to Strabo, the same as that of the Persians, i.e., dualism. They worshiped, besides the sun-god Mithras, the moon, a goddess corresponding to Aphrodite, fire, the earth, winds, and water. The oldest capital of Media was Rhagae, on the site of modern Tehran. Deïoces moved the capital to his new city of Ecbatana (modern Hamadan), in the W part of the country, which remained the summer residence of the Persian and Parthian kings. To Media belonged also Behistun (ancient Baghistan), famous from the trilingual cuneiform inscription discovered there.

*Mediolanum* (mē-di-ọ-lā′num). [Modern name, *Milano;* English, *Milan.*] In ancient geography, a town of the Insubres, in Cisalpine Gaul, situated in the plain between the Addua and Ticinus rivers. It was taken (222 B.C.) by the Romans under Scipio, and fell under Roman dominion permanently in 194 B.C.

*Mediterranean Sea* (med″i-tẹ-rā′nẹ-ạn). [Latin, *Mare Internum, Mare Mediterraneum.*] Sea, the most important extension of the Atlantic, separating Europe on the N from Africa on the S, and communicating with the Atlantic Ocean by the Strait of Gibraltar, and with the Black Sea by the Dardanelles, Sea of Marmara, and Bosporus. It is divided into two major basins, the western reaching from Gibraltar to Sicily and Tunisia, and the eastern from there to Syria. Its chief

fat, fāte, fär, fåll, àsk, fāre; net, mē, hèr; pin, pīne; not, nōte, mȯve, nôr; up, lūte, pùll; oi, oil; ou out; (lightened) ẹlect, agǫny, ūnite;

branches are the Tyrrhenian Sea, Ionian Sea, Adriatic Sea, and Aegean Sea. The chief islands are the Balearic Islands, Corsica, Sardinia, Sicily, Malta, the Ionian Islands, Crete, Cyprus, and the Dodecanese Islands. The chief tributary rivers are the Ebro, Rhône, Po, and Nile. The Mediterranean has an important influence on the climate of the surrounding islands; it has given its name to a type of climate which characterizes these lands, with hot, sunny, dry summers and mild winters. Most of the rainfall occurs in autumn, winter, and early spring. The lands surrounding the Mediterranean basin are generally mountainous, and this enhances the scenery, already famous because of the brilliant blue of the skies and the water. The water of the Mediterranean is about ten percent more saline than that of the oceans. Tides are small; the connection with the Atlantic at the Strait of Gibraltar is only about nine miles wide. Each of the two major basins has a deep zone; the greatest known depth of the E Mediterranean, W of Crete, is about 14,450 feet; of the W Mediterranean (Tyrrhenian Sea), about 12,240 feet. Length, about 2200 miles; greatest width of sea proper, about 700 miles; area, about 963,600 square miles; average depth, about 4890 feet.

***Meduacus Minor*** (med-ū-ā′kus mī′nôr). [Modern name, ***Bacchiglione.***] River in NE Italy which flows past Vicentia (Vicenza) and Patavium (Padua) and empties into the Gulf of Venice.

***Megalopolis*** (meg-a̱-lop′ō̱-lis). In ancient geography, a city of Arcadia, Greece, situated on the Helisson River, not far from Mount Lycaon. The city was founded by Epaminondas after the battle of Leuctra (371 B.C.), in which he had defeated the Spartans. The new city was intended to form a link (with Messene, also a new city founded by Epaminondas, and with Mantinea) in a chain of strong cities to blockade Sparta. It was built on both banks of the river and was encircled by a double wall. The encircling mountains gave it added protection. The villages and towns of Arcadia were joined in a league, and populations of whole villages and levies from the chief cities (Tegea, Clitor, Mantinea, Orchomenus) were moved to the great new city, whose name means "Great City." The new inhabitants brought their local cults and images with them; altars were set up, temples were raised, a stadium was laid out, and public buildings were erected. The Arcadian cities and villages of the league were to be governed by an assembly in a federal system. The sessions of the assembly were held in the Thersilion. But the great plan of Epaminondas and the Arcadian League for a federal system and a strong city was a failure in practice. The peasants who had moved from their old homes became discontented and returned to their villages. The city was subjected to siege many times and was at last destroyed. When the traveler Pausanias passed that way in the 2nd century A.D. the city lay in ruins. Remains of a large theater, capable of accommodating 20,000 spectators, and of a great sanctuary of Zeus Soter *(Savior)* have been uncovered. The extraordinary design of the Thersilion, a vast roofed assembly hall whose supporting columns were artfully arranged in lines radiating from the *bema* (speaker's platform), has evoked the admiration of historians of architecture.

*Megara* (meg′a̱-ra̱). Town on the Isthmus of Corinth in central Greece, situated between the Halcyon Sea, the Corinthian Bay, and the Saronic Gulf. The town, whose name is the plural of the Greek word *megaron* (the great central hall of the bronze-age palaces), is about 21 miles west of Athens. The ancient city, whose early inhabitants were Carians, was situated on the route leading from central Greece to the Peloponnesus.

The Megarians were among the first to send out colonies to the Euxine (Black) Sea region. They founded Chalcedon on the Thracian Bosporus first; then, scolded by the oracle for their blindness, founded Byzantium (667 B.C.) on the opposite and more advantageous shore. The founding of this city that controlled the entrance to the Euxine Sea, assured the penetration of Greek colonists in the region. They also founded Selymbria on the north coast of the Propontis, and Heraclea on the coast of Bithynia. This last, according to legend, had been named Heraclea by Lycus, king of the Mysians, because Heracles had helped him in a war against the Bebryces. The Megarians colonized it in obedience to instructions from the priestess at Delphi. She told them to found a colony on the Pontus (another name for the Black Sea) in a land dedicated to Heracles. In the west the Megarians established the colonies of Hybla Minor (Megara Hyblaea) and Selinus in Sicily. Theagenes, tyrant of Megara (640–600 B.C.), beautified the city and brought water to it by an aqueduct, parts of which remain. His daughter married Cylon, a noble who attempted to seize the citadel at Athens (c632 B.C.). He failed, and in the ensuing wars with Athens Megara was weakened and lost much of its power and influence. Under the inspiration of Solon, the Athenians wrested Salamis from Megara and further weakened it, for this island, in the possession of one, was a threat to the other city. Following a dispute with Corinth, Megara accepted an Athenian garrison and constructed (459 B.C.) the Long Walls that linked the city with her port Nisaea. Shortly afterward, Megara quarreled with the Athenians again and drove out the garrison. In retaliation, Pericles promulgated (432 B.C.) a decree that excluded Megara from Athenian markets. This was a disastrous economic blow. In addition, the Athenians annually ravaged the land and blockaded their coasts. Megara appealed to Sparta, and this was one of the causes of the Peloponnesian Wars, in which Megara served as a battleground for Sparta and Athens. Ultimately, the city fell into the hands of the Macedonians and afterward the Romans controlled it. Megara was the birthplace of Euclid, the founder of the Megarics, or Megarian school of philosophers, and of Theognis, the poet. The Megarians were noted for their gay temperament, and Megara was said to be the birthplace of comedy. The area surrounding Megara is called the *Megaris* (q.v.) or *Megarid.*

*Megara Hyblaea* (meg′ạ-rạ hī-blē′ạ). See *Hybla Minor.*

*Megaris* (meg′ạ-ris). In ancient geography, a district in Greece which formed part of the isthmus connecting the Peloponnesus with C Greece and lay SW of Attica and NE of Corinthia. The surface is largely mountainous. Chief town, Megara.

*Melas* (mē′lạs), *Sinus.* [Modern name, *Gulf of Saros.*] In ancient geography, the name of a gulf in the extreme NE part of the Aegean Sea, formed by the Thracian Chersonese.

*Melita* (mel′i-tạ). [Modern name, *Malta.*] Island in the Mediterranean Sea, about 60 miles S of Sicily. It was colonized by the Phoenicians c1000 B.C. Greek colonies were established in the 8th century B.C. but the Greeks were driven out by the Carthaginians and the island remained a Carthaginian stronghold until taken by Rome in 218 B.C., during the Second Punic War. The *Acts of the Apostles,* Chs. 27, 28, tell how Saint Paul was shipwrecked on the island (c60

A.D.) and converted many of the inhabitants to Christianity. It was occupied successively by Vandals, Goths, Byzantines, Arabs, and Normans, and when the Turks expelled the Knights of St. John from Rhodes, the Emperor Charles V, in 1530, presented Malta to them; they have since been known as the Knights of Malta. Among the ancient remains are substantial stone ("megalithic") structures of the second millennium B.C., and some have proposed to identify Melita with Ogygia, the island on which the nymph Calypso detained Odysseus. (JJ)

*Melitene* (mel-i-tē'nē). In ancient geography, a district in E Cappadocia, Asia Minor.

*Melos* (mē'los). [Italian, *Milo*.] Volcanic island of the Cyclades, SE Greece. The great harbor which the island partially encircles was caused by volcanic action. Remains of three prehistoric cities have been found at Phylakopi on the island. The two oldest date from the early Minoan period (3400–2100 B.C.) and the Middle Minoan period (2100–1580 B.C.) and indicate a Minoan civilization that developed independently of Crete. The latest of the three cities dates from the Mycenaean period. Obsidian produced on Melos was early used in the manufacture of knives and spear-points, and was an important item of export. Melos was a Dorian colony from ancient times, and was never under the control of Athens as the other islands were following the Persian War. In the Peloponnesian Wars it remained neutral until an Athenian armament came to attack it. Thucydides presents a discussion between Athenian and Melian envoys, which clearly indicates the desire of Melos to remain at peace and in liberty and the undisguised intention ofAthens to force the island into submission. The crux of the Athenian argument was that "the strong do what they can and the weak suffer what they must." The Melians, relying on the justice of their cause and the gods, decided to resist (416 B.C.). After a siege of some months they surrendered. All the adult males were put to death by the Athenians, and the women and children were enslaved. Later the Athenians sent out colonists and took the island for themselves. Melos is noted for the Venus of Melos (Venus de Milo) found in the ruins of the ancient city of Melos in 1820, now in the Louvre at Paris. Area of the island, about 57 square miles.

*Mende* (men'dē). In ancient geography, a city on the Pallene

fat, fāte, fär, fåll, åsk, fāre; net, mē, hėr; pin, pīne; not, nōte, möve, nôr; up, lūte, pùll; oi, oil; ou out; (lightened) ēlect, agǫny, ūnite;

peninsula, in Chalcidice. It revolted from Athens, 423 B.C., and gave allegiance to the Spartan general Brasidas.

*Menderes* (men-de-res'). Modern Turkish name of the *Maeander,* and also of the *Scamander.*

*Menderes, Little.* See *Caÿster.*

*Menelaeum* (men-ẹ-lā'i-um). A hill on the banks of the Eurotas River in Laconia, on which the hero-shrine of Helen and Menelaus has been found. The cult of Helen and Menelaus was observed there until the Dorian invasion, c1100 B.C. On the site, remains of a small temple of the 5th century B.C. have been found. Other remains indicate that this temple replaced a much earlier one, in which Helen and Menelaus were honored. Nearby, traces of houses of the Mycenaean period have also been found.

*Mesopotamia* (mes″o-pọ-tā′mi-ạ). [From Greek, meaning "Between Rivers"; Hebrew, *Aram Naharaïm.*] Country between the Euphrates and Tigris. It is usually divided into Upper Mesopotamia (ancient Chaldea) and Babylonia. It is a great lowland plain, and was formerly very extensively irrigated and cultivated; in recent decades there has been a considerable extension of the irrigated area. It was invaded and conquered several times by the Egyptians and has belonged at different times to the Median, Persian, Macedonian, Syrian, Parthian and Roman empires.

*Messana* (mẹ-sā′nạ) and *Messene* (mẹ-sē′nē). [Modern name, *Messina.*] Messene was the name given (c664 B.C.) to the ancient city of Zancle in Sicily, situated on the extreme NE corner of the island, on the strait that separates it from the mainland of Italy. After the Messenians were defeated in the Second Messenian War with Sparta, many of them went to Sicily, according to tradition, on the invitation of the tyrant of Rhegium, a city diagonally S across the strait from Zancle. They defeated the Zancleans, made a treaty of friendship with them, and changed the name of Zancle to Messene, after their own country. Early in the 5th century B.C. the city came under the control of the tyrant of Rhegium, and henceforward it was known as Messana. In the struggle for control of Sicily between Carthage and the powerful Greek city of Syracuse, Messana changed sides many times. In 405 B.C. it was declared independent at the insistence of the Carthaginian general Himilco. When Dionysius, tyrant of Syracuse, renewed the war, 398 B.C., Himilco attacked Messana. Most of the inhabitants had fled, and Himilco took an abandoned city (396 B.C.). He pulled it to the ground, and destroyed its walls and buildings so completely that it was said no one would have known a city ever existed on the site. In the following year Dionysius rebuilt it and settled colonists from Italy and some exiles from Greek Messenia there. It fell again into the hands of the Carthaginians and was freed by Timoleon, 343 B.C. When the wars between Carthage and Syracuse broke out again, it sided with Carthage. It was seized by the Mamertines (288 B.C.), allies of Rome, who sought the aid of Rome and thus initiated the First Punic War. At the end of the war (241 B.C.) it became a free city allied to Rome. In the Roman civil wars following the assassination of Caesar, Messana was on the side of the enemies of Octavian, and was taken and sacked by the forces of Octavian (35 B.C.). Owing to its location the city sprang up many times after destruction, and it soon revived and again became a flourishing port.

*Messapia* (mẹ-sā′pi-ạ). In ancient geography, the peninsula at the SE extremity of Italy, often used as synonymous with Calabria or Iapygia. The name derives from its prehistoric Illyrian inhabitants.

*Messene* (mẹ-sē′nē). A city in Messenia, Greece, on the slope of Mount Ithome, about 19 miles SW of Megalopolis. According to tradition, after the defeat of the Spartans at Leuctra (371 B.C.), their Theban conqueror Epaminondas dreamed that he was instructed to restore the Messenians to their land, from which they had been driven by the Spartans. In his dream he was told to recover a secret thing which the dream directed him where to find, and on that spot to found a city for the Messenians. Epaminondas sent an envoy to find the secret thing of his dream. It turned out to be the Messenian mysteries, buried by Aristomenes before he fled from Messenia after the Second Messenian War. On this spot, which was at Mount Ithome, Epaminondas helped the Messenians, whom he had recalled from their exile, to lay out the foundations of their city (369 B.C.), and to the piping of flutes the heavy walls were raised. The walled city had the practical advantage of serving as a fortress against Sparta. In the city the Messenians dedicated a status of Zeus the Savior in the market-place, and raised temples of Poseidon, Aphrodite, and Demeter, as well as a temple of Messene, daughter

fat, fāte, fär, fåll, ȧsk, fãre; net, mē, hėr; pin, pīne; not, nōte, möve, nôr; up, lūte, pùll; oi, oil; ou out; (lightened) ẹlect, agọny, ūnite;

of Triopas, who had given her name to the Messenians and to their new city. The bones of Aristomenes were recovered from Rhodes at the command of an oracle, and interred in a tomb in the city. Annually certain rites were held at his tomb. A bull was bound to the pillar that stood on the grave of Aristomenes. If the bull, struggling to free himself, rocked the pillar, it was an omen of good fortune for the Messenians. If the pillar was not moved by the struggling bull, misfortune was portended. The ancient city of Messene is noted now for its extensive ruins at the modern village of Mavromati.

**Messene.** City in Sicily, see **Messana.**

**Messenia** (mẹ-sē′ni-ạ). In ancient geography, a division of the Peloponnesus, Greece. It was bounded by Elis and Arcadia on the N, Laconia (separated by Mount Taÿgetus) on the E, and the sea on the S and W. It contained the fertile valley of the Pamisus and enjoyed a milder climate than its neighbor across Mount Taÿgetus. For these reasons it was enviously eyed by the Lacedaemonians whose land was rocky and infertile. According to tradition, Polycaon, son of the Lacedaemonian king, Lelex, married Messene, the daughter of Triopas, an Argive. With a band of Spartans and Argives Polycaon marched into the land west of Mount Taÿgetus and took it, and named it Messenia after his wife. When Polycaon's line died out, the Messenians summoned Perieres, the husband of Gorgophone, daughter of Perseus, to be their king. His throne passed to his two sons, Aphareus and Leucippus, who were supposed to reign as co-kings, but in fact Aphareus was the master. When his twin sons Idas and Lynceus died without heirs, the kingdom passed to Nestor, son of Neleus. The descendants of Nestor held the kingdom until the Dorian invasion and the return of the Heraclidae to the Peloponnesus. In the Dorian invasion, the sons of Aristomachus—Aristodemus, Temenus, and Cresphontes—drew lots to decide which of the three regions of the Peloponnesus each would receive. Cresphontes, by a trick, got Messenia, which was regarded as the choicest portion of the Peloponnesus. In later times the Messenians and Lacedaemonians quarreled. The Lacedaemonians claimed that Messenians attacked a group of Lacedaemonian maidens who were on their way to a festival of Artemis at a sanctuary shared by both Messenians and Lacedaemonians

and ravished the maidens, and killed the Spartan king, Tele-
clus, who tried to protect them. The Messenians claimed
this was not the case at all. They said a band of Spartan
youths, disguised as maidens, set upon them and that the
Messenians killed them in self-defense. This incident was a
cause of much friction, and in the next generation war broke
out between the two kingdoms. The real cause of the war
was the desire of the Spartans to control the rich areas of
Messenia. The war, which some say began in 743 B.C., and
certainly took place in the 8th century B.C., was carried on
sporadically for 20 years. The Messenians protected themselves as best they could but were weakened by their losses
and by disease. They withdrew to Ithome and carried on the
war from there. All the omens predicted Spartan victory.
The oracles told the Messenians that since they had won the
land by guile (Cresphontes' trickery with the drawing of
lots), they would lose it by guile. Unfavorable omens appeared: the shield on the armed statue of Artemis fell to the
ground; when the king was about to sacrifice victims to Zeus
at Ithome, the citadel of the Messenians, the rams rushed
into the flames of their own accord; dogs howled every night
and at last fled to the Spartan camp. Aristodemus, the king
of Messenia, was informed by an oracle that the willing
sacrifice by her father of a Messenian virgin would save
Messenia. He proposed to sacrifice his daughter, but her
affianced husband, in an effort to save his beloved, said she
was not a virgin but was about to become the mother of his
child. Aristodemus was enraged at this slur on his honor. He
slew his daughter and opened up her body to prove that she
was not about to bear a child. But his impious act, carried
out in a rage on the daughter he loved, did not satisfy the
demands of the oracle for a voluntary sacrifice, and the
death of his daughter was in vain. He was visited by evil
dreams and, despairing for the fate of Messenia, he committed suicide on his daughter's tomb. About 724 B.C., according to some accounts, the war came to an end in Spartan
victory. The Messenians fled from Ithome. The Spartans
razed it to the ground and captured other towns. The victors
compelled the Messenians to take an oath that they would
never rebel and that they would give one-half of the produce
of their fields to Sparta. In addition, the Messenians were
compelled to attend the funerals of Spartan officials in the

fat, fāte, fär, fȧll, ȧsk, fâre; net, mē, hėr; pin, pīne; not, nōte, mōv
nôr; up, lūte, pùll; oi, oil; ou out; (lightened) ēlect, agǫny, ūnit

future, a particularly humiliating illustration of their defeat.

In the years that followed, the Messenians chafed under the Spartan yoke so that they welcomed the fiery speeches of Aristomenes, an ardent patriot who grew up in their midst at the beginning of the 7th century B.C. He urged them to revolt and free themselves from Sparta. Under his leadership the Second Messenian War broke out in the first half of the 7th century B.C. Some give the dates of it as 685–668 B.C. In this war Aristomenes performed prodigious feats, on at least one occasion driving the Spartans back in confusion, and several times escaping when he was taken prisoner. The Arcadians were allies of the Messenians, but through bribery their king betrayed the Messenians, without letting his own people, who cherished a warm friendship for the Messenians, know that he was doing so. He ordered the Arcadians to withdraw in the midst of a battle, and led them to the rear through the Messenian lines, thus throwing the Messenians into such confusion as the Arcadians fled through their midst that they were surrounded by the Spartans and suffered heavy losses. The survivors were led to Mount Eira by Aristomenes, and from there carried on their defense. The Messenians were besieged for 11 years, when they were again betrayed, this time by an adulterous woman. They fled to Arcadia, where they were warmly received and where the Arcadians, on learning that their king had betrayed their allies, stoned him to death. Aristomenes went to Rhodes, where he died, and many of the Messenians went to Sicily, where they captured the town of Zancle and changed its name to Messene (664 B.C.). The Spartans now had Messenia and divided it among themselves, except for Asine, which remained separate. Those Messenians who were left were reduced to slavery and became helots. But before Aristomenes flew from Messenia, he took a casket and buried it on a remote spot of Ithome, for an oracle had foretold that if this casket with its secret contents was kept by the Messenians, they would one day recover their country. The hatred of the Messenians for the Spartans never faltered; in 464 B.C. the Messenian helots revolted. This was at a time when Sparta was stricken by earthquakes to punish her for seizing suppliants at the sanctuary of Poseidon at Taenarus and putting them to death. The Messenian helots took refuge in their old fortress of Ithome, and held out against the Spartans for five years. At the end of that time they surrendered, and were allowed to withdraw from the fortress unharmed on condition that they never return to the Peloponnesus. The Athenians offered them a new home at Naupactus on the Corinthian Gulf (455 B.C.). The Messenians aided the Athenians in the Peloponnesian War. It was a Messenian plan that helped the Athenians capture a force of Spartans in Pylus (425 B.C.). With part of the spoil they took from the hated Spartans on this occasion, the Messenians commissioned the sculptor Paeonius to make an image of Victory, hovering in the air over a soaring eagle, which they dedicated in the Altis of Zeus at Olympia. After the Battle of Aegospotami (405 B.C.) in which the Spartans defeated the Athenians, the Messenians were driven from Naupactus. Some went to Rhegium and Sicily, but many went to Libya. At the Battle of Leuctra (371 B.C.), the image of Aristomenes appeared to aid the Thebans against the Spartans. Epaminondas, the Theban general who defeated the Spartans at Leuctra, dreamed that he was instructed to restore the Messenians to the Peloponnesus, and was told in his dream how to find the land he should give them. He sent a servant to the spot indicated to him in his dream; the servant dug there and found the casket hidden nearly three centuries earlier by Aristomenes. The secret contents which Aristomenes had hidden were the mysteries that had originally been brought to Messenia by Caucon in the misty past. Epaminondas recalled the Messenians and restored them to Ithome, where the casket was found. He helped them to lay out (369 B.C.) a new city, Messene, one side of which was formed by the old fortress of Ithome. The Messenians, who had been wandering for generations all over the Greek world, now returned home.

**Messenia, Gulf of.** [Also: *Gulf of Korone.*] Inlet of the Mediterranean, S and E of Messenia, Greece.

**Messina, Strait of.** [Italian, *Stretto* (or *Faro*) *di Messina;* Latin *Fretum Siculum.*] Strait in the Mediterranean, separating Sicily from the mainland of Italy. Width in narrowest part about two miles.

**Mesta** (mes'tä). See *Nestus.*

**Metapontum** (met-a-pon'tum). [Also: *Metapontium.*] In ancient geography, a city in S Italy, situated on the Gulf of Tarentum, about 25 miles SW of Tarentum. It was founded by

Achaeans from the mainland of Greece at an early date. The city became an important manufacturing and shipping center, and enjoyed great prosperity. Two archaic peripteral Doric temples are known at Metapontum: one, of about 520 B.C., attributed to Apollo and now known as the Chiesa di Sansone; the other, of about 500 B.C., of which 15 columns still stand, is now called the Tavole Paladine. In addition, Pliny mentions a temple of Hera notable for having wooden columns. Archaeologists have reported a theater, tombs, and traces of fortification walls. The religious philosopher Pythagoras, forced out of Croton where he had founded his famous brotherhood, took refuge at Metapontum, where he died. The order was later revived at Metapontum, but in the late 4th century B.C. it became finally extinct. (JJ)

*Metaurus* (me-tôr'us). [Modern name, *Metauro*.] Small river in Italy, which flows into the Adriatic about 28 miles NW of Ancona. The battle of the Metaurus was a victory gained at the river, S of Ariminum (Rimini), in 207 B.C., by the Romans under the consuls Marcus Livius Salinator and Claudius Nero over the Carthaginians under Hasdrubal. Nero had eluded Hannibal in S Italy, and made a forced march of 250 miles with 7000 men. Hasdrubal was slain, and his army nearly annihilated. Hannibal was thus left in a hopeless position, unable to get reserves, in S Italy. This victory is ranked as one of the decisive battles of the world.

*Methone* (meth-ō'nē). In ancient geography, a town in Messenia on the coast of the Ionian Sea. In the Peloponnesian Wars the city was besieged by the Athenians (431 B.C.), but it was saved by the arrival of a Spartan force under Brasidas. When Epaminondas restored Messenia after 371 B.C., the city was given to Nauplians.

*Methone* or *Methana* (mē-thā'na). In ancient geography, a peninsula of the Peloponnesus, between Troezen and Epidaurus. It was captured and garrisoned by the Athenian general Nicias, 425 B.C., and served as a base from which the Athenians raided Spartan territory.

*Methone.* In ancient geography, a city of Macedonia, situated near the mouth of the Haliacmon River, on the W side of the Thermaic Gulf. It was called Pierian Methone, from the Pierian forest where the Muses were said to dwell. Some say it was founded by Methon, a son of Orpheus. It was colonized by Euboeans. In the Peloponnesian Wars it was loyal

obscured) errant, ardent, actor; ch, chip; g, go; th, thin; ŦH, then; y, you; variable) ḍ as d or j, ṣ as s or sh, ṭ as t or ch, ẓ as z or zh.

to Athens, and later served, at various times, as a base o
operations against the Macedonians.

*Methone.* In ancient geography, a town of Thessaly, near th
Gulf of Pagasae. The ruins of an ancient acropolis are to b
found here.

*Methydrium* (me̞-thid′ri-um). In ancient geography, a city in
Arcadia, Greece. Methydrium was abandoned some tim
after 371 B.C. when its inhabitants went to dwell in the ne
city of Megalopolis.

*Methymna* (me̞-thim′na̞). In ancient geography, a city in Les
bos.

*Midea* (mid′e-a̞). In ancient geography, a city in C Argolis.

*Mikonos* (mik′o̞-nos, mī′ko̞-nos; Greek, mē′kô-nôs). See *Myco
nus.*

*Milan* (mi-lan′). See *Mediolanum.*

*Milazzo* (me̞-lät′tsō). See *Mylae.*

*Miletus* (mī-lē′tus). In ancient geography, a city in Caria, SV
Asia Minor, situated on the coast opposite the mouth of th
Maeander River. It was the principal settlement of the 1
Ionian cities in Asia. Miletus is thought to have bee
founded about the 12th century B.C. by Ionian Greeks. Th
city was attacked by the Lydian kings from the time of Gyge
(c685–c653 B.C.) to the time of his great-grandson Alyatte
(c617–560 B.C.). Alyattes attacked Milesia (the walled cit
and its surrounding territory) year after year at the time o
the harvest. He marched his forces to the piping of flute
and the strumming of harps through the countryside an
burned the standing grain, but did not destroy the house
as he wanted the owners to return and plant new crops tha
he could again plunder. He harried Miletus in this way be
cause he could not take the city by direct attack, since it wa
strongly walled and commanded the sea, and he thought b
this means to force it into submission. In all this time, onl
Chios of the Ionian cities sent any aid to Miletus. In the sixt
year of Alyattes' war (Lydians had been carrying on the wa
more or less regularly for 12 consecutive years), when th
Lydians set fire to the grain, a violent wind carried th
flames to the temple of Athena Assesia and burned it to th
ground. Afterward, Alyattes fell into a lingering sicknes
and on inquiry at Delphi was told that no answer would b
forthcoming until he rebuilt the temple of Athena Assesi
Alyattes sent a herald to Miletus to ask for a truce, that h

might have time to build the temple. At this time Thrasybulus, the most famous of the Ionian tyrants, was tyrant of Miletus. Under his rule Miletus flourished brilliantly and planted Milesian colonies on the Euxine Sea. Thrasybulus had been informed of the oracle and was expecting that Alyattes would ask for a truce. He arranged for all the meager supply of grain in the area to be brought to the marketplace, and when the herald of Alyattes arrived, he found the Milesians feasting and making merry. The herald was astonished, and reported what he had seen to Alyattes. He too was astonished at the apparent prosperity of the Milesians after so many years of war and destruction of their crops, and decided it was not worthwhile to pursue his war against a people who flourished so in adversity. He ended the war and made an alliance of friendship with Miletus. He then built two temples of Athena at Assesus to make up for the one that had been burned, and recovered from his sickness. Thus, according to Herodotus, the ruse of Thrasybulus with the food was successful in ending the war.

During the reign of Croesus, son and successor of Alyattes, Miletus seems to have submitted to Lydian rule on favorable terms. When Croesus was conquered by Cyrus, Miletus alone of the Ionian cities was not subject to attack, because the Milesians, well aware of the weakness and divisions of Ionia, made an alliance with Persia on the same terms as the one they had with Lydia, rather than joining the weak league of Ionian cities in an attempt to resist. Miletus had reached a great peak of prosperity by the time Darius became king of Persia. Her goods were sent throughout the Greek world; Milesian coins bearing the figure of a lion turned up wherever trade was carried on; over 60 Milesian colonies had been founded, among them were Istria on the Adriatic, Sinope, Trapezus, Cyzicus, and many others on the Euxine Sea, and Abydos on the Hellespont. Milesian traders settled in Naucratis in Egypt, and built a temple of Apollo there. The oracle of Apollo at Branchidae in Milesian territory was famous. But Miletus had suffered much from internal disorders, and asked the Parians to compose the differences between the different factions in their country. The Parians, according to Herodotus, went through the land outside the city walls, noting down the names of the owners of any farms that were prosperous in the midst of the desolation caused by civil strife. When they had completed their survey, they proposed that those who had shown they could maintain their own property in the midst of disorder should be made the governors over the others.

In the time of Darius, Histiaeus was tyrant of Miletus. He had accompanied Darius to the Hellespont when the latter invaded Thrace, and he supported Darius because Darius maintained the tyrants. But later Darius called Histiaeus to his court at Susa and kept him there as his friend and counselor, so he said, and Histiaeus, anxious to return to Miletus but constrained to remain in Susa, became one of the inciters of the Ionian revolt against Persia. Under the guidance of his nephew and son-in-law, Aristagoras, who had succeeded him as tyrant of Miletus, the city played a leading part in the revolt (499 B.C.). The revolt was determined upon for the wrong reasons; it was badly planned and ineffectually carried out. The Persians gave it their full attention and put it down with determination. The Ionians were defeated in a sea battle at Lade by a Phoenician fleet sent against them by Persia. Then the attack was concentrated on Miletus. The city was besieged by sea and land, mines were driven under the walls, and the city was taken in 494 B.C. nearly six years after the revolt broke out. The fall of the city fulfilled an oracle that had been given by the priestess at Delphi:

Then shalt thou, Miletus, so oft the contriver of evil,
Be to many, thyself, a feast and an excellent booty.

For now the Persians killed most of the men, put the women and children into slavery, and plundered and burned the oracle and temple at Didyma (Branchidae). Herodotus, who tells of these things, fairly adds that the Milesians who were carried off to the court of Darius at Susa received no injury at his hands, but were settled by him in another part of his empire. Nor had Darius ordered the burning of Apollo's temple, and he rebuked the officer responsible because, he said, "Apollo had always told the truth to the Persians." The Athenians were grief-stricken over the capture of their daughter city Miletus, and showed their grief in their treatment of the poet Phrynichus. When his drama, *The Capture of Miletus*, was presented, it is said that the entire audience burst into tears. A law was passed that the drama should never be presented again to remind the Athenians of their loss, and Phrynichus was fined.

After the Persian defeat at Mycale in 479 B.C., the Persians withdrew from the coast and Miletus joined the Delian League, from which it revolted in 412 B.C. In 334 B.C. the city was captured by Alexander the Great. Miletus was a flourishing trading city, a great colonizer, and a center of literature and philosophy. It was the birthplace of the philosophers Thales and Anaximander, and of the traveler Hecataeus, and the courtesan Aspasia.

*Milo* (mē'lō). Italian name of *Melos.*

*Milvian Bridge* (mil'vi-an). [Also: *Mulvian Bridge;* Italian, *Ponte Milvio;* Latin, *Pons Milvius* or *Mulvius.*] Ancient bridge across the Tiber River N of Rome, built, to replace an earlier wooden structure, by Aemilius Scaurus in 109 B.C., at the crossing of the river by the Via Flaminia. It was the site of the victory of Constantine over Maxentius (312 A.D.) and of the vision of Constantine of a cross in the sky, which led him to embrace Christianity. The bridge was reconstructed in the 13th century, and was again repaired in the 19th century. Of the four original main arches, two survive, and the bridge continues in use for heavy traffic.

*Milyas* (mil'i-as). In ancient geography, a region in SW Asia Minor, of uncertain extent, usually including parts of Lycia and Pisidia.

*Mincius* (min'shi-us). [Italian, *Mincio.*] River in N Italy, a tributary of the Padus (Po), which it joins about 11 miles SE of Mantua.

*Minturnae* (min-tėr'nē). The Roman historian Livy mentions three *oppida* (cities) of the Aurunci or Ausones, an Italic people of Ausonia, on the border between Latium and Campania, which were captured by the Romans on the same day, he says, and by the same stratagem, in 314 B.C. These three *oppida* were Ausona, Vescia, and Minturnae or Menturnae. A Roman citizen colony was founded at Minturnae in 295 B.C. The site of Minturnae has never been lost; it lies in the Vescian Plain, on the right bank of the river Liris (the modern Garigliano) a mile from its mouth. Before excavation enough classical remains survived above ground (three temples, a theater, an amphitheater, an aqueduct, and, if anyone had looked for them, sections of the fortification wall) to suggest the size and importance of the ancient city. On the right bank of the Liris, near its mouth, excavations by Mingazzini in the 1920's revealed the primitive temple of the obscure local Dea Marica, now explained as the Goddess of the Marsh, with extensive deposits of votive offerings.

Excavations sponsored by the University of Pennsylvania Museum in 1931–1934 identified at the river's edge the colony of 295 B.C., in a *castrum* or fortified camp plan strikingly similar to the famous 4th century B.C. *castrum* of Ostia but walled in polygonal limestone, much enlarged later in the 3rd century B.C. by an extension of the fortifications in ashlar tufa. The *decumanus,* the principal street and east-west axis of the colony, was the Via Appia, surveyed in 312 B.C. and thus anterior to the Roman settlement. In the enlarged city, a block fronting on the Via Appia became the forum with a small temple of Jupiter and *tabernae* (shops or booths) which burned about 200 B.C. Following this fire the temple of Jupiter was replaced by a larger Capitolium, dedicated to the "Capitoline Triad," Jupiter, Juno, and Minerva, and to replace the *tabernae* a large three-winged porticus, or colonnade, was erected. In the time of the Gracchi Minturnae was the scene of a slave insurrection, ruthlessly crushed by the crucifixion of the leaders. The city is famous as the locale of one of the adventures of the dictator Caius Marius, who fleeing from Sulla in 88 B.C., was trapped in the Minturnese marshes and imprisoned in the city, where he so awed his guards and the town fathers that they released him and provided safe transportation to Africa.

Destroyed in another fire, which according to the excavators occurred about 45 B.C., the forum buildings were rebuilt in the fashion of the Augustan period. In the block east of the forum, straddling the foundations of the by then dismantled colony wall, was built a temple of Julius Caesar enclosed, like the Capitolium, within the wings of a three-winged porticus. In a trapezoidal area north of the forum between the porticus and the city wall, a theater was erected the back of whose scene was the wall of the porticus. At about the same time an aqueduct in reticulate masonry, still one of the striking sights of the countryside, was built to bring water from copious springs on the slopes of the Montes Aurunci, about nine miles away to the north. A little later a new temple, dedicated probably to Augustus, or to Augustus and Livia, was squeezed into the forum, between the Capitolium and the east wing of the forum porticus; in the foundations of this temple were reused 29 altars from the *compitalia,* street-corner shrines which had been damaged in the fire of c45 B.C. These altars, inscribed with the names of more than 300 slaves and freedmen and the names of their patrons, are at once a directory of prominent families and a mine of information about the ethnography of Minturnae in the early 1st century B.C.

During the empire additional temples, baths, and an amphitheater were built, the forum expanded into the area south of the Via Appia, the city gates were embellished, water from the aqueduct was conducted in underground lead conduits to fountains throughout the city, and the familiar forests of statues and other dedications crowded the public areas. The country outside the walls was dotted with villas of the well-to-do, and a few hundred yards upstream the Liris was bridged with a single great masonry arch. Minturnae became Christian and had its own bishop, but before 590 A.D. the site was abandoned and the see was merged with that of Formia. The Liris bridge having fallen, ferry service was reëstablished and from this the deserted site received the name of Traetto, which passed also to the medieval town growing, thanks to stones removed from the ruined city, on a hilltop three miles inland. In the 19th century the name was changed to Minturno.

As for the other *oppida* of the Aurunci, Ausona and Vescia, they disappeared long ago. The modern hamlet of Ausonia, on the Via Ausonia, which crosses along the base of the Montes Aurunci from the Via Appia to the Via Latina, has no connection with ancient Ausona. Suessa, or Sessa Aurunca, a Latin colony on the slopes of the extinct volcano known as Roccamonfina, may stand on the approximate site of ancient Vescia, and perhaps reflects an alternate pronunciation of the ancient name. (JJ)

**Minyeius** (min-i-ē′i-us). In ancient geography, a name given by Homer to the Anigrus River in Elis. Its waters were said to cure certain skin diseases and other maladies. Fish living in its evil-smelling waters were inedible. See *Anigrus.*

**Misenum** (mī-sē′num). [Modern name, *Miseno.*] A promontory at the NW entrance to the Bay of Naples, sheltering a small harbor also known as Misenum. In the period of Greek activity it served as a port of Cumae, but was presently eclipsed by Puteoli, whose greater harbor area enabled it to serve a vast and growing commercial enterprise. Misenum became a fasionable resort for well-to-do Romans, whose

custom it shared with Baiae, Puteoli, and Pausilypus Mons
(modern Posilipo). In 31 B.C. Agrippa established the head-
quarters of the imperial fleet at Misenum, and it was from
here in 79 A.D. that Pliny the Elder, as fleet admiral, sailed
to his death in the eruption of Vesuvius. (JJ)

*Mistretta* (mēs-trāt'tä). See *Amestratus.*

*Modena* (mô'dä-nä). See *Mutina.*

*Moesia* (mē'shi-ạ). In ancient geography, a northeastern province of the Roman Empire, lying N of the Balkans, S of the
Danube, and W of the Black Sea, corresponding to the N
and C parts of modern Bulgaria and Serbia. It was made a
Roman province c16 B.C., was divided under Domitian into
Moesia Superior (in the W) and Moesia Inferior (in the E),
and was overrun by Goths in the 3rd and 4th centuries A.D.

*Molurian* (mol-ö'ri-ạn) *Rock.* A cliff over the sea near Megara
on the Saronic Gulf. It was from this rocky crag that Ino is
said to have leaped into the sea with her son Melicertes
when she fled from her maddened husband Athamas of
Orchomenus. The Molurian Rock was also famous as the
spot from which Sciron hurled travelers into the sea, until
he himself was thrown from it by Theseus.

*Mopsuestia* (mop-sọ-es'chi-ạ). [Later Latin name, *Hadriane
Mopsuhestia;* modern village name, *Misis.*] In ancient geography, a city of Cilicia, S Asia Minor, on the Pyramus River
E of Tarsus. The city was favored by the emperor Hadrian
and received special privileges from him; it was renamed in
his honor.

*Morgantina* (môr-gạn-tē'nạ). City in Sicily, in the district
known as Serra Orlando, near Aidone, under excavation by
an expedition from Princeton University, which has revealed
the market-place, public buildings, houses, fortifications,
and a cemetery. The culture is native Sicilian under Greek
influence; after the Roman annexation of Sicily, Morgantina
rapidly declined. The identification of the site as Morgantina, not known previously, emerged from study of the coins
found in the excavations. (JJ)

*Motya* (mot'yạ). [Modern name, *S. Pantaleo.*] In ancient geography, a Carthaginian city of western Sicily. It was situated
on an island in a small bay on the extreme western coast of
Sicily. The island is almost completely enclosed in the bay;
an arm of the mainland stretches across the north and ends
in a long spit of land and protects the bay to the W, or sea

side. The city on the island was completely walled, and was connected to the mainland by a causeway. In 398 B.C. Dionysius the Elder, tyrant of Syracuse, marched at the head of a large force and besieged it. To protect themselves from his siege engines, the inhabitants destroyed the causeway. Dionysius drew his ships ashore on the bay and set to work to build a new causeway, a much larger one than that destroyed, in order to attack the city, not with his fleet, but with his siege engines. The Carthaginians sent a fleet to the relief of Motya and blockaded the fleet of Dionysius in the bay. Instead of launching his galleys against the Carthaginian fleet Dionysius marched his army around the bay and attacked them from the shore with catapults that hurled great stones against the ships. This was a new weapon with which the Carthaginians were not prepared to cope. They sailed out of the bay and lurked out of reach of the catapults. Dionysius then put his own ships on great rollers and hauled them across the arm of land to the north, and launched them in the sea on the other side. The Carthaginians decided not to engage him. Leaving the Motyans to their fate, they sailed back to Carthage. Dionysius was now free to besiege the city, his mole having been completed. Because the space in the city was limited, the inhabitants built up into the air. Stone towers as high as six stories studded the city. The towers were out of reach of ordinary siege engines. Dionysius redesigned his engines, putting the operating force atop siege towers of a height to be effective against the towered city. The siege he thus mounted against Motya became a kind of aerial warfare with the besieged and besiegers struggling from the tops of the towers. Those on the siege towers rained stones on the city with catapults, while below the rams of Dionysius battered at the walls. Those defending the city retaliated with flaming pitch hurled at the wooden siege towers, but to no avail. The forces of Dionysius breached the wall and entered the city. This by no means was the end. From their towers the defenders rained missiles and fire on the invaders. The attackers brought in their siege engines and flung bridges across to the towers of the defenders, so that much of the fighting was carried on on these bridges high in the air. Many were flung to their death. Every tower had to be taken individually as the Motyans had no thought of surrender. Day after day the struggle was

obscured) errȧnt, ardḙnt, actọr; ch, chip; g, go; th, thin; ŦH, then; y, you; variable) ḍ as d or j, ṣ as s or sh, ṭ as t or ch, ẓ as z or zh.

renewed and each night it ceased as both forces rested. The Motyans could not hope to drive off the Greeks, but the were determined to make a Greek victory costly. Many o Dionysius' men were slain, and he decided on a night attack He entered a part of the town that was still being defended and completely surprised the Motyans. His forces poured in and massacred the inhabitants, who continued their heroi resistance to the end. At last Dionysius stopped the slaugh ter. Those who survived were sold into slavery, and the cit was given over to his soldiers to plunder. It was a grea victory for Dionysius and his new methods of siege warfare but the next year the Carthaginians returned and recaptured Motya. They, however, did not restore it. Instead the founded a new city, Lilybaeum, on the south side of the bay

**Motyca** (mō′ti-ka̤) or **Mutyca** (mū′ti-ka̤). [Modern name *Modica.*] In ancient geography, a town of Sicily, situated or a hill between two valleys, near the Mauro River, in the SI corner of Sicily. It was a town of the ancient Sicels.

**Munda** (mun′da). In ancient geography, a town in S Spain, o undetermined location. It is noted for the victory gained (4! B.C.) there by Julius Caesar over the sons of Pompey.

**Munychia** (mū-nik′i-a̤). One of the three harbors serving Athens in the vicinity of Piraeus. The name *Munychia* is also given to the citadel (height, 284 feet) of Piraeus. On the hil at Munychia was a temple of Artemis. After the death o Hipparchus, Hippias fortified the hill of Munychia, in 51( B.C. The democratic opponents of the Thirty Tyrants seized the hill of Munychia, occupied the temple of Artemis, anc in the following conflict (403 B.C.) inflicted such damage or the Thirty that they were thrown from power and sough refuge at Eleusis.

**Mutina** (mū′ti-na̤). [Modern name, *Modena.*] City of Italy, situ ated on the Via Aemilia, NW of Bononia (Bologna). Nea here, 44–43 B.C., Decimus Junius Brutus was blockaded b Mark Antony, and was relieved by Hirtius, Pansa, and Oc tavian (the future Augustus), who defeated Antony.

**Mutyca** (mū′ti-ka̤). See **Motyca.**

**Mycale** (mik′a̤-lē). In ancient geography, a mountain in Lydi Asia Minor, N of Miletus. Here were gathered about 60,00( of the forces of Xerxes, left behind to guard Ionia after th defeat of the Persians at Salamis (480 B.C.). Part of th Persian fleet, not wishing to risk another naval fight with th

fat, fāte, fär, fåll, a̤sk, fãre; net, mē, hèr; pin, pīne; not, nōte, möve nôr; up, lūte, pu̇ll; oi, oil; ou out; (lightened) ẹlect, agǫny, ūnite

Greeks also withdrew to Mycale. There the ships were dragged ashore and a rampart was built around them to protect them and to form a defense for the soldiers. The Greek fleet under Leotychides pursued the Persians to Mycale. Seeing that the Persians did not venture out to meet them, the Greeks disembarked. As the Greeks prepared for battle, a rumor spread through the camp that the Greeks had defeated the Persians at Plataea on that very day. A herald's wand was found lying on the beach, according to Herodotus, which was an indication of the miraculous means by which the news had come from Plataea to Mycale so swiftly. Heartened by the rumor and the sign, the Greeks rushed eagerly into the battle. The struggle was grim and hard-fought on both sides, with neither giving ground at first. When the Athenians on their wing succeeded in breaking through the line of Persian wicker shields, the Persians withdrew into the entrenchment they had created with the ships and the surrounding rampart. The Athenians were so hot in pursuit they swarmed into the entrenchment after them and took the fortress. The Persians fled, and the Greeks fired their ships and took great booty. Thus on the same September day in 479 B.C., or so the story goes, the Persians in Greece under Mardonius were defeated at Plataea, and the Persians in Ionia were defeated at Mycale.

**Mycalessus** (mī-ka̧-lē′sus). In ancient geography, a city in Boeotia. It is said to have been so-named from the Greek word for "low," because the cow guiding Cadmus in Boeotia lowed at this place. Diïtrephes, the Thracian, came to Mycalessus as he led his Thracians back to their country (c413 B.C.). He took the town and put the entire population to the sword. It is for this reason that the statue of Diïtrephes set up on the acropolis at Mycalessus showed him pierced by many arrows. At Mycalessus was a remarkable sanctuary of Demeter Mycalessia.

**Mycenae** (mī-sē′nē). In ancient geography, a city in Argolis, Greece, about 14 miles SW of Corinth. It was a very ancient settlement, dating from perhaps the 20th century B.C., and was conspicuous in Greek legend and history. According to tradition, Argolis was inhabited by Pelasgians, who fell under the domination of Danaus when he arrived from Egypt with his 50 daughters. The kingdom of Danaus in Argolis was subsequently divided among his descendants. Acrisius

became ruler of Argos. His brother Proetus ruled the neighboring region of Tiryns. When Perseus, grandson of
Acrisius, unwittingly killed Acrisius, he did not wish to remain in Argos. He exchanged his inheritance with his cousin
Megapenthes and became ruler of Tiryns. As Perseus proceeded toward Tiryns, he was overcome by thirst. He
stooped to pluck a mushroom and drank the water from its
cap. Pleased that he thus quenched his thirst, he founded a
city on the spot and named it Mycenae for the mushroom
(*mykos*). Nearby the spot where this occurred is a spring
called by the ancients *Persea*, which still gives sparkling water
to the inhabitants. Some say, however, that Perseus named
his city from the cap of his sword, which happened to fall off
at this spot, and which has a Greek name very similar to the
word for mushroom. At all events, he fortified the city
which was on an eminence rising from the fertile plain, easily
defendable and in a position to command routes to and
from the sea. He secured the aid of the Cyclopes to build the
wall of the city, which is sometimes called "the Cyclopean
City," from the huge irregular stones that form its wall.
Sthenelus, son and successor of Perseus, received Atreus
and Thyestes, sons of Pelops, into his realm when they fled
from their father. On the death of Eurystheus, son of
Sthenelus, Atreus became king, ended the Perseid dynasty
and established that of the Pelopidae, which became the
equal of any kingdom in the Peloponnesus. Signs of fire
found in the excavations at Mycenae are attributed to the
struggles that took place when Atreus assumed mastery.
Atreus was followed by his brother Thyestes, who in turn
was succeeded by Agamemnon, son of Atreus and brother
of Menelaus. The rulers between Perseus and Agamemnon
cover the period of time between about the middle of the
14th century, when the city was founded by Perseus, and the
fall of Troy, the traditional date of which is 1183 B.C. In the
time of Agamemnon, Mycenae was at its apogee. Tiryns,
Argos, and Midea were subject to him, as was most of the
Peloponnesus and the neighboring islands. As master of a
strong maritime empire he exercised influence over most of
the Greek mainland and the islands, and drew supporters
from the entire area when he led the expedition to Troy to
recover Helen. The murder of Agamemnon on his return
from his successes at Troy by his wife Clytemnestra and her

fat, fāte, fär, fåll, åsk, fãre; net, mē, hèr; pin, pīne; not, nōte, möve
nôr; up, lūte, pùll; oi, oil; ou out; (lightened) ēlect, agǭny, ūnite

lover Aegisthus, provides the material for some of the most dramatic pages of Greek tragedy. After an interval in which Mycenae was ruled by Clytemnestra and Aegisthus, Agamemnon was succeeded by his son Orestes and his grandson Tisamenus. During the reign of Tisamenus the Dorians invaded the Peloponnesus, took Mycenae, and destroyed its citadel. Thereafter, the influence and power of Mycenae was in eclipse.

As in many cases, history and legend are closely intertwined at Mycenae. Archaeologists consider that the earliest city to occupy the site dated from about the 20th century B.C. In succeeding centuries close relations were established between Mycenae and Crete, and remains of a distinctly Cretan character, dating from 1600–1400 B.C., have been found in tombs on the site along with other evidences of Cretan domination in this period. Following the establishment of the city of Perseus, c1350 B.C., a distinctively Mycenaean culture developed throughout the area and spread to Asia Minor in the east and to Sicily in the west. In the period of its greatness the kings of Mycenae were the peers of the kings of Egypt and Babylon. From the end of the 12th century B.C. the importance of Mycenae declined so completely that nothing more is heard of it until the Persian Wars, when 80 Mycenaeans went to the aid of Leonidas at Thermopylae and later 200 shared in the victory at Plataea (479 B.C.). The Argives, roused to jealousy by the pride which the Mycenaeans took at having their names inscribed on the tripods at Delphi after the Battle of Plataea, attacked Mycenae and destroyed it c470 B.C. The city never recovered from this attack. Only a village remained on the site. The traveler and writer Pausanias visited there in the 2nd century A.D., and saw parts of the old walls and the Lion Gate (which was never completely obscured). He also claimed to have seen the graves of Atreus and Agamemnon in the citadel, as well as the graves of Clytemnestra and Aegisthus outside the walls (for they, as murderers, could not be buried in the citadel). Modern scholars doubt that Pausanias actually saw the graves, for they must have been covered over; rather, it is thought that they were described to him by local inhabitants who knew of them by tradition. From the time of Pausanias until the 19th century Mycenae was a forgotten village. In that century the site was rediscovered by travelers, and various objects that were uncovered were carried off. It was not until the end of the century that the city as a famous and immensely valuable historical and archaeological site again came to the attention of the world. The original excavations were made by Heinrich Schliemann in 1876–77. Following the account of Pausanias, Schliemann discovered the Grave Circle of Mycenae with its royal shaft graves. Five graves were rapidly cleared and yielded a rich treasure. Later work was done on the site by the Archaeological Society of Athens. The Mycenae of the *Iliad*, "that well-built city and fortress," the "golden" "wide-wayed" city especially loved by Hera, as well as the city of much earlier times, has been steadily emerging through archaeological expeditions ever since, notably those undertaken by the British Archaeological Society under Prof. A. J. B. Wace, which were interrupted in 1939 by the outbreak of World War II, and those of the Greek Archaeological Society in the 1950's. In the latest excavations (1952 and following years) a new grave circle has been disclosed, which includes the graves of the ruling families of the 17th and 16th centuries B.C. The shaft graves found by Schliemann and those in the new grave circle uncovered in 1952 were cut into the rock, sealed off, and covered over. They contained many skeletons and objects of value that decorated the bodies of the dead when they were interred. This is of interest as it shows that at the time of these burials the Mycenaeans did not burn their dead, as they did according to the Homeric poems of a later age. Rather, they buried them with all the accoutrements of the living—ornaments, utensils, and weapons. However, once the flesh had disappeared from their bones, no more concern was expressed for their souls or for their journey to the other world, and it appears that the skeletons were somewhat unceremoniously moved to one side to make room for new arrivals in the tombs. Excavations at the site of Mycenae have supplied some of the oldest material for the study of Greek architecture and art. The site consisted of an acropolis, occupying the apex of a hill, and the lower town, the confused ruins of which are spread over its slopes. The acropolis is triangular, and is surrounded by a massive wall of huge stones (Cyclopean stones), partly shaped. It is entered by the Gate of the Lions, which dates from the 14th century B.C. This gate is at the end of a walled passage so placed that the right, or unshielded, side of an enemy would be exposed to the defenders within the citadel. The opening of the gate is about ten feet wide and high, tapering toward the top, with monolithic jambs and a huge lintel. Above the lintel a large triangular opening is formed by corbeling, and the great slab, two feet thick, which fills this, bears the remarkable relief of two facing rampant lions separated by a column. Close inside of this gate, in a double circle of upright stones 80 feet in diameter, were found shaft graves containing golden ornaments and masks, inlaid swordblades, and other objects whose discovery astonished the scientific world. According to legend, these were the tombs of Atreus, Electra, Agamemnon, Cassandra, and others of the period. Modern scholars place the date of the tombs earlier than the time of Agamemnon, between the 19th and 16th centuries B.C. Excavations have disclosed on the acropolis a prehistoric palace resembling that at Tiryns, and remains of palaces and temples of later periods that were superimposed on it. Remains still exist of the ramp on which, perhaps, Clytemnestra placed the royal purple for the feet of Agamemnon on his triumphant return from Troy. The bath in which she almost immediately thereafter slew him disappeared when part of the acropolis was destroyed in a landslide. This is the acropolis that the tutor points out to Orestes, in Sophocles' *Electra,* as "a treasure-house of gold . . . the ancestral home of the family of Pelops, a house of death if ever there was one." The most important monuments of the lower town are the great "beehive" tombs, commonly called treasuries. Of these, one sometimes called "the treasury of Atreus" and sometimes "the tomb of Agamemnon," is a typical example. The interior is a circle about 50 feet in diameter and slightly less in height, covered with a pseudodome formed by corbeling in the horizontal courses of the wall. Indications are that the inner surface of the tomb was decorated with medallions in metal and painted designs. The discoveries at Mycenae threw a flood of light upon the earliest Greek art, particularly in pottery. They were the first important finds of their class, which has since been recognized in a large proportion of Greek settlements of sufficient age, and is everywhere distinguished as Mycenaean. Mycenaean ornament includes geometric decoration, foliage, marine and animal forms, and the human figure. Mycenaean art was practiced and developed through several centuries, and existed contemporaneously with the succeeding dipylon style of decoration, which began c1000 B.C. Among the objects found in the second grave circle, excavated 1952 and following years, are: bronze daggers, spears, swords, and the remains of a leather scabbard; pottery, including painted vases, amphorae, and jars; engraved gems; gold ornaments, including bands, buttons, and ear clips; beads of semi-precious stones; rock crystal bowls and pins with rock crystal heads; and gold cups. In 1970 it was reported that remains of several Bronze Age frescoes had been discovered in the ruins of a house believed to have been destroyed about 1200 B.C. A two-foot section of one fresco, now undergoing restoration, depicts a half-figure of a goddess or priestess; there were also fragments found of stylized motifs previously found only in palaces and royal houses. The chief objects found at Mycenae are in the National Museum at Athens.

*Myconus* or *Mykonos* (mĭk′ọ̄-nos, mī′kọ̄-nos). [Also: *Mikonos*.] Island in the Aegean Sea, one of the Cyclades. Area, about 33 square miles. It lies E of Delos, and according to legend was one of the moorings which anchored Delos, hitherto a floating island, to the sea floor when Leto went to Delos to bear her twin children, Apollo and Artemis. The body of Ajax the Less, which had been recovered from the sea, was buried here by the sea-goddess Thetis.

*Mylae* (mī′lē). [Modern name, *Milazzo* or *Melazzo*.] Seaport on the N coast of the island of Sicily, about 18 miles W of Messana. Near here the Roman fleet under Duilius gained its first naval victory over the Carthaginians in 260 B.C., and Agrippa defeated Sextus Pompey's fleet in 36 B.C.

*Mylasa* (mī-lā′sạ). [Also: *Mylassa;* modern town name, *Milâs*.] In ancient geography, an inland town in SW Asia Minor, in Caria. It was the capital of the later Carian kingdom.

*Myonnesus* (mī-ọ-nē′sus). In ancient geography, a promontory on the coast of Ionia, W Asia Minor, about 27 miles NW of Ephesus. Near it the Romans gained (190 B.C.) a naval victory over the Syrians under Antiochus III.

*Myra* (mī′rạ). In ancient geography, a city in Lycia, SW Asia Minor, situated near the S coast. An ancient theater here is among the finest in Asia Minor.

*Myrina* (mi-rī′nạ). Very extensive Greek necropolis, near Izmir

(Smyrna), Asia Minor, discovered c1870, and systematically excavated by the French School at Athens between 1880 and 1882, known for terra-cotta figurines.

*Myrina.* In ancient geography, a city of the island of Lemnos. The site is now occupied by the town of Kastron.

*Myrtoan Sea* (mẻr-tō′ạn). [Latin, *Mare Myrtoum.*] In ancient geography, that part of the Aegean Sea S of Argolis, Attica, and Euboea.

*Mysia* (mish′i-ạ). In ancient geography, a district in NW Asia Minor. It was bounded by the Propontis on the N, Bithynia on the NE, Phrygia on the E, Lydia on the S, the Aegean Sea on the W, and the Hellespont on the NW. The region is traversed by mountain ranges. There were many Greek cities on the coasts. It belonged successively to Lydia, Persia, Macedon, Syria, Pergamum, and Rome. The Mysians were probably allied to the Lydians. They assisted the Khita (Hittites) against Rameses II.

*Mytilene* (mit-i-lē′nẹ). [Also: *Mitylene, Mytilini;* former name, *Kastro.*] Town on the E coast of the island of Lesbos. In ancient times it was the chief city of Lesbos, the home of Sappho, and an important maritime power of the Aeolian Greeks. It revolted from Athens in 428 B.C., and was subjected in 427 B.C.

*Myus* (mī′us). In ancient geography, one of the 12 Ionian cities of Asia Minor. It was in Caria, situated on the Maeander River, about 11 miles NE of Miletus. According to tradition, it was colonized by Ionians from Attica, under the leadership of Cyaretus, son of Codrus, the legendary king of Athens. The city took part in the Ionian revolt against the Persians, and was subdued. In later centuries, the arm of the sea on which Myus was located was silted over, and turned the inlet into a lake. The lake became a breeding ground for gnats, and they became such a pest that the people of Myus abandoned their city, taking their gods with them, and withdrew to Miletus.

——N——

*Naples* (nā'plz). See *Neapolis*.

*Nar* (när). [Modern name, *Nera*.] A shallow, sulphurous river in Umbria.

*Narbo* (när'bō). [Modern name, *Narbonne*.] A city in Gaul near the Mediterranean coast, known in pre-Roman times as a Celtic market town and in 118 B.C. refounded by the Romans as Colonia Narbo Martius. After Caesar's Tenth Legion had been settled there, the province of Gallia Narbonensis was established, with Narbo as its capital, a distinction later lost to Nemausus. (JJ)

*Narbonensis* (när-bō-nen'sis). [Also: *Gallia Narbonensis*.] Province of the Roman Empire, occupying the S and SE parts of Gaul, named for its first capital Narbo. It extended from the Alps SW along the Mediterranean to the Pyrenees. The N border was near the line of the Cebenna (Cevennes), the Rhodanus (Rhône), and the Lacus Lemanus (Lake of Geneva). The area of the province corresponds approximately to French Provence. Among its leading cities were Massilia (Marseilles) and Narbo (Narbonne), on the coast; Arelate (Arles), Nemausus (Nîmes), Arausio (Orange), and Vienna (Vienne), in the valley of the Rhodanus (Rhône); and Tolosa (Toulouse), inland to the west. The Roman ruins of Provence are famous: at Arles, a theater, an amphitheater, the forum, and town walls; at Nîmes, a fine temple, the so-called Maison Carrée, erected by Agrippa in 16 B.C., an amphitheater, and a gate, and nearby the splendid aqueduct known as the Pont du Gard; at Orange, a theater, a municipal arch, and fortifications; at Vienne, a well-preserved temple and a circus. Narbo became a Roman colony in 118 B.C.; colonies were later established at Arelate, Arausio, and Nemausus, and probably also at Vienna and Tolosa. (JJ)

*Narni* (när'nē) or *Narnia* (när'ni-ạ). See *Nequinum*.

*Naucratis* (nô'krạ-tis). In ancient geography, a city in Egypt situated on the Canopic mouth of the Nile, not far from Saï and about midway between modern Cairo and Alexandria

fat, fāte, fär, fâll, àsk, fāre; net, mē, hèr; pin, pīne; not, nōte, mōve nôr; up, lūte, pùll; oi, oil; ou out; (lightened) ẹlect, agǫny, ūnite

It is believed to have been founded by Milesian colonists not later than the 7th century B.C., and was described by Athenaeus and Herodotus as celebrated for its potters and florists. According to Herodotus, Amasis II (fl. c569–525 B.C.) encouraged the Greeks to settle in Naucratis, the only city where the Greeks were allowed to trade, and gave them land for their temples and altars. The site remained unknown till it was discovered by W. M. Flinders Petrie in 1884. The very extensive and important remains that have been excavated include ruins of the famous Hellenium, a temple built jointly by the Ionians, Dorians, and Aeolians, who owned the temple and appointed the governors of the port; temples of Zeus, Hera, Apollo, and Aphrodite, built by the Aeginetans, Samians, and Milesians; and pieces of pottery in great variety and profusion.

*Naupactus* (nô-pak′tus). [Also: *Naupaktos, Navpaktos, Lepanto*.] City in Locris, Greece, situated on the Gulf of Corinth, opposite Patrae. According to some accounts, the Dorian invasion of the Peloponnesus was launched from here. The name of the city means "city of ship-building," and some say it was Cresphontes, others say it was Aristomachus, and still others say it was Temenus, who here built the vessels for the Dorian invasion. Just west of the city was a sanctuary of Asclepius, and a rock covered with inscriptions expressive of gratitude to the god of healing may still be seen there. In the 5th century B.C. the Athenians established a naval base here, having taken the city from the Ozolian Locrians, and thus won a strategic base for the control of the Gulf of Corinth. About 464 B.C. the Messenians had revolted against Sparta. Athens went to help the Spartans put down the revolt, but as the Spartans feared growing Athenian power more than the revolting Messenians, the Athenians were requested to withdraw. The Athenians got their revenge for this snub by giving Naupactus to the Messenians who were defeated and compelled to leave Ithome, where they had resisted Sparta. In the Peloponnesian Wars (431–404 B.C.), the Messenians offered Naupactus to Athens as a naval base against Sparta. It was a band of Messenian scouts who led the Athenians around to the Spartan rear when the latter were besieged on the island of Sphacteria, and brought about their surrender (425 B.C.). In gratitude for thus humiliating their agelong enemies the Messenians of Naupactus dedicated the famous statue of Victory, by Paeonius, at Olympia. After the defeat of the Athenians at Aegospotami (405 B.C.), the Spartans drove the Messenians out of Naupactus.

*Nauplia* (nô′pli-ạ). [Also: *Nafplion, Nauplion, Navplion.*] Town in S Greece, situated at the head of the Gulf of Nauplia (also called Gulf of Argolis), about 25 miles SW of Corinth. It was the port of ancient Argos. South of the city a rocky cliff rises to a height of about 700 feet above the gulf. This was the ancient citadel of the city. Its name, Palamidi, recalls Palamedes, that son of Nauplius who was treacherously killed by his fellow Greeks in the Trojan War.

*Nauplia, Gulf of.* [Also: *Gulf of Argolis* (or *Argos*); Greek, *Argolikos Kolpos;* Latin, *Argolicus Sinus.*] Arm of the Aegean Sea, indenting the E coast of the Peloponnesus, Greece. Length, about 30 miles.

*Navarino* (nä-vä-rē′nō). See *Pylus.*

*Naxos* (nak′sọs). [Also: *Naxia.*] Island in the Aegean Sea, about 170 square miles in area. It is the largest and most fertile of the Cyclades, and is celebrated for its wine, olives, fruit, and vegetables. According to some accounts, it was anciently known as Strongyle, and was seized by Butes, a son of Thracian Boreas. Thracians dwelt on Naxos for 200 years, when they were driven out by a prolonged drought. It was afterward settled by Carians, whose king was Naxos, and for whom they in their turn renamed the island. The grandson of this king is said to have been the king who hospitably received Theseus and Ariadne when they stopped there on their way from Crete to Athens. The Naxians claimed that Dionysus was reared on their island by the nymphs Coronis, Philia, and Clide. For this reason Dionysus especially loved Naxos and caused its wine to be noted for its excellence, as the island became noted as a center of the worship of Dionysus. The Naxians were celebrated warriors and distinguished themselves at the battles of Salamis (480 B.C.) and Plataea (479 B.C.). Naxos was a member of the Confederacy of Delos, and revolted but was subdued by Athens c467 B.C. Near it Athens won a naval victory over Sparta in 376 B.C.

*Naxos.* [Also: *Naxia.*] Chief town of the island of Naxos, in the Cyclades, situated on its NW coast.

*Naxos.* [Also: *Naxus.*] In ancient geography, a seaport on the east coast of Sicily, just north of Mount Aetna. It was founded by Chalcidians who were accompanied by Ionians

fat, fāte, fär, fåll, ȧsk, fāre; net, mē, hėr; pin, pīne; not, nōte, möve; nôr; up, lūte, pùll; oi, oil; ou out; (lightened) ẹlect, agọny, ūnite

from the island of Naxos. The traditional date of its founding is 735 B.C. It was always especially highly regarded by the Greeks because it was their first settlement in Sicily. Colonists from Naxos founded the Sicilian cities of Catana and Leontini. Naxos sided with the Ionian cities of Sicily against Syracuse and the Dorian cities, and was one of the few allies of Athens in the Sicilian expedition of 415 B.C. In 403 B.C. traitors inside the city accepted gold to open the gates to Dionysius the Elder, tyrant of Syracuse. Dionysius destroyed its walls and its dwellings, sold most of the inhabitants as slaves in Syracuse, and gave the land to the Sicels to win their support. The few Naxians who managed to escape at length found a home in the new town of Tauromenium.

*Neapolis* (nē-ap′ō-lis). [Also: *Parthenope;* modern *Naples.*] In ancient geography, a city of S Italy, situated on a magnificent bay, S of Rome. It was founded by colonists from the Greek settlement of Cumae, c600 B.C., and was first called Parthenope. When new colonists came from Chalcis and Athens and built themselves a settlement, Parthenope came to be known as Palaeopolis, the "old city," and the new settlement was called Neapolis, the "new city." In 327 B.C. Palaeopolis was besieged and taken by the Romans, and its name disappeared from history. Neapolis became a dependency of Rome, to whom she was a faithful ally. It was a strongly fortified town and resisted the efforts of Pyrrhus to take it, 280 B.C. In the civil wars it was betrayed to the partisans of Sulla (82 B.C.) They entered it and slaughtered the inhabitants. However, the city soon revived and became once more a prosperous port. Because of its climate and the beauty of its surroundings ("See Naples and die," Italian proverb) the city was a favorite resort of wealthy Romans and of the emperors. Vergil, who wrote most of the *Georgics* here, wished to be buried on a hill overlooking the city. The glorious beauty of the Bay of Naples, with Mount Vesuvius rising dramatically in the background, has for centuries been celebrated by poets and writers.

*Nemausus* (nē-mô′sus). [Modern name, *Nîmes.*] An important Roman town in the valley of the Rhodanus (Rhône) River, in the Roman province known as Provincia (modern Provence). Established as a colony in 16 B.C., Nemausus prospered greatly, as the impressive remains of Roman buildings indicate: The "Maison Carrée," a handsome and well-preserved hexastyle Corinthian temple built by Agrippa, an amphitheater, a gate, and a great aqueduct, one imposing section of which survives as the Pont du Gard. Eventually Nemausus replaced Narbo as capital of the province of Gallia Narbonensis. (JJ)

*Nemea* (nē'mē-ạ, nẹ-mē'ạ). In ancient geography, a valley in Argolis, Greece, about 11 miles SW of Corinth. As the first of his 12 labors for Eurystheus, Heracles here choked the Nemean Lion to death. It was also the site of the Nemean Games. Of the 4th century B.C. Doric temple of Zeus three columns still stand. Excavations by French and American archaeologists have revealed the plan of the temple, notable for its sunken *adytum* or crypt at the rear of the cella, and a great altar, a palestra, a gymnasium, and an athletes' bath. The stadium lies in a recess in the neighboring hills.

*Nemorensis, Lacus* (nem-ọ-ren'sis, lā'kus). [Italian, *Lago di Nemi;* English, *Lake Nemi.*] A small lake about 17 miles SE of Rome, noted for its beauty. It occupies the crater of an extinct volcano in the Alban Mountains. Nearby is a lonely wood in which there was a temple to Diana where all the Latins joined in her worship. Among the many legends connected with this shrine was one that in the wood there was a tree which bore a golden bough. Whoever plucked the bough and slew the priest of the shrine succeeded him as the new priest and retained the honor until he in his turn was slain. It was in the hope of finding analogies which might provide an explanation of this cult that Sir J. G. Frazer embarked upon the extended research in primitive religion and magic which culminated in the publication of his monumental *Golden Bough.* The "golden bough" itself has, with some plausibility, been explained as mistletoe.

*Neocastro* (ne"ô-kas'trô). See *Pylus.*

*Nequinum* (nẹ-kwī'num). [Also: *Narnia;* modern name, *Narni.*] In ancient geography, a town of Umbria in C Italy, on the Via Flaminia. It was situated on the Nar River about 43 miles N of Rome. The Umbrian town was captured by the Romans, 299 B.C., and colonized by them. The Roman name of the town was Narnia.

*Nera* (nā'rä). [Ancient name, *Nar.*] Small river in C Italy, a tributary of the Tiber. Terni is situated on it.

*Neritos* (ner'i-tos). In ancient geography, a small island near Ithaca, whose sheer cliffs rise abruptly from the sea. Accord-

fat, fāte, fär, fåll, åsk, fãre; net, mē, hėr; pin, pīne; not, nōte, möve, nôr; up, lūte, pùll; oi, oil; ou out; (lightened) ẹlect, agọny, ūnite;

ing to Greek legend, it belonged to Laertes in his young days.

*Nestus* (nes'tus). [Also: *Mesta.*] River in SE Europe, rising in SW Bulgaria and flowing generally SE through NE Greece to the Aegean Sea opposite the island of Thasus.

*Nicaea* (nī-sē'ạ). [Anglicized, *Nice;* Greek, *Nikaia;* modern Turkish name, *Iznik.*] In ancient geography, a town in Bithynia, Asia Minor, situated on Lake Ascania, about 58 miles SE of Constantinople. It was founded in the 4th century B.C., and was one of the chief cities of Bithynia. It was the seat of the two Councils of Nicaea, at the first of which (325 A.D.) the Nicene Creed was formulated and decreed.

*Nicaea.* [Modern name, *Nice.*] In ancient geography, a town on the coast of Liguria, founded by colonists from Massilia (present Marseilles) in the 5th century B.C.

*Nicaria* (nī-kār'i-ạ). See *Icaria,* island.

*Nicopolis* (ni-kop'ō-lis, nī-). Ancient city in Cappadocia, Asia Minor, founded by Pompey to commemorate his victory there over Mithridates VI in 66 B.C.

*Nicopolis.* In ancient geography, a city in Epirus, Greece, situated on the Gulf of Arta. It was founded by Octavian (later the emperor Augustus) in commemoration of his victory at Actium in 31 B.C. The site contains many Roman antiquities.

*Nicopolis.* Ancient city near Alexandria, Egypt, founded (24 B.C.) by Augustus to commemorate his defeat of Antony.

*Nineveh* (nin'ẹ-vẹ). [Latin, *Ninus.*] In ancient geography, an important city, for a long time the capital of the Assyrian Empire, situated on the E bank of the upper Tigris opposite what is now Mosul, and surrounded in ancient times by a shallow river (Khosr). The site, now marked by the two mounds of Kuyunjik and Nebi Unus, was first identified in 1820 by J. C. Rich, political resident of the East India Company at Baghdad. The first attempts at Excavation were made in 1842 by Paul Emile Botta, who, however, met with slight success; these were followed on a more extended scale by Sir Austen Henry Layard (1845–47, 1849–51), by Hormuzd Rassam (1854), by George Smith (1873–76), the work being again taken up by Rassam on the death of Smith, and by King and Thompson (1903–05). As a result of these excavations, the general outline of a city about three miles long, the remains of four palaces and numerous sculptures, and thousands of tablets (principally from the so-called li-

(obscured) errạnt, ardẹnt, actọr; ch, chip; g, go; th, thin; ᴛн, then; y, you; (variable) ḍ as d or j, ṣ as s or sh, ṭ as t or ch, ẓ as z or zh.

brary of Assurbanipal) were discovered. The greater part of
these are now in the British Museum. The city had a perime-
ter of from seven to eight miles, the ruins of the walls showing a height in some parts of 50 feet. It was in existence as
early as the time of Hammurabi (c1950 B.C.). Shalmaneser
I (1330 B.C.) built a palace at Nineveh and made it the city
of his residence. Shamshi-Adad V (824–811) decorated and
restored the temple of Ishtar, famous for a special phase of
the cult of the goddess. Adadnirari III (811–782 B.C.) built
a new palace on the site of the mound Nebi Yunus. For a
time Nineveh was neglected, Sargon II (722–705 B.C.) the
founder of the new dynasty, abandoning it as the capital for
a new town Dur Sharrukin (Khorsabad) which he built and
made his residence. His son, Sennacherib (705–681 B.C.),
was, however, a special patron of Nineveh. He surrounded
it with a wall, replaced (695 B.C.) the small palace at the NE
wall by a large one, built another palace which he filled with
cedar wood and adorned with colossal bulls and lions, and
beautified the city with a park. Thd Old Testament (2 Kings,
xix. 36, Isa. xxxvii, 37) mentions Nineveh as the residence
of Sennacherib. Esarhaddon (680–668 B.C.) finished a temple, widened the streets, and beautified the city, forcing the
kings whom he conquered to furnish materials for adorning
the city and palaces. Nineveh succumbed (c608 B.C.) to the
combined attack of the Medes under Cyaxares and the
Babylonians under Nabopolassar.

*Nisa* (nī'sạ). Ancient name of *Megara.*

*Nisaea* (nī-sē'ạ). In ancient geography, a region in Media (perhaps near the Caspian Gates), famous for its breed of
horses.

*Nisaea.* The port of the ancient city of Nisa (later *Megara*),
founded by Nisus, according to Greek tradition, and named
for him.

*Nisibis* (nis'i-bis). [Modern names, *Nisibin, Nusaybin.*] In ancient geography, a town in Mesopotamia. At various times
an Armenian, Parthian, and Persian stronghold, it was taken
by Lucullus in 68 B.C., and afterward (from the Persians) by
Trajan.

*Nisyrus* (ni-sī'rus). An island near Cos in the Dodecanese.
According to tradition, it was formed during the war between the Giants and the gods when Poseidon broke
off a piece of Cos with his trident and hurled it at the

Giant Polybutes, burying Polybutes under it.

*Nocera Inferiore* (nō-che'rä ēn-fä-rē-ō'rä). See *Nuceria Alfaterna.*

*Nola* (nō'lạ). Town in Campania, S Italy, about 15 miles NE of Neapolis. Possibly founded by Etruscans, it became subject to Rome in 313 B.C. It was the scene of battles (216, 215 B.C.) between Marcellus and Hannibal in the First Punic War, and was also the site of the death of Augustus in 14 A.D.

*Nomentum* (nọ-men'tum). In ancient geography, a town of Latium, about 13 miles NE of Rome. The village of Mentana later occupied this site.

*Nonacris* (nọ-nak'ris). In ancient geography, a city in N Arcadia, Greece.

*Nora* (nō'rạ, nôr'ạ). In ancient geography, a fortress in Cappadocia, Asia Minor, situated at the foot of Mount Taurus, near Lycaonia. Eumenes was besieged (320–319 B.C.) here by the forces of Antigonus.

*Norba* (nôr'bạ). In ancient geography, a city in Latium, Italy, on a spur of the Lepini Mountains, overlooking the Pontine Marshes, about 35 miles SE of Rome. Norba is noted for its well-preserved fortification walls of massive polygonal ("Cyclopean") masonry in local limestone, with an imposing main gate and sally ports, which were formerly held to be of very early date, the 6th or 7th century B.C., but are now assigned to the late 4th or early 3rd century B.C. Within the outer circuit are many retaining walls and foundations in polygonal limestone, including the substructures of at least two temples. Norba was destroyed by Sulla during the civil wars; on the next eminence to the E lies its successor, the medieval town of Norma. (JJ)

*Norcia* (nôr'chä). See *Nursia.*

*Noricum* (nor'i-kum). In ancient geography, a country in Europe, bounded by Germany (separated by the Danube) on the N, Pannonia on the E, Pannonia and the land of the Carni on the S, and Vindelicia and Rhaetia (separated partly by the Inn) on the W. It corresponded mainly to the later Lower and Upper Austria S of the Danube, Salzburg, Styria, Carinthia, and parts of Tirol and Bavaria. It was conquered by the Romans c15 B.C., and made a Roman province.

*Notium* (nō'shi-um). In ancient geography, the port of Colophon, near Ephesus. Near it the Spartan fleet under Lysander defeated (407 B.C.) the Athenians.

*Nuceria Alfaterna* (nū-sir'i-ạ al-fạ-tẽr'nạ). [Modern name, *Nocera Inferiore.*] In ancient geography, a town in S Italy, situated about 20 miles SE of Neapolis. An ancient Oscan town, it was occupied by the Romans in 307 B.C., destroyed by Hannibal in 216 B.C., sacked by the revolting slaves under Spartacus in 73 B.C., and recolonized by Augustus and Nero.

*Numantia* (nū-man'shạ). In ancient geography, the capital of a Celtiberian people, the Arevaci, situated on the Durius (Douro) River near what is now Soria, Spain. It was famous on account of its siege by the Romans under Scipio Aemilianus, beginning in 134 B.C. It was taken and destroyed in 133 B.C.

*Numidia* (nū-mid'i-ạ). In ancient geography, a country of N Africa, corresponding nearly to the modern Algeria. It was bounded by the Mediterranean on the N, the territory of Carthage on the E, the desert on the S, and Mauretania on the W. The peoples in the E and W were united in a kingdom under Masinissa. This was dismembered after the defeat of Jugurtha in 106 B.C., and the E part became a Roman province shortly after the death of its king Juba in 46 B.C.

*Nursia* (nẽr'shạ). [Modern name, *Norcia.*] An ancient Sabine city, about 42 miles SE of Perusia (Perugia).

——O——

*Oaxes* (ō-ak'ses). A river of Crete. According to some accounts, the nymph Anchiale bore the Dactyls in a cave near this river.

*Oceanus* (ō-sē'ạ-nus). In the belief of ancient geographers, a swift and unbounded stream that encircled all the world, from which all earthly rivers were believed to rise. Oceanus was later taken to be the outer sea, which we know as the Atlantic Ocean.

*Oenoë* (ē-nō'ē). An island of the Cyclades in the Aegean Sea.

*Oenophyta* (ē-nof'i-tạ). In ancient geography, a place in Boeotia, Greece, about 23 miles N of Athens. Here the Athenians under Myronides defeated (456 B.C.) the Boeotians.

*Oenotria* (ē-nō'tri-ạ). In ancient geography, a name given by the Greeks to the S part of Italy, which was colonized by Oenotrians. The name was ultimately changed to Italy.

*Oeta* (ē-tạ), *Mount.* A mountain in S Thessaly. Here Heracles built his own funeral pyre when he was suffering from the agonies caused by the poisoned garment sent to him by his wife. Since he was too strong to die, he cast himself on a pyre of his own building and prevailed on Philoctetes to set it alight. A cloud descended on the pyre and when it had lifted, all trace of Heracles had vanished. Nearby is the pass of Thermopylae, into the stream of which Heracles had flung himself to get relief from his burning pain. Its waters brought no relief to Heracles. On the contrary, he caused the waters to bubble and steam, hence the name, which means "burning" or "hot passage."

*Oetylus* (ē'ti-lus). An ancient town in Laconia, on the Taenarum promontory.

*Ogygia* (ọ-jij'i-ạ). In classical geography, the island of Calypso, referred to in the *Odyssey.* Plutarch says it lies due west, beneath the setting sun.

*Olbia* (ol'bi-ạ). In ancient geography, a city in Scythia, a Greek colony from Miletus, near the confluence of the Borysthenes (the modern Dnieper) River and the Hypanis (modern Bug).

*Olbia.* An ancient settlement on the northeast coast of the island of Sardinia. It had the best harbor on the coast and its traditional founding is attributed to an expedition from Thespiae and Attica led by Iolaus. (AH)

*Olenus* (ō'lẹ-nus). In ancient geography, a town on the coast of Achaea. It was one of the 12 towns occupied by the Achaeans after the Ionians had left the region. Olenus did not grow in size and was finally abandoned by its inhabitants because it was so small as to be defenseless.

*Oliarus* (ō-li-ār'us) or *Olearus* (ō-lẹ-ār'us). [Modern name, *Antiparos.*] Island in the Cyclades, SW of Paros, celebrated for a stalactite grotto. Length, about eight miles.

*Olonos* (ọ-lō'nos). See *Erymanthus.*

*Olympia* (ọ-lim'pi-ạ). In ancient geography, the site of a celebrated sanctuary of Zeus and of the Olympic Games, the most important of the great public games of classical antiquity. Situated in Elis in the valley of the Alpheus River at its confluence with the Cladeus River, its location and importance caused it to be spared the incessant warfare that harassed most of the rest of Greece. The area was originally a part of Pisatis, whose capital was Pisa, but came, after many engagements between Eleans, Pisans, Spartans, and Argives, under the control of Elis early in the 6th century B.C. Through centuries of warfare and change in Greece, Olympia remained a relatively peaceful spot, remote from political upheavals and protected by its geographical location. It was primarily a religious center, where the athletic contests in honor of the gods gradually took on more importance than the religious ceremonies that brought them into being. The site is a peaceful valley, cooled by numerous pine trees, once washed by two rivers, and protected at the north by the low wooded Hill of Cronus. The origins of the sanctuary and of the games are anterior to history; according to tradition the games were reorganized, in obedience to the Delphic oracle, in the 9th century B.C. The list of Olympic victors goes back to 776 B.C., which is the first of the four years of the first Olympiad, but the Olympiad system of chronology did not come into accepted use until much later. South of the Hill of Cronus at Olympia was the Altis, a sacred enclosure that was the religious center. It was surrounded by a low wall, the location of which was changed from time to time through the centuries to enlarge the enclosure. Inside the Altis was the 6th century B.C. Doric temple of Zeus, built from the spoils that were taken from the Pisans by the Eleans. Libo, the architect who designed the temple shortly after the Elean victory, did not live to see its completion, which was not accomplished until the middle of the 5th century B.C. The greatest treasure of the temple, which was richly decorated within and without, was the statue of *Olympian Zeus* by Phidias. In front of the temple, facing the east, were many statues given as votive offerings at various times. Among them was the *Nike* of Paeonius, given by the Messenians to celebrate a victory over the Spartans. Inside the north wall of the Altis was the ancient temple of Hera, in the cella of which stood the famous *Hermes and the Infant Dionysus,* by Praxiteles. Between the temples of Zeus and Hera, on a slight rise, was a sanctuary of Pelops, enclosed by a pentagonal stone wall. Black rams were here sacrificed to Pelops, who was honored at Olympia only slightly less than Zeus, and in memory of whom, some say, the first games were instituted. East of the temple of Hera stood the *Metroum,* a temple dedicated to the Mother of the

fat, fāte, fär, fåll, àsk, fāre; net, mē, hėr; pin, pīne; not, nōte, mŏve, nôr; up, lūte, pùll; oi, oil; ou out; (lightened) ęlect, agǫny, ūnite;

Gods, and south of the Metroum, roughly in the middle of the Altis, was a very ancient altar of Zeus made of ashes of victims mixed with the waters of the Alpheus River. In addition, there was a profusion of statues of gods, heroes, and victors scattered within the Altis, as well as numerous other buildings that were erected in later times. Outside the Altis, to the west, was the *Bouleterium,* dating from the 6th and 5th centuries B.C. Here sat the Upper Council, or Boule, that managed affairs at Olympia. Also to the west were a gymnasium and palestra where the athletes trained for the contests. At the northwest corner of the Altis stood the *Prytaneum,* the chief administrative building at Olympia, where the priests and other officials took their meals and where visitors of importance and victors were entertained. In half the building was the sacred hearth of Hestia, on which a fire was kept burning at all times. To the east of the Altis was the stadium, capable of seating 20,000 spectators, where the foot races were held. German archaeologists have uncovered the marble starting line, marked off in equal spaces for the contestants, and the finish line, 192.27 meters away. South of the stadium was the hippodrome, where the chariot races were run. In addition, the site at Olympia was occupied by a number of *thermae,* chiefly of Roman date, the treasuries of various Greek cities and states, numberless statues and works of art, and steles with commenorative inscriptions. The Olympic Games were formally abolished (394 A.D.) by the emperor Theodosius as a relic of paganism. The monuments were much shattered by earthquakes in the 6th century, and as time went on were progressively buried by landslides from Cronus and inundations of the Cladeus (now dry), and the Alpheus, in one of which the hippodrome was entirely washed away. Sand and earth were deposited to a depth of from ten to 20 feet over the ruins. Nor was man free from responsibility in the destruction of the monuments. The heads of many statues were lopped off to destroy the pagan idols, and much material from the temples and other buildings was carried away for use in humbler structures. The French *Expédition de Morée* made (1829) some superficial excavations, and recovered some sculptures (now in the Louvre) from the temple of Zeus. In six seasons of work after 1874, the German government laid bare down to the ancient level the greater part of what survives of the

sanctuary. The sculptural finds include the *Hermes* of Praxiteles and the *Nike* of Paeonius, which are now in the Museum at Olympia, along with large fragments from the
pediments of the temple of Zeus as well as fragments of
metopes from the same temple. In the departments of architecture and epigraphy the German excavations, resumed
after World War II, rank as the most important that have
been made. The antiquities discovered are preserved on the
site. Olympia as a religious and athletic center did not seek
to exercise influence on political affairs, and it was perhaps
for this reason that it was respected as a peaceful island in
the midst of the constantly warring Greek city-states, that
armed soldiers were not permitted to pass through its territory, and that guarantees of safe conduct through hostile
areas could be given to contestants and spectators going to
the games. For centuries, the festival at Olympia gave one
point of unity to the Greeks perpetually at odds with each
other. In its Golden Age, Olympia developed a high stand-
ard of personal excellence in the games, and served as a
widely-attended showplace for the presentation of Greek
ideas and for the exhibition of some of the finest achievements in Greek art, poetry, literature, and philosophy.

*Olympus* (ọ-lim'pus). In ancient geography, the name of various mountains, but especially of one (elevation, about 9794
feet) on the borders of Macedonia and Thessaly, regarded
as the especial home of the chief gods of Greek mythology.
Hence the word is often used to mean heaven. The Mysian
Olympus was on the borders of Mysia, Bithynia, and Phrygia
in Asia Minor. Others were in Lydia, Lycia, Cyprus, Laconia,
and Elis. There are believed to have been 14 in all.

*Olynthus* (ọ-lin'thus). In ancient geography, a city in Chalcidice, Macedonia, situated near the head of the Toronaic
Gulf near the neck of the Pallene peninsula. It was a city of
the Bottiaeans, a Thracian tribe, until 479 B.C. At that time
Artabazus, the Persian general who had escorted the defeated Persian king to the Hellespont, returned to Chalcidice and, suspicious that Olynthus was about to revolt
against Xerxes, captured the city and sacked it. The inhabitants were led to a nearby marsh and slaughtered. Artabazus
then handed the city over to the Chalcidians, who had been
loyal to Persia, and from this time Olynthus became a Greek
city. The city revived under the Macedonian king, Perdiccas.

fat, fāte, fär, fâll, àsk, fãre; net, mē, hèr; pin, pīne; not, nōte, mŏve,
nôr; up, lūte, pùll; oi, oil; ou out; (lightened) ẹlect, agọny, ụnite;

He instigated a revolt of the cities of Chalcidice against Athens and persuaded the inhabitants of the neighboring cities to unite within the walls of Olynthus against Athens (c433 B.C.). Perdiccas later appealed to Sparta for aid against Athens, and Olynthus became the base for the operations of the Spartan general Brasidas in the area. With his successes Perdiccas turned against Sparta and renewed his alliance with Athens. Olynthus became independent and the center of a powerful Chalcidian League. The league, at first an association of equals, soon came to be dominated by Olynthus, which sought to compel neighboring cities to join. They appealed to Sparta and a force was sent against the city, 382 B.C., and Olynthus was compelled to surrender, 379 B.C., but only after having inflicted heavy losses on the Spartans. The city soon recovered its power and its place as the head of a confederacy even more powerful than the earlier one. It was allied with Philip II of Macedon, who had sought its favor by giving it the city of Potidaea. However, as Philip's power grew, Olynthus became alarmed and abandoned her alliance with him. When he demanded the surrender of his half-brother, who had found refuge in the city, the Olynthians refused his demand and he marched against the city. Olynthus appealed to Athens for aid. In the Olynthiac Orations Demosthenes urged the Athenians to send aid to Olynthus. His main argument was that Philip must be crushed before he became so powerful as to threaten Athens, and that the place to crush him was Olynthus, far from the borders of Attica. Athens sent soldiers to the north, but had delayed their departure too long. The city was captured by Philip (348 B.C.) before the Athenians arrived. He so completely destroyed the city that a few years later it would have been hard to realize a city had ever existed on the spot. The inhabitants that were not slain were sold as slaves or scattered in neighboring cities.

**Onchestus** (on-kes′tus). In ancient geography, a city of Boeotia, Greece, near Thebes. It was named for a son of Poseidon, was sacred to that god, and contained a temple and image of Onchestian Poseidon.

**Opus** (ō′pus). In ancient geography, a town on the Gulf of Euboea. It was the capital of Opuntian Locris.

**Orchomenus** (ôr-kom′e̯-nus). In ancient geography, a city in Arcadia, Greece, about 33 miles W of Corinth. Arcadians from Orchomenus took part in the Battle of Plataea (479 B.C.) and had their names inscribed, with others, on the pedestal of an image of Zeus that was dedicated at Olympia.

*Orchomenus* (ôr-kom′ę-nus). In ancient geography, a city in Boeotia, Greece, situated on the Cephissus River, about 55 miles NW of Athens. It became a member of the Boeotian Confederacy at the beginning of the 7th century B.C. In the Persian War it was on the side of the Persians. Up to the time of the Peloponnesian Wars, Orchomenus was the equal of Thebes, but following that long struggle Thebes became a democracy, and the aristocracy that ruled Orchomenus took the side of Sparta and became an enemy of Thebes, fighting against that city at Coronea and Haliartus. When the Thebans defeated Sparta at Leuctra (371 B.C.) they would have destroyed Orchomenus, but Epaminondas persuaded them to spare it. However, in 364 B.C. they destroyed it without mercy. It was rebuilt in 353 B.C. by the Phocians, but was destroyed again by the Thebans in 349 B.C. Philip of Macedon rebuilt it anew, but the city never recovered its former power and wealth. In 87 B.C., Sulla defeated Archelaus, the general of Mithridates VI, king of Pontus, before the walls of Orchomenus. The site contains important remains of antiquity, going back to the Neolithic Age. Modern excavations have uncovered one city built atop another, as at Troy, the oldest of which dates from before 3500 B.C. Fragments of vases and frescoes, on which are depicted buildings and scenes of bull-leaping, and designs similar in style to those of Cnossus and Tiryns, have been recovered at the site. The so-called treasury of Minyas is a very ancient tomb of the Mycenaean beehive type. The plan is circular, 45 feet in diameter, covered by a pseudo-dome formed by corbeling in the stones of the wall.

*Oreus* (ō′rę-us). In ancient geography, a city on the NW coast of Euboea, Greece, situated opposite Thessaly. See *Histiaea.*

*Oropus* (ǫ-rō′pus). In ancient geography, a seaport in Attica, Greece, bordering on Boeotia, situated on the Euripus, about 23 miles N of Athens. It belonged originally to Boeotia, but in the struggles for it between Attica and Boeotia, the former won control of it. Near Oropus was a sanctuary of Amphiaraus, whose divinity was first established by the Oropians, who gave the cult to the rest of Greece. In the sanctuary was a temple and a white marble image of Amphiaraus, and the oracle of Amphiaraus, the Amphareum, was very famous. Sometimes the oracle gave responses in verse, but generally responses were given in dreams. The questioner at the oracle purified himself, sacrificed to Amphiaraus and to all those whose names were on the altar. He next sacrificed a ram, flayed it, and spread its skin on the ground. At night the questioner stretched out to sleep on the ram's skin and the answer to his question came to him in his dreams. Near the sanctuary was a spring into which those who had been cured of diseases as the result of responses from the oracle threw gold and silver coins.

*Ortygia* (ôr-tij′i-a̱). In ancient geography, a small island at the entrance to the great harbor of Syracuse, Sicily. It was famous in the sieges of that city. It is the site of the fountain of Arethusa, a sacred spring. Arethusa was transformed by Artemis into a spring as she fled from the river-god Alpheus. The spring flowed under the sea from Greece and arose in Ortygia. Alpheus pursued her under the sea and the waters of the Alpheus of Elis at last mingled with those of Arethusa in Ortygia. It was said that a flower thrown into the Alpheus River in Greece would float under the sea and rise in Arethusa's spring in Ortygia.

*Ortygia.* An ancient name of Delos. It means "Quail," and was so named because Asteria, daughter of Coeus the Titan, leaped into the sea to escape the embraces of Zeus and was transformed into a quail. The island where she came safely ashore was named for her.

*Orvieto* (ôr-vye′tō). See *Urbibentum.*

*Osroene* or *Osrhoene* (oz-rō-ē′nē). [Also: *Orrhoene.*] In ancient geography, a region in the NW part of Mesopotamia. Its chief city was Edessa (modern Urfa).

*Ossa* (os′a̱). Mountain in the E part of Thessaly, Greece, situated NW of Pelion and separated from Olympus on the N by the Vale of Tempe. According to myth, Pelion was piled atop Ossa by the giants when they stormed Olympus. Elevation, about 6400 feet.

*Ostia* (os′ti-a̱). In ancient geography, a city in Latium, Italy, situated on alluvial soil on the left bank of the river Tiber near its ancient mouth, about 15 miles SW of Rome. According to Roman tradition it was the oldest colony of Rome, founded by Ancus Marcius, fourth king of Rome (640–616 B.C.), but extensive excavations have revealed nothing ear-

(obscured) errạnt, ardẹnt, actọr; ch, chip; g, go; th, thin; ᴛʜ, then; y, you;
(variable) ḏ as d or j, ṣ as s or sh, ṭ as t or ch, ẕ as z or zh.

lier than the 4th century B.C. To the period of about 340 B.C. is assigned the plan of the earliest Roman settlement, in the form of a Roman camp *(castrum)*, consisting of a rectangular fortification bisected by a north-south street, the *cardo*, and by a west-east street, the *decumanus*. The walls, and the four gates where these streets enter the castrum, are of the ashlar tufa masonry which is so typical of Republican construction in and near Rome that it is of little use as a criterion of dating, the most that can be said of it being that it would not be out of place any time between 500 and 50 B.C. Parallel to the walls, both inside and outside the castrum, are strips of land about 40 feet wide, reserved for military purposes and forbidden to private construction, clearly defined by streets, the external and internal pomerial streets, so called because they mark the defense zone known as the *pomerium*. Of the four areas corresponding to city blocks within the walls, part was taken up by temples and a forum or market, the rest being available for residential purposes; but the population quickly outgrew the fortified space and expanded outside the walls. During the Punic Wars, especially the Second Punic War, Ostia became a naval base of crucial importance to Rome. In the disturbances of the time of Sulla, during which Ostia was sacked by Marius, a new and greatly enlarged fortification wall was built in ashlar tufa masonry strikingly similar to that of the 4th century castrum, enclosing an area now calculated at c170 acres, in spite of which Ostia was sacked again in 68 B.C., this time by pirates, an act of unprecedented boldness which led to Pompey's *imperium* in 67 B.C.

Rome's increasing need for grain, other foodstuffs, and building materials imported from Spain, North Africa, Sicily, and Egypt, caused the rapid growth of Ostia as the commercial port of Rome. Ostia built a theater and behind it a vast colonnade where the corporations which organized the import and export trade and the barge services on the Tiber had their offices. Vulcan remained the chief god of Ostia, but the cosmopolitan and polyglot population introduced the oriental cults of Magna Mater, Isis, Mithras; and, soon after, if not before 200 A.D., Christ. To overcome continual silting by the Tiber, Claudius and later Trajan constructed artificial harbors, connected to the sea and to the Tiber by canals. In the 2nd century A.D. Ostia reached its

peak as one of the greatest cities of the Empire; the population then exceeding 200,000 and perhaps approached 300,-
000. The growing population caused crowding that was only
partly relieved by the development of great five-story *insulae*
(apartment houses), with central courts, interior staircases,
windows, and balconies, directly anticipating those of modern cities. Before 300 A.D., however, there is evidence of
depression; taxes and liturgies became increasingly oner-
ous, and the population began to decline.

On an island in the Tiber, the Isola Sacra, was the cemetery of the prosperous freedmen who made up the bulk of
the commercial class. It has been meticulously excavated,
like much of Ostia itself, by the distinguished Italian archaeologist Guido Calza. There is a small museum of sculpture,
and important collections of Latin and Greek inscriptions.
Outside the walls stands the small modern village of Ostia,
but the area within the walls is unoccupied and the shore has
advanced two miles from its ancient line. The Tiber has
eroded a small sector along the northern boundary of Ostia,
and for centuries Ostia was quarried by Roman princes for
building materials and objets d'art, but it remains one of the
most impressive archaeological sites of ancient Italy. (JJ)

**Othrys** (oth'ris). Mountain range in the S part of Thessaly,
Greece, due S of Ossa and SW of Pelion. Peak elevation,
about 5665 feet.

**Otranto** (ô'trän-tō). See *Hydrus.*

# ——P——

**Pachynus** (pạ-kī'nus). Rock-strewn cape at the southeastern
extremity of Sicily, now called Cape Passero.

**Pactolus** (pak-tō'lus). In ancient geography, a small river of
Lydia, Asia Minor, a tributary of the Hermus. It was long
celebrated for its gold, but its sands had ceased to produce
by the time of Augustus. In Greek legend, it was the river
in which Dionysus told Midas to bathe in order to free himself of the gift, which had become a curse, of having everything he touched turn to gold. This was the reason why the

sands of the river afterwards bore grains of gold.

**Padua** (pa'dū-ạ). English form of Italian Padova, Latin Patavium (q.v.).

**Padus** (pā'dus). A Latin name of the Po; equated with the mythical Eridanus River by Greek and Roman writers.

**Paeonia** (pē-ō'ni-ạ. In ancient geography, the land between the Strymon and Axius (modern Vardar) rivers, lying on the north border of Macedonia and the western border of Thrace. The Paeonians claimed descent from colonists from Troy, and fought as allies of the Trojans in the Trojan War. According to Herodotus, they practised polygamy, and, among other deities, they worshiped Dionysus and Artemis. Also according to Herodotus, several tribal chieftains struggled for control of Paeonia. Two brothers sought the aid of the Persian king, Darius, to win power. In a typically devious manner, they dressed their sister, a tall and beautiful woman, in rich clothing and sent her to draw water for them by a way which passed the spot near Sardis where Darius was sitting in state. On her head she bore a pitcher, with one arm she led a horse, and all the while as she walked she spun flax. Darius was struck by her beauty and her industry. He sent men to follow her and observe what she did. When she came to the river she watered the horse, filled the pitcher and set it on her head, and returned by the way she had come, spinning all the while. Darius commanded that she be brought to him. She arrived with her brothers. Darius asked of what nation the woman was. Her brothers said she was their sister and that they were all Paeonians. Darius had never heard of Paeonia. He asked where it was and what had brought them to Sardis. They told him Paeonia was a land not far beyond the Hellespont, and that they had come to put themselves under his protection. They added, in answer to his questions, that all the women of Paeonia were as beautiful and industrious as their sister. Thereupon Darius resolved to have the hard-working Paeonians moved from Europe into Asia, and sent word to his general Megabazus in Thrace to bring the Paeonians to him. Megabazus did, in face, make war on Paeonia, and conquered the lower part of it. He could not conquer the Paeonion tribes on Mount Pangaeus or the Paeonion lake-dwellers. Herodotus says the lake-dwellers had their houses built on platforms resting on piles in the middle of the lake. The platforms were con-

nected to the land by a single narrow bridge. The independent Paeonians in later times raided Macedonia and united
with the Illyrians to harass Macedonia until they were finally
subdued (358 B.C.) by Philip II of Macedon. Paeonia became
a district of Macedonia after the Roman conquest.

*Paestum* (pes'tum). City in Lucania, in southern Italy, situated
near the sea. Founded as Posidonia, a colony of Sybaris,
c600 B.C., it quickly achieved prosperity, as its great Doric
temples indicate. These temples include: a temple of Hera,
c530 B.C., known in later times as the Basilica; a temple of
Athena, c510 B.C., known later as a temple of Ceres; a temple dedicated to Hera, c450 B.C., but later called the temple
of Poseidon. Each of these temples preserves its peristyles,
or outer colonnades, intact, and the temple of Poseidon
(Hera) further preserves its interior supports, small Doric
columns in two stories. Excavations of two more temples of
Hera at the mouth of the river Silarus (Sele), five miles to
the north, have produced delightful sculptured metopes in
the archaic style that are now displayed in the Paestum museum. Together, these temples form an outstanding gallery
of Doric architecture, surpassed in impressiveness and
wealth of information only by the Periclean buildings of
Athens. Yet no ancient writer ever happened to mention
them. Beginning about 400 B.C. native Italian tribes, the
Lucani, attacked Posidonia and soon gained control of the
city, whose inhabitants they are said to have oppressed. The
greater part of the city fortifications, two and a half miles in
circuit and still preserved throughout their entire length,
appears to be of Greek construction, with extensive repairs
attributed to the Lucanians. Four main gates survive, as well
as a number of posterns and sally ports, some blocked up,
and many towers. Of these towers, those later adapted for
use as farm buildings have survived almost intact. From this
period date also a number of painted Lucanian tombs. After
the collapse (275 B.C.) of Pyrrhus' invasion of Italy, Posidonia fell under the domination of the Romans, who established there (273 B.C.) a Latin colony under the name of
Paestum, the name by which it is now usually known (Italian,
Pesto). To the period of Roman domination belong new
temples, an amphitheater, houses, and paved streets. Under
the Empire, however, malaria increased and the population
declined. To this circumstance we must credit the partial

survival of the three great temples and the superb fortifications, which a more vigorous population would surely have
dismantled to obtain their stones for building material. The
temple of Athena (known as the temple of Ceres) became a
church, and still contains traces of Christian tombs, but after
a destructive Saracen raid in the 9th century the site was
deserted. Paestum's temples remained unknown to western
scholarship until 1745, when the Italian traveler Antonini
described them. Recent excavations by Claudio Pellegrino
Sestieri have revealed streets, Roman houses, fresh data on
the history of the fortifications, painted tombs, and an extraordinary underground ritual chamber containing a bed
and jars of offerings. (JJ)

*Pagae* (pa'jē). In ancient geography, a seaport on the Gulf of
Corinth, surrounded by the hills of the Megaris. In the Persian War a force from the army of Mardonius was lost in the
hills nearby at night. In fear of hostile forces, they fired off
a volley of arrows. The arrows struck a rock at Pagae which,
according to tradition, Artemis caused to groan. The Persians, thinking they were hitting their enemies, shot off all
their arrows, and when day broke they were easily overcome, having exhausted their ammunition, and were slain
by the Greeks. The rock at Pagae, bristling with the Persian
arrows, was shown for centuries as one of the sights of the
region. In gratitude for her help, the inhabitants of Pagae
raised a bronze image of Artemis Savior at Pagae.

*Pagasae* (pag'ạ-sē). A principal seaport in Thessaly, in NE
Greece. Many ancient ruins of the city remain. Near it is the
modern city of Volos.

*Palatine* (pal'ạ-tīn) *Hill.* See *Palatium.*

*Palatium* (pạ-lā'shi-um). [Also: *Mons Palatinus.*] One of the
seven hills of Rome, SE of the Capitoline and dominating
the Forum from the S; traditionally, the hill at whose foot
Romulus and Remus were washed ashore, where Romulus
took the auspices, where he plowed the magic furrow that
marked the *pomerium,* and the site of the first settlement at
Rome. Archaeological confirmation for this is lacking, and
the suggestion that the Palatium had still earlier been a
pasture is commended by no more than a dubious
etymology—*pascere,* "drive to pasture." Much built over in
later times, the Palatium preserves of primitive structures a
few courses of fortification walls in tufa and little else. Since

householders on the hill could reach the Forum in a few moments, it became the fashionable residence of the wealthy and the politically ambitious, and we hear of many prominent citizens of the late Republic who had houses there: M. Fulvius Flaccus, Q. Lutatius Catulus, M. Livius Drusus whose house was bought by Crassus and then by Cicero, Cicero's brother Quintus Cicero, Q. Hortensius, M. Aemilius Scaurus, Mark Antony, and many others. When Octavian established the principate he acquired the house of Hortensius and added to it to form a suitable imperial residence; later emperors extended these quarters until they occupied almost the whole of the Palatium. Romans who had business at the offices of the emperor spoke of going *ad Palatium* (to the Palatium); from this came the secondary meaning of palatium as the residence of any head of state or church, English "palace." The Palatium also had temples of Jupiter, Victoria, Magna Mater (Cybele), Apollo, and other divinities, and relics of Romulus, whose locations are still in controversy. (JJ)

*Palermo* (pä-ler′mō). See *Panormus.*

*Palestrina* (pal-ęs-trē′nạ; Italian, pä-läs-trē′nä). See *Praeneste.*

*Palinurus* (pal-i-nur′us) or *Palinurum* (-um). [Modern names, **Cape Palinuro, Cape Spartimento.**] Promontory on the W coast of Italy, situated in Lucania. It was the scene of shipwrecks of Roman fleets in 253 and in 36 B.C., and of the legendary burying of Palinurus.

*Pallanteum* (pạ-lan-tē′um). A town in Italy, founded by Arcadians from Greece, descendants of Pallas. According to legend, Evander, to whom Aeneas came when he reached Latium after his flight from Troy, was king in the town. The site of the town was later known as the Palatine Hill in Rome.

*Pallantium* (pạ-lan′shi-um). In ancient geography, a city in Arcadia, founded by Pallas, a son of Lycaon. According to legend, from here Evander, son of Hermes and a nymph, daughter of the river-god Ladon, was sent out to found a colony. He went to Italy, and there on the banks of the Tiber River founded a town, Pallanteum, which he named for his native town in Arcadia.

*Pallene* (pạ-lē′nē). See *Cassandra.*

*Pamisus* (pạ-mī′sus). Chief river of Messenia, Greece. Its waters made the Messenian fields fertile, and in honor of it the

(obscured) erra̧nt, ardȩnt, acto̧r; ch, chip; g, go; th, thin; ᵺH, then; y, you; (variable) ḏ as d or j, ṣ as s or sh, ṭ as t or ch, ẓ as z or zh.

kings of ancient Messenia made annual sacrifices to it. It flows into the Gulf of Messenia.

*Pamphylia* (pam-fil'i-ạ). In ancient geography, a mountainous region in Asia Minor, bounded by Pisidia on the N, Cilicia on the E, the Mediterranean Sea on the S, and Lycia on the W. It was successively under the rule of Lydia, Persia, Macedon, Syria, Pergamum, and Rome.

*Pamphylian Gulf* (pam-fil'i-ạn). [Also: *Pamphylian Sea.*] Ancient name of *Antalya, Gulf of.*

*Pamphylicus Sinus* (pam-fil'i-kus sī'nus). Latin name of *Antalya, Gulf of.*

*Pandataria* (pan-dạ-tär'i-ạ). [Modern name, *Ventotene.*] In ancient geography, an island in the Tyrrhenian Sea, W of Naples. It was the place of banishment of Julia, the licentious daughter of Augustus; Agrippina, Julia's daughter and wife of Germanicus; and Octavia, daughter of Claudius and Messalina.

*Pandosia* (pan-dō'shạ). In ancient geography, a town in Bruttii, Italy, situated on the Acheron River, near what is now Cosenza. Here Alexander I, king of Epirus, was defeated and slain (326 B.C.) by the Bruttians.

*Paneas* (pan'ē-ạs). [Roman name, *Caesarea Philippi;* modern name, *Baniyas.*] Village in SW Syria, at the foot of Mount Hermon, about 40 miles SW of Damascus: said to have been named by the Greeks for the god Pan.

*Pangaeus* (pan-jē'us) or *Pangaeum* (-um), *Mount.* A mountain in Thrace, near the mouth of the Strymon River on the shore of the Aegean Sea. The mountain was rich in gold and silver. Philip II of Macedon in 358–357 B.C. seized it and from its mines secured the funds to build his military organization.

*Pannonia* (pạ-nō'ni-ạ). In ancient geography, a Roman province, bounded by the Ister (Danube) on the N and E, Moesia and Illyricum on the S, and Noricum on the W. It was made a Roman province by Tiberius (c9 A.D.), and divided by Trajan into Upper Pannonia in the W and Lower Pannonia in the E (c106 A.D.).

*Panopeus* (pan'ō-pūs). In ancient geography, a city of Phocis. Among the wonders of Panopeus described by Pausanias, who visited it when the city was in ruins, were two very large, clay-colored stones that gave off an odor like the smell from the skin of a man. The people of Panopeus claimed these stones were all that remained of the clay from which Prome-

fat, fāte, fär, fåll, ȧsk, fãre; net, mē, hèr; pin, pīne; not, nōte, möve, nôr; up, lūte, pull; oi, oil; ou out; (lightened) ẹlect, agǫny, ụnite;

theus fashioned the human race. Panopeus was destroyed by
the Persians (480 B.C.), rebuilt, destroyed by Philip of Macedon following the Sacred War (346 B.C.), and never recovered from the destruction of Sulla (86 B.C.).

*Panormus* (pạ-nôr'mus). In ancient geography, a city on the N
coast of Sicily, lying at the foot of a mountain. Harbors on
both sides of the ancient city accounted for its name, which
means "All-haven." The city was founded in very ancient
times by the Phoenicians, came under the power of Carthage, and was one of the most important Punic centers in
Sicily. It remained a Punic city until 254 B.C., when it was
taken by the Romans. The modern city on the site is
Palermo, noted for its mild climate and the beauty of its
location.

*Pantelleria* (pän"tel-le-rē'ä). [Also: *Pantalaria, Pantellaria*.] Island in the Mediterranean Sea, off the W tip of Sicily. It was
highly favored as a place to which members of the imperial
family and other prominent persons were banished in the
time of the Roman empire. See *Cossura*.

*Paphlagonia* (paf-lạ-gō'ni-ạ). In ancient geography, a country
in Asia Minor, bounded by the Euxine Sea on the N, Pontus
(separated by the Halys) on the E, Galatia on the S, and
Bithynia on the W. According to Homer, the inhabitants
were specially noted as breeders of mules. The country was
semi-independent under Persian and Macedonian rule. It
passed later to Pontus, and to Rome in 65 B.C.

*Paphos* (pā'fos). In ancient geography, the name of two cities
in Cyprus. Old Paphos was situated near the SW coast.
According to legend, it was founded by Cinyras, the grandson of Pygmalion, and it was he who built the celebrated
temple of Astarte, or Aphrodite, of unburned brick and
wood on a stone foundation measuring 164 by 220 feet. The
famous image of the goddess was a *baetylus* (a conical mete-
oric stone). The temple stood in a large enclosure whose
walls were likewise of sun-dried brick on a massive stone
foundation. Cinyras named the city for his father Paphos,
who was the son of Pygmalion and Galatea. The city was
sacred to Aphrodite and was one of her favorite haunts. New
Paphos was situated on the W coast eight or ten miles NW
of Old Paphos. It was a commercial center. Aphrodite is said
to have risen from the sea near Paphos.

*Parma* (pär'mạ). [Latin: *Parma, Colonia Julia Augusta*.] City in

N Italy, situated between Bononia (Bologna) and Placentia (Piacenza). It became a Roman military colony in 183 B.C. and was of great strategic importance because of its location on the Via Aemilia. It was destroyed by Mark Antony in the civil wars, and was rebuilt by Augustus under the name of Colonia Julia Augusta.

**Parnassus** (pär-nas'us). [Also: *Liakoura*.] Mountain ridge in Greece, about 83 miles NW of Athens, and situated mainly in ancient Phocis. The mountain was sacred to Apollo, the Muses, Dionysus, and the nymphs, and hence was regarded as the seat of music and poetry. On its slopes was located the most famous of all Greek oracles, that of Apollo at Delphi. The mountain was a favorite place for the orgies that were celebrated in honor of Dionysus. On its slopes was the Corycian cave, sacred to Pan. In the Persian Wars, the Delphians took refuge in the mountain peak when Xerxes sent an army against Delphi, but the mountain itself, according to Herodotus, protected the sacred oracle: two enormous crags broke off from it, rolled down, and crushed the Persian forces (480 B.C.). Guerrilla bands hid out in the mountain and used it as a base from which to make damaging raids on the armies of Mardonius before the battle of Plataea (479 B.C.). Highest summit, Lycoria (8068 feet).

**Paros** (pär'os). Second largest island of the Cyclades; in the Aegean Sea W of Naxos. It is composed of a single mountain, famous in ancient times for its white marble. According to tradition, the island was first colonized by Arcadians. These were later joined by Ionians from Athens. Colonists from Paros, including the poet Archilochus, went to the island of Thasus early in the 7th century B.C. Because Paros had been an ally of the Persians at Marathon (490 B.C.), the victorious Athenian general Miltiades attacked it after the defeat of the Persians, but was unable to take the island. In 480 B.C. Paros again sided with the Persians. After the expulsion of the Persians from Greece (479 B.C.) Paros was forced by the Athenians to pay a heavy fine, to join the Confederacy of Delos, and to pay the highest tribute to the Confederacy treasury of any of the islands. Remains of many ancient structures have been found on the island, among them sanctuaries of Asclepius, Aphrodite, and of Delian Apollo, and a grotto of Ilithyia. Parian marble was exported from the 6th century B.C., and was used by the most famous of the Greek sculptors. Some of the tunnels in the mountain by which the marble was quarried can still be seen. One of the most interesting finds made on the island was that of the Parian Chronicle, a marble tablet, found 1627, on which were engraved a number of dates relating to Greek history, especially literary and religious history, from the time of Cecrops, king of Athens, to the time of the Athenian archon Diognetus, 264 B.C. Area of the island, about 81 square miles; length, about 15 miles.

*Parthenia* (par-then′i-a). Another name for the island of Samos.

*Parthenius* (pär-then′i-us). A river of Paphlagonia; a gentle river, where Artemis bathed to refresh herself after hunting.

*Parthenius, Mount.* In ancient geography, a mountain in Arcadia. Near the sanctuary of Pan on Mount Parthenius, Phidippides, the Athenian runner, met the god when he was on his way to Sparta to seek aid for Athens just before the battle of Marathon (490 B.C.), and Pan assured him of his interest in the Athenians. The mountain was noted for its many tortoises, the shells of which would make good lyres, but the people of the mountain would not permit the tortoises to be taken because they were considered sacred to Pan.

*Parthia* (pär′thi-a). In ancient geography, a country in W Asia, situated E of Media and S of Hyrcania. It was the nucleus of the Parthian Empire.

*Patara* (pat′a-ra). In ancient geography, a city in Lycia, Asia Minor, situated on the coast. There are remains of a theater dating from the time of Hadrian.

*Patavium* (pa-tā′vi-um). [Modern name, *Padova;* English, *Padua.*] City in NE Italy, situated on the Meduacus Minor River, about 20 miles W of Venetia (Venice). According to legend, it was founded by Antenor, who came to this place when he was spared by the Greeks in the sack of Troy. It became a capital of the Veneti, and by 174 B.C. it was subject to Rome. It was the birthplace of the Roman historian Titus Livius (Livy), 59 B.C.–17 A.D., whose literary style the rival historian Asinius Pollio ridiculed as *Patavinitas* (Patavinity), and of Asconius Pedianus. (JJ)

*Paternò* (pä-ter-nô′). Town on the island of Sicily, situated on the S slope of Mount Aetna. Nearby is the site of the ancient Hybla or Hybla Major.

*Patmos* (pat′mos; Greek pät′môs). [Also: *Patino;* Italian,

**Patmo.**] Island of the Dodecanese, situated in the Aegean Sea, about 20 miles SW of Samos. It was colonized first by Dorians, who were later joined by Ionian colonists. In the Roman period the barren volcanic island was frequently used as a place of banishment for political exiles. There is a monastery bearing the name of Saint John the Divine, and a cave pointed out where, according to legend, the apostle saw the visions of the Apocalypse. Area of the island, about 22 square miles.

**Patrae** (pā'trē). [Modern name, **Patras.**] A city on the N coast of Achaea in the Peloponnesus, at the western end of the Gulf of Corinth. In the Peloponnesian War Patrae supported Athens. After occupation by Rome Augustus established a Roman colony at Patrae, which had been abandoned for some time. The city was, and still is, an important port for travelers from Italy.

**Patrai** (pä'trē) or **Patras** (pa̤-tras', pat'ra̤s). See **Patrae.**

**Patroclus** (pa̤-trō'klus). Uninhabited island off the Cape of Sunium. It was named for Patroclus, an admiral in command of an Egyptian fleet that came to help the Athenians c267–263 B.C. There was an ancient fortification on the island.

**Paxos** (pak'so̤s, päk-sôs'). [Also: **Paxoi.**] Small island of the Ionian Islands, about eight miles SE of Corfu. It is noted for the production of olive oil. According to a famous story found in Plutarch and mentioned by Rabelais and Milton among others, it was from Paxos that mariners heard the great voice announcing "Pan is dead."

**Peiraeus** (pē-rē'us) or **Peiraieus.** [Greek, **Peiraievs.**] See **Piraeus.**

**Pelasgia** (pe̤-laz'ji-a̤). Ancient name of Arcadia, said to have been called this after Pelasgus, the first king of the area.

**Pelasgiotis** (pe̤-laz-ji-ō'tis). In ancient geography, a division of C Thessaly, Greece.

**Pelion** (pē'li-o̤n). Mountain in Thessaly, N Greece, near the coast, SE of Ossa. It was the legendary home of the centaurs, and known especially as the dwelling place of Chiron, the wise centaur who was tutor to Achilles. It was near his cave on Mount Pelion, that Peleus and the sea-nymph Thetis were married. The two mythical giants known as the Aloidae piled Mount Ossa on Olympus and then Pelion on Ossa in their attempt to reach heaven.

**Pella** (pel'a̤). In ancient geography, the capital of Macedonia

fat, fāte, fär, fâll, a̤sk, fāre; net, mē, hėr; pin, pīne; not, nōte, möve; nôr; up, lūte, pu̇ll; oi, oil; ou out; (lightened) e̤lect, agǫny, ūnite;

(c400–167 B.C.). It was the birthplace of Alexander the Great.

*Pellegrino* (pel-lā-grē′nō), *Monte.* See *Ercta.*

*Pellene* (pẹ-lē′nẹ). In ancient geography, a town in E Achaea, on the borders of Sicyon. The town was one of the 12 towns occupied by the Achaeans after the Ionians left the region. Pellene was on the lower slopes of a hill, and boasted an ivory-and-gold image of Athena in the temple that was said to have been made by Phidias before he made the famous statue of Athena in the Parthenon. The Pellenians claimed that a deep shrine beneath the pedestal of this statue was filled with damp air, and this dampness preserved the ivory of the image. Behind the temple was a grove of Artemis Savior, and nearby was a sanctuary of Dionysus Lampteros (*Torch-bearer*). The Pellenians held a festival in his honor, during which they took blazing brands to the sanctuary at night, and set bowls of wine throughout the city. The Pellenians also held games in honor of Apollo Theoxenius (*God of Strangers*), whose shrine was in their city. In addition, there were sanctuaries of Artemis and Ilithyia. Pellene fell under the dominion of Alexander the Great, who appointed one of their own sons despot over them. Thereafter the Pellenians would not even mention his name, though he had won two prizes at the Isthmian games and four at the Olympian, because he had permitted the conqueror to set him up as a tyrant over his own countrymen.

*Peloponnesus* (pel″ọ-pọ-nē′sus). [Also: *Morea, Peloponnesos, Peloponnese.*] Leaf-shaped peninsula forming the S part of continental Greece. It is practically an island, attached to the mainland only by the narrow rocky Isthmus of Corinth, and separated from it by the Gulf of Corinth and the Saronic Gulf on the north. To the east is the Aegean Sea; to the west the Ionian Sea. It has an area of 8356 square miles, and measures about 160 miles in its greatest length. Sharp high mountains divide the parts of the peninsula one from the other and in ancient times communication was easier by sea than by land. The chief rivers are the Eurotas (or Iri) and the Alpheus. According to legend, when Pelops, son of Tantalus, was driven out of his land in Paphlagonia by barbarians he settled on Mount Sipylus in Lydia. But the Trojan king would not permit him to remain, and he came to the country of Oenomaus, ruler of Pisa and Elis in the Peloponnesus. He won Hippodamia, daughter of Oenomaus, in a chariot race and succeeded to Oenomaus' throne. His kingdom became rich and powerful, and he subjugated the surrounding country which he then renamed *Peloponnesus* (Pelops' island). In ancient times the principal divisions of the Peloponnesus were, in clockwise order, Argolis, Laconia, Messenia, Elis, and Achaea, all of which bordered on the sea. Arcadia, occupying the mountainous center of the peninsula, alone was without an exit to the sea. Of the ancient Pelasgian population of the peninsula, only that of Arcadia, which boasted of its pure race, remained relatively unmixed by successive invasions. The Achaeans and Aeolians moved into Argolis, Laconia, Messenia, and Elis. Danaus and Pelops represented invaders from Egypt and Asia Minor. The so-called Mycenaean civilization that developed in the Peloponnesus, centered about Mycenae, was equalled only by the earlier Minoan civilization of Crete. Under the rule of Agamemnon, grandson of Pelops, Mycenae dominated all of Argolis, most of the Peloponnesus and the islands, and extended its influence to continental Greece. Such was the influence of Agamemnon that when he sailed against Troy to recover Helen, princes from all over Greece rallied to his cause and joined his expedition. In succeeding generations, the Peloponnesus was invaded by the Epeans who came from Aetolia and of whom Augeas was a king, by the Caucones who spread out from Arcadia into Elis, and by Ionians, said to have come from Attica. About 1100 B.C. the Dorian invasion of the Peloponnesus took place. This invasion by people from the north is also called the "return" of the Heraclidae. The basis of the claim of the Heraclidae to the Peloponnesus was that their ancestor Heracles had conquered large parts of it and left it in trust for his descendants. All of the Peloponnesus except Arcadia, which made an agreement with the Heraclidae, fell under Dorian domination. By the 7th century B.C. the Peloponnesus was divided into the city-states of Corinth, Sicyon, Argos, Sparta, Elis, and the 12 Ionian cities of Achaea. Arcadia, divided into independent cities, retained its homogeneity as a race. In the 7th century B.C. Argos was the dominant power. By the next century its power had been eclipsed by that of Sparta. For the next 300 years affairs in the Peloponnesus revolved around the activities of Sparta. After the downfall of Sparta at Leuctra (371 B.C.) the cities and states of the Peloponnesus united in various leagues, against Sparta, against Macedonia, and against the Romans. The Peloponnesus was conquered by the Romans, 146 B.C., and became the Roman province of Achaea.

*Pelusium* (pẹ-lö′shi-um). In ancient geography, a city at the NE extremity of the Nile delta, Egypt, SE of modern Port Said, at what was called the Pelusiac mouth of the Nile. It was a frontier fortress of Egypt toward Syria. Herodotus tells of an Egyptian king, Sestos, who was a priest of Hephaestus, who scorned and neglected the warrior class in Egypt, and took from them the rich land that had been granted to them. When, therefore, Sennacherib led a force of Arabians and Assyrians against Egypt, the warriors refused to respond to the call of Sestos for their aid. The king, in despair, entered the temple of Hephaestus and lamented. He fell asleep in the temple and dreamed that the god came to him and told him not to despair, to march against the Assyrians with whatever forces he could muster, and that the god would come to his aid. Sestos called together the traders and artisans and marched with them to Pelusium, relying on the god's help. The two armies encamped opposite each other. During the night an army of field mice attacked the camp of the Assyrians; they devoured the strings of their bows and ate the straps of their shields. Next day great numbers of Assyrians were slain as they had no weapons with which to defend themselves, and the rest fled. According to Herodotus, there was in his time a statue of Sestos holding a mouse in his hand, in the temple of Hephaestus, and bearing an inscription admonishing the beholder to look on him and "learn to reverence the gods." It was at Pelusium that Assurbanipal defeated Tirhaka of Egypt; and it was here that Cambyses, son of Cyrus, defeated the Egyptians under King Psammetichus, the last Egyptian king (525 B.C.), and reduced Egypt to a Persian province.

*Peneius* (pẹ-nē′us). See *Peneus.*

*Peneus* (pẹ-nē′us). [Also: *Peneius.*] River in the Peloponnesus, Greece, sometimes also called the Gastuni. It drains into the Ionian Sea.

*Peneus.* [Also: *Peneius.*] Principal river in Thessaly, Greece, sometimes also called the Salembria. It traverses the Vale of

(obscured) errạnt, ardẹnt, actọr; ch, chip; g, go; th, thin; ᵺн, then; y, you;
(variable) ḍ as d or j, ṣ as s or sh, ṭ as t or ch, ẓ as z or zh.

Tempe and flows into the Gulf of Salonika about 26 miles NE of Larissa.

*Pentapolis* (pen-tap'ọ̄-lis). State consisting of five cities, or a group of five cities; the term was used in ancient geography in speaking of a variety of groups: 1) In Cyrenaica, Africa, a district comprising Cyrene, Apollonia, Barca, Arsinoë (near what is now Bengasi), and Berenice (or Hesperides; modern Bengasi), with their neighboring territories. 2) In Palestine, five cities including Sodom, Gomorrah, Admah, Zeboim, and one other. 3) Five cities of the Philistines: Ashkelon, Gaza, Gath, Ekron, and Ashdod. 4) Five Dorian cities in Asia Minor: Cnidus, Cos, Lindus, Camirus (on the island of Rhodes), and Ialysus. 5) Five cities in Italy: Rimini, Ancona, Fano, Pesaro, and Sinigaglia, with part of the exarchate of Ravenna; this, also called Pentapolis Maritima, was later included in the States of the Church (Papal States).

*Pentelicus* (pen-tel'i-kus). [Also: *Brilessus, Mendeli.*] Mountain in Attica, Greece, about 12 miles NE of Athens; noted especially for a variety of white marble resembling Parian, but denser and finer-grained, apparently inexhaustible quarries of which have from antiquity been worked in this mountain. The Parthenon, the Propylaea, and other Athenian monuments are built of it, and from it are carved the famous sculptures known as the Elgin Marbles. Elevation, about 3638 feet.

*Peparethos* (pep-ạ-rē'thos). [Modern name, *Skopelos.*] Island in the Aegean Sea, about 16 miles from Euboea, and SE of Thessaly. It was famous in ancient times for its wines. According to legend, the island was part of the realm of Rhadamanthys of Crete, brother of King Minos, and was bequeathed by him to Staphylus, son of Ariadne and Dionysus, god of wine.

*Peraea* (pē-rē'ạ). In ancient geography, a maritime district on the coast of Caria, Asia Minor, opposite Rhodes.

*Perga* (pėr'gạ). [Also: *Perge.*] In ancient geography, a city in Pamphylia, Asia Minor, long noted for the worship of Artemis. A Roman theater here is one of the finest surviving.

*Pergamum* (pėr'gạ-mum). [Also: *Pergamus;* modern name, *Bergama.*] The word appears to mean "citadel" or "stronghold." In ancient geography, a city in Mysia, Asia Minor, about 50 miles N of Smyrna. The city was raised to importance by the famous victory of Attalus I over the Gauls in the latter half of the 3rd century B.C. Attalus I celebrated this victory by dedicating a series of bronze statues on the acropolis of Pergamum, and later a second series at Athens. Of some of these statues marble copies survive: *The Dying Gaul* in the Capitoline Museum, Rome; the *Ludovisi Gaul,* and the head of the *Dying Asiatic,* in the National Museum (Museo delle Terme), Rome; another *Dying Gaul* and *Dying Asiatic,* and a *Dead Amazon,* in the National Museum, Naples; and others elsewhere. To the son of Attalus, Eumenes II, are due the great extension of the city as well as its architectural adornment, and during his reign occurred the remarkable development of Pergamene sculpture, on lines much more modern in spirit than the older Greek art. The same king founded a famous library here. His chief buildings were placed on a succession of terraces on the summit of the acropolis, which rises 900 feet above the plain, and on the other lower terraces immediately outside the powerful acropolis walls. The city remained prosperous under the Romans, and under the empire many fine buildings were erected on the acropolis, and beside the river below. In 1878 the Prussian government sent to the site an exploring expedition under Alexander Conze and Karl Humann. Their investigations were continued for several years, and to them are due the rediscovery of Pergamene art and the mass of information regarding later Greek architecture which together form one of the most remarkable archaeological acquisitions of that century. There are also a Greek theater, a Roman amphitheater, and remains of several temples. An Ionic temple of the finest Greek design is on the slope of the acropolis; the cella with its ornamented doorway remains unusually perfect. The temple of Athena Polias, a Doric peripteros of six by ten columns, of late Greek date, measuring 42½ by 72 feet, occupied a terrace surrounded on two or three sides by a handsome stoa of two stories, Doric below and Ionic above, with a balustrade sculptured with warlike trophies in the second story. The Great Altar of Zeus, with its high-relief sculptures of the *Battle of Gods and Giants,* is one of the landmarks of Hellenistic art. The continuous frieze is seven feet high and 400 feet long. The temple of Trajan, occupying a large terrace toward the summit of the acropolis, was a Corinthian peripteros of white marble.

*Pergamum, Kingdom of.* Ancient Greek kingdom in Asia Minor. It rose to prominence under Attalus I in the 3rd century B.C. Attalus III died in 133 B.C., and bequeathed the kingdom to Rome. It was made a Roman province under the name of Asia.

*Perinthus* (pḗ-rin'thus). [Also: *Heraclea Perinthus.*] In ancient geography, a city in Thrace, strongly situated on a cliff on a peninsula on the Propontis about 55 miles W of Byzantium. It was part of the realm of Darius the Great, and revolted against him when he was on his expedition in Scythia. After the Persian Wars (479 B.C.) it became a member of the Confederacy of Delos, to which it paid tribute. The city made a successful defense against Philip II of Macedon in 340 B.C. Eski Eregli is the name of the town now occupying the site.

*Persepolis* (pẽr-sep'ọ-lis). In ancient geography, one of the capitals of the Persian Empire, about 35 miles NE of what is now Shiraz. It became the capital under Darius I, was captured by Alexander the Great, c330 B.C., and subsequently burned, and is still noted for the ruins of its palaces. The most remarkable monuments are grouped on a terrace of smoothed rock and masonry, approximately rectangular in plan, though with irregular projections, measuring 940 by 1550 feet, and attaining in front the height of 43 feet, of fine polygonal masonry, while at the back it is dominated by the rock of the foothills behind. The chief buildings on the terrace were the Propylaea and the great hypostyle hall of Xerxes, the Hall of 100 Columns, attributed to Darius, and the residence palaces of Darius and his successors. In the palace of Darius carved reliefs of men fighting animals occur, based on Assyrian originals; in that of Xerxes the sculptures represent subjects pertaining to royal luxury. Great figures of bulls, often set up before the portals, recall the Assyrian practice. The chief explorations are due to Eugène Napoléon Flandin and P. Coste in 1840–41, and to F. Stolze and Andreas prior to 1882. In 1891 some excavations were made by Herbert Weld Blundell, and casts of the sculptures and inscriptions taken by a private expedition sent out from England. The site was carefully investigated in the 1930's by an expedition representing the University of Chicago and the University of Pennsylvania, under Ernst Herzfeld and Erich F. Schmidt.

*Persis* (pėr′sis). In ancient geography, a country in Asia, lying
SE of Susiana, S of Media, and W of Carmania. It was the
nucleus of the Persian Empire, and corresponded nearly to
the modern Fars.

*Perugia* (pā-rö′jạ). Italian name of *Perusia* (q.v.).

*Perusia* (pė-rö′shạ). City in C Italy, situated on hills above the
Tiber River, N of Rome. The ancient city was one of the 12
principal cities of the Etruscan federation. The city submitted to Roman rule in 309 B.C. In 41 B.C. Octavian, the future
Augustus, besieged and captured it; this is the Perusine War
of the historians. Eventually becoming a colony, its name
thereafter was Colonia Vibia Augusta Perusia.

*Pescara River* (pās-kä′rä). [Also, in its upper course, *Aterno*.]
River in C Italy which flows into the Adriatic near the town
of Pescara.

*Pessinus* (pes′i-nus) or *Pesinus* (pe-sī′nus). In ancient geography, a city in Galatia, Asia Minor, situated near the Sangarius (Sakarya) River about 80 miles SW of what is now
Ankara. It was long noted for the worship of Cybele.

*Petra* (pē′trạ). In ancient geography, a city in Arabia Petraea.
The site was early occupied on account of its proximity to
the caravan route between Arabia and Egypt. From the 3rd
century B.C. or earlier it was a stronghold of the Nabataeans.
The site consists of a precipice-enclosed valley on the NE
side of Mount Hor, approached only through narrow
gorges. The sandstone rocks are brilliantly colored in many
different hues, and are greatly worn by the action of water.
Petra is famous for its rock-cut architectural remains, dating
from after the establishment of Roman rule in 105 A.D.
These remains have been looked upon by many as those of
temples and palaces, but are merely the façades, many of
them considerable in scale and elaborate in ornament, of
rock tombs, with motifs borrowed from Assyrian, Egyptian,
and Greek architecture. They gain in effectiveness by their
situation and by the marvelous coloring of the rock. The
buildings of the town are in an extreme state of ruin, except
for the rock-cut theater.

*Phaestus* (fes′tus). [Also: *Phaistos*.] In ancient geography, a city
of Crete, situated in the middle of the south side of the
island, on a hill 300 feet above the plain of Mesara. To the
N and W, Cretan Mount Ida, where some say Zeus was born,
rises above the plain. The city is mentioned by Homer in the

*Iliad* as one which sent men against Troy under the leadership of Idomeneus. It was one of the most ancient cities of Crete. According to legend it was founded by Minos, whose nephew Gortys, son of Rhadamanthys, later destroyed the citadel and added the area to his realm. Remains at the site show that there were three distinct periods of occupation. The first structures date from the neolithic age. In the second period, c2000 B.C., a palace was built on the site, remains of which indicate a highly developed and prosperous civilization. This palace was destroyed, or partly destroyed, c1700 B.C., by some catastrophe, either by earthquake, or by enemy raids. However, the interruption in the prosperity of Phaestus was temporary, and a second and larger palace was constructed on the ruins of the first. This too was destroyed by means unknown, c1400 B.C.; after this the site was relatively unoccupied and was ultimately crowned by a temple of the classical period. Among present remains are traces of the structures of all three periods. Work on the excavation of the site, begun in 1900 by the Italians under Federigo Halbherr and continued in subsequent years, is still proceeding. The palace, which lies on terraces of differing levels connected by large and small staircases, follows the general plan of that at Cnossus but on a smaller scale and with more refinement. The general plan of the installations on the site includes a large paved court where dances and games were held, a theater, rooms for the performance of sacrifices, with channels to collect the blood of victims, gypsum shelves for the exhibition of statues and cult objects, an ingenious system for supplying the area with water and an intricate drainage system. The palace itself, approached through a propylaeum, had a large central court with porticoes, at least on the east and west sides, a great colonnaded reception hall that was approached by a majestic stairway, *megaron* (central hall), guest rooms, baths, storage areas, and other chambers for the use of the royal family and those occupied in serving it. The women's quarters were separate from the men's. Only the king, by a private stairway, could pass the sentry who guarded the women's quarters. Remains of a bathroom and bath have been found. The bath was a sunken chamber, with steps leading down to it, surrounded by a balcony on which a maid might stand to pour water over her mistress. Some say, however, that such a sunken chamber had ceremonial significance, and was used for purification rites. As at Cnossus, careful and brilliant provision was made for insulating the palace against the hot sun of summer and the bitter winds that swept down from the north in winter. The plaster of the walls was mixed with straw to provide air spaces, even as is done today in the houses of the Cretan farmers. Two sets of doors, with an air space between them, protected the main chambers from drafts or heat. For light and ventilation the palace had light wells, covered at the top and with openings cut in the walls below the roof. Of the many finds at Phaestus, a clay disc that had been hardened and preserved in the fire that destroyed the palace was unique. On the two faces of the Phaestus Disc appear pictographic inscriptions in spiral form, which, according to a recent effort at decipherment, can be read as Greek, and list Cretan shrines to be visited by the pious traveler.

*Phalerum* (fạ-lir'um). [Also: *Phaleron.*] In ancient geography, a seaport in Attica, Greece, on a small bay S of Athens and E of Piraeus. According to legend, Theseus sailed from here on his way to Crete with the tribute of youth and maidens demanded by King Minos. Shrines of Nausithous and Phaeax, pilots of Theseus on this voyage, were erected in Phalerum, and the Cybernesia *(Steering Festival)* was held in their honor. It was from this port also that Menestheus set sail with his fleet for the Trojan War. In ancient times Phalerum was the port of Athens, but after the time of Themistocles it was abandoned as the port of Athens because he built up and fortified the Piraeus, a more advantageous and better protected location.

*Phanagoria* (fan-ạ-gō'ri-ạ). In ancient geography, a Greek colony situated on the peninsula now called Taman, opposite the Crimea.

*Pharae* (fā'rē, fär'ē). See *Pherae.*

*Pharos* (fā'ros, fär'os). An island in the mouth of the Nile, opposite ancient Alexandria. Ptolemy I and Ptolemy II, Greek kings of Egypt, erected a celebrated lighthouse on Pharos, which was one of the seven wonders of the ancient world.

*Pharsala* (fär'sä-lä). See *Pharsalus.*

*Pharsalus* (fär-sā'lus). In ancient geography, a city in Thessaly, Greece, about 23 miles S of Larissa; the modern Pharsala.

It is celebrated for the great battle fought near it, June 29 or Aug. 9, 48 B.C., in which Caesar with 22,000 legionaries and 1000 cavalry totally defeated Pompey and his army of 45,000 legionaries and 7000 cavalry.

**Phaselis** (fạ-sē′lis). In ancient geography, a seaport in Lycia, Asia Minor, situated on the W shore of the Pamphylian Gulf (the modern Gulf of Antalya).

**Phasis** (fā′sis). [Modern name, *Rion*.] In ancient geography, a river of Colchis emptying into the Euxine Sea.

**Pheneüs** (fe′nẹ-us). In ancient geography, a city in N Arcadia, Greece, on a river of the same name.

**Pherae** (fē′rē). In ancient geography, a city in Thessaly, Greece, about 25 miles SE of Larissa. In the 4th century B.C. it became an important power under the tyrant Jason, who united Thessaly under his command. The later revolt of Thessaly against the tyrants of Pherae presented Philip II of Macedon with an opportunity to extend his power into Greece.

**Pherae** or **Pharae** (fa′rē). [Modern name, *Kalamai* or *Kalamata*.] City in Messenia, on the Gulf of Messenia, said to have been founded by Pharis, a son of Hermes. At Pherae there was an oracle of Hermes, which was much consulted by the sick. The first chance words that were heard on leaving the oracle constituted the oracular answers to questions that had been asked of it.

**Phigalia** (fi-gā′li-ạ). In ancient geography, a town in the SW corner of Arcadia, Greece. Near Phigalia was a temple of Apollo designed by Ictinus.

**Philippi** (fi-lip′ī). In ancient geography, a city in Macedonia, about 73 miles NE of Thessalonica. It was founded by Philip II of Macedon in 358 B.C., and is famous as the site of the two battles in 42 B.C., in which Octavian and Mark Antony defeated the republicans under Brutus and Cassius. A Christian church was founded here by Paul, who addressed to the congregation the Epistle to the Philippians.

**Phintias** (fin′ti-ạs). [Modern name, *Licata*.] Greek city on the S coast of Sicily, at the mouth of the river Himera (modern Salso), between Gela and Acragas. It was founded c284 B.C. by Phintias, tyrant of Acragas, who in 282 B.C. settled there the refugees from the destruction of Gela by the Mamertines. (JJ)

---

*Phlegraean* (flĕ-grē′ạn) *Fields* or *Plain*. [Italian, *Campi Fle-grei*.] Volcanic district lying W of Naples, Italy, bordering on the Bay of Naples, where according to some accounts, the Battle of the Giants and the Gods was brought to a conclusion with the defeat of the Giants. According to other accounts, the battle was finished on the Phlegraean Plain of Chalcidice, in northeastern Greece, under the generalship of Athena.

*Phliasia* (fli-ā′shi-ạ). In ancient geography, a small district in the Peloponnesus, Greece, NW of Argolis, NE of Arcadia, and S of Sicyonia. The Phliasians were Argives originally, but when the Dorians conquered the Peloponnesus they came to terms with them and became Dorian.

*Phlius* (flī′ūs). In ancient geography, a city in Phliasia, Peloponnesus, Greece, about 14 miles SW of Corinth, situated on the upper reaches of the Asopus River. It was founded by Dorians from Argos. Phlius, usually an ally of Sparta, drove out its oligarchs after the Peloponnesian Wars. The Spartan king Agesilaus reduced it by siege and forced it to receive a Spartan garrison (381–379 B.C.). Henceforth it was either allied to Sparta or remained neutral.

*Phocaea* (fō-sē′ạ). In ancient geography, the most northerly of the 12 Ionian cities of Asia, situated on the Aegean Sea about 28 miles NW of Smyrna. The inhabitants were Phocians by descent. To commemorate Psamathe the Nereid, they put the figure of a seal on their earliest coins, because Psamathe had transformed herself into a seal to escape the embraces of Aeacus. Her efforts were unsuccessful; she bore Phocus, the ancestor of the Phocians in Greece. When the Phocians emigrated to Asia and colonized Phocaea they won their land by agreement with the natives and settled among them without warfare. Phocaea was admitted to the league of Ionian cities when the inhabitants accepted a descendant of Codrus, legendary king of Athens, as their ruler. The Phocaeans were great sailors and according to Herodotus were the first of the Greeks to explore the coasts of the Adriatic and Tyrrhenian Seas, and to set out colonies in that area. Phocaea was the mother-city of Massilia, later Marseilles, France. The Phocaeans even sailed to the shores of Spain. According to Herodotus, when they arrived at Tartessus, a colony founded by the Phoenicians in Spain, the ruler was so impressed by them that he invited them to leave

Phocaea and settle in his country. When they declined his invitation he gave them money to wall their city in Asia. When Phocaea was attacked by Harpagus, general of Cyrus, in 540 B.C., their wall momentarily protected them, and they asked for a day in which to consider whether they would submit to Persian domination. This was granted them, and the Phocaeans, rather than submit to slavery, used their day of grace to load their families, and as much of their goods as possible, aboard their vessels and sailed away. Harpagus, on entering the city next day, found it empty. After a brief stop at Chios the Phocaeans decided to go to Cyrnus (Corsica), where years before they had established a colony, Alalia, and settle there. Before they left, however, they sailed back to their own city, surprised the Persian garrison and put them to the sword. Then they dropped a huge mass of iron in the sea and swore they would not return to Phocaea until the iron floated to the surface. But some of the Phocaeans were so saddened at the thought of leaving their homes that they immediately broke their oath and deserted their comrades and returned. The remainder went to Cyrnus and settled there for a time, but found it expedient to withdraw, following a sea-battle with the Carthaginians and Etruscans, to Rhegium. It is said that the Carthaginians landed the Phocaean captives they took in the sea-battle on the shore and stoned them to death. Afterward, men and animals passing the spot where the stoning took place were afflicted: their bodies became palsied or their limbs paralyzed. The people sent to Delphi to inquire about this matter and were told to honor the dead Phocaeans with funeral rites and games, a practice which was followed annually for many years. The Phocaeans finally established themselves at Elea in Italy.

**Phocis** (fō'sis). In ancient geography, a region in S central Greece. It was bounded by Locris on the N, Boeotia on the E, the Corinthian Gulf on the S, and Doris and Locris on the W. Before the Persian invasion of Greece, according to Herodotus, the Phocians fought against the Thessalians. They buried empty water jars just beneath the surface of the ground, and when the Thessalian cavalry charged, their horses, falling into the jars, were lamed or crippled and the cavalry was thrown into complete confusion. Enraged, the Thessalians gathered a large army to hurl against the Pho-

cians. The latter consulted the oracle at Delphi and were
told:

"I will match in fight mortal and immortal,
And to both will I give victory, but more to the mortal."
Puzzled by this equivocal response, the Phocians sent 300
picked men against the Thessalians. All perished. Terrified,
the Phocians gathered their women, children, and valuables
and made a huge pyre. They left 30 men to guard it and gave
them orders to set it alight and cause all to burn if the
Phocians should lose in the battle they were about to engage
in with the Thessalians. This gave rise to the expression
"Phocian despair," for a forlorn hope. With the picture of
their women and children before their eyes, the Phocians
attacked desperately, and won. Thus the oracle was fulfilled,
for the watchword of the Thessalians was "Itonian Athena,"
and the watchword of the Phocians was "Phocus," a mortal's
name. In gratitude, the Phocians sent offerings to Delphi. In
a later attack, the Phocians smeared themselves with chalk
and put on white armor. When they appeared at night the
Thessalians thought they were spirits, not their enemies
from Phocis, and the Phocians slaughtered them wholesale.
When the Persians made their successful way into Greece
the Phocians were compelled to join them, but they deserted
as soon as possible and afterward took part in the Greek
victory at Plataea (479 B.C.). The Phocians had periodically
controlled and lost Delphi. In 357 B.C. they seized it again.
The Thebans fought against them for ten years until at last
Philip of Macedon intervened on the pretext of restoring
order to Greece and put an end to the war, 348 B.C. This war
was called the Phocian War and also, the Sacred War. The
cities of Phocis—Lilaea, Hyampolis, Anticyra, Parapotamii,
Panopeus, and Daulis—were captured and destroyed. Only
Abae, whose citizens were free from impiety, was spared as
it had not shared in the seizure of the sanctuary. The Phocians now lost their share in the sanctuary and in the assembly. Their votes in the Amphictyonic League were given to
the Macedonians. In the following years some of the cities
of Phocis were rebuilt. The Phocians allied themselves with
Athens and took part in the disastrous battle of Chaeronea
where the allies were defeated by Philip. In the 3rd century
B.C., when the Gauls attacked, the Phocians fought savagely
in order, some say, to defend Delphi and atone for their

(obscured) errạnt, ardẹnt, actọr; ch, chip; g, go; th, thin; ᴛʜ, then; y, you;
(variable) ḏ as d or j, ṣ as s or sh, ṭ as t or ch, ẓ as z or zh.

earlier crimes against the sanctuary. The region is moutainous and contains Mount Parnassus. As a region it was especially important because of its chief place, Delphi.

**Phoenicia** (fẹ-nish′ạ). In ancient geography, the strip of land on the coast of S Syria, between Mount Lebanon and the Mediterranean Sea. It was about 200 miles in length, and its width did not exceed 35 miles at the maximum; area, about 4000 square miles. But the rivers (fed by the snows of Lebanon) which irrigated it, and the energy and enterprise of its inhabitants, made this narrow tract of land one of the most varied in its products, and gave it a place in history out of proportion to its size. The principal rivers were the Leontes (Litani), N of Tyre, and the Orontes (Nahr el Asy) in the N. The cedars of the mountains furnished building material; the coast furnished sand for glass and the purple snail for dyeing; and the inland plains were covered with orchards, gardens, and grain fields. Though the coastline was not deeply indented, the skill of the inhabitants secured them harbors. The ancient inhabitants of Phoenicia, the Phoenices of the classical writers (*Poeni* or *Puni* designating the Carthaginians), are now considered by many scholars to have been Semites of the Canaanites, and their country Canaan. In Greek legend, the Phoenicians are counted as the descendants of Phoenix, the son of Agenor and Telephassa, and the brother of Cadmus and Europa. When Europa was carried off he went, at his father's command, in search of her. He traveled westward from his native Canaan, to what later became known as Carthage, whose people took the name Punic from him. But since he did not find Europa he returned to Canaan, after his father's death, and the land was named Phoenicia in his honor, and its people Phoenicians. According to classical writers, the Phoenicians emigrated from the Erythraean Sea. This would favor the assumption that the Phoenicians were identical with the Punti of the Egyptian monuments. The language of the Phoenicians was closely akin to Hebrew. They worshiped as principal divinities Baal and Astarte, besides the seven planets under the name of Cabiri. Phoenicia never formed a single state under one head, but rather a confederacy of cities. In the earliest period (1600–1100 B.C.) Sidon stood at the head of Phoenician cities; c1000 Sidon lost the hegemony to Tyre; in 761 B.C. Aradus was founded in the

N extreme of the country; and from these three cities Tripolis (the modern Tripoli in Lebanon) was settled. South of Tripolis old Byblos was situated, while Berytus (Beirut) in the N did not become prominent before the Roman period. To the territory of Tyre belonged Akko or Acco (Acre), later called Ptolemaïs. Separated from the rest of Phoenicia lay Joppa (Jaffa), on the coast of Palestine, which the Maccabees united with Palestine. The constitution of these Phoenician townships was aristocratic, headed by a king. The earliest king of Tyre mentioned in the Old Testament was Hiram, a contemporary and friend of David and Solomon. After Hiram six kings are supposed to have ruled until Ethbaal or Ithobal, the father of Jezebel, wife of Ahab. Under Ethbaal's grandson, Pygmalion, contentions about the throne led to the emigration of his sister Elissa (Dido in Vergil) and the foundation of Carthage, the mighty rival of Rome. In the middle of the 9th century B.C., Phoenicia shared the fate of Syria at large. After the battle of Karkar (853 B.C.) it became tributary to Assyria. It made a struggle for independence under Shalmaneser IV, but was brought to submission by his successor, Sargon. In 609 B.C. Phoenicia came for a short time into the hands of Necho II, king of Egypt. Tyre was besieged for 13 years (585–572 B.C.) by Nebuchadnezzar. Cyrus brought Phoenicia with the rest of the Babylonian possessions under Persian supremacy. But, owing to their skill in navigation, the Phoenicians retained an independence of sorts. In 351 B.C. Sidon was destroyed by Artaxerxes III. The same fate befell Tyre at the hands of Alexander the Great in 332 B.C. In 64 B.C. Phoenicia was annexed by Pompey to the Syrian province of the Roman Empire. Less original and productive in the domain of thought and higher culture, the Phoenicians excel other members of the Semitic family in contributions to material civilization. They were the merchants and manufacturers of antiquity. They were the most skillful shipbuilders and boldest navigators. All along the Mediterranean, even beyond Gibraltar, they established colonies. They sent colonies to Cyprus, Crete, and England, and it is not improbable that they worked the tin mines of Cornwall. They even ventured to circumnavigate Africa. The principal articles of their commerce were precious stones, metals, glassware, costly textiles, and especially purple robes. Their skill in architecture was exhibited in the temple of Solomon. Their alphabetic writing became the parent of all the European alphabetic systems now in use. According to the Greek legends, the alphabet was brought to Crete by Cadmus, when he was searching for Europa, and from there to Greece. The Phoenicians also transmitted a knowledge of mathematics and of weights and measures to other nations. Of the Phoenician literature only a few fragments in Greek translation have come down to us. Among the numerous Phoenician inscriptions, the most important is that of the sarcophagus of the Sidonian king Eshmunazar (who reigned in the 4th century B.C.), found in 1855, and now at Paris.

*Phoronicum* (fôr-ō′ni-kum). A city in the Peloponnesus, founded by Phoroneus, brother of Io. Its name was later changed to Argos. It was said to have been the first market town, and the first in the Peloponnesus to establish the worship of Hera.

*Phreattys* (frē′at-is). In ancient geography, a place near the sea at Piraeus. Here exiled men, against whom some new charge had been brought, stood on a ship at sea and defended themselves while the judges listened from the shore.

*Phrygia* (frij′i-ạ). In ancient geography, a country in Asia Minor, of varying boundaries. In the Persian period it comprised Lesser Phrygia, on the Hellespont, and Great Phrygia in the interior, bounded by Bithynia and Paphlagonia on the N, the Halys River on the E, the Taurus Mountains on the S, and Mysia, Lydia, and Caria on the W. Later the Galatians settled in the NE part. The inhabitants (Phrygians) were of undetermined origin, but are believed to have come from Europe. The country was overrun by the Cimmerians in the 7th century B.C., and was ruled later by Lydia, Persia, Macedon, and Rome. Gordius, who tied the Gordian knot, and Midas, his son, who possessed the golden touch, were legendary kings of Phrygia.

*Phthia* (thī′ạ). In ancient geography, a district and town in Thessaly.

*Phthiotis* (thī-ō′tis). In ancient geography, a region of Thessaly, bordered on the E by the Maliacus Sinus (Gulf of Lamia). It was in ancient times a home of the Achaeans.

*Phyle* (fī′lē). In ancient geography, a fortified place in Attica, on Mount Parnes, commanding the shortest route between Athens and Thebes. It was one of a series of fortresses that guarded the mountainous border of Attica. When (404 B.C.) the Thirty Tyrants ruled Athens Thrasybulus, who had sought refuge in Thebes, resolved to overthrow the tyrants. With 70 partisans he left Thebes and seized the fortress of Phyle. The tyrants sent a force against him and prepared to force his surrender by a blockade of the fortress. However, a snowstorm compelled the attackers to withdraw. Some months later another expedition was sent against Phyle but they were ambushed by Thrasybulus and suffered heavy losses. From Phyle Thrasybulus marched to Piraeus, seized Munychia, and succeeded in overthrowing the Thirty (403 B.C.).

*Phyllis* (fil′is). In ancient geography, a river of Bithynia.

*Phyllis.* In ancient geography, a mountain of Thessaly, the source of the Apidanus and the Enipeus Rivers.

*Piacenza* (pyä-chen′tsä). See *Placentia.*

*Picenum* (pī-sē′num). In ancient geography, a territory in Italy, lying between the Adriatic Sea and the Apennines. It was bounded by Umbria on the NW and W, the Sabines on the SW, and the Vestini on the S. It was reduced by Rome in 268 B.C., and took part in the Social War against Rome in 90 B.C. Capital, Asculum Picenum.

*Pieria* (pī-ir′i-a). In ancient geography, a district in N Thessaly, Greece. It was the legendary birthplace of Orpheus and of the Muses. Mount Olympus was in the district.

*Pillars of Heracles,* or *Hercules* (her′kū-lēz). In ancient geography, the two opposite promontories Calpe (Gibraltar) in Europe and Abyla in Africa, situated at the E extremity of the Strait of Gibraltar, at the outlet from the Mediterranean into the Atlantic. According to some accounts, a land bridge once joined the two continents and Heracles carved it apart to let the waters of Ocean mingle with those of the inner sea. Others say the waterway between the two continents was once much wider and Heracles narrowed it to keep ocean monsters out of the inner sea.

*Pimplea* (pim′plē-a). In ancient geography, a city and fountain in Pieria sacred to the Muses.

*Pincian Hill* (pin′shi-an). [Latin, *Mons Pincius.*] Hill in the N part of Rome, extending in a long ridge E from the Tiber River. It was not one of the traditional Seven Hills, though separated by but a narrow interval from the Quirinal. In antiquity, as at the present day, it was noted for its beautiful

(obscured) errant, ardent, actor; ch, chip; g, go; th, thin; ᵼн, then; y, you; (variable) ḍ as d or j, ṣ as s or sh, ṭ as t or ch, ẓ as z or zh.

gardens. The view from it toward Saint Peter's is famous.

**Pindus** (pin'dus). Range of mountains in Greece, between Thessaly on the E and Epirus on the W. Greatest elevation, about 7665 feet.

**Pirae** (pī'rē). The name of a village between Formia and Minturnae on the Via Appia, mentioned once by the Latin author Pliny the Elder, who describes it as deserted in his time (1st century A.D.). It has been identified with a substantial fortification of polygonal limestone at the modern seaside village of Scauri, five miles W of Minturnae. The existence of a town of this name in the 1st century B.C. has been confirmed by the Minturnae excavations, in whose inscriptions the name of a slave owner Pirana or Peirana, "woman from Pirae," appears four times. (JJ)

**Piraeus** (pī-rē'us). [Also: *Peiraeus, Peiraieus, Peiraievs, Piraieus.*] Seaport of Athens and the chief port of Greece, situated on the Saronic Gulf about 5 miles SW of Athens, on the west side of the Munychian peninsula. The ancients believed the Piraeus was once an island, and its name is taken to mean "land across the water." In ancient times Phalerum, which could be seen from the Acropolis, was the port of Athens, but Themistocles recognized the advantages of the Piraeus with its three harbors, even though it was farther away from Athens than Phalerum, and built it into a formidable port. The three harbors of the Piraeus were the great harbor on the west side of the peninsula, and the smaller, circular harbors of Munychia and Zea on the east side. Because of these harbors Themistocles himself thought the Piraeus even more important than Athens, and perhaps if he had been a tyrant would have compelled the Athenians to give up their city and move to the port. He advised them if they were ever hard-pressed to withdraw to the Piraeus, but they never did. During his archonship (493–492 B.C.) he fortified the harbor and built it up as a port. In c450 B.C. Hippodamus of Miletus remodeled the city, laying out the streets in squares or rectangles, the so-called gridiron system. The great ship sheds there were one of the glories of Athens. Among the artifacts found on the site of the ship sheds are marble plates, with a great eye painted on them. These plates were fastened to the bow of the ships, providing an eye so that the ship could see where it was going. The port was connected to Athens by long walls, and ultimately the whole area, Athens, Piraeus, Munychia and Zea, was enclosed in a single fortification. At the end of the Peloponnesian Wars (404 B.C.), the Spartans destroyed the fortifications. They were rebuilt in 394 B.C. by Conon, who also founded a sanctuary of Aphrodite near the SE rim of the great harbor. Sulla destroyed the fortifications (c86 B.C.) and they were never rebuilt. At the Piraeus there was a sacred precinct of Athena Savior with a bronze image of the goddess holding a spear; and there was a precinct of Zeus Savior with a bronze image of the god holding a staff and Victory. Annually a public sacrifice was offered to Zeus Savior with a public festival, boat races, and a procession. Those who had been saved during storms at sea made offerings at the sanctuary of Zeus Savior. Themistocles founded a sanctuary of Aphrodite at the NE extremity of the Piraeus. There were, among other religious sites, at least two theaters of Dionysus there. The bones of Themistocles who died in Magnesia in Asia, were brought back to Greece by his sons and buried at Piraeus. In 1959 it was reported that a cache of ancient statues had been discovered at Piraeus by workmen digging during street repairs. From the charring of the walls of the chamber in which the statues were found and the fact that the statues are of various ages, archeologists have conjectured that the statues had been collected in a warehouse and then abandoned after a fire there, possibly in the 1st century B.C. The most notable of the statues is the Apollo, a bronze figure of excellent workmanship that dates from the last quarter of the 6th century B.C. It is probably the oldest full-size bronze figure in the world. Several statues dating from the 4th century B.C. were found; these include a bronze female figure, a marble statue of a maiden, a five-foot-high bronze statue of Artemis, and an eight-foot-high bronze of Athena, her helmet etched with intricate designs. Several hermae of marble and bronze, thought to be 1st century B.C. Roman copies, were also found there.

*Pirene* (pī-rē′nē) *Spring.* A spring behind Aphrodite's temple on the Acrocorinth, the citadel of Corinth, or one just outside the city gate. Some say it was caused to flow to supply Corinth with water forever by the river-god Asopus. He did this in return for information supplied him by Sisyphus about the fate of Aegina, a daughter of Asopus, who had been carried off by Zeus. Others say the spring gushed forth

(obscured) errant, ardent, actor; ch, chip; g, go; th, thin; ᴛʜ, then; y, you;
(variable) ḍ as d or j, ş as s or sh, ţ as t or ch, ẓ as z or zh.

when Pegasus, the winged horse, struck the ground with his hoof. It was while Pegasus was drinking at this spring that Bellerophon slipped the golden bridle over his neck and captured him. American archaeologists heve found what is undoubtedly the Pirene Spring of the classical period within the city, just off the agora.

*Pisa* (pē'sä). [Ancient name, *Pisae.*] City in C Italy, situated on the Arno River. Ancient Pisae, on the same site, was only two miles from the sea, but deposits in the delta of the Arno have so built out the land that the city is now six miles from the Mediterranean Sea. The ancient city was one of the 12 federated towns of Etruria. It became a Roman colony in 180 B.C., and was important for its location on the Aemilian Way and as an outpost against the Ligurians.

*Pisae* (pī'sē). Ancient name of *Pisa,* city in C Italy.

*Pisatis* (pī'sa̱-tis). In ancient geography, a region in the NW of the Peloponnesus. It became a part of Elis.

*Pisidia* (pi-sid'i-a̱). In ancient geography, a territory in Asia Minor. It was bounded by Phrygia on the N, Isauria and Cilicia on the E, Pamphylia on the S, and Lycia on the SW, and was traversed by the Taurus Mountains. It was conquered by Rome.

*Pistoria* (pis-tôr'i-a̱). [Modern name, *Pistoia.*] City in C Italy, situated near the Umbro River, about 20 miles NW of Florence. It was colonized by the Romans in ancient times. Nearby the conspiracy of Catiline was crushed (62 B.C.) when his forces were destroyed and he was killed.

*Pithecusa* (pith-e̱-kū'sa̱) or *Pithecusae* (-sē). [Also: *Aenaria.*] In ancient geography, a volcanic island in the Tyrrhenian Sea, situated about 16 miles W of Naples. The name, given it by the Greeks, means "Apes' island." According to legend, Zeus became disgusted with the Cercopes, a people notorious for their lying and cheating habits. He changed them into apelike animals covered with long yellow hair, deprived them of speech so that they could no longer plague humanity with their lies, and exiled them to this island which bears their name. Modern name of the island is *Ischia.*

*Pityusa* (pit-i-ū'sa̱). [Modern names, *Spetsai, Petza, Spetzia.*] Island in S Greece, at the entrance to the Gulf of Nauplia, about 28 miles SE of Nauplia. Length, about 5 miles.

*Placentia* (pla̱-sen'sha̱). [Modern name, *Piacenza.*] City in N Italy, situated on the Padus (Po) River E of its junction with the Trebia (Trebbia) River, about 40 miles SE of Mediolanum (Milan). Founded by the Romans in 218 B.C. as a fortress against the Gallic tribes, it served as a place of retreat for the remnants of the Roman army after the defeat at the Trebia (218 B.C.) by Hannibal. In 207 B.C. Hasdrubal unsuccessfully besieged it; in 200 it was burned by the Gauls; and in 190 B.C. it was recolonized, and a few years later was made a terminus of the Aemilian Way. In the time of Augustus part of the ancient city was named Julia Augusta.

*Plataea* (plạ-tē′ạ). [Also: *Plataeae*.] In ancient geography, a city in Boeotia, Greece, situated at the foot of Mount Cithaeron, about 30 miles NW of Athens. The Plataeans played a valiant part in the Persian War. They helped the Athenians defeat the Persians at Marathon (490 B.C.). The part they played in the battle of Plataea (479 B.C.) was so glorious they were awarded the meed of valor after the defeat of the Persians. With their share of the booty from the victory they raised a temple of Athena Area *(Warlike)*, and in it placed a wooden image of the goddess, with head, hands, and feet of marble, said by some to have been made by Phidias. On the walls of the temple was a painting by Polygnotus, showing Odysseus after he had slain the suitors, and a painting by Onasias which depicted the expedition of the Seven against Thebes. Because of their valor at the battle of Plataea the Plataeans were excused from all further contributions to the war against the Persians, and undertook to celebrate the anniversary each year. Annually deputies came from all parts of Greece to sacrifice to Zeus Savior. No slaves were allowed to take part in this ceremony that was sacred to the memory of men who died for liberty. On the day of the celebration a trumpet call to battle was sounded at dawn. Immediately, a procession was formed, in which chariots laden with myrtle boughs were followed by a black bull and young men carrying wine and milk for libations. The procession marched to the entrance of the city where the graves of those who fell in the battle were located near an altar of Zeus, God of Freedom. There the archon washed the little pillars on the monuments of the dead with water and rubbed them with oil and perfumes. Then the black bull was slain and the archon called on the shades of the dead to come and feast on its blood. Next he poured wine from a bowl and presented it to the men who had died for the liberty of Greece. This ceremony was performed annually at least until the 1st century A.D. Every fifth year games, called Eleutheria, were celebrated in honor of Zeus Eleutherios (*God of Freedom*), in which races by men in armor were the most important contest. The Plataeans also celebrated the festivals known as the Great and Little Daedala. Plataea was unsuccessfully attacked by the Thebans in 431 B.C., besieged by the Spartans and their allies in 429 B.C., taken and destroyed by them in 427, and restored in 387 B.C. In 373 B.C. the Plataeans, wary of the Thebans, went out of their city to the fields only when they knew the Thebans were meeting in assembly and would not attack. The Thebans, learning of this policy, went to their assembly armed, marched out of it, and attacked Plataea while the inhabitants were at work in the fields. They took the city, destroyed all but its sanctuaries, and barred the gates against the Plataeans, so that though they lost their city they at least kept their lives, and many of them went to Athens. They were restored to their own city and rebuilt it after Philip of Macedon conquered Thebes and her allies at Chaeronea (338 B.C.).

**Plavis** (plā′vis). [Modern name, *Piave*.] River in Italy, which flows into the Adriatic Sea about 20 miles NE of Venetia (Venice).

**Pnyx** (niks). Hill between the Museum Hill and the Hill of the Nymphs, above the Agora, in the group SW of the Acropolis, at Athens, Greece; also, a famous ancient place of public assembly established on the N slope of this hill, beneath the summit. The place of assembly consists of a terrace, bounded at the back by a vertical cutting 13 feet high in the rock at the summit of the hill, and supported by a curved retaining wall, built of well-jointed polygonal masonry in huge blocks. Some of the courses of this retaining wall have disappeared, so that the terrace now slopes downward while originally it was level or ascended slightly toward the back. The length of the terrace is 395 feet and its width 212 feet. The back wall is not straight, but forms an open obtuse angle, at the apex of which projects a huge cube of rock, rising from three steps and ascended by a small flight of steps in the angle at each side. This is the *bema*, or orators' platform, from which Demosthenes and other great Athenian political orators delivered their harangues.

*Po* (pō). [Latin, **Padus, Eridanus.**] Largest river in Italy. It rises in Monte Viso *(Mons Vesulus)* in the Alps on the French border, flows NE and then generally E, traversing a wide, fertile, and nearly level plain, and empties by several mouths into the Adriatic Sea *(Mare Adriaticum)*. Its chief tributaries are the Tanaro *(Tanarus)* and Trebbia *(Trebia)* on the right, and the Dora Baltea *(Duria Major)*, Sesia *(Sessites)*, Ticino *(Ticinus)* (draining Lake Maggiore, *Lacus Verbanus*), Adda *(Addua)* (draining Lake Como, *Lacus Larius*), Oglio *(Ollius)* (draining Lake Iseo, *Lacus Sebinus*), and Mincio *(Mincius)* (draining Lake Garda, *Lacus Benacus*) on the left. The chief places on its banks are Turin *(Taurosia)*, Piacenza *(Placentia)*, and Cremona.

*Pometia* (pō-mē′shi-ạ) or *Pometii* (-ī). A city of the Volsci in S Latium. The Volscian town became a Roman colony in 382 B.C. In ancient times the city was also called Suessa Pometia, perhaps the modern Torre Petrara, or Mesa.

*Pompeii* (pom-pā′ē). Ancient city in Italy, situated on the Bay of Naples 13 miles SE of Naples, nearly at the foot of Mount Vesuvius. It was a flourishing provincial town, containing many villas. It was severely injured (63 A.D.) by an earthquake, and was totally destroyed (79) by an eruption of Vesuvius. Owing to the preservation of the ruins practically intact to the present day by the layer of ashes and pumice that buried them, the remains of Pompeii afford in many ways the most complete information we possess of Roman material civilization. Some excavations were made on the site in antiquity, in the effort to recover buried treasure, but Pompeii and its tragic end were soon forgotten. In 1748 some peasants came accidentally upon a few ancient works of art in a ruined house, and the Bourbon sovereigns of Naples thereupon caused searches to be made for similar objects. Between 1808 and 1815 Joachim Murat instituted the first scientifically conducted excavations. After his fall the work went on more or less irregularly until the Bourbon kingdom ended in 1860. It thereafter progressed with system and regularity under Giuseppe Fiorelli. Most of the oval area included within the walls has now been thoroughly explored. Excavators have now uncovered about two-fifths of the city which in 79 had an area of about 160 acres. The great theater, of the time of Augustus, is one of the most perfect of Roman antiquity, semicircular in plan, with a diameter of 322 feet. The temple of Isis is a small Corinthian tetrastyle prostyle structure raised on a basement in a peristyle court upon which open the lodgings of the priests. Many interesting objects connected with the cult were found here, and skeletons of the priests amid surroundings indicating that they had sought, too late, to flee. The so-called House of Castor and Pollux is curious as being a double house with a large peristyle court common to the two parts. Each part has its atrium and all its subdivisions complete. The exterior contrasts with the usual plainness by its stucco decoration in panels and arabesques. The so-called House of Marcus Lucretius is a double house, remarkable also for having had three stories, and for its beautiful reception room (*tablinum*) and dining room. The so-called House of Meleager is notable for its paintings and other decorations. In the atrium there is a marble table supported by winged griffins. The peristyle court, with 24 Ionic columns, is the finest in Pompeii. The so-called House of Pansa is one of the largest and most elaborate dwellings of Pompeii, measuring 120 by 300 feet. The so-called House of the Faun is perhaps the best in style of the ancient city. The usual wall paintings are here replaced by mosaics. The famous *Dancing Faun* and the mosaic of the *Battle of Issus* came from this house.

**Pomptinae Paludes** (pomp-tī′nē pạ-lö′dēz). [English, *Pontine Marshes*.] Marshy district in the region of Latium, C Italy, between the Tyrrhenian Sea and the Volscian Mountains and extending about 31 miles from Tarracina to near Velitrae. From ancient times it had been a notoriously malarial swampland, due to a lack of natural drainage, and from 160 B.C. many attempts were made to drain it, notably those by Cethegus and Trajan. The area, finally drained and improved in the 1920's and 1930's is traversed by the Appian Way.

**Pontiae** (pon′shi-ē) or **Pontia** (-shạ). [Modern name, *Ponza*.] Chief island of the Pontine group, situated in the Tyrrhenian Sea about 67 miles W of Naples: a place of exile for state prisoners under the early Roman emperors.

**Pontine Islands** (pon′tin, -tīn). [Modern name, *Ponza Islands*.] Group of small volcanic islands W of Naples.

**Pontine Marshes.** See **Pomptinae Paludes**.

**Pontus** (pon′tus). In ancient geography, a country in Asia Minor. It was bounded by the Pontus Euxinus (Black Sea) or the N, Colchis on the E, Armenia on the SE and S, Cappadocia on the S, Galatia on the SW, and Paphlagonia on the W. It became independent of Persia in the 4th century B.C., and rose to great power with extended boundaries under Mithridates VI. After the victories of Pompey (66 B.C.) it was reduced to its former limits, and was eventually made a Roman province.

**Pontus Euxinus** (ūk-sī′nus). [Latin form of the Greek name of the **Euxine Sea**, or **Black Sea**.] The Greek word *euxeinos* may be translated "friendly to strangers." The Black Sea having been notably treacherous to Greek mariners with their keelless ships, the legend arose that it had once been called the *Axeinos*, "hostile to strangers." It was said that its name had been changed in the hope of placating its spirit, as the Greeks were said to have changed the name of the Erinyes (Furies) to Eumenides "the Kindly-Disposed." (JJ)

**Populonia** (po-pū-lō′ni-a). In ancient geography, a town of the Etruscans, situated on the coast of Etruria on the N end of a promontory projecting into the Mediterranean Sea and opposite the island of Elba. According to the *Aeneid* it was one of the Etruscan towns that lent assistance to Aeneas in his war with the Latins. Sulla took the town by siege about the beginning of the 1st century B.C., and thereafter it declined. Tombs dating from the 9th century B.C. have been found near the site of the ancient town.

**Poros** (pô′ros). See **Calauria.**

**Portici** (pôr′tē-chē). Town and commune in S Italy, in the Campania, situated on the Bay of Naples about 5 miles SE of Naples; a seaside resort. Near here is the site of ancient Herculaneum, covered in 79 A.D. by ashes from the eruption of Vesuvius, which, wet with rain and flowing as warm mud, filled the streets and houses and there hardened into stone.

**Portoferraio** (pôr-tō-fer-rä′yō). See **Argoön.**

**Porto Torres** (pôr′tō tôr′räs). See **Turris Libisonis.**

**Portus Trajani** (pōr′tus tra̧-jā′nī). See **Centumcellae.**

**Posidonia** (pos-i-dō′ni-a). Original name of **Paestum.**

**Potidaea** (pot-i-dē′a̧). [Also: **Cassandrea.**] In ancient geography, a city in Macedonia, situated on the Pallene peninsula, the most westerly of the peninsulas of Chalcidice. The city was founded by colonists from Corinth (c600 B.C.). The Persians, on their way back to the Hellespont after their defeat at Salamis (480 B.C.) attempted to take Potidaea and

besieged it, but after three months gave up the siege and
withdrew. As a result of a quarrel between Athens and Cor
inth over Corcyra, Potidaea revolted against Athens (43;
B.C.), of whom she had become a tributary ally after the
Persian War. Athens sent a force to subdue the city. Corintl
sought the aid of Sparta to defend it. The revolt of Potidae;
was one of the precipitating causes of the Peloponnesia
Wars. The Athenians besieged the city for a year and re
duced its inhabitants to starvation. According to Thucydi
des, they were so driven by their hunger that in certai
instances they ate human flesh. The city surrendered (43(
B.C.). By the terms of the surrender the inhabitants and thei
auxiliary soldiers were allowed a free passage out of the city
the men with one garment apiece, the women with two, and
a fixed sum of money was allotted them for the journey
Later the Athenians sent colonists to repopulate the city
The city joined the Chalcidian League early in the 4th cen
tury. In 364–362 B.C. it fell again under Athenian dominion
Philip II of Macedon captured it (c356 B.C.) and handed i
over to Olynthus. The city was largely destroyed, probabl
during the Olynthian War (348 B.C.), but was rebuilt b
Cassander, son of Antipater, who renamed it Cassandrea fo
himself. For a time it was very powerful, but it was finall
destroyed by the Huns. Ruins of the ancient wall are to b
found on the site.

*Potniae* (pot'ni-ē). In ancient geography, a city of Boeotia
Greece.

*Pozzuoli* (pōt-tswô'lē). See *Puteoli.*

*Pozzuoli, Bay of.* Northwestern arm of the Bay of Naples.

*Praeneste* (prē-nes'tē). [Modern name, *Palestrina.*] In ancien
geography, a city in Latium, Italy, situated on a lofty hil
about 23 miles ESE of Rome. According to legend, it wa
founded by Caeculus, a son of Vulcan. It was built probabl
as early as the 8th century B.C., and was often opposed t(
Rome, especially in 380 B.C. when it was captured by Camil
lus, and in the Latin War (340–338 B.C.), and was later alliec
with Rome until the time of the Social War (90–88 B.C.)
when it received the Roman franchise. It was taken by th
partisans of Sulla from the Marians under the younge
Marius in 82 B.C. With its clear air and refreshing breezes
it became a favorite summer resort of the Roman nobilit
(the residence of Augustus, Horace, Tiberius, and Hadrian)

and was celebrated for the temple of the goddess Fortuna Primigenia. Connected with the temple was an oracle, the *sortes Praenestinae* (Praenestine lots), which was consulted in the following manner: Contained in a receptacle were a number of small oak tablets, on which were inscribed enigmatic sentences. When a petitioner wished to consult the oracle, a child drew one of these and handed it to him. He was at liberty to interpret it as he saw fit. Ruins of ancient Praeneste are still visible. These include long sections of fortification wall in polygonal limestone masonry, assignable to the 4th or 3rd century B.C., the vast sanctuary of Fortune, majestically constructed in ascending terraces on the hill slope and still the subject of endless study and discussion, and a large Nile landscape in mosaic. From the cemetery have come the famous Praenestine cists (decorated caskets, as the Ficoroni Cist) and the Praenestine fibula (ornamental clasp), with the earliest inscription in Latin. (JJ)

**rasiae** (prā′si-ē) or **Prasia** (-ą). A coast town of Laconia.

**rasiae.** In ancient geography, a place in Attica where there was a temple of Apollo especially connected with Hyperborean Apollo. First fruits of the Hyperboreans, wrapped in wheaten straw, were sent here. From here, the Athenians took them to Delos. There was a monument to Erysichthon at Prasiae, for he died on the return voyage from Delos after having delivered the Hyperborean first fruits there.

**riene** (prī-ē′nē). In ancient geography, one of the 12 Ionian cities of Asia. It was in Caria, N of Miletus. According to tradition, it was colonized by Ionians and Thebans, who went there under the leadership of a grandson of Codrus, the legendary king of Athens. In the 4th century B.C. the city was rebuilt on the rectangular "gridiron" plan. The site contains many ruins and is a fine example of ancient town planning. The temple of Athena Polias, dedicated 340 B.C., was an Ionic peripteros of six by 11 columns, of marble, graceful in proportion and with delicate decorative sculpture.

**rivernum** (prī-vẹr′num). In ancient geography, a town of C Italy, about 47 miles SE of Rome. It was an ancient Volscian town. The modern town near the ancient site is Priverno.

**rochyta** (prok′i-tą). Ancient name for Procida, an island at the entrance of the Bay of Naples.

*Procida* (prô'chē-dạ). [Ancient name, *Prochyta.*] Island at th
entrance of the Bay of Naples, about 13 miles SW of Naple;
belonging to the province of Napoli, Italy. The surface i
rocky and volcanic.

*Proconnesus* (prō-kọn-nē'sus). [Modern name, *Marmara.*] I;
land in the W part of the Propontis. It has marble quarrie:
for which it has been noted since ancient times. Area, abou
50 square miles.

*Propontis* (prō-pon'tis). [Modern name, *Sea of Marmara* o
*Marmora.*] Sea communicating with the Euxine Sea on th
NE by the Thracian Bosporus, and with the Aegean Sea o
the SW by the Hellespont. Length, about 170 miles; greate:
width, about 50 miles.

*Provincia* (prō-vin'shi-ạ, -shạ). [Also: *Gallia Provincia, Pr*
*vincia Gallica.*] In ancient geography, the part of Gaul cor
quered by the Romans at the end of the 2nd century B.C. I
corresponded originally to the later Provence, Dauphiné
and Languedoc.

*Psophis* (sō'fis). In ancient geography, a town in NW Arcadiạ

*Psyttalia* or *Psyttaleia* (sit-ạ-lī'ạ). An islet lying between Salami
and the mainland of Greece. With the Greek fleet anchore
in the harbor at Salamis the Persians, planning a sea figh
sent a body of troops to Psyttalia, partly for the purpose (
enclosing the Greeks and partly in the hope of destroyin
them as the wrecks of their fleet drifted to the island afte
the battle. In the event, the Persian fleet was beaten, and th
Persian troops on Psyttalia were attacked and cut to piece
by the Greeks under the command of Aristides and totall
destroyed (480 B.C.).

*Pteria* (tir'i-ạ). In ancient geography, a place in Cappadociạ
Asia Minor: the modern Bogazkale, Turkey. It was the scen
of a battle between Cyrus the Great and Croesus c554 B.c

*Ptolemaïs* (tol-ẹ-mā'is). In ancient geography, a city i
Cyrenaica, W of Cyrene.

*Ptolemaïs.* [Also: *Ptolemaïs Theron.*] In ancient geography,
town on the W coast of the Red Sea.

*Puteoli* (pụ-tē'ọ-lī). [Modern name, *Pozzuoli.*] Ancient town i
S Italy, situated on the Bay of Pozzuoli about seven miles \
of Naples; commercial center for Rome's eastern trade an
a fashionable villa resort. Founded by political refugee
from the Greek island of Samos, c521 B.C., Puteoli becam
a Roman colony in 194 B.C. and developed into one of th

fat, fāte, fär, fâll, ȧsk, fāre; net, mē, hėr; pin, pīne; not, nōte, mōv
nôr; up, lūte, pùll; oi, oil; ou out; (lightened) ẹlect, agọny, ụnit

greatest ports of Italy (it was the port of the town of Cumae), and a winter and seaside resort for wealthy Romans; it declined later in competition with the Roman port of Ostia. The site is noted for its ruins, including harbor installations, amphitheater, houses, and temples (the so-called Temple of Serapis is really an ancient market-place).

*ydna* (pid'na). In ancient geography, a town in Macedonia, situated near the Thermaic Gulf, about 30 miles SW of Thessalonica. It is notable for the victory gained near it in 168 B.C. by the Romans under Aemilius Paulus over the Macedonians under Perseus, causing the overthrow of the Macedonian monarchy.

*ylae Ciliciae* (pī'lē si-lish'i-ē). Latin name of the *Cilician Gates*.

*ylus* (pī'lus). In ancient geography, a town in N Messenia, Greece, situated N and E of the Gulf of Navarino. The "sandy Pylus" of the *Iliad* and the *Odyssey*, it was about two and a half miles from the Bay of Pylus. (The bay has since been converted into a lagoon by a sandbar that blocks its mouth.) According to legend, this Pylus was founded by Pylas, who came into the region from Megara and whose companions were Leleges. It later fell into the hands of Neleus, who raised the city to such renown that Homer called it "the city of Neleus," and later into the hands of his son Nestor. In ancient times Pylus was a place of considerable importance. Nestor's palace was the peer, in size and wealth, of the palace of Agamemnon at Mycenae. Until 1939 the location of the palace of Nestor had been a matter of dispute; some placed it farther north, in Elis, and some placed it on the western promontory of the Gulf of Navarino that was known in ancient times as Coryphasium. In 1939 Prof. Carl W. Blegen, of the University of Cincinnati, located the palace of Nestor at Epano Englianos, a plateau about two and one-half miles from the modern village of Chora, when he and a Greek team uncovered the foundations and floor of the palace there. In 1952 and succeeding years, excavations under Prof. Blegen's direction have revealed the existence of a large palace dating from about 1300 B.C. Remains uncovered give a clear outline of the size and ground plan of the palace. Lying in a NW-SE direction on the plateau, the palace is roughly a huge rectangle that is divided lengthwise into three unequal parts. The central and largest portion is occupied, beginning at the SE end, by a portico, vestibule, great hall, and storage magazines. A narrow aisle on the southerly side has many small chambers On the northerly side a wider aisle holds, from the southeas to the northeast, the queen's apartments, a bathroom, stair ways to the upper floors, and more storage spaces. It i thought the palace had at least two stories, the walls of th first story being of soft limestone blocks, and those of th upper story being of crude brick. Fragments of pottery of al sizes and descriptions have been dug up. In one pantr alone, over 2800 drinking cups were found; these wer shaped like champagne glasses, and the number of them wa ascertained by counting the stems. The work of the excava tors has revealed that the floors and walls of the palace wer covered with plaster and decorated with paintings of dol phins, octopuses and other marine creatures, linear designs floral patterns, winged griffins, and human figures in armor The great hall, or throne room, was surrounded by an insid balcony from which the ladies, whose apartments were o the second floor, could observe the men. There was a intricate drainage system by which water from the roofs an terraces of the palace was collected and carried off by under ground limestone conduits. A large, circular, decorate hearth was found in the throne room where, presumably slices of bulls' thighs wrapped in fat were roasted whe Nestor entertained. A smaller circular hearth was found i the queen's apartments. Fragments of terra-cotta chimne pots to carry off the smoke from the hearth fires have als been discovered. The remains of a bathroom, in which ther was an unbroken tub, have also been found. In a wing con nected to the palace by a kind of ramp, another tub has bee located. A huge altar unearthed in a portico before this win indicates that this area may have been the household shrine One of the most important finds in the excavation of th palace was the discovery of what was apparently an archiv room. In this were hundreds of clay tablets and fragment inscribed with the Linear Script B. These tablets were th first to be found on the mainland of Greece and prove tha the Greeks had a written language at least as early as 130 B.C. At the time the tablets were found the Linear Script I so-named by Sir Arthur Evans who found it in Crete, had nc been deciphered. It was at last deciphered in 1952. Th inscriptions on the tablets list inventories of olive oil, whea figs, and other stores of the royal household, as well a

fat, fāte, fär, fåll, åsk, fâre; net, mē, hėr; pin, pīne; not, nōte, möv nôr; up, lūte, půll; oi, oil; ou out; (lightened) ēlect, agǫny, ůnit

accounts of work to be done and goods to be supplied to the palace. Pylus is in earthquake country. The stone blocks of the lower part of the walls were laid in courses that were separated, horizontally at least, by wooden beams that served as springs and took up the shock in case of earthquake. It is thought that olive oil stored in huge vessels in the palace caught fire, perhaps in an attack from outside, and burned with such heat that the wooden beams were ignited, burned, and the courses of stone collapsed. The height of the first story was calculated from counting the courses as they lay in parallel rows where they had fallen. That the palace was destroyed by fire is evident from the fused condition of the stone. The heat was so intense that the tablets of sun-dried clay in the archive room were baked to hardness and preserved. The site was never again occupied, so that the outline of the original structure has not been confused by the remains of later buildings, as at Mycenae and Tiryns. In the neighborhood of the palace many tombs have been discovered, some of which have been excavated. In them were found swords with ivory handles, bits of gold leaf, small art objects, and other funerary offerings. Skulls have been found that may even be those of the heroes of Homer. The modern seaport of Pylos, on a promontory at the SE end of the Gulf of Navarino, is a town founded early in the 19th century. In the neighborhood is a vast cave, with oddly shaped rock formations. This is said to be the cave where the cattle of Neleus and Nestor were kept. Because the sandy soil, whence its name "sandy Pylus," was unfit for growing grass, the cattle were driven to this area for grazing and were sheltered in this grotto. The modern Pylos has also been called *Navarino* and *Neocastro*.

*Pyrgi* (pir'jī). In ancient geography, a town of Etruria, situated on the coast W and N of Caere. It was celebrated for its rich temple of Leucothea which was plundered by Dionysius the Elder (384 B.C.).

*Pyrgos* (pir'gôs). [Also: *Pirgos*.] See *Letrini*.

# —Q—

*Quirinal* (kwir'i-nạl). [Latin, *Mons Quirinalis.*] Farthest north and the highest of the seven hills of ancient Rome, lying N of the Capitoline and NW of the Viminal. It takes its name from an old Sabine sanctuary of Quirinus.

# —R—

*Ragusa* (rä-gö'zä). See *Hybla Heraea.*

*Raphia* (rạ-fī'ạ). [Modern name, *Rafa.*] In ancient geography a city on the coast of Palestine, SW of Gaza. Near it Ptolemy IV defeated (217 B.C.) Antiochus III.

*Raudian Fields* (rô'di-ạn). [Latin, *Campi Raudii.*] In ancient geography, a noted plain in N Italy, probably near Vercelli but by some located near Verona. It was the scene of a battle in 101 B.C., in which the Cimbri were annihilated by the Romans.

*Ravenna* (rä-ven'nä). City in N Italy, about six miles from the Adriatic Sea. It was probably founded by the Etruscans, and came later (c191 B.C.) into the hands of the Umbrians and the Romans, who developed it into the chief naval station of the upper Adriatic coast. The historical importance of Ravenna really begins in 404 A.D., when because of its defensibility and the protection of the fleet, the emperor Honorius (395–425 A.D.) moved the imperial residence there.

*Reate* (rē-ā'tē). [Modern name, *Rieti.*] In ancient geography, a town of C Italy, situated on the Velino River, about 42 miles NE of Rome, in a region celebrated by Vergil and Cicero for its fertility. The town was the chief town of the Sabines.

*Reggio di Calabria* (rād'jō dē kä-lä'brē-ä). See *Rhegium.*

*Reggio nell'Emilia* (nel-lä-mē'lyä). See *Regium Lepidum.*

fat, fāte, fär, fåll, åsk, fāre; net, mē, hėr; pin, pīne; not, nōte, möv nôr; up, lūte, půll; oi, oil; ou out; (lightened) ēlect, agǫny, ūni

*Regillus* (rĕ-jil′us), *Lake.* In ancient geography, a small lake near Rome (perhaps near Frascati). It is traditionally the scene of a victory of the Romans over the Latins c496 B.C. that gave Rome preëminence in Latium.

*Regium* (rē′ji-um). See *Rhegium.*

*Regium Lepidum* (lep′i-dum). [Modern names, *Reggio nell′ Emilia, Reggio, Reggio Emilia.*] City in N Italy, supposed to have been founded by Marcus Aemilius Lepidus, c187 B.C., in the course of the construction of the Aemilian Way, on which it lies.

*Rhaetia* (rē′shạ). [Also: *Raetia.*] In ancient geography, a province of the Roman Empire. It was bounded by Vindelicia (at first included in it, but afterward made a separate province as Rhaetia Secunda) on the N, Noricum on the E, Italy on the S, and Helvetia on the W, corresponding to the modern canton of Graubünden, Switzerland, the N part of Tirol province, Austria, and part of the Bavarian and Lombard Alps. It was conquered by Tiberius and Drusus in 15 B.C., and was made a Roman province soon after.

*Rhaetian Alps* (rē′shạn alps). [Latin, *Alpes Raeticae.*] Term of varied signification, applied in ancient times to the mountainous regions of Rhaetia, but in modern times generally to the chain of the Alps extending from the neighborhood of the Splügen Pass to the valley of the Adda, divided by the Engadine and Bergell into the Northern and Southern Rhaetian Alps. Peak elevation, Piz Bernina (about 13,295 feet), in the Bernina group.

*Rhaetia Secunda* (sĕ-kun′dạ). See *Vindelicia.*

*Rhamnus* (ram′nös). In ancient geography, a place in Attica, at the head of a wooded glen overlooking the Euripus, and not far from Marathon. There were two temples here: one was a temple of Nemesis and the other, smaller one, was perhaps a temple of Themis. Nemesis was a goddess implacable to men of violence. Some say her wrath fell on the Persians who landed at Marathon (490 B.C.), and that she helped the Athenians defeat them because the Persians were so sure of defeating the Athenians that they brought marble with them to make a trophy. In her anger at their pride, Nemesis caused their defeat. Phidias used the marble they had brought with them to celebrate their victory to make a statue of Nemesis. On her head was a crown with deer and small images of Victory. In her left hand she held an apple branch;

in her right, a cup engraved with figures of Aethiopians. On the pedestal of the image Helen was shown being led by Nemesis, said by some to be her mother, to Leda. The temple of Nemesis here was a Doric hexastyle peripteros with 12 columns on the flanks, measuring 37 by 98 feet. The cella had pronaos and opisthodomos.

*Rhegium* (rē′ji-um) or *Regium*. [Modern name, *Reggio di Calabria*.] In ancient geography, a city in Bruttii, S Italy, situated on the Straits of Messina, on the tip of the toe of the Italian boot. The city was founded by Greek colonists in the 8th century B.C. as a sister city to Zancle, and became an important port and prosperous city. It was allied to Athens by treaty (433 B.C.) and took part with Athens in action against Syracuse (427 B.C.) which was waging war on the Athenian ally Leontini, but in the later Athenian expedition against Syracuse (415 B.C.) Rhegium remained neutral. In 391 B.C. the city was besieged by Dionysius the Elder, tyrant of Syracuse, who not only wanted it for its dominating position on the straits, but also desired to punish Rhegium for an insulting refusal to give him a maiden of their city in marriage. At the time, the Italian cities came to the aid of Rhegium, and the siege was raised. Two years later (389 B.C.), in the continuing struggle with Dionysius, Rhegium was compelled to surrender her fleet, and in 387 B.C. he besieged the city. The inhabitants held out for ten months when they were compelled by starvation to surrender. Those who could not raise the money to ransom themselves were sold into slavery. The city was soon rebuilt and its activity as a port revived. In 280 B.C. the city was seized and its male inhabitants massacred following the revolt of a Roman mercenary garrison that had been admitted within the walls during the invasion of Italy by Pyrrhus. In 270 B.C. the Romans successfully besieged it and freed it from the mercenaries. Rhegium remained a loyal ally of Rome throughout the Punic Wars. It kept its Greek character into the time of the Roman Empire.

*Rhenia* (rē′ni-a̤). In ancient geography, an uninhabited island near Delos, thought by some to be the island once known as Ortygia, where Artemis was born. The island served as a graveyard for the Delians, since no one was allowed to die or to be buried in the sacred island of Delos. When Polycrates, tyrant of Samos, captured Rhenia he dedicated it

Apollo and bound it to Delos with a chain.

***Rhipaei Montes*** (ri-pē'ī mon'tēz). Range of snowy mountains supposed by the ancient Greeks to be at the extreme north of the world. Their exact location was never agreed upon. As the area of the known world increased, they were pushed farther and farther north. They did not finally disappear from maps until the Renaissance.

***Rhodes*** (rōdz). [Greek: ***Rhodos, Rodos;*** Italian, ***Rodi;*** Latin, ***Rhodus.***] Island in the Aegean Sea, SW of Asia Minor and separated from the coast by a channel about seven miles wide. One of the Dodecanese Islands, it is about 45 miles long and about 545 square miles in area. The surface is mountainous and hilly. It is noted for its fertility and has an active commerce. The inhabitants are largely Greek. According to traditional accounts, Rhodes was first inhabited by the Telchines, who nursed the infant Poseidon there. When he grew up he fell in love with Halia, a sister of the Telchines, and by her had six sons and one daughter, Rhode or Rhodos. These six sons outraged the goddess Aphrodite and committed other evil deeds. To punish them, Aphrodite drove them mad, and Poseidon sank them under the ground. Some say that when Zeus was parceling out the lands to the gods he absentmindedly forgot to award any to Helius, and when he thought of it, he was distressed. Helius offered to take an island that was just then rising from the great flood Zeus had sent over the world. Helius went there and found Poseidon's daughter Rhode, with whom he fell in love and for whom he named the island Rhodes. Thus, the island came to be known as "the Bride of the Sun." Rhodes is the scene of many myths and legends. Danaus, fleeing with his daughters from Egypt, stopped there and founded a temple of Athena at Lindus. Cadmus, searching for Europa, also touched at the island. He founded a temple to Poseidon in fulfillment of a vow he had made during a storm at sea, and also dedicated a bronze cauldron inscribed with Phoenician letters. According to some accounts, this was how the Phoenician alphabet was brought to the Greek world. Althaemenes, the son of Catreus of Crete, fled to Rhodes to escape an oracle that predicted he would kill his father. He built a temple to Zeus on Mount Atybrus, the highest point on the island, from which it was claimed he could see his beloved homeland. The flight of Althaemenes to Rhodes and his settlement there provide a legendary explanation for prehistoric colonization of the island by Cretans. Tlepolemus, the son of Heracles, also sought refuge on Rhodes, and became its king before he sailed to join Agamemnon in the war against Troy. His followers founded the three cities of Lindus, Camirus, and Ialysus and laid the legendary basis for the Dorian invasion of Rhodes about 1000 B.C. Some say that Helen, after the death of Menelaus, fled from Sparta because of the enmity with which she was regarded, and sought asylum in Rhodes with her former friend Polyxo, wife of Tlepolemus. But Polyxo now hated her because of the death of Tlepolemus in the Trojan War, and inspired her maids to hang Helen. At one time Rhodes was so infested by serpents that it was called "Ophidea." The inhabitants sent to the oracle of Apollo at Delphi for relief, and were told to admit Phorbas, son of Lapithes, to colonize the island. The Rhodians sent for Phorbas, who came with his companions and destroyed the serpents. After his death he was accorded a hero's honors by the grateful people. Some say the three chief cities of the island—Ialysus, Lindus, and Camirus—were named for three daughters of Danaus who died there. Others say they were named for three grandsons of Helius, and that they founded the cities after a great flood and divided the island into three parts, each of the cities being the center of the area which each of the brothers ruled.

In prehistoric times Rhodes was colonized by Phoenicians and Cretans, and later by Dorians, and its three cities formed, with Halicarnassus, Cnidus, and Cos, the "Dorian Hexapolis." At the beginning of the 6th century B.C. the island fell under the domination of the Persians. After the Persian War it joined the first Athenian Confederacy, 478 B.C., from which it withdrew by revolt at the end of the 5th century. In 408 B.C. Lindus, Ialysus, and Camirus founded the city of Rhodes on the NE tip of the island. The new city became the capital, replacing Lindus, and rapidly grew into a flourishing commercial, religious, and political center thanks to its location and its wide commerce throughout the Mediterranean. The city later came under the influence of Sparta, from which it freed itself in 394 B.C. In 378 it entered the second Athenian Confederacy, from which it withdrew in 356 B.C. After the death of Alexander the Great, who had imposed a garrison on Rhodes as an ally of Persia against the Macedonians, the Rhodians allied themselves to Egypt and successfully withstood a year's siege by the Macedonians. Following this success, Rhodes entered into relations with Rome, and it was in this period that it reached the height of its importance and influence. Its commerce was carried on throughout the Mediterranean world. The code of maritime law developed by Rhodes was so good that 300 years later the Emperor Augustus adopted it for his entire empire. The city became an outstanding artistic and literary center. Lysippus the sculptor made his famous *Chariot of the Sun* there, and a distinctive Rhodian school of sculpture developed that numbered among its members Chares of Lindus, who made the famous *Colossus of Rhodes;* Philiscus, author of a group of the Muses; Apollonius and Tauriscus of Tralles, who executed the famous statue of the Dirce group, the so-called *Farnese Bull;* and Athenodorus, Polydorus, and Agesander, creators of the massive *Laocoön* group. Aeschines, the Athenian exile, founded a school of rhetoric at Rhodes that was later attended by Cato, Cicero, Caesar, Brutus, and other Romans. Splendid examples of Mycenaean pottery, dating from the 10th century B.C. and earlier have been found at Rhodes, and a distinctive style of glazed vases decorated with deer, the lotus flower, palm trees, and geometric designs, was in full flower by the 7th and 6th centuries B.C. The island was wholly sacred to Helius. Chariot-races, athletic and musical contests were held annually in the summer at the festival celebrated in his honor. Four horses were hurled into the sea each year at the festival as a sacrifice to him. About 278 B.C. the colossal bronze statue by Chares of Lindus was erected to Helius. This *Colossus,* one of the Seven Wonders of the ancient world, stood on the breakwater which protected the harbor of the city of Rhodes. It stood until 224 B.C., when it was hurled down by an earthquake; its fragments were melted down in 656 A.D. Augustus recognized Rhodes as a city allied to Rome. The emperor Vespasian incorporated it into the Roman Empire.

**Rhodope** (rod′ō̇-pē) *Mountains.* Mountains of NE Greece, sacred to Dionysus. According to legend, Rhodope was the wife of Haemus, king of Thrace, who was changed into a mountain because she considered herself more beautiful than Hera.

*Rieti* (rye′tē). Modern name of *Reate.*
*Rimini* (rē′mē-nē). Modern name of *Ariminum.*
*Rion* (rē-ôn′). See *Phasis,* river.
*Rodope* or *Rodopi* (rod-ō′pē). See *Rhodope Mountains.*
*Rome* (rōm). City in C Italy, the capital and center of the
Roman republic and empire of ancient times. It is situated
on both banks of the Tiber River, about 15 miles from its
mouth. Evidence exists of settlements on the site dating
from c1000 B.C. The legendary date of the foundation of the
city is April 21, 753 B.C., when Romulus, the first king of
Rome, built his settlement on the Palatine Hill known as
*Roma Quadrata* (Square Rome) because the fortifications of
his settlement enclosed it in a square. To gain wives for his
followers Romulus invited the Sabines to a celebration of
sacred games and, in the midst of it, captured the women
and drove off the men. The women brought about a recon-
ciliation between the Romans and Sabines; the latter were
united in one race with the Romans and took up settlements
on the Capitoline and Quirinal Hills, the former of which
was added to the city. The area between the Palatine and
Capitoline served as a common Forum. Traditionally, the
seven kings of Rome were: Romulus (753–715 B.C.); Numa
Pompilius (715–672 B.C.); Tullus Hostilius (672–640 B.C.)
who destroyed Alba Longa, joined the Albans to the Romans, and added the Caelian Hill to the city; Ancus Marcius
(640–616 B.C.), who added the Aventine Hill, the Janiculum
and the port of Ostia; Tarquinius Priscus (616–578 B.C.)
who laid out the Circus Maximus; Servius Tullius (578–534
B.C.), who added the Quirinal and Viminal Hills and, so
some say, the Esquiline Hill also, and built the Servian Wall
that enclosed all the seven hills of Rome; and Tarquinius
Superbus (534–510 B.C.), who laid the foundations of the
temple of Capitoline Jupiter, and who was expelled by
Lucius Junius Brutus, the founder of the Roman Republic
(509 B.C.). The early history of the Republic is one of almost
continuous warfare with the various tribes of Italy and with
the Gauls of the north. About 390 B.C. the Gauls, under
Brennus, captured and burned the city. It was hastily rebuilt
as soon as the Gauls were driven out. By 265 B.C., having
defeated the Etruscan and Latin federations, the Samnite
tribes, and the Greek cities in S Italy, Rome had become the
ruler of Italy, which was ultimately linked to the city by a

fat, fāte, fär, fâll, àsk, fãre; net, mē, hèr; pin, pīne; not, nōte, mõve
nôr; up, lūte, pùll; oi, oil; ou out; (lightened) ēlect, agǫny, ūnite

network of magnificent roads. Among the many splendid roads were the Appian Way (Via Appia), which ran south and terminated at Brundisium, the Flaminian Way (Via Flaminia), running northeast to Ariminum on the Adriatic Sea, the Aurelian Way (Via Aurelia), running northwest to Pisa and continued by Augustus into Gaul, and the Latin Way (Via Latina), which was an inland road that ran south and joined the Appian Way at Capua. Rome clashed with Carthage, the leading maritime power of the Mediterranean, in the three Punic Wars (264–241 B.C., 218–201 B.C., and 149–146 B.C.), and with the final defeat of Carthage became not only the dominant sea power in the Mediterranean, but also the most powerful state in the ancient world.

By 61 B.C., when Julius Caesar became propraetor in Spain, Rome held sway over all Italy, Narbonensis, all of Spain and Portugal except the north coast of the Iberian peninsula, North Africa from Carthage east to the Nile, Phoenicia, large areas of the Parthian empire, Media, Armenia, Pontus, Bithynia, much of Asia Minor, all of Greece, and the eastern shore of the Adriatic Sea. Under Caesar and, after the replacement of the Republic by the Empire, under Augustus, Trajan, and Hadrian, Rome became the capital of a dominion which encompassed at its height virtually all of the world as it was then known to most people: the entire Mediterranean basin; to the N, Gaul, Britain, and what was later to be W Germany and the Netherlands along the banks of the Rhine River; the Alpine countries; to the E the Danube basin down to the Black Sea, the Balkans, Greece, Asia Minor, Syria, and Palestine; the North African shore from Egypt to Morocco; and all of Spain and Portugal. The Roman legions were unquestionably the best disciplined and most effective major military force known in the world to that time. The fact that they did not penetrate to India, as did the army of Alexander the Great, is probably chiefly attributable to what was long a basic Roman strategic attitude toward its military efforts, namely that the legions should take, fortify, and hold territory, which would then be developed and colonized as integral portions of a single economic and (eventually) cultural unit. Compared to those of the early Roman emperors, Alexander's conquests were a brilliant military tour de force, but comprised an empire which it was far beyond actual Macedonian power to hold

obscured) errant, ardent, actor; ch, chip; g, go; th, thin; ᴛʜ, then; y, you; variable) d̩ as d or j, ş as s or sh, t̩ as t or ch, z̧ as z or zh.

together. The Romans, who understood far better than anyone before them the logistic perils of too extended lines of communication, were not interested, for most of their history, in conquests which could not be consolidated and brought within the defensible empire. The existence of India and China was certainly known to the scholars and geographers of Rome under the emperors, but the thought of bringing them into the Empire was hardly one which would occur to leaders as shrewd and thrifty, in a military sense, as the early Roman emperors. It was during the period of early and middle Empire that the wealth of all these countries poured into Rome, and that the buildings which became the admiration of the centuries were erected.

Among the many existing remains of the Roman city are the Forum Romanum, with the arches of Titus, Septimius Severus, and Constantine, the Flavian Amphitheater or "Colosseum," Forum of Trajan, the temples of Concord, Fortune, Saturn, and Neptune, the Basilica of Constantine, the palace of Caligula, Christian and Jewish catacombs, and others; the Thermae (Baths) of Diocletian are near the Central Station; outside the old Servian Wall are the Theater of Marcellus, the well-preserved Pantheon, the Mausoleum of Augustus, and the Thermae (Baths) of Caracalla; the monument of Hadrian is on the right bank of the Tiber River.

*Rubi* (rö'bē). [Modern name, *Ruvo di Puglia*.] In ancient geography, a town of Apulia, SE Italy. Many ancient Apulian vases of the 5th–2nd centuries B.C. have been discovered here.

*Rubicon* (rö'bi-kon). In ancient geography, a small river in Italy, near Rimini. In the later Roman Republic it was the boundary between Italy proper and Cisalpine Gaul. The crossing of it by Julius Caesar, in 49 B.C., took place despite contrary orders to Caesar from the Senate, and signalized Caesar's irrevocable decision to proceed against Pompey, which meant civil war. From this event, the phrase "cross the Rubicon" has since come to describe any act or decision of irrevocable import. It has been identified with the Rugone, Uso, and Fiumicino rivers.

*Rufia* (rö-fyä'). See *Alpheus River*.

*Rusellae* (rö-sel'ē). In ancient geography, a city of the Etruscan League, situated near the Umbro (Ombrone) River about six miles NE of what is now Grosseto. It was conquered (c300 B.C.) by the Romans. There are various remains of antiquity on the site.

***Ruvo di Puglia*** (rö′vō dē pö′lyä). See ***Rubi.***

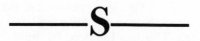

***Sabine Mountains*** (sā′bīn). Range of mountains E of Rome, near the E border of Latium. It is a branch of the Apennines. The highest point in the range is about 4200 feet.

***Sacer*** (sā′sėr), ***Mons.*** Latin name of the ***Sacred Mount.***

***Sacred Mount.*** [Latin, ***Mons Sacer.***] Hill about three miles NE of Rome, beyond the Anio (Aniene) River. It is noted in Roman history as the place of temporary emigrations of the plebeians, undertaken in order to extort civil privileges. The first (c494 B.C.) led to the establishment of the tribunate; the second (449 B.C.) resulted in the abolition of the decemvirate.

***Sacriportus*** (sak-ri-pōr′tus). In ancient geography, a locality in Latium, Italy, near Praeneste. Here Sulla decisively defeated (82 B.C.) the forces of the younger Marius.

***Saepinum*** (sē-pī′num). [Modern name, ***Altilia.***] Small place in C Italy about 20 miles N of Beneventum. The Roman walls of the ancient town remain practically perfect.

***Saguntum*** (sạ-gun′tum). [Modern name, ***Sagunto.***] In ancient geography, a town in E Spain, situated near the Mediterranean Sea, about 15 miles N of what is now Valencia. A Roman theater and the ruins of an ancient citadel are preserved; there are scattered remains also from the Iberian, Carthaginian, and Moorish periods. The ancient town, according to legend founded by Greeks, actually is more likely to have been an Iberian town. Around 228 B.C. the town, disturbed by the growth of Carthaginian power, concluded an alliance with Rome. The Carthaginian leader Hannibal attacked the town in 219 B.C. and conquered it after a siege of eight months. The Romans rebuilt the town after 214 B.C., but it failed to regain its former importance.

***Salamis*** (sal′ạ-mis). [Also: ***Koulouri.***] Island of Greece, in the Saronic Gulf, S of Attica and opposite the harbor of Athens.

It is about ten miles long. The island was said to have been named for Salamis, daughter of the river-god Asopus. In early times, Salamis was independent, and was contended for by the Megarians and Athenians; for whichever of the two cities controlled Salamis menaced the other city. Solon aroused the Athenians to "recover" Salamis. A force was organized, of which Pisistratus was one of the generals. Under his command, Nisaea, the Megarian port opposite Salamis, was taken. This was followed by the occupation of the island itself. The Megarians and Athenians made peace and agreed to submit their dispute to arbitration. The Spartans, called on to judge the merit of their claims, awarded the island to Athens (c596 B.C.) because of the lines in the *Iliad* that connect Salamis and Athens, they read:

Ajax from Salamis led his warships; twelve was the number,

Led them and stationed them where the Athenians stood in battalions.

After the destruction of Athens in the Persian War the Persian fleet of Xerxes assembled off Salamis, with the intention of engaging the Greek fleet. The Athenians had withdrawn to the island with their families before the Persian advance on Athens, and wanted to make a stand against them there. The Greeks of the Peloponnesus were reluctant to fight, as they thought, for the benefit of the Athenians, and preferred to protect the Peloponnesus by constructing a great wall across the isthmus. Themistocles, the great Athenian commander, feared that the vote in the assembly would go against his plan to fight at Salamis, and that the allies would elect instead to withdraw and defend the Peloponnesus. He first threatened to withdraw the Athenian fleet and when that failed to change the plans of his allies, he resorted to stratagem. He sent a confidential messenger to the Persians to tell them that the Greeks were disorganized and in panic, as indeed they were, and to advise them that this would be the time to attack. The Persians promptly accepted the advice. They sent a force to occupy the island of Psyttalia, which lies between the jutting promontory of Salamis and the mainland, ordered their Egyptian allies to sail around Salamis and cut off a Greek retreat through the Bay of Eleusis, and moved their own ships in to block the Greeks behind the island of Psyttalia. While the Greeks, unaware of these

fat, fāte, fär, fâll, àsk, fãre; net, mē, hėr; pin, pīne; not, nōte, möve, nôr; up, lūte, pùll; oi, oil; ou out; (lightened) ĕlect, agǫny, ūnite;

maneuvers, were still disputing in council, Aristides arrived from Aegina and announced that it was now too late to argue, as they were surrounded. Themistocles had chosen the narrow waters of Salamis for the engagement with the Persians because it was best suited to the Greek ships, and in the narrow space the Persian ships would be at a disadvantage. In addition to his determination to protect Megara, Aegina, and Salamis, which would be abandoned if the Greeks withdrew to the Peloponnesus, he considered the strait of Salamis the ideal spot and opportunity for a decisive battle with the Persians. Demaratus, the Spartan king who had been exiled and who had fled to the court of Xerxes, accompanied him on his expedition into Greece. Some say that before the battle of Salamis he was walking with an Athenian exile in the plain near Athens. They observed a huge dust storm, raised as if by the feet of thousands of marching men, rising in the direction of Eleusis, and out of it they heard a great cry, like the cry given at the festival of Eleusis. Demaratus asked his Athenian companion what the dust and the cry could mean. The Athenian answered that it was a token of disaster for the forces of Xerxes, for as there were no men where the dust rose it must have come by divine means, and the cry was certainly a divine one; and since both came from Eleusis it was a message of good fortune for Athens. If the dust moved off in the direction of the Peloponnesus it indicated defeat for the land forces of Xerxes; if it went toward the ships it indicated disaster for the fleet. As the two watched the dust formed a great cloud, rose in the air, and moved toward the ships. Now Demaratus and his companion knew that the fleet of Xerxes would suffer defeat, but they decided not to tell Xerxes of the omen, lest in his anger he cut off their heads. When the Greeks saw that they no longer had a choice they prepared for battle. At dawn, Sept. 20, 480 B.C., the Greeks put to sea in their fleet. The Persians attacked, and at once the Greeks started to back water as Themistocles had told them to do to lure the Persians through the narrow strait. Then one ship, either Athenian or Aeginetan, darted out from the line and attacked the enemy. As it was engaged the other Greek ships came to its aid and battle was joined. Some say that at this time a phantom in the shape of a woman appeared to the Greeks and cheered them on in a voice that was heard from one end of the line to the other, but first she rebuked them, saying, "Strange men, how long are you going to back water?" And some say that Cychreus appeared in serpent form during the battle and aided the Greek fleet. The Persians fought bravely, for Xerxes was watching the battle from the mainland, but their heavy ships were unable to maneuver in the narrow space, and those in the van who tried to withdraw were soon entangled with those that were eagerly forcing their way forward from the rear. By the end of the day a large part of the fleet was either destroyed or disabled. The Persians were compelled to withdraw to Phalerum, having suffered an overwhelming and decisive defeat. After the Persian War Salamis remained under Athenian control until it passed to Macedon in 318 B.C.; it was restored to Athens c230 B.C.

**Salamis.** In ancient geography, a city on the E coast of Cyprus, near what is now Famagusta. Teucer, the half-brother of Telamonian Ajax, was banished by his father on his return to Salamis from the Trojan War, because he had not brought back the bones of Ajax for burial. He sailed to Cyprus and was given permission to found a city, which he named Salamis after his homeland. In the Roman period the city was rebuilt as Constantia. Near it, a naval victory was gained (306 B.C.) by Demetrius Poliorcetes over Ptolemy I and his allies.

**Salembria** (sạ-lem'bri-ạ). See *Peneus.*

**Salentinum Promontorium** (sal-ẹn-tī'num prom-ọn-tō'ri-um). A Latin name of *Santa Maria di Leuca, Cape.*

**Salerno** (sạ-lêr'nō), *Gulf of.* [Also: *Gulf of Paestum;* Italian, *Golfo di Salerno.*] Arm of the Mediterranean Sea, on the W coast of Italy, SE of the Bay of Naples.

**Salernum** (sạ-lêr'num). [Modern name, *Salerno.*] Town in S Italy, situated on the Gulf of Salerno SE of Naples. It became a Roman colony in 194 B.C.

**Salina** (sä-lē'nä). [Ancient name, *Didyme.* ] One of the Lipari Islands, in the Mediterranean Sea about four miles NW of Lipari. Length, about six miles.

**Salonika** (sal-ō-nē'kạ, sạ-lon'i-kạ). [Also: *Salonica, Saloniki, Thessalonike, Thessaloniki.*] See *Thessalonica.*

**Salonika, Gulf of.** See *Thermaic Gulf.*

**Samarkand or Samarcand** (sam-ạr-kand'). See *Maracanda.*

**Same** (sä'mē). Another name for Cephallenia, an island in the

Ionian Sea west of the Gulf of Corinth. Under this name it is mentioned in the Odyssey as the home of some of Penelope's suitors.

**Samicon** (sam'i-kǫn) of **Samicum** (-kum). In ancient geography, a city of Triphylia in Elis, Greece, situated on a high plateau of Mount Makistos. It was the meeting place of the six Minyan cities of Triphylia, and was noted for its temple of Samian Poseidon. Still visible are parts of the fortifications, built by the Eleans as a defense against the Spartans and Arcadians, probably in the 4th century B.C.

**Samnium** (sam'ni-um). In ancient geography, a mountainous district in C Italy. It was bounded by the country of the Marsi, Paeligni, and Frentani on the N, Apulia on the E, Lucania on the S, Campania on the SW, and Latium on the W, and was originally inhabited by the Samnites.

**Samos** (sā'mos). Island in the Aegean Sea, off the W coast of Asia Minor, from which it is separated by a narrow strait; colonized by Ionians, c1100–1000 B.C. The island, with an area of 181 square miles, is mountainous (highest point, 4725 feet), but has land of notable fertility. Samos was one of the chief seats of the worship of Hera, and one of her most ancient temples was here. It was raised, some say, by the Argonauts, and the ancient image within it was brought by them from Colchis. In the time of Herodotus the temple of Hera on Samos was the largest then known. Among the offerings in the temple was an embossed bronze bowl, sent by the Spartans as a gift to Croesus, king of Lydia. The Spartans claimed the Samians stole the bowl when the ship carrying it to Croesus touched at their port. The Samians said it arrived in their island after Croesus had been defeated by Cyrus, and that it was sold by the Spartans to some Samians, who then offered it to the temple. Amasis, king of Egypt, sent two wooden statues of himself to the temple, because of his friendship with Polycrates, tyrant of Samos. A linen corselet, in which was woven the figures of many animals and which was embroidered in gold and silver thread, was also dedicated in the temple. This was also a gift of the Spartans, but it had been intended for Amasis, and the Spartans said the Samians stole it. Mandrocles, a Samian engineer, built a bridge across the Bosporus for Darius when he was preparing to march against Thrace. Darius honored him with great gifts, part of which Mandrocles used to have a picture painted in the temple of Hera. The picture showed the bridge, with Darius sitting on a seat of honor and watching his army cross over into Thrace. Under the picture was the following inscription:

The fish-fraught Bosporus bridged, to Hera's fane
Did Mandrocles this proud memorial bring;
When for himself a crown he'd skill to gain,
For Samos praise, contenting the Great King.

The Samians were great sailors, and ventured as far west as Tartessus. With part of the proceeds of such a voyage they caused to be made a bronze vessel, with griffins embossed on it, and resting on three ten-foot kneeling figures wrought of bronze; this they dedicated in the temple. Ionians and Epidaurians colonized Samos in very early times, and it became a flourishing commercial and shipping center. Polycrates made himself master of the island c540 B.C., built up a great fleet, captured many of the neighboring islands, and overcame the Lesbians in a sea fight. He compelled his Lesbian prisoners, weighted down with chains, to dig a moat around his castle. In making himself master of Samos he caused many prominent men to go into exile. They sought help from Sparta to secure their return and overthrow Polycrates. The Spartans, to punish the Samians for the theft of the bronze vessel intended for Croesus and the theft of the linen corselet intended for Amasis, agreed to help the exiled Samians. The Corinthians, because of an old grievance, joined the Spartans. They assembled a fleet and besieged Samos. When the place had not fallen after a siege of 40 days the Spartans and their allies withdrew and sailed back to the Peloponnesus. Polycrates, who had slain one of his brothers and banished another, Syloson, in winning control of Samos, had an alliance of friendship with Amasis, king of Egypt. According to legend, this friendship was broken off by Amasis because he feared lest the unfailing good fortune of Polycrates bring down on him the wrath of the gods, who are ever jealous of and seek to humble the pride of men. Legend aside, the friendship between Samos and Egypt ended during the reign of the successor of Amasis, when Polycrates offered his aid to Cambyses, the enemy of Egypt.

The Samians were great and daring sailors, versatile traders, and under Polycrates maintained a luxurious court of which the poet Anacreon was an ornament. During his rule some remarkable feats of engineering were executed. An underground aqueduct over 1000 feet long beneath a hill 900 feet high was constructed to bring water into the city. He completed the magnificent temple of Hera, the largest of its time. Another engineering triumph carried out by the Samians was the construction of a great mole to protect their harbor. The fears of Amasis that the gods would bring evil to his too fortunate friend Polycrates were fulfilled. Oroetes, the Persian satrap at Magnesia, lured him there with the promise of great treasure for his fleet, seized him upon his arrival, and caused him to be slain. Maeandrius, successor of Polycrates, raised an altar to Zeus the Protector of Freedom and prepared to grant Samos a democratic government, but when he saw that if he gave up the tyranny someone else would seize it, he kept his despotic power. Samos was the first city, Greek or barbarian, to fall under the sway of Darius I. Some say Darius attacked Samos as a favor to Syloson, banished brother of Polycrates. This Syloson had performed a friendly act for Darius while the latter was still unknown and powerless. When Darius became king of the Persians Syloson reminded him of the incident and asked the return of Samos as a reward. Henceforth Samos was subject to the Persians. During the Ionian Revolt the Samians rose, and engaged their fleet with other Ionian units in defense of Miletus, but in consequence of an agreement made by the Samian captains with the Persians, when the battle was joined all but 11 of the Samian ships deserted their Ionian allies and sailed away (494 B.C.). This treachery was humiliating to many Samians. Furthermore, they did not enjoy living under Persian dominion. They honored the captains who had remained to fight with their allies, and then many of them left Samos and went to settle in Zancle in Sicily. Samos remained under Persian control, and fought, at the battle of Salamis (480 B.C.), under Persian command. The following spring the Persian fleet mustered at Samos, but by this time the Samians had had enough of Persian rule. They sent envoys to the Spartan admiral Leotychides, urging him to free the Ionian cities, promising that the Ionians would rise up, and assuring him of the friendship and help of Samos. Leotychides agreed; some say he was convinced by the good omen that appeared in the name of the Samian envoy: he was Hegesistratus, "Leader of Ar-

mies." The Greek fleet sailed and when it appeared off
Samos the Persians, rather than risk battle, withdrew to join
their land army at Mycale opposite Samos. As the Greeks
pursued them and prepared to engage them on land, the
Persians disarmed the Samians who were in their army.
They suspected them of complicity, because they could not
help but note that the Samians had ransomed many
Athenian prisoners taken by the Persians and returned them
to Greece. Even though disarmed, the Samians did all in
their power to help the Greeks at Mycale, and the Persians
suffered a disastrous defeat (479 B.C.). After the Persian War
Samos was one of the leading maritime members of the
Confederacy of Delos, from which it revolted, 440 B.C. Pericles besieged it, 439 B.C., put down the revolt and established a democratic government there. In the last years of
the Peloponnesian Wars it was one of the most faithful
friends of Athenian democracy, but afterward it was besieged by the Spartan Lysander, who restored the oligarchy
(404 B.C.), and fell under Spartan influence. It was retaken
by Athens, 366 B.C., and colonized by Athenians. After the
death of Alexander the Great it fell to the sway of his general, Ptolemy, later bowed to Philip V of Macedon, was given
by the Romans (189 B.C.) to the kings of Pergamum, and
became part of the Roman province of Asia, 133 B.C. Mark
Antony captured and sacked it, 39 B.C., and Augustus restored its freedom. Among the famous sons of Samos were
the philosopher Pythagoras, the astronomer Conon, and the
sculptor and architect Rhoecus, who is said to have invented
casting in bronze and who was the architect of the famous
temple of Hera.

*Samos.* [Also: *Same.*] Ancient city in Cephallenia.

*Samosata* (sạ-mos'ạ-tạ). In ancient geography, a fortified town
in Commagene, Syria, situated on the right bank of the
Euphrates; residence of the kings of Commagene and important commerical center. It was the birthplace of Lucian.

*Samothrace* (sam'ọ-thrās). [Also: *Khora, Samothrake, Samo-
thraki.*] Wild, rocky island in the N part of the Aegean Sea,
belonging to Greece, opposite the mouth of the Hebrus
River and NW of the island of Imbrus. The island was famed
in ancient times as the center of highly revered mysteries,
those of the Cabiri, concerning which little is known. The
rocky and difficult coast of the island, and the lack of anchor-

fat, fāte, fär, fåll, ȧsk, fãre; net, mē, hėr; pin, pīne; not, nōte, mȯve,
nôr; up, lūte, pùll; oi, oil; ou out; (lightened) ẹlect, agọny, ụnite;

ages, protected it from invasion, rendered it politically unimportant, and conserved the ancient mysteries intact. These mysteries assumed great importance under the Hellenistic rulers, and came to rival those of Eleusis in importance. It was when he went to Samothrace to be initiated into the mysteries that Philip II met Olympias, who became his wife and the mother of Alexander the Great. Arsinoë Philadelphus, the daughter of Ptolemy I who married her brother Ptolemy II, was banished to Samothrace and became patroness of the sanctuary. She subsequently escaped and married Ptolemy II, but continued her benefactions to Samothrace. She and Ptolemy dedicated the most important buildings on the island. Perseus, last king of Macedonia, fled to Samothrace after his defeat by Aemilius Paulus (168 B.C.) and sought refuge in the sanctuary; he was captured there and taken prisoner. At Samothrace a French expedition found (1863) the famous statue called the *Victory of Samothrace,* now in the Louvre. Among the remains discovered on the island are the ruins of a temple dating from the 6th century B.C., ruins of a later temple, probably that dedicated by Ptolemy II, and a few rows of seats of an ancient theater. A New York University expedition directed by Karl Lehmann has, in a number of excavation campaigns since 1939, exposed the central area of the sanctuary. The area of the island is about 71 square miles; its highest point, 5248 feet.

**Santa Maria di Leuca** (sän′ta mä-rē′ä dē le′ö-kạ), *Cape.* [Also: *Cape Leuca;* Latin, *Salentinum Promontorium.*] Cape at the SE extremity of Italy.

**Santa Maura** (mou′rạ). See *Leucas.*

**Santorin** (san-tō-rēn′). See *Thera.*

**Sardinia** (sär-din′i-ạ). [Italian, *Sardegna;* Greek: *Ichnousa* or *Ichnusa, Sardo;* Latin, *Sardinia.*] Island in the Mediterranean Sea, situated between Corsica and Tunisia, about 150 miles W of the Italian mainland. The surface is largely mountainous, particularly in the E part of the island. It has an area of 9302 square miles. It was called Ichnusa by the Greeks who traded there in ancient times, because it is shaped like a man's footprint *(ichnos).* Sardinia was conquered by the Carthaginians (c500 B.C.) and the Romans (238 B.C.). According to legend, there were no snakes and no wolves on the island, and only one poisonous plant. This plant was something like celery, and those who ate of it were said to die laughing, hence the expression, "sardonic laughter."

***Sardis*** (sär'dis). [Also: ***Sardes***.] In ancient geography, the capital of Lydia, Asia Minor, situated at the foot of Mount Tmolus, on the Pactolus near the Hermus. It was a flourishing city under Croesus. Cyrus the Great defeated the forces of Croesus before the walls of Sardis (546 B.C.), and after a short siege took the city. According to Herodotus, Croesus, who had been rescued from a blazing funeral pyre, watched the Persians plundering Sardis. He turned to Cyrus and asked, "What is it, Cyrus, which those men yonder are doing so busily?" "Plundering your city," Cyrus replied, "and carrying off your riches." "Not my city," answered Croesus, "nor my riches. They are not mine any more. It is your wealth which they are pillaging." Cyrus was so struck by this view he halted the plundering. In the revolt of the Ionian cities against Darius (499 B.C.) the Athenians and Eretrians marched with a revolting Ionian force to Sardis and burned the city (c498 B.C.). The Athenians and Eretrians then returned home, but the burning of Sardis brought the wrath of Darius on the Greeks of Europe and was an important cause of the Persian Wars against Greece. The city was rebuilt and became the residence of the Persian satraps of W Asia. It submitted to Alexander the Great without a struggle in 334 B.C. The tomb of Alyattes at Sardis is a conical tumulus 1180 feet in diameter and 142 feet high, with a sloping base-revetment of massive masonry. The Temple of Cybele, a famous sanctuary, in its existing remains of Hellenistic date, was an Ionic dipteros of eight by 17 columns, with three ranges of columns on the front, and measured 144 by 261 feet. The columns are 6½ feet in diameter and about 58½ feet high.

***Sarmatia*** (sär-mā'shạ). In ancient geography, according to Ptolemy, a territory extending from the Vistula River on the W to the Rha (Volga) River on the E, and N to the Mare Suevicum (Baltic Sea). It comprised a large part of what is now S Russia and E Poland, and was occupied by the Sauromatae and Scythians.

***Sarnus*** (sär'nus). In ancient geography, a small river in Italy, which flows into the Bay of Naples near Pompeii; the modern Sarno. Near it the Goths were totally defeated (553 or 552 A.D.) by the Romans.

***Saronic Gulf*** (sạ-ron'ik). Arm of the Aegean Sea, lying SW of

Attica and NE of Argolis, Greece. It contains the islands of Salamis and Aegina. Also called Gulf of Aegina.

*Sarsina* (sär′si-na̱). In ancient geography, a town of C Italy, in Umbria. The Roman poet Plautus was born there, c251 B.C.

*Scione* (ski-ō′nē̱ or si-ō′nē̱). In ancient geography, a city on the Pallene peninsula, in Chalcidice. It revolted from Athens, 423 B.C., and gave allegiance to the Spartan general Brasidas. He was received as a hero there, covered with garlands, and crowned with a golden crown.

*Scylacium* (si-lā′shum) or *Scylaceum* (sil-a̱-sē′um). [Modern name, *Squillace*.] In ancient geography, a town on the coast of Bruttii, in the toe of the Italian boot, near the Gulf of Tarentum. It is mentioned in the *Aeneid* as "ship-wrecking," from its rocky coast. It was founded by Ionian colonists and became part of the dominions of Dionysius the Elder of Syracuse.

*Scylla* (sil′a̱). [Modern names, *Scilla* or *Sciglio*.] Promontory in S Italy, projecting into the Strait of Messina.

*Scyllaeum* (si-lē′um). In ancient geography, a promontory in Argolis, Greece, projecting into the Aegean: the easternmost point of the Peloponnesus. According to tradition, it was named for Scylla, who betrayed her father Nisus for love of Minos, king of Crete. When, thanks to Scylla's betrayal, Minos had defeated the forces of Nisus, he refused to take Scylla back with him to Crete, on the grounds that she was a parricide. Scylla swam out to his ship, but he ordered his men to drive her off. Some say she drowned, and that her body was washed up on this promontory, and that it was not buried but torn to pieces by sea birds. Others say she was transformed into a sea bird.

*Scyrus* (sī′rus) or *Scyros* (-ros). Island in the Aegean Sea about 25 miles E of Euboea. The island was conquered (469 B.C.) by the Athenians under Cimon, who also found there bones proclaimed to be those of Theseus. He restored them to Athens. Length of the island, about 19 miles.

*Scythia* (sith′i-a̱). In ancient geography, a name of varying meaning. It designated at first a region in what is now S European Russia and Rumania, inhabited by the Scythians. They resisted the invasion of Darius I of Persia. Since they had neither forts nor cities, carried their tents with them wherever they went, and were accustomed to fight from horseback, their method of avoiding destruction from in-

(obscured) errant, ardent, actor; ch, chip; g, go; th, thin; ᴛʜ, then; y, you;
(variable) d̠ as d or j, s̠ as s or sh, t̠ as t or ch, z̠ as z or zh.

vaders was to refuse to stand and make a fight. When Darius invaded their country they decided, according to Herodotus, not to meet the Persians in open conflict but to retreat by a distance of one day's march before the enemy, destroying the wells and driving off their cattle as they withdrew. In this way they led the Persians all over their land, never engaging them. Darius, at his wits' end at this strange manner of warfare, sent heralds to the Scythians. They sent back presents to him: a bird, a mouse, a frog, and five arrows. Asked the meaning of these presents, the Scythian herald refused to give it. They were at last interpreted in this way: unless the Persians could turn into birds and fly away, or into mice and burrow in the ground, or into frogs and retreat to the marshes, they would never escape from Scythia but would be killed by the Scythian arrows. Ultimately Darius came to the conclusion that this was indeed the case, and retreated from Scythia, without having subdued the country. After the time of Alexander the Great Scythia was subjugated by the Sarmatians and others. Later Scythia denoted N Asia and much of C Asia, divided by the Imaus Mountains into Scythia Intra Imaum and Scythia Extra Imaum. As a Roman province it comprised the lands immediately S of the mouths of the Danube.

*Scythica* (sith'i-ka̤), *Chersonesus*. An ancient name of the Crimea.

*Segesta* (sē-jes'ta̤). In ancient geography, a city in Sicily, situated near the coast, about 27 miles W of Panormus. According to some accounts, it was founded by Acestes, son of the Trojan woman Egesta and the river-god Crimisus, and was therefore Trojan, and not Greek, in origin. Segesta was often at war with Selinus, and was an ally of Athens in the Peloponnesian War, the disastrous Sicilian expedition of 415 B.C. of the Athenians being allegedly to aid Segesta. It became a dependent of Carthage c400 B.C., was sacked (307 B.C.) by Agathocles, and had its name changed to Dicaeopolis, and passed under Roman supremacy in the time of the First Punic War. There are ruins near the modern Alcamo and Calatafimi. The Greek temple, though never finished, is one of the most complete examples surviving. It is Doric, hexastyle, with 14 columns on the flanks, on a stylobate of four steps. The architectural details are of the best period. All the 36 peristyle columns are still standing, and the entablature and pediments are almost whole. There is also a Greek theater, of the 4th century B.C., with Roman modifications. In plan it is more than a semicircle; the diameter is 209 feet, that of the orchestra 54 feet; the length of the stage is 91 feet. The cavea is in great part rock-hewn.

*Segni* (sā'nyē). See *Signia.*

*Seistan* (sā-stän'). [Also: *Sistan.*] See *Drangiana.*

*Seleucia* (sē-lö'shạ). [Also: *Seleuceia.*] In ancient geography, a city in Cilicia, Asia Minor, situated near the coast, about 70 miles SW of Tarsus. There are remains of a Roman hippodrome.

*Seleucia.* [Also: *Seleuceia.*] In ancient geography, a city in N Pisidia, Asia Minor, near the frontier of Phrygia.

*Seleucia.* [Also: *Seleuceia;* sometimes called *Seleucia Pieria.*] In ancient geography, a city in Syria, situated on the coast N of the mouth of the Orontes: the port of Antioch. It was built by Seleucus I. There are many antiquities on the site.

*Seleucia.* [Also: *Seleuceia.*] In ancient geography, a city near the Tigris, about 17 miles below Baghdad. It was built largely from the ruins of Babylon by Seleucus I, 312 B.C., and was one of the largest cities of the East. It was plundered by Trajan, and was destroyed by Avidius Cassius in 164 A.D.

*Selinus* (sē-lī'nus). In ancient geography, a city in SW Sicily, situated near the coast about 48 miles SW of Panormus (Palermo), near what is now Castelvetrano. The city, named for the wild celery that abounds in the region, was the westernmost settlement of the Greeks in Sicily. It was built (c628 B.C.) by colonists from Megara and Hybla Minor and soon became rich and powerful. A quarrel between it and Segesta brought about the Athenian expedition (415 B.C.) to Sicily in the Peloponnesian War. In 410–409 B.C. the city was besieged by a huge Carthaginian force under Hannibal (grandson of Hamilcar), and after stubborn resistance was stormed and sacked. Most of the inhabitants were slaughtered, a few were sold into slavery, and a few escaped to Acragas. Selinus was the first of the Greek cities of Sicily to fall to Carthage. The following year it was rebuilt and fortified by Hermocrates, but under a treaty of 405 B.C. it became a subject city to Carthage. It never recovered its prosperity, and was utterly abandoned in the First Punic War when its few inhabitants were moved to Lilybaeum. Besides remains of the walls built by Hermocrates, the site retains the ruins of seven important Doric temples, several of them among the most archaic examples of the style known, and metopes, also in the archaic style, from an eighth temple have also been found. These temples were thrown down by earthquakes and lie in complete ruin, except that part of the peristyle of Temple "C" was restored some years ago, and since 1958 the complete peristyle and entablature of Temple "ER" have been spectacularly re-ërected from its fallen stones. The metopes are now in the museum at Palermo.

**Sellasia** (se̜-lā′zha̜). In ancient geography, a place in Laconia, Greece, a few miles NE of Sparta. Here the Lacedaemonians under Cleomenes III were totally defeated (222 B.C.) by the Macedonians and their allies under Antigonus III.

**Selymbria** (se-lim′bri-a̜). In ancient geography, a city on the north coast of the Propontis, founded in the 7th century B.C. by colonists from Megara.

**Sentinum** (sen-tī′num). In ancient geography, a city in Italy, near the Apennines, about 37 miles SW of Ancona, near what is now Sassoferrato. It is noted for the decisive victory gained (295 B.C.) there by the Romans under Quintus Fabius Maximus Rullianus and Publius Decius Mus over the allied Samnites and Gauls.

**Sepeia** (se̜-pī′a̜). In ancient geography, a place in Argolis, Greece, situated on the Gulf of Argolis, W of Nauplia. Cleomenes I, king of Sparta, believing he had received assurance from an oracle that he would take Argos, marched his forces to this place and prepared to attack (c494 B.C.). Such was the reputation of the Spartans that the Argives were terror-stricken. They could think of no plan to counter-attack or defend themselves and at length resolved that each time they heard the Spartan herald shout a command to the Spartan troops they would give the same command and execute the same maneuver. When Cleomenes observed their tactics he was at first perplexed but soon thought of a way to trick the Argives. He ordered his herald to shout the command to the Spartans to disarm and take their midday meal. The Argives thankfully gave the same command and fell to eating. Whereupon Cleomenes, who had secretly given another order, set upon the Argives and drove them headlong before him. They took refuge in a sacred grove. Cleomenes attempted to lure them out by calling out the names of the leading warriors and announcing that they had been ransomed. When they came out he seized them. The Argives within the grove learned from their scouts what was happening to those who responded to Cleomenes' call and thereafter refused to answer when they heard their names. Cleomenes did not wish to invade the sacred grove. Instead he set fire to it and burned the Argives who had sought sanctuary in it. Six thousand Argives perished. Afterward Cleomenes thought to inquire to whom the grove was sacred. When he learned it was sacred to Argus he concluded that the oracle was fulfilled, some say. He had taken Argus but would not take Argos. He withdrew his forces. From this disaster Argos never fully recovered its former power and equality with Sparta.

*Sepias* (sep'i-as). A cape or promontory in Thessaly. Here, according to legend, Peleus caught Thetis as she slept in a cave and, although she transformed herself to many shapes, he clung to her. The name comes from the sepia fluid of a cuttlefish into which she last changed herself. The cape was sacred to the Nereids.

*Serbonis, Lacus* (sėr-bō'nis, lā'kus). [*Serbonian Lake.*] In ancient geography, a bog or morass between the Isthmus of Suez, the Mediterranean, and the Nile delta. According to legend the monster Typhon lies under it.

*Seriphus* (sẹ-rī'fus) or *Seriphos* (-fos). Island of the Cyclades, in the Aegean Sea about 26 miles N of Melos. Here, according to legend, the chest containing Danaë and the infant Perseus was cast ashore. The island was a place of banishment during the Roman Empire. Area, 25 square miles; length, nine miles.

*Serrai* (se'rē). See *Serres*.

*Serres* (ser'ẹs). [Also: *Seres, Serrai.*] Town in N Greece, situated in Macedonia near the N end of the lake Cercinitis. The town is of great antiquity, the site on which it lies having been occupied since pre-Hellenic times. The ancient names of the town, in the territory of the Paeonians, were Siris, or Sirrhae. Xerxes stopped here on his march into Greece, 480 B.C., and left the sacred car and horses of the Sun here for safe-keeping. When he returned after his defeat at Salamis and demanded the return of the chariot and the mares, he learned that they had somehow fallen into the hands of the Thracians.

*Sesia* (se'zyä). See *Sessites.*

*Sessites* (ses'i-tēz). [Modern name, *Sesia.*] River in NW Italy, which rises in the Alps and joins the Padus (Po) about six miles E of Bodincomagus (Casale Monferrato).

*Sestos* (ses'tos) or *Sestus* (-tus). In ancient geography, a town in the Chersonesus Thracica, situated on the European shore of the Hellespont, opposite Abydos. It is noted as the residence of Hero in the legend of Hero and Leander, and as the place of debarkation of the army of Xerxes in his invasion of Europe.

*Setia* (sē'sha). [Modern name, *Sezze.*] In ancient geography, a town in C Italy, situated in the foothills of the Volscian Mountains, SE of Rome. It was a Volscian town, and became a Latin colony in 382 B.C. Sulla captured it in 82 B.C. Among the Roman architectural remains on the site are fortification walls and a theater.

*Seven Hills of Rome* (rōm). The seven hills on which Rome was originally built, included within the circuit of the Servian Wall. They are the Palatine, the Capitoline, the Quirinal, the Aventine, the Caelian, the Esquiline, and the Viminal. The elevations are inconsiderable, the highest, the Quirinal, rising 226 feet above the sea, and the lowest, the Aventine, 151. The Capitoline and the Aventine rise above the left bank of the Tiber, the former to the N. The Palatine lies between them, a little back from the river. N of the Palatine, the furthest N of the seven, is the Quirinal, and on the E are the Viminal, the Esquiline, and the Caelian, respectively NE, E, and SE of the Palatine.

*Sezze* (sät'tsä). See *Setia.*

*Sicily* (sis'i-li). [Latin, *Sicilia;* Greek, *Sikelia;* ancient names, also: *Trinacria* and *Sicania.*] Island in the Mediterranean Sea, SW of the mainland of S Italy, from which it is separated by the Strait of Messina. The surface is largely hilly or mountainous, with the volcanic structure of Mount Etna in the E and several ranges in the N. The largest plain is around Catania. The climate is subtropical, with hot, dry summers and mild, humid winters. In ancient times the island was called Trinacria, "Three Capes," from the three promontories of its roughly triangular shape—Pelorum, Pachynum, and Lilybaeum. It is thought to be the island mentioned in the *Odyssey* as the place where Helius pastured his sacred cattle. The land is very fertile and produced an abundance of grain. According to Sicilian tradition the island was the favorite home of Demeter, who gave the gift of grain to its people before any others, and taught them how to make use of the gift. The Sicilians claimed that the rape of Persephone took place in the meadows about the town of Henna (Enna), which lie in the center of the island. The spot, one of extraordinary beauty and noted for its abundance of violets, was called "the navel of Sicily." Near it were sacred groves, a grotto, and the chasm through which Hades bore Persephone to the Underworld.

The location of Sicily, midway between the eastern and western ends of the Mediterranean and stepping-stone between Italy and Africa, gave it great strategic importance, and made it a battleground for successive waves of colonists and invaders. The earliest inhabitants of which anything is known were the Sicanians, for whom the island was once called Sicania. They were pushed back by the Siceli who moved over from Africa and occupied the eastern half of the island, which henceforth was called for them, Sicily. In the northwest corner were the Elymi, a people who had come perhaps from Asia Minor and occupied the area in very ancient times. At an early date the Phoenicians established settlements on the coasts of Sicily. But the most important of the early immigrants were the Greeks, whose influence endured for centuries. The earliest Greek colonizers were Chalcidians from Euboea who, c735 B.C., founded the town of Naxos, near what later became the Corinthian colony of Syracuse (c734 B.C.). The Greeks pushed the Phoenicians out of their settlements, mostly trading posts, and the latter withdrew to strong areas in the north and west, near the Elymian towns of Eryx and Segesta. Other early Greek settlements on the rugged eastern coast were the Chalcidian cities of Leontini and Catana (729 B.C.), Dorian Megara Hyblaea (726 B.C.), Zancle (715 B.C.), Gela (689 B.C.), Himera, the only Greek settlement on the northern coast (648 B.C.), Selinus (628 B.C.), Camarina (599 B.C.), and Acragas (582 B.C.). The Greek cities flourished; close ties were maintained with the homeland, and the intellectual and cultural vigor of the Greek mainland took firm root and proliferated in Sicily. Behind the Greek cities of the eastern coast were the Sicel and Sicanian settlements. West of them were the strong Phoenician towns of Panormus, Solus, and Motya.

These last looked to the Punic city of Carthage to protect them from the encroachments of the Greeks. In the first half of the 6th century B.C. a large force was sent from Carthage which won some Greek territory for the Punic cities of the island. This century saw also the consolidation of certain areas of Greek Sicily, and by the beginning of the 5th century B.C. large areas were under the sway of tyrants, as those of Acragas, Syracuse, Zancle, and Himera. With Greece engaged in a desperate struggle against the might of Persia, Carthage seized the opportunity presented by a quarrel between Sicilian tyrants to interfere in Sicily and to win additional influence there. Hamilcar invaded Sicily at the head of a great armament. He was resoundingly defeated at Himera (480 B.C.), where he lost his life. For the next 70 years the Carthaginians remained on the sidelines in the struggles between the rival cities of Sicily. In that time Athens engaged in an expedition (415–413 B.C.) to the island designed to curb the growing power of the Corinthian colony of Syracuse and to establish Athenian domination of the island. The Athenian expedition was not only a failure; it was a disaster for Athens. Possibly the greatest effect of it for Sicily was to show the Sicilian cities that they had attained a status of political independence and equality with the city-states of Greece. Political independence was cherished, but not more than the Greek cultural heritage. In 409 B.C. the Carthaginians returned and won firm control of the western part of the island. The history of the next century is of wars with Carthage, in which the leading Sicilian participant was the great city of Syracuse. In the course of the wars mercenaries from Campania settled in Sicily, and later gave the Romans their pretext for interference in the island. In the First Punic War (264–241 B.C.) between Rome and Carthage, Sicily was a battle-ground. When the war ended, Carthage withdrew from the island and the western half became a Roman province (241 B.C.). The eastern half remained free as an ally of Rome. In the Second Punic War (218–201 B.C.), Syracuse revolted against Rome. The revolt was put down after a two-year siege by Marcellus (211 B.C.), and the entire island became a Roman province and the prey of a series of plundering Roman officials.

*Sicinus* (sik′i-nus). [Modern name, *Sikinos.*] An island of the Cyclades, about 19 miles S of Paros. Length, nine miles.

fat, fāte, fär, fȧll, ȧsk, fãre; net, mē, hèr; pin, pīne; not, nōte, mōve, nôr; up, lūte, pùll; oi, oil; ou out; (lightened) ēlect, agǫny, ūnite;

*Siculum* (sik'ū-lum), *Fretum.* Latin name of *Messina, Strait of.*
**Sicyon** (sish'i-on, sis-). In ancient geography, a city in the N
part of the Peloponnesus, Greece, situated near the Gulf of
Corinth, about ten miles NW of Corinth.

After the Dorian invasion Sicyon was part of Argive territory. Early in the 7th century B.C. Orthagoras became tyrant.
He exercised a benevolent despotism and Sicyon flourished.
His dynasty reached a peak of power and influence under
Clisthenes, who contended against Argos, put an end to the
recital of the Homeric poems because they exalted the Argives, suppressed the cult of the Argive hero Adrastus who
had ruled Sicyon for a time, and changed the names of the
Sicyonian tribes so that they should not share the names of
the Argive tribes. He gave his daughter in marriage to Mega-
cles, son of Alcmaeon the Athenian. With the Amphictyonic
League, he went to the aid of Delphi (c590 B.C.), against
Crisa, because Crisa claimed control over the oracle and
exacted tolls from visitors to it. He helped to crush Crisa and
assured the independence of the oracle. In the time of its
greatest prosperity Sicyon had rich treasuries at Delphi and
Olympia and was renowned for its painters, of whom
Eupompus, Pamphilus, and Pausias were the most famous.
After the reign of Clisthenes, Sicyon was so weakened by
internal struggles between the aristocratic and democratic
factions that it was able to play only a minor role in the
Persian War. Afterward, Athens sought to control it. Pericles led an expedition against it but failed to subdue it. In
368 B.C. the city fell under the domination of Epaminondas.
The city was destroyed by Demetrius Poliorcetes, 303 B.C.
He moved the inhabitants away from the harbor to the citadel, which he considered to be healthier and safer, and built
a new city there. Sicyon joined the Achaean League, 251
B.C., was taken with the rest of the Peloponnesus, by the
Romans, and was destroyed, 23 A.D., by an earthquake. An
ancient theater at the foot of the Acropolis where the new
city of Demetrius Poliorcetes stood, was excavated by the
American School at Athens. It is a large and important
monument. At the bottom of the cavea there is a row of seats
of honor, in the form of benches with backs and arms. Access to the cavea from without is facilitated by two vaulted
passages. There is a covered underground passage from the
middle of the orchestra to the interior of the stage structure.

Other excavators have found remains of a council chamber and of a Doric temple of Artemis.

*Sicyonia* (sish-i-ō'ni-ạ, sis-). In ancient geography, the territory surrounding Sicyon, Greece, and bounded by the Gulf of Corinth on the NE, Corinthia on the E, Argolis and Phliasia on the S, Arcadia on the W, and Achaea on the NW. The Dorians entered Sicyonia c1100 B.C. but did not devastate it because its ruler at that time was, as the invaders claimed to be, a descendant of Heracles. Under the Dorians it was made part of Argive territory.

*Side* (sī'dē). In ancient geography, a town in Pamphylia, Asia Minor, situated on the Gulf of Pamphylia, near what is now Antalya, Turkey. The site contains a Roman theater, in part excavated from a hillside and in part built up of masonry. The cavea, greater than a semicircle, has 26 tiers of marble seats below the precinction and 23 above it. A number of vaulted passages lead from the precinction to the exterior. The diameter is 409 feet; that of the orchestra, 125 feet.

*Sidon* (sī'dọn). [Modern name, **Saida.**] Oldest city of ancient Phoenicia. From the 17th century B.C. to c1100 B.C. it held supremacy in Phoenicia, and established most of the Phoenician colonies. Later it was surpassed by Tyre, but long continued to hold an important position among the mercantile cities of the ancient world. In 351 B.C. it was destroyed in consequence of a revolt against the Persian king Artaxerxes III, but was rebuilt and was still a wealthy city about the beginning of the Christian era. During the Crusades it was several times destroyed. The ancient necropolis, long known and exploited, has yielded numerous monuments of the most diverse ages and civilizations, from the oldest Phoenicians still under Egyptian influence, through the various stages of Greek art. In 1887 an important discovery was made, consisting of an intact subterranean mausoleum of several chambers, containing 22 sarcophagi, several of them bearing polychrome sculptures in relief of the best Greek art, and almost uninjured. The sarcophagi were transported to the museum at Constantinople, where they form one of the most important existing collections of ancient art. The Greek sarcophagi were not executed at Sidon, but were imported from different places and at different times. Their usual form is that of a temple. Four only are completely covered with sculpture; but these four rank with the finest

fat, fāte, fär, fâll, ȧsk, fãre; net, mē, hėr; pin, pīne; not, nōte, möve; nôr; up, lūte, pull; oi, oil; ou out; (lightened) ēlect, agọny, ūnite;

existing productions of Greek art, and are the only sarcophagi known which belong to the best period of sculpture.
The oldest is of Lycian form, with centaurs and Lapiths, and
hunting scenes. The second, dating from the beginning of
the 4th century B.C., is called "the Sarcophagus of the Weeping Women," from the graceful figures in the intercolumnia-
tions of its Ionic colonnade. The third bears varied scenes
from the life of an Oriental ruler. The fourth is so splendid
that its discoverers may be pardoned for proclaiming it the
sarcophagus of Alexander. Four of its six sculptured panels
represent hunting or battle scenes in which the portrait of
Alexander, almost contemporaneous, actually figures. It is
no doubt the tomb of an Oriental prince who had enjoyed
the companionship of the Macedonian conquerer.

**Siena** (sye'nä). [Ancient names: *Sena Julia, Colonia Julia Senen-
sis.*] City in C Italy. It was founded by the Etruscans, and
became a Roman town in the time of Augustus.

**Sigeum** (sī-jē'um). In ancient geography, a promontory and
town in the Troad, at the mouth of the Hellespont about five
miles NW of Troy. It was the legendary station of the Greek
fleet during the Trojan War and, according to tradition, the
tomb of Achilles was here. Sigeum was colonized by settlers
from the island of Lesbos. With the encouragement of Miletus, Athens seized Sigeum, but lost it early in the 6th century
B.C. when Pittacus, tyrant of Mytilene, won it back for Lesbos. Athens regained control (c535 B.C.), during the rule of
Pisistratus.

**Signia** (sig'ni-ạ). [Modern name, *Segni.*] In ancient geography,
a town in C Italy, situated near the Volscian Mountains,
about 30 miles SE of Rome. It is notable for important Italic
remains, which include massive fortifications in polygonal
limestone masonry, with a picturesque corbelled gate—the
Porta Saracinesca—a postern gate, and several sally ports,
other fortifications in ashlar tufa, and an Italic triple-cella
temple of the late 3rd or early 2nd century B.C. The cella
walls of the temple, of ashlar tufa, incorporated in the ancient church of San Pietro, survive to nearly their original
height. The temple stands on a double terrace of rough
polygonal limestone (Cyclopean) construction, once
thought to indicate an earlier building period but now considered contemporary with the existing temple. Signia was
said to have received a Latin colony in 495 B.C., and the

polygonal fortifications were formerly assigned to this period, though some scholars, deceived by their primitive appearance, considered them earlier still. It now appears safer to refer them to the period of the Punic Wars in the 3rd century B.C., when Signia was an important defensive outpost of Rome. (JJ)

**Silarus** (sil′ạ-rus). [Modern names, *Sele, Silaro*.] River in S Italy which flows into the Mediterranean about 17 miles SW of Salernum. Near it, in 71 B.C., Spartacus was defeated and slain by the Romans under Crassus.

**Simois** (sim′ō-is). A small stream near Buthrotum in Epirus.

**Sinope** (si-nō′pẹ). [Modern name, *Sinop*.] An ancient city and seaport located on a peninsula in the Pontus Euxinus (Black Sea). It has an excellent harbor. It was colonized by Milesians in the 8th century B.C. and became an important Greek commercial and colonizing center. One of its chief exports was cinnabar, which takes its name from Sinope. In 183 B.C. it was conquered and became the capital of Pontus. It was later (70 B.C.) subdued by Lucullus and became a Roman city. According to myth, Sinope was named for the daughter of the river-god Asopus.

**Siphnus** (sif′nus). [Also: *Siphnos*.] Island of the Cyclades, in the Aegean Sea about 24 miles NE of Melos. In ancient times there were rich mines of gold and silver in the island, the yield of which, according to Herodotus, was annually divided among the citizens and made them the richest of the islanders. The Siphnians furnished a treasury at Delphi which was equal to the grandest there, and at the time asked the oracle how long their wealth and good things would last. The answer of the priestess was as follows:

> When the Prytanies' seat shines white in the island of Siphnos,
> White-browed all the market—need then of a true seer's wisdom—
> Danger will threat from a wooden host, and a herald in scarlet.

The Prytanies' seat referred to the prytaneum, or town-hall. About this time the building was covered with Parian marble. In the war of the Samian exiles to overthrow Polycrates, tyrant of Samos, the exiles, seeing they were temporarily at a stand, sailed to Siphnus in their scarlet-painted wooden ships. They asked the Siphnians to lend them money out of their great store. The Siphnians refused. The Samian exiles made war on them and defeated them; thus was the oracle fulfilled. The Siphnians, Ionians of Athenian stock, were among the few Ionian islanders who refused to give earth and water to the Persians as tokens of submission. In the Persian War they contributed a 50-oared ship to the Athenian fleet at Salamis. The area of the island is 29 square miles; its length is ten miles.

*Sipylus* (sip'i-lus). In ancient geography, a mountain in Lydia, Asia Minor, near Smyrna. A female image, believed by the Greeks to represent Niobe, was here carved out of the mountain rock. The limestone rock out of which it was carved dripped with moisture after rain, and as the water flowed over the face of the figure, disintegrating and disfiguring the stone as it ran, the Greeks considered that they beheld in it Niobe weeping for her children. The figure was, in fact, originally that of the great goddess of Asia Minor, known usually as Cybele.

*Sirbonis* (sėr-bō'nis), *Lacus*. See *Serbonis, Lacus*.

*Siris* (sī'ris). In ancient geography, a city of Magna Graecia, Italy, situated at or near the mouth of the Siris River.

*Siris River*. [Modern Italian name, *Sinno*.] In ancient geography, a small river in Italy, flowing into the Gulf of Tarentum in what is now the province of Potenza. Near it Pyrrhus defeated (280 B.C.) the Romans in the battle of Heraclea.

*Siros* (sē'rôs). See *Syrus*.

*Sistan* (sē-stän'). See *Seistan*.

*Skopelos* (skop'e-los). See *Peparethos*.

*Skyros* (skē'ros). See *Scyrus*.

*Smyrna* (smėr'na). [Modern name, *Izmir*.] In ancient geography, a city on an arm of the Aegean Sea, in Lydia, Asia Minor. It had been one of the 12 Aeolian cities, but was seized by Ionians from Colophon (shortly before 688 B.C.) and compelled to join the Ionian League. Thanks to its location it became a flourishing and rich commercial city, and hence a target for the Lydian kings who were extending their power over the Ionian cities. The Lydian king Alyattes (c617–560 B.C.) conquered and destroyed it. Almost 300 years later a vision came to Alexander the Great commanding him to rebuild the city and to bring back the people of Smyrna. The vision having been verified by the oracle at Clarus, Alexander sent his generals Lysimachus and An-

(obscured) errant, ardent, actor; ch, chip; g, go; th, thin; ₮ℋ, then; y, you; (variable) ḍ as d or j, ṣ as s or sh, ṭ as t or ch, ẓ as z or zh.

tigonus to rebuild and enlarge the city, and it became one
of the chief cities of Asia Minor. It was destroyed by earthquakes in 178 and 180 A.D. and again restored by Marcus
Aurelius. Smyrna was one of the cities that claimed to be the
birthplace of Homer. It was also the first Ionian city to send
to the Olympic Games a contestant who won the victor's
crown (688 B.C.).

*Sogdiana* (sog-di-ā'nạ). [Also: *Sogdiane.*] In ancient geography,
a large region in C Asia, lying N of Bactriana, between the
Oxus (modern Amu Darya) and Jaxartes (modern Syr
Darya), in the vicinity of Bukhara and Samarkand. It was
invaded by Alexander the Great.

*Soli* (sō'lī). In ancient geography, a city on the coast of Cilicia,
Asia Minor, about 26 miles SW of Tarsus. It was destroyed
by Tigranes of Armenia, and was rebuilt by Pompey and
called Pompeiopolis. The corruptness of the Greek spoken
there was proverbial, whence the word "solecism."

*Solus* (sō'lus). [Also: *Soluntum.*] In ancient geography, a city on
the N coast of Sicily, about 12 miles SE of Panormus. It was
an ancient Phoenician colony.

*Sora* (sō'rä). Town of C Italy, situated on the upper Liris river,
about 62 miles SE of Rome. It was an ancient Volscian town.
The Romans captured it three times, in 345, 314, and 305
B.C. In 303 B.C. they finally secured its annexation to Rome
by sending a strong colony there. In the time of Augustus,
soldiers from the Fourth Legion colonized it.

*Soracte* (sō-rak'tē). [Italian, *Monte Soratto, Monte Sant'
Oreste.*] Mountain in Italy, near the Tiber river, about 25
miles NE of Rome. There is an extensive view from its summit, and it was known in ancient times for its temple of
Apollo. Elevation, 2260 feet.

*Sorrento* (sôr-ren'tō). See *Surrentum.*

*Sounion* (sön'yôn). See *Sunium.*

*Sparta* (spär'tạ). Ancient city in Laconia, Greece, situated on
the Eurotas River. From the city the entire kingdom (which
was called Lacedaemon as well as Laconia and Laconica)
came to be known as Sparta. Sparta was famous in myth and
legend. Among the many monuments of the ancient city
were the grave of Orestes near a sanctuary of the Fates; a
sanctuary of Athena Celeuthea (*Lady of the Road*) founded by
Odysseus in gratitude for having won the race in Sparta by
which he also won Penelope for his bride; the Hellenium, in

fat, fāte, fär, fåll, ȧsk, fāre; net, mē, hėr; pin, pīne; not, nōte, mōve,
nôr; up, lūte, pùll; oi, oil; ou out; (lightened) ẹlect, agọny, ūnite;

which, some say, the Greeks deliberated before sailing to Troy to secure the return of Helen (and others say the Greeks deliberated here when they were preparing to repel Xerxes in 480 B.C.). Near the Hellenium was the tomb of Agamemnon's herald Talthybius. And there were many other sites and monuments connected with mythological and legendary figures, as well as many religious sites. The famous temple of Athena of the Bronze House, said to have been begun by Tyndareus, was on the acropolis at Sparta. The Spartans claimed it was Aristodemus, the son of the Dorian Aristomachus, who marched into the Peloponnesus and claimed Sparta; but others say he had died on the eve of the invasion, and that it was his twin sons, Procles and Eurysthenes, who won Sparta as their territory in the drawing of the lots with their uncles Cresphontes and Temenus. It was for this reason (that Procles and Eurysthenes shared the throne), that Sparta alone of the Greek states had two kings and two royal houses.

By the legislation of the semi-legendary Lycurgus, Sparta became a powerful state. A conservative, aristocratic governmental system was developed, in which every moment of the lives of its citizens was strictly regulated. The purpose of the regulation was to develop a nation continually poised for war. In this Sparta was eminently successful. In the first place, the citizen was freed from the necessity of gaining his livelihood. The land was divided into lots. Each Spartan obtained a lot, which then belonged irrevocably to him and his descendants. It could not be sold or divided. The land was cultivated by the helots, virtual slaves, who belonged to the Spartan master and could not be either sold or freed by him; but under certain circumstances the state might emancipate a helot. Of the produce which the helots drew from the land certain amounts of grain, wine, and fruit went to the Spartan lot-holder. Any over these specified amounts was left to the helots who cultivated the land. Trade and commerce were carried on by the Perioeci (*Dwellers-around*) who, though free, enjoyed none of the rights of citizenship. Thus the Spartan citizen was free to devote himself to the service of the state. When a child was born it was examined by representatives of the state, and if it was found to be weak or imperfect it was exposed on Mount Taÿgetus to die. At the age of seven years boys were given into the care of the

(obscured) errant, ardent, actor; ch, chip; g, go; th, thin; ŦH, then; y, you; (variable) ḍ as d or j, ṣ as s or sh, ṭ as t or ch, ẓ as z or zh.

state, and their training was entirely directed to the ends of complete obedience and the cultivation of devotion to the state. This training was supported by exposing the children to all sorts of hardships to strengthen them and make them invulnerable to hardships. A well-known story of Spartan self-control and self-discipline is of the Spartan boy who stole a fox, hid it under his cloak, and stood motionless and silent while the fox gnawed at his vitals. At the age of 20, Spartan youths were permitted to marry, but since at the same time they entered military service and were compelled to live in barracks, they could not enjoy a home or family life. At 30 the Spartan was considered a man and won the full rights of citizenship. Thenceforward however, he continued to eat with his army comrades at public messes. Spartan women were also subjected to a discipline by the state. They were encouraged to develop their bodies in gymnastic exercises, so that they might bear strong sons. Their devotion to their country surpassed their maternal instinct. In the development of Sparta as an armed camp there was no place for luxury or soft living, and Spartan simplicity became proverbial. As a further effect, the concentration on developing superb soldiers left no room for the encouragement of original thinkers—poets, dramatists, artists. The valor of the Spartan fighting man also became proverbial. The Greeks in general, for centuries, could not imagine a Spartan surrender or a Spartan captive. The death of the 300 Spartans under Leonidas at Thermopylae (480 B.C.) was considered typical of the Spartan way in war, and illustrated on a large scale the command of the Spartan matron to her son about to go to war, to come back with his shield or on it. Yet contrary to expectation, though always in a state of preparedness, Sparta was reluctant to initiate war and, on the whole, rather slow to engage in it even when her own interest was manifestly affected. In the 8th and 7th centuries B.C. Messenia was conquered. Arcadia, Messenian ally, later acknowledged Spartan supremacy. In the 6th century B.C. Sparta succeeded in conquering Tegea, the most powerful of the Arcadian cities. According to legend, Tegea had previously been invulnerable to Spartan attacks. An oracle told the Spartans they must bring back the bones of Orestes to Sparta if they would conquer Tegea. When this was accomplished, through the agency of the Spartan Lichas, Tegea was overwhelmed.

By the middle of the 6th century B.C. Sparta had established its supremacy over Argos, and was the leading Greek state and acknowledged as such by the other states. The Spartans had an alliance with Croesus. When the Ionian cities revolted they sought, in vain, the aid of Sparta. When the Persian invasion threatened (490 B.C.), the Spartans were prevented by a religious holiday from assisting the Athenians at Marathon. By the time the holiday was over and the Spartans came hurrying up, the Athenians had utterly routed the Persian forces. The Spartans were filled with admiration, and closely examined the battlefield where the great victory had taken place. With the approach of the second Persian invasion (480 B.C.), Sparta was the acknowledged leader of the Greeks and played a leading part in the Persian War and the Greek victory therein. After the Persian War Sparta retained its place as the leading land power, but the sea power of Athens had developed and now seemed to threaten Spartan supremacy. With various allies, Sparta fought against Athens in the Peloponnesian Wars (431–404 B.C.) and emerged victorious. The years 404–371 B.C. followed as the period of Spartan hegemony in Greece. At the height of its power the city of Sparta remained unwalled. It is said that when someone asked Agesilaus, the Spartan king (398 B.C.), why Sparta was unwalled, he pointed to the citizens in arms and replied, "These are the walls of Lacedaemon." But the period of Spartan ascendancy was short. Sparta had many enemies, and the arid military policy prevented the natural growth of the state. In 371 B.C. the Spartans were defeated at the battle of Leuctra by the Thebans under Epaminondas. At this time the two stars symbolizing the Dioscuri, patrons of Sparta, fell from their place in the temple and disappeared forever. This was the end of Spartan power. Sparta passed under Roman rule in 146 B.C.

**Sperchius** (sper-kī′us). [Also: *Hellada, Spercheius, Sperkhios*.] River that rises in Mount Othrys and flows through Thessaly into the Gulf of Lamia near Thermopylae.

**Sphacteria** (sfak-tir′i-ạ). [Also: *Sphakteria, Sphagia*.] Small island off the promontory of Messenian Pylus. Here the Spartans were cut off by the Athenians. They took refuge on what was thought to be an impregnable height at one end of the

(obscured) errạnt, ardẹnt, actọr; ch, chip; g, go; th, thin; ŦH, then; y, you;
(variable) ḍ as d or j, ṣ as s or sh, ṭ as t or ch, ẓ as z or zh.

island. Their ancient enemies the Messenians, who were aiding the Athenians, discovered a perilous path up the cliffs in the rear of the Spartan position. They led the Athenians up the cliffs so that they now commanded the rear as well as the van of the Spartans and the Spartans surrendered (425 B.C.). Though the force of Spartans that surrendered was comparatively small, the victory was enormous, for up to this time the Spartans had such a reputation for fighting to the death that it was thought they were never taken alive. A bronze shield, found in a cistern near the temple of Hephaestus in Athens, bears an inscription recording its dedication by the Athenians, "from the Lacedaemonians at Pylus."

*Spoletium* (spō-lē'shum). [Modern name, *Spoleto.*] Town of C Italy, situated on a branch of the Via Flaminia, about 60 miles NE of Rome. It was attacked (217 B.C.) by Hannibal after the battle of Trasimenus, but he was driven off. The town was a battleground during the civil wars and its territory was annexed by Sulla, 82 B.C. Under the empire it again became a prosperous town. There are many Roman remains in Spoletium, including a theater, amphitheater, bridge, a triumphal arch of Drusus and Germanicus (21 A.D.), houses, and parts of walls.

*Spoleto* (spō-lā'tō). See *Spoletium.*

*Sporades* (spor'a-dēz). Group of Greek islands in the Aegean and neighboring seas. The name is variously applied. It includes Melos, Thera, Cos, and others, and sometimes Samos, Chios, Lesbos, and others.

*Squillace* (skwēl-lä'chä). See *Scylacium.*

*Stagira* (sta-jī'ra). [Also: *Stagirus.*] In ancient geography, a city on the coast of Chalcidice, Macedonia, about 43 miles E of Thessalonika: the birthplace of Aristotle. It was colonized from Andros.

*Stamphane* (stäm'fä-ne) or *Stamphanes* (stäm'fä-nes). See *Strophades.*

*Stenyclaros* (sten-i-klä'ros). [Also: *Stenyclerus, Stenyclarus.*] In ancient geography, a city in Messenia.

*Strongyle* (stron'ji-lē). [Modern name, *Stromboli.*] Northernmost of the Aeoliae Insulae (Lipari islands), N of Sicily: famous for its constantly active volcano (elevation, about 3038 feet).

*Strongyle.* An ancient name of the island of *Naxos.*

fat, fāte, fär, fåll, åsk, fāre; net, mē, hėr; pin, pīne; not, nōte, möve, nôr; up, lūte, půll; oi, oil; ou out; (lightened) ēlect, agōny, ūnite;

*Strophades* (strof′ạ-dēz; Greek, strô-fä′thes). [Also: *Stamphane,*
*Stamphanes, Strofadhes;* Italian, *Strivali.*] Group of small is-
lands W of the Peloponnesus, Greece. Hither the sons of
Boreas were said, in Greek legend, to have pursued the
Harpies, and here they turned back from their pursuit. The
Harpies remained on the islands, which took the name,
meaning the islands of turning, from the fact that the Borea-
dae, Calais and Zetes, turned back here.

*Strymon* (strī′mọn). [Modern name, *Struma.*] A river of Thrace
which empties into the Aegean Sea. It was reputed to be the
nesting ground of the cranes which fought the Pygmies.

*Strymonic Gulf* (strī-mon′ik). [Also: *Gulf of Orfani;* Latin,
*Strymonicus Sinus.*] Arm of the Aegean Sea, indenting the
coast of Macedonia, Greece, E of the peninsula of Chalcidice, at the mouth of the Strymon River.

*Stymphalus* (stim-fā′lus). In ancient geography, a district and
lake in the NE part of Arcadia, Greece. About the spring and
lake of Stymphalus dwelt the savage, man-eating Stym-
phalian birds that were shot down as one of the Labors of
Heracles. The birds were carved on the sanctuary of Stym-
phalian Artemis, and behind the sanctuary stood figures of
maidens, in white marble, with the legs of birds. The Stymphalus River, the source of which is a spring, disappears,
says Pausanias, into the earth through a chasm, and reap-
pears in Argolis as the Erasinus River.

*Subura* (sö-bū′rạ). Valley in ancient Rome, on the N side of the
Fora, and extending between the Viminal and Esquiline
hills. It was drained by the Cloaca Maxima.

*Suessa Aurunca* (swes′ạ ạ-rung′kạ). A town on the SW slopes of
the extinct volcano now known as Roccamonfina, commanding the pass between Roccamonfina and the Mons Massicus
of wine-growing fame. On this site was established in 313
B.C. the Latin colony of Suessa Aurunca, which survives
today as Sessa or Sessa Aurunca. It was the birthplace of the
Latin satirist Caius Lucilius. To the imperial period belong
an amphitheater and numerous architectural fragments
from temples and other buildings, while in the neighborhood is a celebrated Roman bridge, the Ponte Ronaco (=
Aurunco), still in daily use. It has been suggested that
Suessa preserves an alternate pronunciation or dialectal
form of Vescia, a lost city of the Ausones, and if so Suessa
may stand over or near the site of ancient Vescia; but no

traces of a pre-Roman Suessa have been identified. If, as a single late reference indicates, Roccamonfina last erupted in 269 B.C., Vescia may have been buried by ash, like Pompeii, and may still be awaiting the discoverer's spade. (JJ)

**Suessula** (swes′ū̯-la̯). In ancient geography, a place in Campania, Italy, about 13 miles NE of Naples. It is the traditional scene of a Roman victory over the Samnites in the First Samnite War (343–341 B.C.).

**Sulmo** (sul′mō). [Modern names; **Sulmona, Solmona.**] Town of C Italy. It was a Roman town, in the region of the Sabines, from ancient times. The town was taken and sacked by Hannibal, 211 B.C. It is the birthplace of the poet Ovid, its most famous son.

**Sunium** (sö′ni-um) or **Sunium Promontorium** (prom-o̯n-tō′ri-um). [Also: **Sounion, Cape Colonna.**] In ancient geography, a lofty headland running into the sea at the SE extremity of Attica. At the summit, enclosed by a fortification wall and approached through propylaea or formal entrance gates, are the striking ruins of a splendid Periclean Doric hexastyle temple of the sea-god Poseidon, designed by the *Theseum Architect*, constructed c444 B.C. to replace an earlier temple, and conspicuous far out to sea. It is built of a local marble which unlike Pentelic marble has not weathered to a russet patina, but retains its dazzling whiteness. The view of the Aegean and its islands from the temple terrace is superb. Outside the sanctuary, at a little distance, are the foundations of an Ionic temple of Athena, unusual in that it had exterior columns on the front (E) and one flank (S) only. According to Homer, Phrontis, pilot of Menelaus, was struck down by the arrows of Apollo as his ship rounded Sunium on the return from Troy. (JJ)

**Surrentum** (su-ren′tum). [Modern name, **Sorrento.**] Town in S Italy, situated on cliffs high above the Bay of Naples, about 16 miles SE of Naples. It has been famous since ancient times for its location and its wine, and has always been a popular resort. In ancient times its most celebrated temples were those of Athena and of the Sirens. It has numerous Roman remains, including villas and temples.

**Susa** (sö′za̯, sö′sa̯). [Biblical name, **Shushan.**] In ancient geography, the capital of Susiana or Elam, "the City of Lilies," situated near the Choaspes (Karkheh) River, S of modern Dizful in Iran. It was destroyed in 645 B.C. by Assurbanipal.

---

fat, fāte, fär, fåll, ȧsk, fāre; net, mē, hėr; pin, pīne; not, nōte, möve; nôr; up, lūte, pủll; oi, oil; ou out; (lightened) e̯lect, ago̯ny, ūnite;

The Achaemenid kings of Persia made it their winter residence, and provided it with a citadel. It was still flourishing in the 12th century A.D. It is frequently mentioned in the books of Daniel and Esther. The site at present exhibits a group of high and large mounds, forming together a diamond-shaped figure about 3½ miles in circuit. Excavations were made in 1851 by Loftus in one of the mounds, disclosing the palace of Artaxerxes II, the chief feature being a fine colonnade of 340 feet front. The excavations of M. A. Dieulafoy, between 1884 and 1886, laid bare beneath these ruins those of the palace of Darius the Great, and showed that the upper strata of the mound are formed by superposed layers of ruins.

**Susiana** (sö-zi-ā′nạ, -an′ạ). Province of the Persian Empire, corresponding to the Biblical Elam and to the region of modern Iran known as Khuzistan. It was an independent state after the first destruction of Nineveh, and was subdued by Sargon II. Its capital was Susa.

**Sybaris** (sib′ạ-ris). In ancient geography, a city of Magna Graecia, S Italy, situated near the Gulf of Tarentum. It was founded (720 B.C.) by Achaean and Troezenian colonists. It was celebrated for its wealth, and its inhabitants were proverbial for their luxury (whence the epithet "Sybarite"). It was destroyed (510 B.C.) by the Pythagorean inhabitants of Croton. A second Sybaris rose upon the ruins of the first, but it never flourished, and was finally absorbed in the Athenian colony of Thurii (443 B.C.). Herodotus is said to have been one of the colonists. The site has been covered so deeply by earth eroded from the nearby hills that no sign of occupation appeared above ground, and archaeologists had searched in vain for its precise location, until in 1953 Donald F. Brown explored the plain with a coring tool and brought up specimens of datable pottery which established its position and approximate limits beyond reasonable doubt. The modern village near the site is Terranova di Sibari. (JJ)

**Sybota** (sib′ọ-tạ). In ancient geography, a small town on the coast of Epirus, Greece, opposite the S end of Corcyra (Corfu). Near it was fought (432 B.C.) a naval battle between Corcyra (aided by Athens) and Corinth. The Corinthians won the sea fight, but withdrew the next day.

**Syme** (sī′mē). [Also: **Simi, Symi.**] Small island off the SW coast of Asia Minor, about 15 miles N of Rhodes.

**Synnada** (sin'ạ-dạ). [Modern name, **Eskikarahisar.**] Ancient city in Phrygia, famous for its ruins of old palaces. The city was known for its marble quarries, and from the time of Constantine was the capital of Phrygia Salutaris.

**Syracuse** (sir'ạ-kūs, -kūz). [Italian, **Siracusa;** Latin, **Syracusae.**] City of Sicily, situated on the island of Ortygia off the E coast of Sicily. In ancient times the largest and wealthiest city of Sicily, it was a Dorian city, founded (c734 B.C.) by Corinthian colonists under the leadership of Archias, on a site that was seized from earlier settlers. In the next century Syracuse began founding her own colonies in Sicily, and laid the foundations for the dominating position she attained among the Greek cities of the island. The government of the city was oligarchic and democratic by turns. Gelo (died c478 B.C.), tryant of Gela, in answer to an appeal by Syracusan nobles who had been expelled by the people, made himself master and tyrant of Syracuse in 485 B.C. The splendid location of Syracuse made it a center of commerce and shipping. The island on which it stood was in the northeast part of a bay about five miles in circumference. Gelo connected the island by a causeway to Achradina, a mainland height on a promontory that commands the island. The island now became a peninsula that dropped down and enclosed the bay on the northeast. He built a wall that ran down to the bay across the promontory behind the fortified height of Achradina and enclosed it, the causeway, and the island of Ortygia in one unit. The Great Harbor of Syracuse, as the bay became, was thus protected on the north by the citadel of the city on the island and by fortified Achradina, and on its southern side by the promontory called Plemmyrion. Safe inside the Great Harbor was anchorage for a vast number of ships. On the sea side of the causeway was another, smaller harbor. Gelo shifted at will populations from cities he had conquered to populate his enlarged city, giving the nobles he imported the citizenship and making slaves of the common people who were compelled to settle in Syracuse. He joined with Theron, tyrant of Acragas, to drive the Carthaginians out of Greek Sicily, and defeated them at Himera, 480 B.C. After his victory he brought Syracuse to a peak of power and prosperity and extended its dominion. Under his successor, his brother Hiero I (ruled 478–467 B.C.), who defeated the Etruscans and destroyed their influence in southern Italy, the magnificent court of Syracuse attracted and welcomed such poets from the mainland of Greece as Aeschylus, Pindar, Simonides, and Bacchylides. Spiritual and cultural ties to the great shrines of Greece were jealously preserved by the thriving city in the west. Hiero I was followed by his brother Thrasybulus, whose lack of capacity coupled with a harsh and cruel rule precipitated a revolution. He was overthrown, a democratic government was established, and to celebrate freedom regained the Syracusans set up a huge statue of Zeus Eleutherius *(Deliverer)* and instituted annual games in his honor. Syracuse flourished and continued to expand, by colonizing and by extending its influence over neighboring areas, until the great expedition (under Nicias, Alcibiades, and Lamachus) was sent (415–413 B.C.) from Athens to check the Syracusan advance, to gain influence in Sicily, and as an attack on Athens' enemy Corinth. The Athenian expedition was a disaster for Athens. The vast armament that set out from Athens with such splendor and such hope was completely destroyed. The prisoners taken by the Syracusans were set to work in the huge quarries that are still a feature of Syracuse.

Syracuse took its place now, not as the equal of the cities of Greece, but as a strong power to which they could turn, as did Sparta, for assistance. Syracuse was triumphant, but greatly weakened by the long struggle with Athens, and almost immediately had to defend herself against attack from Carthage. The democracy which had been joyfully restored after the defeat of the Athenians seemed unable to cope with the Carthaginians. Dionysius I was named sole general to counter the Carthaginian menace (405 B.C.). The fortunes of Syracuse vis-à-vis Carthage rose and fell. Dionysius made himself absolute ruler. In the course of his reign he defended Syracuse from a siege by the Carthaginians (397 B.C.), defeated them, and drove them out of all but the western corner of Sicily. Under Dionysius (c430–367 B.C.), Syracuse became the most powerful city in the Greek world, which is to say, the most powerful state in Europe at the time. At its greatest extent, the empire of Syracuse included most of Sicily and the southern part of the peninsula of Italy, into which Dionysius had successfully penetrated. The various parts of the empire were attached to Syracuse in varying degrees of dependence, alliance, and association. Dionysius enlarged and beautified the city, and improved its defenses to make it the best fortified, as well as the most magnificent, city in Sicily. He also improved the docks and increased the fleet to give Syracuse the strongest naval force in the Mediterranean. In succeeding years Syracuse suffered under the tyranny of Dionysius the Younger (c395–after 343 B.C.), son of Dionysius I, expelled him, and was governed for a time by Dion (c408–353 B.C.), a follower of Plato and a theoretical democrat who had tried to make of Dionysius the Younger a constitutional monarch. Syracuse fell again to Dionysius the Younger, but was then freed by Timoleon, a Corinthian general sent out by the mother city to free Syracuse from tyranny and from an invading Carthaginian force (343 B.C.). About 317 B.C. Agathocles (361–289 B.C.), with an army of Campanian mercenaries and Greek exiles, and with the encouragement of Carthage, made himself tyrant. He restored order to the city, which had been rocked by revolution. Under Hiero II (c307–216 B.C.), Syracuse enjoyed more than 50 years of peace, and flourished greatly under his beneficent rule. In the First Punic War between Rome and Carthage (264–241 B.C.; Syracuse had suffered her own Punic Wars), Syracuse was on the side of Rome, but Hieronymus (grandson of Hiero II), finding Rome a greater threat than Carthage ever was, changed sides in the Second Punic War (218–201 B.C.). He was dethroned in 215 B.C., and his family was murdered. Marcellus, the Roman consul and general, made such demands that the Syracusans, abetted by Carthage, determined to resist. Marcellus laid siege to the city in 214 B.C. The city was heroically defended; the inventions of the great Archimedes played havoc with the Roman ships in the Great Harbor. The city held out until the defenders, weakened by plague and lack of supplies, were compelled to submit (211 B.C.). Marcellus allowed his army to plunder the city, and many of its treasures were carried off to Rome. Though Marcellus had given strict orders to spare and protect Archimedes, in the confusion he was slain as, oblivious of the turmoil about him, he worked out a problem in the sand. Syracuse now became a Roman city in what was ultimately the Roman province of Sicily. Syracuse is famous for its Greek antiquities, including, on the island of Ortygia, remains of Doric temples of Apollo (6th century

fat, fāte, fär, fâll, ȧsk, fāre; net, mē, hėr; pin, pīne; not, nōte, möve, nôr; up, lūte, pùll; oi, oil; ou out; (lightened) ĕlect, agǫny, ūnite;

B.C.) and Athena (5th century B.C., the modern cathedral) that rest on foundations of even older temples. There are also a Greek theater, a Roman amphitheater, parts of walls and aqueducts, remains of a great fortress on the slope inland from Achradina, Roman houses, and numerous other remains. On the west side of the island of Ortygia is the celebrated fountain of Arethusa, which according to legend represents the nymph Arethusa. She fled the embraces of the river-god Alpheus and was transported to Syracuse by Artemis, where she was changed to a fountain. The river-god dove under the sea and came up in Ortygia to mingle his waters with those of the fountain of Arethusa. Through the marshes about Syracuse runs the stream Cyane. According to legend, the nymph Cyane saw Pluto (Hades) carrying off Proserpina (Persephone). She tried to persuade him to release Proserpina but he ignored her and plunged into the earth with his captive. Cyane wept so that she was changed into a fountain, the source of the stream.

**Syria** (sir'i-a). The region of this name described by the ancients lay probably between the Euphrates and the Mediterranean and between the N part of Arabia and the Taurus Mountains, and thus included Lebanon, Palestine, and Jordan. The inhabitants were Hittites, Arameans, Canaanites, Hebrews, and Phoenicians. (Sometimes lower Mesopotamia was included, and the names Assyria and Syria were used interchangeably by some ancient writers; this larger region is also called Aram in the Bible.) Syria became subject to Assyria c733 B.C. and was later under Babylon, Persia, and Macedon. Part of it was conquered by Seleucus Nicator and the name Syria was given to the whole realm of his descendants, the Seleucids, which had Antioch as its capital and embraced a great part of the Macedonian conquests in Asia. It was conquered by Pompey (c65 B.C.) and annexed to the Roman Empire.

**Syrus** (sī'rus) or **Syros** (sī'ros). [Also: **Siros, Syra.**] The most populous and richest island of the Cyclades. The philosopher Pherecydes, the teacher of Pythagoras, was born on the island, and a cave on the north of the island called the Grotto of Pherecydes, is said to have been his home. The chief town of the island is Hermoupolis, "Hermes' city." Area of the island, about 31 square miles; length, 11 miles.

**Syrtis** (sèr'tis). In ancient geography, a large embayment of the

Mediterranean Sea, in Libya, the N coast of Africa. According to legend, it was a vast quicksand, where the *Argo* was driven by a great storm when the Argonauts were on their roundabout way home to Iolcus from Colchis.

———T———

**Taenarus** (tē′na̱-rus) or **Taenarum** (-rum). Locality, city, cape, and river, at the extremity of Laconia, Greece. Near the river in this locality, according to ancient legend, there was a back entrace to Tartarus which was used by those who evaded Hermes, the conductor of the dead to Tartarus, and by those who had no coin under their tongues to pay Charon to ferry them across the Styx. It was a cave-like temple.

**Tainaron** (te′nä-rôn). See **Taenarus**.

**Tanagra** (tan′a̱-gra̱, ta̱-nag′ra̱). In ancient geography, a town of Boeotia, Greece, situated near the Asopus River, about 24 miles NW of Athens. The inhabitants in ancient times claimed descent from Apollo and Poseidon, and said their town was named for Tanagra, a daughter of Aeolus or, as some say, of the river-god Asopus. Among the temples of Tanagra in antiquity were those of Themis, Apollo, Aphrodite, Hermes, and Dionysus. In the last was a marble image of the god by the sculptor Calamis. There was also an image of a headless Triton. According to legend, a Triton attacked the women of Tanagra when they went to bathe in the sea to purify themselves before celebrating the rites of Dionysus. The women called on the god to protect them; he came and killed the Triton after a great struggle. But others say the Triton used to come from the sea and attack the cattle of the Tanagraeans. To catch him, a bowl of wine was set on the beach. The Triton drank of it and fell into a drunken slumber on the sand, whereupon a man of Tanagra cut off his head. Some say the tomb of Orion was at Tanagra. The tomb of the lyric poetess Corinna was also there, with a painting depicting her binding her hair with the victor's crown after a contest with Pindar. A victory was gained here in 457 B.C. by the Spartans over the Athenians and their allies. Its extensive necropolis has made this obscure town famous, for from it came (c1874) the first of the charming Tanagra figurines of terra-cotta which drew attention to the antiquities of this type. Such figurines, previously ignored, have since been eagerly sought and found in great quantities not only at Tanagra but upon a great number of sites in all parts of the Greek world.

*Tanais* (tan′ā-is). Ancient Greek (Milesian) colony near the head of the Palus Maeotis. The colony dates from c500 B.C. and was probably founded by settlers from Panticapaeum.

*Tanais.* [Modern name, *Don.*] In ancient geography, a river of Scythia, flowing generally south to empty into the Palus Maeotis. A trade route to Central Asia was said to follow the valley of this river.

*Tanarus* (tan′a̱-rus). [Modern name, *Tanaro.*] River in NW Italy. It rises in the Ligurian Alps and empties into the Po.

*Taormina* (tä-ôr-mē′nä). See *Tauromenium.*

*Taphiae* (tā′fi-ē). [Also: *Teleboides.*] In ancient geography, a group of the Ionian Islands W of Acarnania, Greece. Homer called the people of the islands "Lovers of the oar."

*Taranto* (tä′rän-tō). See *Tarentum.*

*Tarentinus Sinus* (ta-ren̪-tī′nus sī′nus). [Modern name, *Gulf of Taranto.*] Arm of the Mediterranean, on the S coast of Italy. It separates the "heel" of the peninsula from the "toe," projecting into the "foot" about 85 miles.

*Tarentum* (ta̱-ren′tum). [Also: *Taras;* modern name, *Taranto.*] In ancient geography, a city of SE Italy, situated on a sheltered harbor on the N coast of the Gulf of Tarentum. The ancient name of Taras was given to it, according to some accounts, in honor of a son of Poseidon of that name. According to tradition, this ancient Dorian city was founded by Phalanthus, c707 B.C., who led a colony across the sea from Laconia and raised the city. It prospered, owing to its fertile soil, its protected harbor, and its manufacture of fabrics, dyed wools, and pottery, which were known throughout the Mediterranean area. Tarentum established colonies of her own on the east coast of Italy, and became the most powerful city of Magna Graecia. In the 4th century B.C. the city was threatened by the Lucanians, appealed to Sparta for aid, and received a force from there under the command of King Archidamus. The Spartan expedition was ineffectual. King Archidamus fell in battle (338 B.C.). Tarentum next appealed to Alexander of Epirus, uncle of Alexander the Great. He beat back the Italian tribes with great energy. The speed and vigor with which he established his control came to seem a greater threat to Tarentum than the Italian tribes had been. However, having greatly weakened the enemies of Tarentum, Alexander was treacherously slain and Tarentum was freed from both native and foreign threats for a time. At the beginning of the 3rd century B.C. the growing power of Rome became a menace. The Tarentines invited Pyrrhus, king of Epirus, to come and command them in a war against Rome. He arrived to find the city luxuriating in its wealth and making no great effort to arm itself for the coming war. After great but costly successes against Rome, Pyrrhus went to Sicily. Tarentum was defeated by the Romans, 272 B.C., and became a Roman ally. In the Second Punic War the city was captured by Hannibal. It was taken (209 B.C.) and plundered by Fabius Cunctator, thanks to betrayal by some Bruttians in the city. Fabius slew many of the Tarentines and sold 30,000 others into slavery. Among the spoils which he removed from the city was a statue of Heracles. This he sent to Rome and caused it to be set up near a statue of himself. In 123 B.C. the city was colonized by Rome with the new name Colonia Neptunia, and an attempt was made to revive its industry. Architectural remains of antiquity include a Doric temple on an island in the harbor, and a Roman aqueduct.

**Tarpeian Rock** (tär-pē′an). [Latin, *Mons Tarpeius.*] Originally, the name of the entire Capitoline Hill in Rome, or at least of the peak occupied by the citadel, in memory of the treason of Tarpeia in connection with the Sabine siege; later, that part *(Rupes Tarpeia)* of the cliff of the Capitoline over whose precipice, according to tradition, condemned criminals were hurled; now unrecognizable owing to artificial and natural changes in the rocks.

**Tarquinii** (tär-kwin′i-ī). [Former name, *Corneto Tarquinia,* modern name, *Tarquinia.*] City in Latium, in C Italy, about 44 miles NW of Rome. The town, surrounded by walls and fortifications, has numerous Etruscan and Roman antiquities, and a necropolis of great interest, containing notable murals. One of the 12 chief Etruscan cities, it submitted to Roman rule in the 3rd century B.C.

**Tarracina** (tar-a-sī′na). [Also: *Anxur;* modern name, *Terraci-*

*na.*] In ancient geography, a town of C Italy, situated on the Mediterranean Sea about 58 miles SE of Rome. It was an ancient Volscian town and was taken by the Romans in 406 B.C. Roman remains include the ancient forum, whose original paving survives as the paving of the piazza in front of the cathedral (the dedicatory inscription, A. AEMILIVS. A.F., can be clearly read in the channels cut for the inlay of bronze letters, though the letters themselves were long ago pried up as scrap metal); a temple on whose foundations stands the cathedral; another temple, of the Augustan or post-Augustan period, with three cellas, exposed by World War II bombing; extensive city walls of polygonal limestone masonry of various periods, the earliest probably to be referred to the founding of a Roman citizen colony in 329 B.C.; paved stretches of the Via Appia; tombs; on the hill above the city, further fortification walls of concrete and rubble ("opus incertum") of c100 B.C., and the imposing substructure of a large temple of Jupiter Anxur, of about the same date; on the shore road just east of the city is a famous piece of Roman engineering—the scarp or vertical cut in the rock face made to permit the Via Appia to pass at sea level. (JJ)

**Tarsus** (tär'sus). In ancient geography, the capital of Cilicia, Asia Minor, situated on the Cydnus River. It was an important city in the Persian period, became partly Hellenized and the seat of a school of philosophy, and received important concessions from the Romans. It was the birthplace of the apostle Paul.

**Tartessus** (tär-tes'us). In ancient geography, a city and region in the SW part of the Iberian Peninsula, near the Pillars of Hercules. It was noted for its commerce. It is associated with Gades (modern Cádiz) and also with the Biblical Tarshish.

**Taurica** (tô-ri-kạ), **Chersonesus.** An ancient name of the Crimea (peninsula).

**Tauromenium** (tô-rọ-mē'ni-um). [Modern name, **Taormina.**] In ancient geography, a city on the NE coast of Sicily, just N of Mount Aetna. It was founded by the Carthaginian general, Himilco, 397 B.C., on the hills above the old Greek city of Naxos which had been destroyed by Dionysius the Elder of Syracuse. Himilco intended it as a stronghold for the Sicels and as a bastion against the Greeks. A few years later it was unsuccessfully besieged by Dionysius, to whom it was ultimately awarded, 392 B.C., in the conclusion of a peace treaty with Carthage. Dionysius settled his mercenaries there. After the death of Dionysius it became independent and received (358 B.C.) the former inhabitants of Naxos within its walls to revive ancient Naxos in Tauromenium. In the Punic Wars between Rome and Carthage it was allied with Rome. It was a place of refuge for the rebellious slaves in the Roman civil war, and in the reign of Augustus it became a Roman colony. There are architectural remains of antiquity, especially two Roman theaters, one of which rests on Greek foundations, remains of a 3rd-century B.C. Greek temple, known as the temple of Serapis, into which the church of S. Pancrazio has been built, and walls, houses, and tombs of the Roman period. The modern city of Taormina, on the ancient site, is famous for the magnificent views it commands of Mount Aetna to the south and the mountains of Calabria across the sea in the Italian peninsula.

*Taurus* (tô′rus) *Mountains.* Great mountain range in Asia Minor, along the S coast. It extends from the SW extremity of the peninsula to near the NE angle of the Mediterranean Sea. The Anti-Taurus is an offshoot to the NE. The chief pass is known as the Cilician Gates. Highest point, about 12,250 feet.

*Taxila* (tak′si-la). In ancient geography, a city in the Punjab, India, in the vicinity of the modern Rawalpindi. Alexander the Great reached it, 326 B.C., in his march into India, and was obsequiously received.

*Taÿgetus* (tā-ij′e-tus). Highest mountain range in the Peloponnesus, Greece. It is situated in the W part of Laconia, on the border between Laconia and Messenia, extending into Arcadia. Length, 70 miles; highest point, Hagios Elias (about 7903 feet). On the wild slopes, haunt of deer, bears, wild goats, and other animals, weak and sickly Spartan infants were exposed to die, so that the state would not have the burden of rearing any children that would not be fit soldiers.

*Tegea* (tē′jē-a). In ancient geography, a city in E Arcadia, Greece. Tegea was the site of a famous temple of Athena Alea, founded by Aleus. The ancient temple was burned, c394 B.C., and as restored by Scopas it was a Doric peripteros of six by 13 columns, measuring 72 by 154 feet. There were many sanctuaries, as of Aphrodite, Artemis, Demeter and the Maid, and many images. In the sanctuary of Ilithyia was an image of "Auge on her Knees," because, some say,

fat, fāte, fär, fâll, àsk, fāre; net, mē, hèr; pin, pīne; not, nōte, möve; nôr; up, lūte, pùll; oi, oil; ou out; (lightened) ẹlect, agǫny, ūnite;

when Aleus gave her to Nauplius to take her off and drown her because she had profaned the temple of Athena Alea with Heracles, she fell on her knees before the temple of Ilithyia and gave birth to a son. But others tell a different tale. Most of the altars of the Tegeans stood on a lofty site in their city, and here the Tegeans feasted annually.

The Tegeans were the first of the Arcadians to defeat the Lacedaemonians. Charillus, king of Sparta, deceived by an oracle into thinking he could conquer Tegea, took fetters with which to bind his Tegean prisoners and attacked Tegea. His attack was unsuccessful. Aided by the Tegean women, who took up arms, the Tegeans defeated the Lacedaemonians and took many captives. In honor of their capture of the Spartans the Tegeans thereafter held a festival, the *Halotia* (Capture Festival). The fetters the Spartans had brought were placed on themselves, and they were forced to till the fields of the Tegeans as slaves. Many times the Spartans sought to conquer the Tegeans, but each time they were repulsed. According to legend, there were two reasons why Tegea was invulnerable to Sparta. First, some say that Athena gave Cepheus, king of Tegea and the son of Aleus, a lock of the hair of Medusa and that this protected the city. The sanctuary of Athena Poliatas *(Keeper of the City)* was also called Eryma *(Defense)* for this reason. Second, some say that the bones of Orestes were buried in Tegea and that as long as they rested there the Spartans could not defeat the Tegeans. At last the Spartans learned from the priestess of Delphi that they must secure the bones of Orestes and restore them to Sparta if they would conquer Tegea. Lichas, a Spartan, by trickery discovered that the bones of Orestes were buried beneath a forge in Tegea, secured their removal, and restored them to Sparta. After this, whenever the Spartans contended with the Tegeans, they were always victorious.

In the Persian War, 500 Tegeans served under Leonidas at the Pass of Thermopylae but did not take part in the final struggle and defeat there, as they were sent away with the other allies when Leonidas learned that the Persians had been led around the mountain and were about to cut off the Greeks in the pass. At the Battle of Plataea (479 B.C.) the Tegeans claimed the right to command one wing of the army facing the Persians. They based their claim to this distinction on the feat of their ancestor Echemus, who had slain Hyllus when the Heraclidae first invaded the Peloponnesus. Their claim did not prevail; the Athenians put forth more cogent reasons why they should have the honor. However, the Spartans, whose right to command one wing no one questioned, placed the Tegeans next to themselves in recognition of their courage. They did well in doing so, for in the great struggle at Plataea that decided the fate of Greece, through a confusion in commands the Spartans alone were left to face the army of Mardonius, and their Tegean allies remained firmly at their side and rushed into the fray with them. The Tegeans were the first to enter the wooden fortress to which the Persians had been driven by the onrush of the Spartans and the Tegeans, and they were the first to reach and plunder the tent of Mardonius. Among the booty given to the Tegeans for their part in the battle was a bronze manger from which the Persian horses fed. The Tegeans placed it in the temple of Athena Alea at Tegea. According to Herodotus, of the 1500 Tegeans who took part in the engagement, 16 fell and were buried with full honors in a common grave on the field at Plataea. Tegea sided with Sparta in the Peloponnesian and Corinthian wars, was later a member of the Arcadian Confederacy against Sparta, fought against Sparta at Mantinea in 362 B.C., and was a member of the Aetolian and Achaean leagues.

*Telamon* (tel′ạ-mon). In ancient geography, a place on the coast of Etruria, Italy, about 76 miles NW of Rome. Near here the Romans nearly annihilated (225 B.C.) an army of Gauls.

*Telmessus* (tel-mes′us). In ancient geography, a town on the coast of Lycia, Asia Minor. The town was noted for its oracle of Apollo. Croesus, withdrawing to Sardis after an indecisive engagement with Cyrus, found that the outskirts of Sardis were swarming with snakes. The horses left the pastures and went to feed on the snakes. Croesus sent to the soothsayers of Telmessus to learn the meaning of this strange portent. The Telmessians sent word that the prodigy meant that foreign invaders would come and subdue his people, for the serpent, they said, is a child of earth, and the horse is a warrior and an alien. But by the time the message from the Telmessian soothsayers arrived, Croesus had already been captured by Cyrus and the Persians were plundering his capital. Among the important antiquities on the site of the ancient town is an ancient theater, well preserved and of good style.

**Tempe** (tem′pē), **Vale of.** Valley in E. Thessaly, Greece, deeply cleft between Olympus on the N and Ossa on the S, and traversed by the Peneus (or Salambria) River. It has been celebrated from ancient times for its beauty and savage grandeur. Tempe was one of the chief seats of the cult of Apollo. Length, about five miles.

**Tenea** (ten′ē̠-a̠). In ancient geography, a town in the region of Corinth.

**Tenedos** (ten′ē̠-dos). A small island in the Aegean Sea situated off the Troad, on the NW coast of Asia Minor. Historically, the island was settled by Aeolians, was subjugated by the Persians, and was in alliance with Athens in the 5th century B.C. Length, about seven miles.

**Tenos** (tē′nos). [Also: **Tino, Tinos.**] An island of the Cyclades, SE of Greece. In modern times the island is one of the most prosperous of the Greek islands, and exports marble and wine. Length, about 17 miles; area, 79 square miles.

**Tentyra** (ten′ti-ra̠). [Also: **Tentyris;** modern names, **Dendera, Denderah.**] Town in Upper Egypt, situated on the Nile. It is celebrated for its temple of the cow-goddess Hathor, which notwithstanding its late date, begun by Ptolemy XII (Ptolemy Auletes), and the great *pronaos* (columned hall outside the temple proper) added as late as the time of Tiberius, is one of the most interesting buildings in Egypt, owing to its almost perfect preservation, even to the roof. The imposing hexastyle pronaos has four ranges of Hathoric columns; on its ceiling is a noted sculptured zodiac, combining Egyptian and classical elements. Next to the pronaos is a hypostyle hall (ceiling supported on columns) of six columns, from which three chambers open on each side, and beyond this is a vestibule before a large hall in which stands an isolated cella. This hall is surrounded by a series of chambers, one of which in the middle of the back wall contained the emblematic *sistrum* (an instrument in the form of a metal rattle) of the goddess. The whole interior surface is sculptured, the art, however, being inferior. On the roof there is a small six-chambered temple to the local divinity Osiris-An.

**Teos** (tē′os). In ancient geography, one of the 12 Ionian cities of Asia Minor, situated on the W coast, about 25 miles SW of Smyrna. According to tradition, it was first inhabited by Minyans from Orchomenus who went there with Athamas, descendant of that Athamas who was the son of Aeolus. They were later joined by Ionians, Athenians, and Boeotians. The Teians fell under the dominion of the kings of Lydia. When Croesus was attacked by Cyrus, the Ionian cities rejected the overtures of Cyrus, thinking he could not defeat Croesus, and when Cyrus conquered Croesus he set out to bring the Ionian cities under his sway. All, except Miletus, resisted. Harpagus, general of Cyrus, approached Teos and prepared to take the walled city by building a mound of earth up around the wall. The Teians, rather than submit to slavery under the Persians, abandoned their city. They embarked all the inhabitants in their ships and sailed off to Thrace, where they founded Abdera. Among the ruins at Teos is a noted temple of Dionysus, a beautiful Ionic hexastyle peripteros on a stylobate of three steps.

**Termini Imerese** (ter′mē-nē ē-mā-rā′sä). See **Thermae Himeraeae.**

**Terracina** (ter-rä-chē′nä). See **Tarracina.**

**Testaceus** (tes-tạ-sē′us), **Mons.** [Modern name, **Monte Testaccio.**] Hill in the S part of Rome, SW of the Aventine Hill, on the left bank of the Tiber. It is about 115 feet in height above the surrounding area, and 2500 feet in circumference, and is formed entirely of the fragments of pottery vases, chiefly amphorae, from the extensive warehouses which once lined the neighboring quay. The potters' stamps on the fragments show that this rubbish heap was still used in the 4th century A.D., and it is believed to have been begun about the inception of the empire.

**Teuthrania** (tū-thrā′ni-ạ). In ancient geography, a region of Mysia, Asia Minor.

**Teutoberg** (tū′tọ-bėrg) **Forest.** [German, **Teutoburger Wald** or **Teutoburgerwald.**] Low, wooded mountain range in NW Germany, extending from the vicinity of Osnabruck in Hanover SE through North Rhine-Westphalia. It is known in different parts as the Lippischer Wald, Osning, and by other names. A victory was gained in this area (exact locality undetermined) in 9 A.D. by the Germans under Arminius (Hermann) over the Romans under Varus, the Roman army being nearly annihilated. Peak elevation, about 1535 feet.

**Thalamae** (thal′ạ-mē). In ancient geography, a place on the

promontory of Taenarum in Laconia, where there was an
oracle of Pasiphaë, which, in this case, was a title of the
moon. This oracle was consulted during sleep and responses were given in dreams.

*Thapsacus* (thap'sạ-kus). [In the Bible, *Tiphsah;* modern village, *Dibse.*] In ancient geography, a town in Syria on the W
bank of the Euphrates. It was an important crossing place in
ancient times. Here Xenophon crossed when he accompanied the expedition of Cyrus the Younger; and here also
Alexander the Great crossed the Euphrates.

*Thapsus* (thap'sus). In ancient geography, a town in N Africa,
situated on the coast about 30 miles SE of what is now
Sousse. Here Julius Caesar totally defeated (46 B.C.) the
remnants of the army of Pompey that had been reorganized
under Cato, Scipio, and Juba, and ended the African phase
of the civil war. It is said that Caesar's forces were in a near
panic when they learned of the size of the army Juba was
leading against them. Caesar's psychology for encouraging
his men was to exaggerate the size of the enemy's forces,
giving exact figures, as he claimed, to keep them from
spreading rumors, and also to spur them to fight for their
lives before an overwhelming force. Any who doubted their
ability to win or the facts he had given them were invited to
embark on a leaking ship and put to sea where they would
be the plaything of the winds. As noted above, this psycho-
logical approach was effective.

*Thasus* (thā'sus). An island in the N part of the Aegean Sea, S
of E Macedonia, lying about four miles from the mainland.
The surface is mountainous. It was colonized by Ionians
from Paros about the end of the 8th century B.C., who either
subdued or expelled the Thracian aborigines. Herodotus
mentions having seen the rich gold mines that provided
such a source of wealth to the inhabitants. Thasus carried on
a prosperous trade with the Thracians, the Egyptians, and
the Phoenicians, and by the 6th century B.C. had developed
a flourishing civilization of its own. Histiaeus the Milesian
fortified (c494 B.C.) the chief city (which had the same name
as the island) with marble walls to protect it from attack.
Darius the Great compelled the Thasians to dismantle the
fortifications (491 B.C.); they were reconstructed, but again
partly destroyed (464 B.C.) at the command of the Athenians. However, large parts remain to this day. During the

Persian Wars Thasus was under the dominion of the Persians. The island later belonged to the Delian League, revolted c465 B.C. but was besieged and subjugated by Cimon. During the Peloponnesian Wars it changed hands between Athens and Sparta several times. It was subject to Philip V of Macedon, and later became a free city under the Romans, who accorded it a favorable position because, unlike the rest of Greece, it had favored Rome in the Mithridatic Wars. Polygnotus the painter (beginning of the 5th century B.C.) and Stesimbrotus the writer (end of the 5th century B.C.) were natives of the island. The French School of Athens engaged in excavations at Thasus from 1910. Among the notable remains are the ruins of the walls about the ancient citadel, with a block engraved with the name of the builder, a Hellenistic theater, the foundations of a temple of Pythian Apollo (5th century B.C.), and remains of two altars on the terrace of a sanctuary of Poseidon and a huge altar of Hera as protectress of ports. On the latter it was forbidden to sacrifice goats. There are also remains of sanctuaries of Dionysus and Heracles, and a museum houses numerous statues and fragments. According to legend, the island was colonized by Thasus, for whom it was named. He was a son of Agenor of Phoenicia. Wearied of searching for his sister Europa he settled on the island in accordance with instructions he received from the oracle of Apollo at Delphi. The chief protecting deities of the island in ancient times were Dionysus and Heracles.

*Thasus.* Chief town and ancient capital of the island of Thasus, situated on the N coast.

*Thaumasium* (thou-mā′si-um). In ancient geography, a mountain in Arcadia, Greece. Here, according to some accounts, Rhea gave Cronus a stone wrapped in swaddling clothes. Under the impression that it was his newborn son Zeus, Cronus swallowed the stone.

*Thebae* (thē′bē). Latin form of *Thebes.*

*Thebes* (thēbz). [Modern Greek, *Thevai:* Latin, *Thebae.*] In ancient geography, the chief city of Boeotia in Greece. According to tradition, Cadmus the Phoenician came to Thebes following, in obedience to the command of the oracle of Delphi, a cow that had white moons on its flanks. Where the cow sank to rest, he was instructed to build his city. This it did at Thebes and there Cadmus slew the dragon that guarded the fountain of Ares and sowed its teeth to raise a race of warriors. But some say that before Cadmus came into the land it was occupied by the Ectenes, whose king Ogygus, or Ogyges, was an aborigine who reigned before the great flood that Zeus sent to engulf Hellas. The Ectenes perished by pestilence. The land was occupied by the Hyantes and Aones, and it was in this time that Cadmus came and built the upper citadel, called the Cadmea, where he had his own house. The room in the house where his daughter Semele gave birth to Dionysus was barred to men as late as the 2nd century A.D., when the traveler Pausanias visited Thebes. (Excavations at Thebes have uncovered the remains of what is called the "palace of Cadmus.") The city was first called Cadmea and its inhabitants were known as Cadmeans. Later Amphion and Zethus came and conquered it and built the lower city and the walls. The name was changed to Thebes in honor, some say, of the nymph Thebe, daughter of the river-god Asopus. She was the wife of Zethus. Thebes was celebrated as the birthplace of Dionysus, Heracles, the seer Tiresias, Amphion and Zethus, and many others. It was the scene of the exploits and tragedies of the Labdacids, descendants of Cadmus, the family of which Laius, Oedipus, and his descendants were members. It was the target of the Expedition of the Seven against Thebes, caused by the rivalry between Polynices and Eteocles, sons of Oedipus; and of the war of the Epigoni, undertaken by the sons of the original Seven, in which the Thebans were overcome and the city was taken. King Thersander, grandson of Oedipus, was slain in Mysia in the early years of the Trojan War. His grandson, Autesion, became king of Thebes, but on the advice of the oracle left the city and brought to an end the long line of Labdacid kings of Thebes. Within 60 years of the end of the Trojan War Thebes had become the capital of the cities of Boeotia. The wall of the ancient city was pierced by seven gates—the Electran, Proetidian, Neïstan, Crenaean, Hypsistan, Ogygian, and Homoloid Gates. Outside the Electran Gate, on a slight eminence, was the temple of Ismenian Apollo. The priest in the temple was a boy of noble family who served for one year. He was called a "laurel-bearer," from the wreath of laurel he wore. Heracles was one of these laurel-bearers, according to some accounts, and his foster father Amphitryon dedicated in the temple a bronze tripod in his name which was inscribed with the "Cadmean" letters said to have been introduced into Greece by Cadmus. Before the temple was a stone called "Manto's chair." She was the prophetic daughter of Tiresias; and within the temple was an image of Apollo of cedar wood, made by Canachus. Among the treasures of the temple were a shield, spear, and tripod, all of solid gold, dedicated by King Croesus of Lydia. The site of the temple was discovered in 1910. Among the sights of Thebes were a sanctuary of Heracles decorated with marble sculptures representing most of his great labors; a temple of Artemis Euclia *(Of Good Repute)* with an image by Scopas, before which was a stone lion dedicated by Heracles after he defeated Erginus; the spring where Oedipus washed off the blood that had splattered on him when he slew his father; the spring where Cadmus slew the dragon of Ares and brought down the wrath of that god on his descendants; a shrine and tomb of Amphion outside the Ogygian Gate, and, farther off, a shrine of Iolaus, the companion of Heracles; the tomb, near the Neïstan Gate, of Menoeceus, son of Creon, who voluntarily leaped from the walls of Thebes to his death in order to propitiate Ares and save the city when the Seven attacked it; a sanctuary of Athena near the Hypsistan Gate, where Cadmus, having killed the dragon, sacrificed a cow to the goddess; a temple containing ancient wooden images of Aphrodite, said to have been made from the figureheads of the ships that brought Cadmus to Greece and dedicated by his wife Harmonia; the grave of Trojan Hector near the fountain where Oedipus cleansed his hands, for Hector's bones were brought to Thebes in obedience to an oracle; a temple of Ammon containing an image dedicated by Pindar; and Pindar's tomb.

Modern scholars say Thebes was early settled by Boeotians from Thessaly, and that by the 7th century B.C. it was the capital of a loose confederation of Boeotian cities, from which, however, the wealthy Boeotian city of Orchomenus held aloof. In 509 B.C. the Boeotian city of Plataea sought the protection of Athens and became a staunch ally of that city and the implacable enemy of Thebes. The protection that Athens rendered Plataea caused a quarrel between Athens and Thebes and they became enemies. When Xerxes invaded Greece, Theban troops under Leonidas at Ther-

fat, fāte, fär, fåll, åsk, fãre; net, mē, hėr; pin, pīne; not, nōte, mȯve, nôr; up, lūte, pu̇ll; oi, oil; ou out; (lightened) ḝlect, agọ̈ny, ụnite;

mopylae (480 B.C.) served unwillingly, according to
Herodotus, and after the defeat of the Greek forces there,
the Thebans allied themselves openly with Persia, fought on
the Persian side, and shared in the Persian defeat at Plataea
(479 B.C.). Some say the Thebans fought on the side of the
Persians against their will, compelled by their aristocratic
rulers who hated Athenian democracy. After the Persian
War the rivalry with Athens, now stronger than ever, flared
anew. In a battle at Tanagra (457 B.C.) the Thebans, with the
aid of the Spartans, defeated the Athenians but could not
press their advantage, and were defeated by the Athenians
at Oenophyta in 456 B.C. During the Peloponnesian Wars
Thebes was the bitter enemy of Athens and rendered aid to
Sparta. The partnership with Sparta was an unequal one,
however, and there were many Theban voices raised against
Sparta in the years immediately following the long wars.
Following a defeat at Coronea (394 B.C.) Thebes was forced
to yield to Sparta (392 B.C.). In 382 B.C. the Spartans, by a
conspiracy with malcontents within the city, gained control
of the citadel of Thebes. They arranged to seize it on the day
when the Thesmophoria was being celebrated, for on that
day only women, celebrating the feast, occupied it. The
Spartans thus took it without resistance and established a
government friendly to Sparta. This government, and the
Spartan officials in Thebes, were overthrown (379 B.C.) by
a most daring coup of Pelopidas, the Theban general and
good friend of Epaminondas. Under command of Epaminondas, the Thebans defeated Sparta at the Battle of Leuctra (371 B.C.) and again at Mantinea (362 B.C.), and
established Theban hegemony of Greece. Epaminondas was
killed at Mantinea and those who assumed power in Thebes
exercised power over the Boeotian cities so tyrannously that
they earned for Thebes a hatred that ultimately led to the
destruction of the city. Thebes took part in the Sacred War
(354 B.C.) that was carried on intermittently about Delphi
for ten years. She was allied with Athens in the attempt to
hold back Philip of Macedon and was defeated with her at
Chaeronea (338 B.C.), and was severely treated by Philip,
who stationed a Macedonian garrison in the city. On the
death of Philip the Thebans rebelled. Philip's son, Alexander the Great, marched against it and subdued it. At his
side fought the Boeotian enemies of Thebes. Alexander

(obscured) errạnt, ardẹnt, actọr; ch, chip; g, go; th, thin; ᴛʜ, then; y, you;
(variable) ḍ as d or j, ṣ as s or sh, ṭ as t or ch, ẓ as z or zh.

gave the beleaguered city every opportunity to surrender without bloodshed, but the defenders refused, the citadel was taken, and 6000 Thebans were massacred before Alexander put a stop to the slaughter. He entrusted the fate of the city to the hands of his Greek allies; they decreed that the people be sold into slavery and the city razed to the ground. At the command of Alexander, one house was spared, that of Pindar the poet, which stood alone among the ruins. Before Alexander took the city, the Thebans were warned of their black fate by a prodigy: a spider spun a black web over the entrance to the sanctuary of Demeter, the temple in which, in happier times, the shields of the Spartans who fell at Leuctra had been dedicated by the victorious Thebans. The city was rebuilt by Cassander, who restored the ancient walls, but it lapsed into insignificance under the Roman Empire. Remains of the walls of the ancient city are still to be seen but much of the ancient city now lies buried under 15 to 20 feet of earth. In 1970 the remains of a palace dating from about 1300 B.C. were reported to have been discovered in Thebes. Excavation of the site has thus far yielded several unusual finds, including a clay bathtub and fragments of several Linear Script B tablets. Professor Spyridon Marinatos, director general of Greek antiquities, has assembled three of the tablets, which are notable both for the several new elements of the script found in them and for their palm-leaf rather than rectangular shape.

*Thelpusa* (thel-pū'sạ). In ancient geography, a town in Arcadia, Greece, on a hill near the Ladon River.

*Thera* (thir'ạ, thē'rạ). [Also: *Thira, Santorini*.] Volcanic island in the S part of the Cyclades. The island rises steeply from the sea, and has long been celebrated for its volcanic activity. At an early date, about 1500 B.C. according to some scholars, a catastrophic series of eruptions caused part of the island, including most of the volcano, to sink into the sea. The sea forced a way into the volcanic cone, forming a deep anchorage for ships near the center of the island. At times the water at certain spots can be seen to bubble from the subterranean pressures of the volcano. An eruption of the volcano occurred in 1956. In 1967, near Akrotiri, in the south of Thera, a team of archeologists discovered and began excavating the site of a Minoan city abandoned as a result of the 1500 B.C.(?) eruptions. Its streets and houses

fat, fāte, fär, fâll, àsk, fãre; net, mē, hėr; pin, pīne; not, nōte, möve, nôr; up, lūte, pùll; oi, oil; ou out; (lightened) ḗlect, agǫny, ūnite;

have been preserved by the layer of volcanic ash 100 to 300 feet thick that covers most of the island. Its ancient name as yet unknown, this outpost of Minoan civilization has yielded many valuable finds. Objects discovered range from remnants of food and medicines still in their containers, household utensils, and furniture outlined in the ash, to pottery of relatively sophisticated design and a group of remarkable frescoes. "The Room of the Lilies," one of these frescoes, is the largest nearly intact fresco of that period ever found in Greece. The city may originally have extended about one mile in length and possibly held 20,000 to 30,000 inhabitants. Area of the island, 30 square miles; length, 10 miles.

*Therma* (thèr'mạ). In ancient geography, a city of Macedonia, situated at the head of the Thermaic Gulf (Gulf of Salonika), which was named for the city. Xerxes stopped here in his invasion of Greece, 480 B.C. It was held briefly by the Athenians just before the Peloponnesian Wars. About 316 B.C. Cassander founded the city of Thessalonica nearby and Therma was absorbed in it.

*Thermae Himeraeae* (thèr'mē him-èr-ē'ē) or *Himerenses* (him-èr-en'sēz). [Modern name, *Termini Imerese*.] In ancient geography, a town on the N coast of Sicily. It was founded (407 B.C.) by the Carthaginians, near the site of Himera, which they had destroyed. The town was on the hill above "the hot baths of the Nymphs" mentioned by Pindar. Its name, Thermae, refers to the hot springs, and the name Himeraeae signalizes the old Greek city that was destroyed. Greek settlers soon came to live in the Carthaginian town of Thermae Himeraeae and made of it a Greek town. Much contested between Syracusans and Carthaginians, it finally became a Roman town. Among scanty remains of antiquity are those of a Roman theater.

*Thermaic Gulf* (thèr-mā'ik) or *Thermaicus Sinus* (thèr-mā'i-kus sī'nus). Northwesternmost arm of the Aegean Sea, situated W of the Chalcidice peninsula. Length, about 70 miles.

*Thermodon* (thèr'mọ-don). In ancient geography, a river of Pontus. The area about its mouth was traditionally the home of the Amazons.

*Thermopylae* (thèr-mop'i-lē). Hot salt springs on the border of Locris; the name means "hot gates." According to legend, Heracles, preparing to sacrifice to Zeus after his conquest of

(obscured) errạnt, ardẹnt, actọr; ch, chip; g, go; th, thin; ᴛʜ, then; y, you;
(variable) ḍ as d or j, ṣ as s or sh, ṭ as t or ch, ẓ as z or zh.

Eurytus, donned a ceremonial robe his wife sent to him here. The robe had been secretly anointed by his wife with the dried blood of his fallen enemy, the centaur Nessus. When the heat of the sacrificial fires melted the blood poisoned by one of Heracles' own arrows, the robe clung to Heracles and seared and stung his flesh. Maddened by the burning pain, he leaped into the waters to cool his body, but the heat of his flesh was so intense it caused the waters to bubble and steam. Ever since, these springs have been hot. The springs are at the narrow pass of the same name which runs from Thessaly to Locris, between Mount Oeta and a marsh bordering the Maliacus Sinus (Gulf of Lamia). (The configuration of the land has been somewhat changed in modern times.) Through it passed the only road from N to S Greece. Here occurred (480 B.C.) one of the most famous conflicts of the Persian Wars. A small band of Greeks under the Spartan Leonidas defended the pass against a vast army under Xerxes. Their position was betrayed, and Leonidas sent away his troops, except for 300 Spartans and 700 Thespians. These remained and with unmatched courage resisted the Persians until all were slain. According to Herodotus, two Spartans had been sent to the rear before the final battle, because they were afflicted by diseases of the eye. When they heard of the assault being made against Leonidas, one of them ordered his slave to bring him his armor and lead him to the battle. The slave did so and fled; his master plunged into the fight and perished with his friends. The other Spartan afflicted with a disease of the eyes used his sickness as an excuse to stay away from the battle and later returned to Sparta. There he was greeted with disgrace. No Spartan would give him a light to kindle his fire, nor would any Spartan speak with him. But this man, Aristodemus, redeemed himself later at the battle of Plataea (479 B.C.). Another Spartan who survived because he had been sent as an envoy to Thessaly by Leonidas was in such disgrace when he returned to Sparta that he hanged himself. In 279 or 278 B.C., the allied Greeks attempted unsuccessfully to prevent the passage of the Gauls under Brennus through the pass; and here, in 191 B.C., the Romans under Glabrio defeated Antiochus III of Syria.

*Thespiae* (thes'pi-ē). A city in Boeotia at the foot of Mount Helicon. With Plataea it refused to give earth and water to

fat, fāte, fär, fâll, àsk, fāre; net, mē, hėr; pin, pīne; not, nōte, mŏve, nôr; up, lūte, pùll; oi, oil; ou out; (lightened) ēlect, agǫny, ūnite;

the heralds of Xerxes, and it sent to Thermopylae 700 men who remained and perished with the Spartans. The Thespians fought against the Persians at Plataea in 479 B.C. and against Athens at Delium in 424 B.C. The walls of the city were later destroyed by Thebes. Thespiae was noted for the worship of Eros and the Muses and in it was Eros' most famous shrine.

***Thesprotia*** (thes-prō'shạ). [Also: ***Thesprotis.***] In ancient geography, a region in SW Epirus, Greece, lying near the sea.

***Thessalonica*** (thes"ạ-lọ-nī'kạ, -lon'i-kạ). [Modern names, ***Salonika, Salonica, Thessalonika.***] In ancient geography, a city and seaport of Macedonia, situated at the head of the Thermaic Gulf (Gulf of Salonika). It was founded, c316 B.C., by Cassander near the ancient city of Therma, which was absorbed by the new city. Cassander named his city after his wife, a sister of Alexander the Great. It became a Roman province in 146 B.C. Owing to its location on the Gulf and also on the Via Egnatia (large sections of which remain in the city), the Roman military road that ran from the coast of the Adriatic to the East, it became a flourishing commercial and intellectual center. Cicero went into exile at Thessalonica, 58 B.C., and Pompey took refuge there briefly after his defeat by Caesar, 49 B.C.

***Thessaly*** (thes'ạ-li). [Also: ***Thessalia.***] District which in ancient times formed the NE division of Greece. It was bounded by Macedonia on the N (separated by a range of mountains including Mount Olympus), the Thracian Sea and Magnesia (or including Magnesia) on the E, Doris and Aetolia on the S, and Epirus on the W (separated by Mount Pindus). Thessaly contained the mountains Ossa, Pelion, and Othrys, and was traversed by the Peneus River that flowed through the Vale of Tempe. According to tradition, it was the original home of the Achaeans, who migrated from there to Crete and to other parts of Greece and laid the foundations for a highly developed civilization which did not, however, take root in Thessaly. The fertile land and location of Thessaly as the entrance to the Greek peninsula from the north attracted frequent invasions. Pelasgians invaded it in the 2nd millenium B.C. They were followed by the Minyans, whose story is told in the legends of Iolcus, Pagasae, and the expedition of the Argonauts. Various other tribes came into the region, including Achaeans from Phthia (part of Achilles' realm), and Boeotians. The men of Thessaly took part in the great united Greek expedition against Troy, Thessalus, a son of Heracles and a king in Thessaly, being one of the leaders of the Thessalians. After the Trojan War the land was invaded by a Dorian people of Epirus, who also claimed descent from Heracles. They were called Thessali, and gave their name to the whole region. The newcomers subjugated and enslaved the people of Thessaly, and established themselves as the military and ruling class. "Horse-breeding" Thessaly made cavalry the backbone of its military establishment. Several powerful families were founded, as the Aleuadae at Larisa and the Scopadae at Crannon. They established oligarchic and aristocratic rule, and democracy was much delayed in the region. Pagasae and Pherae became the seats of powerful lords. In the 6th century B.C. these powerful families united in a loose confederation, which in times of emergency united under a common military commander, called a *tagus*. The area was divided into four regions: Thessaliotis, centering about Pharsalus; Pelasgiotis, around Larisa; Hestiaeotis, about Triccala; and Phthiotis, about Othrys. In the Persian Wars Thessaly, the gateway to Greece, was pro-Persian, as much from necessity, owing to its exposed position, as from choice. At times the united Thessalian Confederation presented a threat to Phocis and southern Greece, but more often the confederation was weakened by the ambitions of local leaders. Jason, tyrant of Pherae in the 4th century B.C., won domination of the confederation and for a time threatened southern Greece. Whatever his dreams of conquest may have been, they were cut short by his assassination. The Thessalian cities invoked the aid of Macedonia to resist Jason's successor, Alexander of Pherae. They found it no happier to be under foreign rule, and turned to Thebes. For a time Thessaly existed as a Theban protectorate, divided into tetrads, four political divisions based on geographical divisions. In 353 B.C. Philip II of Macedon entered Thessaly, at the invitation of the Thessalians, and subsequently made himself master of it. It remained more or less a vassal of Macedonia until 197 B.C., when it became a protectorate of Rome. Many of the cities of Thessaly, its mountains and valleys, are celebrated in Greek legend.

*Thisbe* (thiz′bē). In ancient geography, a city of Boeotia, Greece, named for a local nymph.

*Thornax* (thôr′naks), *Mount.* Mountain in Argolis. Here, some say, Zeus, in the form of a cuckoo, wooed Hera. She had rejected his advances when he courted her in his own shape, but took the cuckoo and nestled it in her bosom. Zeus thereupon resumed his own shape and ravished her. Afterward, the name of the mountain was changed to Cuckoo.

*Thrace* (thrās). [Latin, *Thracia;* Greek, *Thraki.*] In ancient geography, a region NE of Macedonia, extending to the Ister (Danube) River on the N and the Euxine (Black) Sea on the E. As a Roman province it was bounded by the Haemus or Balkan Mountains (separating it from Moesia) on the N, the Euxine Sea and Bosporus on the E, the Propontis, Hellespont, and Aegean Sea on the S, and the Nestus or Mesta (separating it from Macedonia) on the W. The principal mountain range is the Rhodope; the principal river, the Hebrus (Maritsa). The climate was known for its severity, and the inhabitants for their ferocity and barbarity. Because of the severe climate and the fierce people Thrace was known as the home of Boreas, the North Wind, and the war-god Ares. The aborigines were scattered by invaders, who were in turn replaced by the various tribes called Thracians between 1600–1400 B.C. The affinities of the ancient inhabitants are unknown; they may have been ancestors of the Wallachs. The wide stretch of country between the lower course of the Ister and the shores of the Aegean and the Propontis was occupied in ancient times by the tribe of the Thracians, which Herodotus regards as the greatest of all peoples next to the Indi. The scanty remains of the Thracian language are enough to establish traces of its Indo-Germanic character, but not enough to define its position in the Indo-European family more closely. Certain it is, however, that from hence a large part of Asia Minor received its Indo-European-speaking population. In the first place, it is known that the Thracians themselves spread eastwards over the strait a considerable distance towards Asia. According to the unanimous opinion of antiquity, again, the Phrygians emigrated from Europe, and were originally connected with the Thracians. According to Greek legend, Orpheus, Linus, and Musaeus came from Thrace. In the Trojan War the Thracians, under their prince Rhesus, were allies of King Priam.

(obscured) errạnt, ardẹnt, actọr; ch, chip; g, go; th, thin; ŦH, then; y, you;
(variable) ḍ as d or j, ṣ as s or sh, ṭ as t or ch, ẓ as z or zh.

From the 8th century B.C. the Greeks visited Thrace, and planted colonies at Byzantium, on the Chersonesus Thracica (Gallipoli Peninsula), and at Abdera, Perinthus, and elsewhere. Darius the Great invaded Thrace and when he withdrew he left his general Megabazus there and the latter subdued the region. The Thracian Greeks furnished 120 ships and many foot soldiers to the armament Xerxes led into Europe in 480 B.C. And it was in Thrace, at the mouth of the Hebrus River, that Xerxes reviewed his vast army, as enumerated by Herodotus. After the defeat of the Persians the Athenians dispersed the Persian garrisons Xerxes had left in Thrace. In the middle of the 5th century B.C. Teres, king of the Odrysae, the most powerful of the Thracian tribes, brought most of Thrace under his rule. During the Peloponnesian War, Sitalces, son of Teres, supplied Athens with troops and invaded Macedonia to little effect. The Spartan general Brasidas made an unsuccessful attempt to win the Athenian cities on the coast of Thrace. In the 4th century B.C. an alliance between Athens and Thrace proved ineffective. Philip II of Macedon won control of the area c340 B.C. Following the death of Alexander the Great, Thrace became for a time part of the dominion of Lysimachus, and then fell to Macedonia. With the defeat of the Macedonian king Perseus (168 B.C.), Thrace became independent under the protection of Rome, and subsequently, a Roman province.

*Thracian Bosporus* (thrā′shạn bos′pọ̄-rus). Ancient name of the *Bosporus.*

*Thracica* (thrā′si-kạ), *Chersonesus.* Ancient name of the *Gallipoli Peninsula.*

*Thronium* (thrō′ni-um). In ancient geography, a city in the Ceraunian Mountains, settled, according to tradition, by Locrians from Thronium on the river Boagrius and by Abantes from Euboea, who, in eight ships, were driven to this place by a storm on their way home from the Trojan War. They named the land about their new city Abantis. Later, they were expelled from their city by their neighbors of Apollonia, a colony of Corcyra.

*Thurii* (thū′ri-ī). [Also : *Thurium.*] In ancient geography, a city in Magna Graecia, Italy, situated near the ancient Sybaris and near what is now Terranova di Sibari. It was founded (452 B.C.) by fugitives from Sybaris who were soon expelled

fat, fāte, fär, fȧll, ȧsk, fãre; net, mē, hėr; pin, pīne; not, nōte, mȯve, nôr; up, lūte, pu̇ll; oi, oil; ou out; (lightened) ẹlect, agǫny, ụnite;

by Croton, and was refounded (c443 B.C.) by colonists from Athens and other cities. Hippodamus of Miletus was said to have drawn the plans for the Athenian colony, and the historian Herodotus was one of the colonists. It was defeated (390 B.C.) by the Lucanians, called Rome to its aid against Tarentum in 282 B.C., and later was subject to Rome. It was plundered (204 B.C.) by Hannibal, and was later the site of a Roman colony.

*Thymbrius* (thim′bri-us). In ancient geography, a small river near Ilium (Troy).

*Tiber* (tī′bėr). [Also: *Tiberis, Tiberinus, Tibris, Tybris;* modern name, *Tevere.*] Second longest river in Italy. It rises in the Apennines about 20 miles NE of Arretium (Arezzo), flows generally S, and empties into the Mediterranean about 16 miles SW of Rome, which is on its banks. Its chief tributaries are the Clanis (Chiana), Nar (Nera), and Anio (Aniene).

*Tibris* or *Tybris* (tī′bris). An ancient name of the *Tiber.*

*Tibur* (tī′bėr). [Modern name, *Tivoli.*] In ancient geography, a town in C Italy, situated on a height above the falls of the Anio River, about 15 miles E of Rome. It was an ancient town of the Latins. Under the Romans it continued to flourish, and was especially known as a resort and celebrated for the picturesque Falls of the Anio. Tibur is also notable for two interesting temples of the republican period, a round temple of Vesta and a rectangular temple, sometimes attributed to Hercules, or to the Sibyl, for many centuries used as a church. At the foot of the hill are extensive deposits of the fine water-laid limestone known by the Romans as *lapis Tiburtinus,* in English as travertine, and at a little distance are sulphurous warm springs, the Aquae Albulae of the Romans, and the extensive remains of the villa of the emperor Hadrian. (JJ)

*Ticinus* (ti-sī′nus). [Modern name, *Ticino.*] River in Switzerland and Italy, formed by the junction of two headstreams flowing from the Alps. It traverses Verbanus Lacus (Lago Maggiore) and the Lombard plain, and joins the Po near Pavia.

*Tifata* (tī-fā′tạ). [Modern name, *Monte di Maddalini.*] Low mountain range near Capua, Italy, about 17 miles NE of Naples. Near it, in 83 B.C., Sulla defeated the Marian general Norbanus.

*Tifernum Tiberinum* (ti-fėr′num tib-ẹ-rī′num). In ancient geography, a city in Italy, on or near the site of the modern Città di Castello, about 20 miles from Arezzo.

*Tigris* (tī'gris). [Biblical name, *Hiddekel.*] River in Mesopotamia (modern Asiatic Turkey and Iraq) which is formed by headstreams that rise in the mountains of Armenia and Assyria, and flows S and SE to the Persian Gulf. The ancient cities of Nineveh, Calah, and Ctesiphon, among others, were on it. According to Greek legend to account for the name of the river, Dionysus crossed it on a tiger's back.

*Tiryns* (tī'rinz). In ancient geography, a city in Argolis, Greece, situated near the coast SE of Argos, and about three miles N of Nauplia. According to tradition, the region was first occupied by Pelasgians, who fell under the domination of Danaus when he came to Argolis from Egypt with his 50 daughters. Following internecine wars, the kingdom of Danaus was divided among his descendants. Acrisius became ruler of the region of Argos and his brother Proetus became king of the area about Tiryns and founded the city. According to legend, he imported Cyclopes from Lycia to build its "Cyclopean" walls of enormous, irregular stones. It fell under the domination of Mycenae but with the Dorian invasion of the Peloponnesus recovered its independence. In the Persian Wars Tiryns sent 200 men to the Battle of Plataea (479 B.C.). Their names were inscribed on the tripods dedicated at Delphi in celebration of the Greek victory. In 468 B.C. Argos, jealous of the honor paid Tiryns for its part in the Persian Wars, in which Argos had played no heroic part, conquered Tiryns and destroyed the city.

The city was built on a low rocky hill that rose above the plain of Argos. The ancient city, occupying the hill and the area of the plain at its base, was older than Mycenae, and dates from the 3rd millennium B.C. After 2000 B.C. the citadel on the summit of the low rock was enclosed by walls, within which remains of a pre-Mycenaean palace have been found. Tiryns is celebrated for its antiquities, including Cyclopean walls, gates, and the palace (excavated by Heinrich Schliemann and Wilhelm Dörpfeld, 1884–85). The citadel is a famous memorial of early Greek civilization. The massive walls, built of great blocks, some of which weigh as much as 13 tons, with the interstices filled with small stones, surround the summit of an oblong hill. In the *Iliad* Homer speaks of Tiryns as "mighty of ramparts." Pausanias, who visited it in the 2nd century A.D., said it was unnecessary to

go to Egypt to see the pyramids when there were such wonders as Tiryns at home. The acropolis at Tiryns is divided
into three terraces, of which the highest was occupied by the
palace and royal quarters, and included the well-known galleries of arcades resembling pointed arches. These galleries
gave on to chambers constructed in the thickness of the
walls and were unique in Greek architecture. They were
used as storage areas in time of peace and as armories and
places of shelter in time of war. The middle terrace, north
and west of the royal quarters, reinforced the acropolis and
was occupied by those connected with the royal household.
To the north, and separated by a wall, was the lower terrace
where the garrison was quartered, and to which the population of the city at the base of the hill withdrew in times of
invasion. As at Mycenae, the principal approach to the
acropolis was by a passageway made of enormous blocks of
stone, more carefully dressed and fitted than the surrounding walls, and was so placed that the right, or unshielded,
side of an approaching enemy was exposed to the defenders
in the citadel. Within the walls of the acropolis there are
remains of an extensive prehistoric palace, with outer and
inner courts, men's apartments, bathroom, and secluded
women's quarters, the whole corresponding with the spirit
of the Homeric picture. The floor plan of the palace is still
plainly visible. A cistern and remains of a drainage system
have been found at Tiryns, as well as a royal altar surrounded by a ditch into which the blood of sacrificial victims
flowed. Wall paintings and other details of high interest
were found by Schliemann.

*Titane* (ti-tā′nē). In ancient geography, a town between Sicyon
   and Phlius in the region of Corinth, Greece.
*Titaresius* (ti-ta̱-rē′si-us). In ancient geography, a river of Thessaly, called by Homer a branch of the dread river of oaths,
   the Styx. The seer Mopsus lived near its banks.
*Tithorea* (ti-thôr′ē-a̱). In ancient geography, a city of Phocis, on
   the slopes of Mount Parnassus.
*Tivoli* (tē′vō-lē). See *Tibur.*
*Todi* (tō′dē). See *Tuder.*
*Tomi* (tō′mī). [Also: *Tomis.*] In ancient geography, a town on
   the coast of the Euxine (Black) Sea, near what is now Con-
   stanta (Constanza), Rumania. It was the place to which the
   outspoken Roman poet Ovid was banished.

*Toronaicus, Sinus* (tôr-ọ̄-nā'i-kus sī'nus). [Also: *Gulf of Cassandra (Kassandra), Toronaic Gulf.*] Arm of the Aegean Sea, between the peninsulas of Cassandra and Sithonia.

*Torone* (tọ̄-rō'nē). In ancient geography, a city on the Sithonian peninsula, in Chalcidice. It was captured by the Spartan general Brasidas, 423 B.C., with the aid of conspirators inside the city.

*Trabzon* (träb-zôn'). [Also: *Trebizond;* ancient name, *Trapezus.*] A seaport in N Turkey, on the Black Sea. See *Trapezus.*

*Trachis* (trā'kis). In ancient geography, a city of Greece, situated at the foot of Mount Oeta near Thermopylae. It was an important strategic point, and the legendary scene of the death of Heracles. The Spartan colony of Heraclea was established there in 426 B.C.

*Trajanopolis* (trā″ją-nop'ọ̄-lis). In ancient geography, a city in Thrace founded by Trajan.

*Tralles* (tral'ēz). In ancient geography, a city of Lydia or Caria, in Asia Minor, situated on a tributary of the Maeander River. According to tradition, it was founded by colonists from Argos and Thrace. A school of sculpture, known as the Trallian school, grew up there, and is best represented by the Farnese Bull, now in the National Museum at Naples.

*Transalpine Gaul* (trans-al'pin, -pīn, gôl). See *Gaul, Transalpine.*

*Transpadane Gaul* (trans'pą-dān, trans-pā'dān). See *Gaul, Transpadane.*

*Trapani* (trä'pä-nē). See *Drepanum.*

*Trapezus* (trą-pē'zus). In ancient geography, a place in W Arcadia. The people of Trapezus refused to abandon their city to join the new Arcadian city of Megalopolis (after 371 B.C.), but when the Arcadians would have compelled them, they left the Peloponnesus entirely and went to the Pontus, and were there welcomed by the city of Trapezus on the Euxine Sea (Pontus) that had the same name as their own Arcadian city.

*Trapezus.* [Also: *Trebizond;* modern name, *Trabzon.*] A seaport on the Pontus. It is picturesquely situated on a tableland between two deep ravines. Next to Smyrna (now Izmir) it was long the chief commercial city in Asia Minor, and a center of transit trade between Europe and Armenia, Persia, and C Asia. It was a dependency of the Greek colony of Sinope, a resting place on the retreat of the Ten Thousand

Greeks, and an important city about the time of Hadrian. (JJ)

***Trasimenus, Lacus*** (tras-i-mē′nus, lā′kus). [Modern names, *Lago Trasimeno, Lago di Perugia;* English, *Lake Trasimeno, Lake Perugia.*] Lake in Etruria, about ten miles W of Perusia (Perugia). Here (217 B.C.) Hannibal almost annihilated a Roman army under the consul Flaminius, who was slain. It has no natural outlet. Elevation, about 850 feet; length, about ten miles; depth, about 25 feet; area, about 50 square miles.

***Trebia*** (trē′bi-ạ). [Modern name, *Trebbia.*] River in N Italy which joins the Po near Placentia (Piacenza). Near it Hannibal defeated the Romans under Sempronius Longus and Publius Cornelius Scipio in December, 218 B.C.

***Trent*** (trent). See *Tridentum.*

***Tricca*** (trik′ạ). [Modern name, *Trikkala.*] In ancient geography, a town of Thessaly, situated N of the Peneus River.

***Tricrena*** (trī-krē′nạ). In ancient geography, mountains near Pheneüs, in Arcadia, where there are three springs (thus accounting for the name). Hermes was thought to have been bathed in these after he was born, and for this reason they were sacred to him.

***Tridentum*** (trī-den′tum). [Modern name, *Trent.*] In ancient geography, a city in NE Italy, situated on the Athesis (Adige) River. It was a Celtic colony, was fortified by the Roman emperor Augustus, and served as a base for the campaign of Drusus (15 B.C.) which incorporated the Alpine countries into the Roman domain.

***Trikkala*** (trik′ạ-lạ). See *Tricca.*

***Trinacria*** (tri-nā′kri-ạ). Old name of Sicily, meaning "Three Points," referring to the three promontories Pachynus, Peloris, and Lilybaeum.

***Triphylia*** (trī-fil′i-ạ). In ancient geography, a region in the S part of Elis, disputed for centuries by Elis and Arcadia. There was a celebrated temple of Samian Poseidon at Triphylia, and it was the seat of a league of six Minyan cities. In the time of Herodotus most of its cities were in ruins. The warrior and historian Xenophon, exiled from Athens, lived for a time at Scillus in Triphylia, and there set down the *Anabasis,* the celebrated history of the march of the Ten Thousand.

***Triton*** (trī′ton). A river in Boeotia. Also, the Nile River was sometimes called Triton.

*Triton.* [Modern name, *Garavos.*] In ancient geography, a river of Crete, rising E of Mount Ida and flowing N into the sea.

*Tritonis* (trī-tō'nis), or *Triton, Lake.* A vast lake that once covered a large part of the lowlands of Libya. Athena was sometimes said to have been born on the edge of this lake, hence her epithet "Tritogeneia." The lake was thought to have been formed by a tidal wave that engulfed the shores of Libya, and to have disappeared ultimately as a consequence of earthquakes. In classical times the lake covered 900 square miles, having shrunk considerably since mythological times. It has now shrunk to a salt lake about 120 miles long in SW central Tunisia, known as Shatt el Jerid, if indeed this body of water is to be identified with Lake Tritonis. Possibly the lake also once included the Shatt el Melghir, another salt lake about 100 miles long in NE Algeria.

*Troad* (trō'ạd). In ancient geography, the region in NW Asia Minor about the city of Troy, which was its capital. It included a number of allied and dependent cities, and extended to the Hellespont and the Aegean Sea. In the Trojan War the Greeks harried the cities of the Troad for nine years before they attacked the capital city itself.

*Troezen* (trē'zẹn). In ancient geography, a city in the Peloponnesus, Greece, situated near the coast, about 39 miles SW of Athens. It was originally an Ionian settlement, but later became Doric. According to Pausanias, the Troezenians were "unrivalled glorifiers of their own country." Troezen early sent out colonists. In Caria they founded the cities of Halicarnassus and Myndus. In the Persian War the Troezenians received the women and children who were sent to them for safety as the Persians approached Athens (480 B.C.). Stone images set up in the agora afterward represented these fugitives and commemorated Troezenian hospitality. The Troezenians played a valiant part in the war. They sent five ships to join the Greek fleet, a thousand men to Plataea, and at the battle of Mycale (479 B.C.), Herodotus says that, after the Athenians, "the most valiant were the men of Corinth, of Troezen, and of Sicyon." In the middle of the 5th century B.C. Troezen came under the dominion of Athens. It was an unwilling partnership, and later the Troezenians took the side of Sparta in the disastrous Peloponnesian Wars.

*Troy* (troi). [Also: *Ilium;* Latin, *Troia, Troja.*] Ancient city in

Asia Minor, famous in Greek legend as the capital of Priam and the object of the siege by the allied Greeks under Agamemnon. According to legend, the city was founded by Teucer, an immigrant from Crete who was the son of the Cretan river Scamander and the nymph Idaea. From him the people were called Teucrians. In the reign of Teucer, Dardanus came to his kingdom from Samothrace. Teucer gave him land in the region and his daughter Batia in marriage. Dardanus built a city at the foot of Mount Ida which he called Dardania. Tros, the grandson of Dardanus, called his people Trojans and named the city Troy. One son of Tros was Ilus, the father of Laomedon and the grandfather of Priam. Another was Assaracus, the ancestor of Aeneas. And a third son was Ganymede, carried off to Olympus by Zeus. Ilion, the city that Ilus founded in obedience to an oracle, was joined with Dardania and Troy and the whole came to be called Troy or Ilium. The location of Troy near the Hellespont and the entrance to the Propontis and the Euxine Sea, gave it command of trade from the Aegean islands and Greece to the region about the Euxine Sea. It was the strongest power on the coast of Asia Minor. The Trojan War, celebrated in the *Iliad* of Homer, is now thought to have been waged to destroy this control and to secure access to the lands about the Euxine Sea. According to Homer, the war lasted ten years. The first nine were occupied in raids on the cities of the Troad which supplied and supported Troy, for Priam's rule extended from the island of Lesbos to the Hellespont to Phrygia. In the tenth year the city itself was attacked and finally fell. The date for its fall is c1200 B.C.

The site of this Homeric city was generally believed in antiquity to be identical with that of the Greek Ilium (the modern Hissarlik); and this view has been supported in later times, most notably by Heinrich Schliemann, who followed the descriptions in the *Iliad* literally and whose explorations (1871 *et seq.*) at Hissarlik laid bare remains of a series of ancient towns, one above the other. The third and later the second from the bottom he identified with the Homeric town, those levels showing the effects of a conflagration and massive ruins. On the other hand, some scholars regarded the situation of Ilium as irreconcilable with Homer's description of Troy, and preferred a site in the neighborhood of the later Bunarbashi, holding Schliemann's results to be

(obscured) errant, ardent, actor; ch, chip; g, go; th, thin; ŦH, then; y, you;
(variable) ḍ as d or j, ş as s or sh, ţ as t or ch, ẓ as z or zh.

inconclusive. More recent investigations indicate, however, that Schliemann was correct about the site, but that the sixth, or more probably, the seventh level was ancient Ilium. Schliemann's and subsequent excavations on the site have revealed that a city existed there as early as the 3rd millennium B.C. Priam's city, erected on the ruins of earlier cities, was on a mound commanding the plains of the Scamander River and its tributary the Simois. It was larger than the earlier cities and was surrounded by a massive wall, built in the reign of Laomedon, according to legend, by Apollo and Poseidon with the aid of Aeacus. The wall was pierced by gates, of which the Scaean Gate is mentioned in the *Iliad.* On the highest point within the walls rose the palace-fortress. On the lower slopes were the houses of the inhabitants of the city, remains of which have been found. Gold ornaments and pottery indicate that the city was of the level of the Mycenaean civilization. The city of Troy remained a center of interest throughout antiquity for its historic and legendary significance. Xerxes stopped there on his way to invade Greece (481 B.C.) and offered sacrifices at the shrine of Ilian Athena to the shades of the ancient heroes of the Trojan War. Alexander the Great stopped there, 334 B.C., and saw the arms the heroes of the Trojan War had carried, including the shield of Achilles. The Romans, claiming descent from Trojan Aeneas, honored it. Lucius Scipio offered sacrifice to Ilian Athena. Sulla rebuilt the city after it had been destroyed by his opponent, the Roman general Fimbria. Augustus honored the city and enlarged its territory. After the 4th century A.D. the city fell into ruins, its site was abandoned, and even the location of the historic city was forgotten and lost until Schliemann's discovery of it.

*Tuder* (tū'dẽr). [Modern name, *Todi.*] In ancient geography, an Umbrian town of C Italy, situated on a height above the Tiber River, about 23 miles S of Perusia (Perugia). It has Etruscan and Roman antiquities, including walls, a temple, and a theater. Objects found here are in the museum at Florence and in the Vatican at Rome.

*Turris Libisonis* (tur'is li-bis-ō'nis). [Modern name, *Porto Torres.*] Town on the island of Sardinia, situated on the Gulf of Asinara NE of modern Sassari. A Carthaginian and then a Roman settlement, the town still has remains of ancient times.

*Tuscan Archipelago* (tus'kạn). Group of islands W of Tuscany, including Elba and some smaller islands.

*Tuscan Sea.* Name sometimes given to the part of the Mediterranean W of Tuscany, Italy.

*Tuscany* (tus'kạ-ni). Region in C Italy, bounded on the N and E by the main range of the Apennines, on the W by the Ligurian and Tyrrhenian seas, and on the S by the regions of Umbria and Latium. It was the home of the Etruscans, and one of the earliest objects of Roman expansion.

*Tusculum* (tus'kū-lum). In ancient geography, a city in Latium, Italy, situated in the Alban Hills about 13 miles SE of Rome, near the modern Frascati. According to tradition its chief, Mamilius, joined Tarquinius Superbus against the Romans. Later it was allied with Rome. Under the Republic and Empire it contained villas of many Romans (Lucullus, Pompey, Brutus, and Cicero). It was destroyed near the end of the 12th century. Its ruins contain a Roman amphitheater and a theater.

*Tyana* (tī'ạ-nạ). In ancient geography, a city in Cappadocia, Asia Minor. Its ruins are about 75 miles NW of the modern Adana. It was the birthplace of Apollonius of Tyana, a 1st-century A.D. wandering teacher and sage.

*Tylissus* (tī-lis'us). In ancient geography, a town on the E slope of Mount Ida on the island of Crete. It was the site of a Minoan palace built about 1600 B.C. Many valuable objects of the Minoan civilization have been recovered from the site.

*Typaeum* (tī-pē'um), *Mount.* Mountain on the road to Olympia, in Elis. According to a law of Elis, any married woman caught observing the Olympic contests on prohibited days was cast to her death from this mountain.

*Tyre* (tīr). [Arabic, *Es Sur;* French, *Sour, Tyr;* Latin, *Tyrus;* Hebrew, *Zor;* called *"Queen of the Sea."*] Most important and, next to Sidon, the oldest city of Phoenicia; now a town in Lebanon. It consisted of a town on the mainland, which was the oldest part, and two rocky islands directly opposite. These islands originally contained only the temple of Melkarth and warehouses. In the 13th century B.C. they were more settled, and were later united by Hiram, the contemporary of Solomon, by an embankment. In the 11th century B.C. Tyre began, under its first king, father of Hiram, to rival its mother city Sidon, and soon supplanted it as queen of the Phoenician cities. Of its magnificence and luxury the prophet Ezekiel gives a detailed description. It established colonies in Sicily, Sardinia, Spain, Africa (Carthage), and sent out mercantile fleets as far as India and Brittany. Under Hiram Tyre reached the height of its prosperity and splendor. It then came into close friendly relations with Israel. Later, Ahab, king of Israel, married Jezebel, daughter of Ethbaal, whose great-granddaughter Elissa (Dido) is said to have founded Carthage. Tyre was often the aim of attacks by Eastern rulers. It became tributary to Assyria under Tiglath-pileser III (745–727 B.C.). Shalmaneser IV (727–722 B.C.) besieged it for five years, apparently without success. Under Nebuchadnezzar it stood a siege of 13 years (585–572 B.C.). Later it came under Persian supremacy. Alexander the Great reduced the city after a siege of nine months (332 B.C.), though he did not completely destroy it. From this blow Tyre never fully recovered, but it continued to have a degree of prosperity through its manufactures of metalwork, fine textiles, and purple dye. In the Roman period Tyre was still a prosperous city, and it retained some importance down to the Middle Ages. During the Crusades it often changed hands between the Christians and the Mohammedans, and was repeatedly destroyed.

*Tyrrhenian Sea* (ti-rē′ni-an). [Latin, *Inferum Mare, Mare Tyrrhenum.*] That part of the Mediterranean Sea which lies W of Italy and is partly enclosed by the islands of Corsica, Sardina, and Sicily.

# ——U——

*Ufens* (ū′fenz). [Modern name, *Ufente* or *Uffente.*] In ancient geography, a river of Latium flowing into the sea west of Tarracina.

*Umbria* (um′bri-a). In ancient geography, a region in Italy, E of Etruria and W of Picenum. The Umbrians took part in the Second Samnite War, but were defeated (308 B.C.) by Rome. After theThird Samnite War they were gradually Romanized.

*Urbibentum* (ėr-bi-ben′tum). [Called in the Middle Ages, *Urbs*

*Vetus,* whence the modern name *Orvieto.*] A walled town in Umbria, about 60 miles N of Rome, on a volcanic hill thought by some to be the site of the once wealthy Etruscan city of Volsinii, which the Romans destroyed in 280 B.C. In the neighborhood have been found prehistoric antiquities and an Etruscan cemetery. Bronzes and Greek vases from the cemetery are exhibited in the local museum. Fragments of architectural decoration in terra-cotta, discovered with the walls, indicate the presence of an Italic (or Etruscan) temple. (JJ)

*Utica* (ū'ti-ḳa). In ancient geography, a city in Africa, situated near the Bagradas (modern Medjerda) River, about 25 miles NW of Carthage. It was founded by the Phoenicians (c1100 B.C.), sided in the Third Punic War with Rome, and succeeded Carthage as the leading city in Africa. It was held by Cato for the Pompeians in 46 B.C. Following the victory of Caesar at Thapsus Cato committed suicide there.

─────**V**─────

*Vadimonis, Lacus* (vad-i-mō'nis, lā'kus). In ancient geography, a small lake in Italy, near the Tiber River; the modern Laghetto di Bassano. Here the Romans under Fabius Maximus Rullianus defeated (310 or 309 B.C.) the Etruscans; in 283 B.C. the Romans defeated the combined north Italians and Gauls here.

*Vale of Tempe* (tem'pē). See *Tempe, Vale of.*

*Veii* (vē'ī). In ancient geography, a city in Italy, the most important of the Etruscan League, about 11 miles NW of Rome. It was frequently at war with Rome, especially in behalf of the restoration of Tarquinius Superbus. It was besieged and taken by the Romans under the leadership of Camillus in 396 B.C. Roman references to Veii as a center of fine sculpture in terra-cotta have been borne out by excavations both clandestine and official, which have produced striking figures of gods, Apollo, Artemis, and others, in the Villa Giulia Museum in Rome. According to Pliny the Elder, a Veientine sculptor named Vulca made terra-cotta statues for the Capitolium in Rome. Under the Empire the city sank into obscurity. In Rome, on the W side of the Piazza Colonna, is a portico of ancient Ionic columns, removed from Veii in 1838 and reërected here. (JJ)

*Velabrum* (ve̞-lā′brum). Area in ancient Rome, between the Capitoline and Palatine hills and the Tiber River, extending NE to the Forum Romanum. It was a marsh before the construction of the Cloaca Maxima.

*Velia* (vē′li-a̞). Locality in ancient Rome, identified as the ridge which extends from the Palatine Hill to the Esquiline Hill, and on which stand the Temple of Venus and Roma and the Arch of Titus. As it now exists, it has been much cut down from its original height.

*Velia.* The Italic name of Elea, a Greek colony on the coast of Lucania in Magna Graecia. It was said to have been founded (540 B.C.) by Phocaeans who emigrated from Asia Minor rather than submit to Persia. It was the center of the Eleatic School of philosophy. (JJ)

*Velinus* (ve̞-lī′nus). [Modern name, *Velino.*] River in C Italy which joins the Nar (Nera) above Interamna (Terni). Near its mouth is the noted waterfall Cascate delle Marmore, consisting of a series of three cascades.

*Venusia* (ve̞-nū′shi-a̞). [Modern name, *Venosa.*] Town in S Italy. It was a station on the Appian Way, and the birthplace of the Roman poet Horace (65 B.C.).

*Verbanus, Lacus* (vėr-bā′nus, lā′kus). [Modern names, *Lago Maggiore, Lago di Verbano.* ] Second largest lake of N Italy. It is traversed by the Ticinus River. It contains the Borromean Islands, and is famous for picturesque scenery. Elevation, about 633 feet; length, about 37 miles; area, about 82 square miles; greatest known depth, about 1220 feet.

*Veroia* (ve′ryä). [Also: *Veria, Verria.*] See *Beroea.*

*Verona* (ve̞-rō′na̞). City in NE Italy, in Cisalpine Gaul, situated on the Athesis (Adige) River. It was a Celtic settlement in ancient times, and became a Roman colony in 89 B.C. It was the birthplace of the poet Catulus. Verona has one of the best-preserved Roman amphitheaters of Italy, and other Roman antiquities, including a theater, gates, and large archaeological collections.

*Vesuvius* (ve̞-sö′vi-us), *Mount.* [Italian, *Monte Vesuvio.*] The only active volcano on the mainland of Europe, and unquestionably the best-known one in the world, situated on the

fat, fāte, fär, fȧll, ȧsk, fāre; net, mē, hėr; pin, pīne; not, nōte, möve, nôr; up, lūte, pŭll; oi, oil; ou out; (lightened) e̞lect, agŏny, ŭnite;

Bay of Naples, Italy, about nine miles SE of Naples. It has
two summits, the volcano proper (about 4200 feet high),
and Monte Somma to the N (3730 feet). It was regarded in
ancient times as extinct. Severe earthquake shocks occurred
in 63 A.D., and the first recorded eruption took place in 79
A.D., destroying Pompeii, Herculaneum, and Stabiae. The
popular belief that Pompeii, Herculaneum, and Stabiae
were overwhelmed by streams of molten lava is mistaken; in
the eruption of 79 A.D., Vesuvius sprayed into the atmos-
phere vast quantities of molten rock in the form of droplets
charged with gases, which expanded as in the cooler air the
drops solidified, forming *lapilli*, "pellets" of light, dry, warm
"ash" (pumice). It was this ash which covered Pompeii to a
depth of 16 to 20 feet, and Stabiae, in some places, to an
even greater depth. On the SW slopes of the volcano, however, it rained, and the wet ash, falling to the ground as
warm mud, flowed downhill and covered the lower slopes,
including the entire resort of Herculaneum, where it hardened into the rock known as tufa, effectively sealing it off
from discovery and clandestine excavation until the 18th
century. Other more or less notable eruptions have taken
place since 79 A.D., the most destructive being those of Dec.
16, 1631, and 1906. (JJ)

*Viminal Hill* (vim′i-nạl). [Latin, *Mons Viminalis*.] Northeastern-
most of the group of seven hills of ancient Rome, E of the
Quirinal and N of the Esquiline. The baths of Diocletian lie
below it to the N.

*Vindelicia* (vin-dẹ-lish′i-ạ, -lish′ạ). [Also: *Rhaetia Secunda*.] In
ancient geography, a Roman province; sometimes united
with Rhaetia. It was bounded by the Ister (Danube), the
Aenus (Inn) (separating it from Noricum), and Rhaetia. Its
chief town was Augusta Vindelicorum (Augsburg). The
early inhabitants were probably of Celtic origin. Vindelicia
occupied in general what is now the S part of Baden, Wurt-
temberg, and Bavaria, and the N part of the Tyrol.

*Volaterrae* (vol-ạ-ter′ē). [Modern name, *Volterra*.] Town in C
Italy. It was one of the 12 leading Etruscan towns. Tombs
of the Villanovan period have been found nearby. The town
fell to Rome in 298 B.C. Ancient walls still surround the
town.

*Volos* (vô′lôs). [Also: *Bolos*.] Town in NE Greece, on the coast
about 32 miles E of Larissa: main harbor of Thessaly. In the

vicinity are many ancient ruins; nearby were the sites of Iolcus and Pagasae, ancient seaports, both of which have been identified as the starting point of the Argonauts, and also of ancient Demetrias.

*Volscian Mountains* (vol'shạn). [Italian, *Monti Lepini.*] Group of mountains in Italy, SE of Rome. They are W of the main chain of the Apennines, and S of the Alban Hills. Elevation, about 4420 feet.

*Volsinii* (vol-sin'i-ī). One of the twelve capitals of the Etruscan Confederacy, destroyed by the Romans in 280 B.C., thought by some scholars to have stood on the site of *Urbibentum,* modern Orvieto. The Romans later refounded it some miles to the SW as Volsinii Novi, modern Bolsena, on the shores of the Lacus Volsiniensis or Lake of Bolsena. (JJ)

*Volterra* (vōl-ter'rạ). See *Volaterrae.*

*Volturnus* (vol-tėr'nus). [Modern name, *Volturno.*] River in Italy which traverses Campania and flows into the Mediterranean Sea about 21 miles NW of Neapolis (Naples).

*Vulcania* (vul-kā'ni-ạ). [Modern name, *Vulcano.*] In ancient geography, an island between the Sicilian coast and Aeolian Lipara. According to legend, it was Vulcan's workshop. It was an island of volcanic origin and was supposed by Vergil to be connected by subterranean channels with Mount Aetna. The island was also called, in ancient times, Hiera.

# X

*Xanthus* (zan'thus). In ancient geography, a city in Lycia, Asia Minor, situated on the Scamander (or Xanthus) River near its mouth. It was besieged and destroyed by the Persian general Harpagus, c545 B.C., and again by the Romans under Brutus, in 43 or 42 B.C. Important antiquities were discovered (c1838) there by Fellows. Among them is the so-called Nereid monument, a cella with a beautiful Ionic peristyle, dating from the middle of the 4th century B.C. The chief frieze, on the basement, represents a battle of cavalry and foot soldiers; the second frieze illustrates a siege; the third frieze, on the cella, is sculptured with sacrificial and

fat, fāte, fär, fȧll, ȧsk, fāre; net, mē, hėr; pin, pīne; not, nōte, möve, nôr; up, lūte, pu̇ll; oi, oil; ou out; (lightened) ẹlect, agǫny, ụnite;

feasting scenes; the fourth frieze, on the entablature, shows
hunting episodes and homage to an official personage. The
principal parts of the monument have been transported to
the British Museum.

*Xanthus.* [Modern name, *Koca.*] In ancient geography, a river
of Lycia, Asia Minor, rising in the Taurus Mountains and
flowing S to empty into the Mediterranean Sea.

*Xypete* (zī′pẹ-tẹ̄). One of the demes or villages of Attica, on the
highway from Phalerum to Athens, in which was a temple of
Hera in Xypete, sacked and burned by the Persians in 480
B.C., and thereafter left in ruin as a reminder of the impiety
of the Persians; still lacking doors and roof, it was seen in
the second century A.D. by the traveler Pausanias. The cult
continued active in its ruined sanctuary; it appears in 5th-
century B.C. financial audits, and possessed a statue of Hera
by the sculptor Alcamenes. (JJ)

*Zacynthus* (zạ-sin′thus). Island of the Ionian group, Greece,
about eight miles S of Cephallenia. It has often been visited
by earthquakes. It was originally colonized by Achaeans,
who roamed the seas and, some say, founded Saguntum in
Spain long before the Trojan War. Its position between the
Peloponnesus and routes to the west made it an important
station. It became a member of the Athenian Confederacy.

*Zakynthos* (zä′kēn-thôs). See *Zacynthus.*

*Zama* (zā′mạ). In ancient geography, a town in N Africa, about
85 miles SW of Carthage. A decisive victory was gained near
it in 202 B.C. by the Romans under Scipio Africanus over
Hannibal. It ended the Second Punic War.

*Zancle* (zang′klẹ̄). In ancient geography, a town in the NE
corner of Sicily, situated on a sickle-shaped harbor that gave
the city its name (from the Greek word for sickle). The
ancient coins of the city (later named Messene) were engraved with a sickle, representing the harbor, within which
a dolphin floated. The town commanded the narrow strait
between Italy and Sicily. Originally occupied by pirates, it

was colonized by Chalcidian Greeks in the 8th century B.C. According to tradition, when the Messenians were defeated by the Spartans in the Second Messenian War those who could escape fled the country. Many of them went to Sicily at the invitation of the tyrant of Rhegium. They defeated the Zancleans in battle, but refused to kill them when they fled to their altars as suppliants. Instead, they exchanged pledges with them to dwell together in peace, raised a temple of Heracles, and changed the name of the city to Messene (c664 B.C.), after their own country.

*Zante* (zan'tē). Another name for *Zacynthus* (q.v.).

*Zariaspa* (za-ri-as'pạ). Another name for *Bactra,* capital of the ancient country of Bactria.

*Zea* (tse'ä). See *Ceos.*

*Zela* (zē'lạ). In ancient geography, a town in Pontus, Asia Minor, at or near what is now Zile, a farm-market town in Turkey. It was the scene of a victory of Mithridates VI over the Romans c67 B.C., and was famous for the victory by Caesar over Pharnaces II in 47 B.C. It was with reference to this battle that Caesar wrote the famous *"Veni, vidi, vici"* (I came, I saw, I conquered).

*Zone* (zō'nē). In ancient geography, a place in Thrace where, according to tradition, wild oaks stand in ranks just as they were left, after having been led to this place from Pieria by the music of Orpheus.